LONDON RECORD SOCIETY
PUBLICATIONS

VOLUME XXXI
FOR THE YEAR 1994

LONDON BRIDGE:
SELECTED
ACCOUNTS AND RENTALS,
1381–1538

EDITED BY
VANESSA HARDING
AND
LAURA WRIGHT

LONDON RECORD SOCIETY
1995

Typeset by
The Midlands Book Typesetting Company, Loughborough, Leicestershire
Printed and bound in Great Britain by
Quorn Selective Repro Ltd, Loughborough, Leicestershire

CONTENTS

INTRODUCTION

The Corporation of London's own archives constitute a great resource for the history of the medieval and early modern city. However, although they are very rich in administrative and legal records, they contain few financial records from before the seventeenth century.[1] A major exception to this is the series of accounts and rentals that record the management of London Bridge and its estates. The series begins in the second half of the fourteenth century and survives almost unbroken thereafter. The records provide a picture not only of the work on the bridge itself, one of the biggest and surely the longest-running building project in London, but also of an organisation reacting to economic and administrative change over a very long period, and give much information on the life of London on and around the bridge. The detailed and continuous nature of the records reveals both short-term events and changes and long-term developments in the areas covered: wages, work and employment practices in the construction industry, building materials and techniques, property values, administrative method, institutional culture. Their value as a quarry for particular kinds of information has long been known,[2] but only limited extracts have ever been printed, and the potential contribution of the series as a whole to the history of London in a more general sense has not been fully exploited.

Two aspects of the records in the period c.1380–1540 are especially worthy of attention, the economic and the linguistic. For the former, the accounts help us to examine changes in the economy of London, providing plentiful evidence for the strength of the property market and for changes in wages and work practices. The experience of an institution whose main income was from rents and whose main expenditure was on wages, in a period when these were moving in opposite directions, must be a topic of some interest to historians of the medieval economy. In the case of language, the fifteenth century saw the development of English as a language of business and professional activity, and these accounts, with their repetitive format and concerns and their specialist vocabulary, document this. The medieval Latin of

---

1. B.Masters, *Chamber Accounts of the sixteenth century* (London Record Society vol. 20, 1984), p. ix.
2. E.g. L.F.Salzman, *Building in England down to 1540* (1952), *passim*; P.E.Jones, 'Some Bridge House properties', *Journal of the British Archaeological Association* 3rd. series 16 (1953), pp. 59–73; C.P.Christianson, *Memorials of the book trade in medieval London: the archives of old London Bridge* (1987).

the early accounts is studded with vernacular words, while the accounts as a whole are written in English after 1480.

This volume offers a selection from the series of accounts for the later middle ages. Although one of the great values of the series is its almost unbroken continuity, it was felt that the best way of displaying the range and detail of the material in a single volume of reasonable length was to present accounts for complete years at intervals: the selection therefore starts with the first surviving account (1381–2) and includes accounts for four more years at roughly 40-year intervals, up to 1537–8. Where two complementary accounts survive, both have been included (this dictated the choice of 1537–8 rather than 1540). Two rentals of the Bridge estate, from the first Rental book and to match the last account, are also printed. Within this framework, accounts for more eventful years were chosen; thus the account for 1420–1 details expenditure on decorating the Bridge for the entry of Henry V and Katherine of France in 1421, while that for 1501–2 refers much more briefly to the entry of Katherine of Aragon.

The records are presented in modern English, somewhat calendared, rather than as a verbatim transcript/translation, but no information has been omitted. There is thus enough material to make comparisons over a long period, while retaining the full detail of individual years' accounts. It would be possible to take the comparison further in time, but arguably the period to c. 1540 is the one to which these records can make the greatest contribution: the evidence is genuinely comparable across the period, while later accounts show a lower level of activity and may be less sensitive to change.[3]

London Bridge and the Bridge House

London's stone bridge was begun in the later 12th century, replacing a previous wooden structure. Its construction was associated with the development of the cult of Thomas Becket, London's native-born saint and martyr (d. 1170; canonised 1173), and one of the bridge's most prominent features was a chapel dedicated to St Thomas, on one of the central piers. Nineteen pointed arches, with variable gaps between them, spanned some 900 ft. (275 m.) of fast-flowing, tidal river. A drawbridge near the southern end could be raised to allow the passage of ships to the upper river and to prevent entry to the city; the gate at the Southwark end could also be barred or chained. From an early period it appears that the bridge was lined with houses and shops. It was completed around 1209, but for the six and a half centuries of its existence, until its replacement in the mid-nineteenth century, it

---

3. Once it became common, as it did in the sixteenth century, to lease property for terms of years, for a fine or income and a fixed rent, with repairs to be done by the tenant, the Bridge employed far fewer workmen, and rent receipts were less variable.

needed constant maintenance and sometimes substantial repair.[4] By the time sixteenth-century visitors were recording their impressions of the city, the bridge was acknowledged as one of the sights of London – 'a remarkable sight even among the beauties of London', 'easily one of the finest bridges in the whole of Europe, both for size and beauty'[5] – and it dominates most early views of the city, even if it is not always accurately represented.[6]

Even before the building of the stone bridge, pious Londoners gave sums of money or property to sustain the wooden bridge, but the association with a popular cult and a major campaign to secure adequate funds helped in the acquisition of a substantial landed estate which generated the greater part of the income necessary to maintain the structure.[7] Much of this estate had been acquired by the middle of the fourteenth century, and by the late fourteenth century, when the surviving accounts series begins, it is clear that the work of the administrators of the bridge was almost as much concerned with managing and exploiting this estate as with organising the repair and maintenance of the bridge's structure. Other sources of income included tolls from carts passing over the bridge and from ships passing through the drawbridge, and the rents from the fish- and flesh-markets at the Stocks, built in the later 13th century by the then mayor, Henry le Waleys.

Unlike for example Rochester Bridge Trust,[8] the administration of London Bridge was not in the hands of an independent charity or corporate body; essentially it was a municipal institution at one remove from the municipality. The stone bridge had been begun at a time when the citizens of London were struggling for recognition as a collective entity, before the institution of the mayoralty and the development of a civic administration, so it is perhaps not surprising that the arrangements for managing the bridge retained some informality.

Essential both to the city's economic health and to its security from attack, London Bridge was often referred to as 'the city's bridge'.[9] Important decisions about the estate and regulations about the bridge's

---

4. G.Home, *Old London Bridge* (1931); C.N.L.Brooke and G.Keir, *London 800–1216: the shaping of a city* (1975), pp. 109–10, 158, 162; John Stow, *A Survey of London* (1603; ed. C.L. Kingsford, 2 vols., Oxford 1908; reprinted 1971), i, pp. 21–6, 42.
5. C.Barron, C.Coleman, and C. Gobbi, 'The London journal of Alessandro Magno, 1562', *The London Journal* 9(2) (1983), p. 142; G.W.Groos, ed., *The diary of Baron Waldstein, a traveller in Elizabethan England* (1981), p. 175.
6. Cf. the reproductions in F.Barker and P.Jackson, *London, 2000 years of a city and its people* (1974), pp. 51, 57, 96–7. For the accuracy of the representations, see Home, *Old London Bridge*, p. 27, pl. f.p. 33.
7. Brooke and Keir, *London 800–1216*, pp. 110, 362. Five guilds of the Bridge were noted in 1179–80: G.Unwin, *The gilds and companies of London* (1908), pp. 47–51.
8. N.Yates and J.M.Gibson, ed., *Traffic and politics: the construction and management of Rochester Bridge, AD 43–1993* (Woodbridge, 1994).
9. E.g. *C[alendar of] L[etter] B[ooks of the City of London: Letterbook] K*, ed. R.R. Sharpe (1911), p. 191.

use were authorised by the mayor, aldermen, and citizens, who kept a close eye on its administration and finances, and defended its interests.[10] The mayor and aldermen made or approved leases of property devoted to the bridge's upkeep, sometimes granting rebates of rent or concessions, and other business concerning the Bridge was issued under the City's common seal.[11] Although the estates pertaining to the Bridge and those to the municipality were kept separate, sums of money from the Bridge revenues were at times given to or appropriated by the City for its own uses.[12] The day-to day running of the Bridge and its estate was in the hands of wardens or masters elected in civic fora and answerable to the commonalty; auditors of their accounts were appointed annually. Nevertheless, though never incorporated as such, the wardens, workforce, properties and rights of London Bridge developed an institutional identity, to which the name 'the Bridge House' was applied from the thirteenth century.[13]

The Bridgemasters or wardens of the bridge

The number, status, and competence of the men appointed to discharge the trust seem to have varied in the late thirteenth century, with references at different times to two or three wardens, to a sub-warden, and to the appointment of a coadjutor.[14] Edward II's charter to the City granted the keeping of the bridge to two worthy men of the city, other than aldermen, and thereafter two wardens were the norm.[15] Fourteenth-century wardens were elected and took their oaths in the Court of Husting, the county court of the City, and rendered their account to auditors approved by the City. From 1404 the wardens were elected on 21 September, by the same congregation that elected the sheriffs and the auditors.[16]

Fourteenth-century wardens often served for a period of some years, and may not have rendered accounts until they left office. Alan Gille served from at least 1336 until 1350, John de Hatfeld, alias John le Chaundeler, from 1353 to 1363, Henry Yevele for perhaps 30 years.[17] In 1404 the wardens' term was limited to two consecutive years, with the possibility of later re-election, but in 1406 the immediate re-election of suitable candidates was permitted.[18] As a result, wardens still commonly served several years at a time, and a handful served for more than ten

---

10. Below; *CLBE*, pp. 179–80, 186, 200, 257, 299.
11. *CLBA*, p. 157; *CLBC*, p. 78; *CLBE*, pp. 41–2; **300, 351**.
12. *CLBE*, p. 52; *Memorials*, p. 591.
13. *CLBA*, p. 2; *CLBB*, p. 216. 'The Bridge House' was also the name of the property in Southwark used as headquarters and chief storehouse for the organisation (**200, 247, 316**, etc.), and of an estate in Lewisham belonging to the Bridge (**318, 428**).
14. *CLBB*, pp. 140–1, 216; *CLBC*, pp. 2, 61, 70.
15. W. de G. Birch, ed., *The historical charters and constitutional documents of the City of London* (1887), p. 49.
16. *CLBC*, pp. 2, 31, 133; *CLBE*, pp. 41, 52, 83, 143–4, 146; *CLBH*, pp. 102 and *passim*; *CLBI*, pp. 33–4.
17. *CLBE*, pp. 41–2, 52, 299; *CLBF*, pp. 227–8; *CLBG*, pp. 13, 155; John H. Harvey, *Henry Yevele, the life of an English architect* (1944), pp. 28–9.
18. *CLBI*, pp. 33–5.

years, sometimes with interruptions.[19] The accounts were nevertheless meant to be rendered and audited annually, within a month from Michaelmas, though this was not being strictly applied in the middle of the fifteenth century.[20]

The wardens seem to have been men of substance, as might be expected, but not necessarily of the top rank in the city. Fourteenth-century wardens often had interests in riverside parishes or waterborne trades: Edmund Horn, Thomas Cros, William Jordan, Robert Swote, John Lovekyn, Alan Gille, owned property in riverside parishes;[21] Gilbert Cros, Robert Swote, John Lovekyn, John Little, Richard Bacoun, were fishmongers.[22] The charter of Edward II of 1319 said that the wardens should not be aldermen, though this had sometimes been the case in the past, and one, John Lovekyn, apparently served as alderman and bridge warden at the same time from 1347.[23] Up to the middle of the fifteenth century several men who had served as wardens subsequently became aldermen, but thereafter, perhaps as the Court of Aldermen became a narrower élite of overseas merchants, the two circles ceased to overlap.[24] Regulations in 1404 for the wardens' election specified 'two good and discreet citizens', and it seems probable that all fifteenth-century wardens were members of Common Council. They normally belonged to one of the leading livery companies.[25] By the later sixteenth century the Bridgemasters (= the wardens), still normally Common Councilmen, could effectively be classed as city officers or bureaucrats; aldermen in the making, 'notable' and 'élite' Londoners, served rather as auditors of the accounts, or sat on the Bridge House Estates and City Lands Committees.[26]

Fifteenth-century wardens swore to serve the city of London in the office of warden of the bridge of the same city; to repair and sustain the bridge, using its lands and rents to its best profit; to do no waste

19. Robert Colbrook, ironmonger, 1421–32; Thomas Cooke senior, draper, 1440–57; Thomas Davy, tailor, 1449–60; Peter Alfold, 1457–68; William Galle, tailor, 1474–87; Simon Harrys, grocer, 1485–97 or later; Christopher Eliot, goldsmith, 1490–after 1502: *CLBI, K, L, passim.* Wardens and other officers of London Bridge for the period 1400–60 are listed in Caroline M. Barron, 'The government of   London and its relations with the Crown, 1400–1450', unpublished Ph.D. thesis, London 1970, pp. 184–6.
20. *CLBI*, pp. 33–4; *CLBK*, pp. 248; cf. Barron, 'Government of London' pp. 589–600.
21. *CLBC*, pp. 2, 70; *CLBE*, pp. 296, 299; *Cal. Wills* i, pp. 129, 140, 166, 673, 685.
22. *CLBC*, pp. 133; *CLBE*, p. 296; *Cal. Wills* i, p. 685; *CLBF*, pp. 2, 216; *Cal Wills* ii, pp. 117–18; *CLBG*, p. 37.
23. Anketin de Gisors and Henry de Gloucestre were already aldermen when they became Bridge Wardens in 1315: *CLBE*, p. 41. John Lovekyn remained warden when he became an alderman in 1347: A.B.Beaven, *The Aldermen of the City of London, temp. Henry III – 1908* (2 vols., 1908, 1913), i, p. 386.
24. John Vyvyen, Walter Neel, John Lovekyn, John Little, James Andreu, Henry Vanner, William Chichele, William Sevenok, Nicholas James: Beaven, *Aldermen,* i, pp. 379–80, 382, 385–6, 398; ii, pp. 4, 6.
25. *CLBI*, pp. 33–4, 245, 261; *CLBK*, pp. 123, 183, 219, 248, 329; *CLBL*, pp. 86, 91, 215, 225, 270, 273, 289.
26. F.F.Foster, *The politics of stability: a portrait of the rulers in Elizabethan London* (1977), pp. 60, 67, 69, 86–7.

to the estate, but increase it if possible; and to make account without concealment, charging themselves with all profits and advantages and asking no unlawful allowance. The office of warden does not appear to have been one of profit, though the form of the oath recognised that the provision of materials might offer opportunities for exploitation: wardens promised to buy stone, timber, iron, etc. at the lowest prices, 'without any increase or winning to your use or profit in any wise'.[27]

The wardens handled very large sums of money, accounting for some £750 a year in the late fourteenth century and around £1,500 in the mid-sixteenth, but their annual fees and rewards still came to less than £30 each by the latter date (**1, 457, 487–8, 491**). There may have been a reward on leaving office, once the accounts had been satisfactorily audited, but at least one warden, William Wetenhale (1434–8), forfeited this because he was judged to have tended the bridge negligently. From 1459 incoming wardens had to provide security of £500.[28] In 1491 Common Council ordered a stricter control of the nominations for warden: the mayor and aldermen were to provide a list of four candidates, from whom Common Council would choose two, rather than the free choice that had prevailed hitherto, since that had led to the admission of 'needy men and unable for the office', whose accounts, by implication, were unsatisfactory.[29]

It is difficult to assess how efficiently the wardens discharged their office over the period covered by the accounts in this book, though it seems likely that quite serious mismanagement occurred in the mid-fifteenth century.[30] Such irregularities aside, the wardens were not expected to balance income and expenditure year to year, only to set down what had come in and what had been spent. The needs of the bridge varied and there might be extraordinary calls on their revenues: the accumulation of 'arrears' (essentially a deficit carried forward) could reflect an increase in needs not matched by any increase in current revenue, not in itself the fault of the wardens. There was no way of budgeting for future expenditure: the idea of maintaining a reserve seems to have been unknown and indeed impracticable, since any surplus would probably have been raided by the City for its own uses.[31]

Of the five accounts printed here, only that for 1501–2 shows an excess of income over expenditure, when arrears and other accounting elements have been subtracted, though the overspend in 1420–1 is almost all accounted for by the £75 spent on decorating the bridge for the royal entry in 1421 (**257–66, 278, 280, 287, 294**). It seems to

---

27. *CLBD*, pp. 184–5.
28. Barron, 'Government of London', pp. 184–5.
29. A.H.Thomas and I.Thornley, ed., *The Great Chronicle of London* (1938, reprinted 1983), p. 245; *CLBL*, pp. 290–1.
30. *CLBK*, p. 248; Barron, 'Government of London', pp. 184–5.
31. It should be said, in any case, that the accountants' calculations contain many small errors, sometimes the result of copying, and possibly some more serious mistakes. The same may be true of my calculations.

have been fairly normal, if not perhaps very sound practice, to allow the account to run into debt, and trust to a future excess of income over expenditure to pay it off. Indeed the excess of £120 in 1501–2 only went a small way towards paying off the huge paper arrears of over £1000 carried forward at the start of the account (**356**), but a series of years in profit had reduced the deficit to almost nothing by 1537.[32] It is not clear who carried the debt – the masters, the bridge's employees or creditors, or the city – and how liabilities were eventually settled. Ultimately the evaluation of the wardens' efficiency must depend on the health of the estate and of the fabric of the bridge.

The Bridge House staff
The headquarters of the operation was at the Bridge House in Southwark, where building materials were stored, accounts kept, and wages paid.[33] The wardens had a staff to carry out the daily business of the Bridge, but the numbers of these, and the way in which they were deployed, varied over time.

There was always at least one rent-collector, paid at least £10 yearly; he also had an allowance for drinking when he collected the weekly rents from the Stocks market. In the middle of the fifteenth century there were two collectors, one for the proper rents and another for the foreign and quit-rents and the Stocks rents. By the end of the century there was one receiver, allowed £23 6s. 8d. a year for his fee and drinking (**2, 294, 349, 395, 487**). The passage-tolls over and under the bridge appear to have been collected by a man referred to as the clerk of the drawbridge or tollkeeper, who rendered them weekly to the wardens, receiving a salary of 20d. a week, later £3 6s. 8d. a year (**3–107, 189–241, 254, 267, 280, 294, 310, 349**). The tolls were farmed from 1488 (**359, 448**). Another clerk wrote up the accounts; in 1420–1 both these tasks were undertaken by clerks of the chapel, but in 1461–2 and later the clerk of the works had an extra allowance for writing the accounts (**67, 82, 93, 107, 254, 267, 280, 292, 294, 351, 396, 488**).

The office of clerk of the works first appears by name c. 1440,[34] but it seems possible that John Silkeston was acting in this capacity in 1420–1, even though he is not directly attributed a salary. Silkeston sold materials from the Bridge House store and apparently presided over the weekly accounting (**190, 192, 194, 197, 217, 220, 226, 243–94**), though John Hethingham, a clerk of the chapel, wrote up the account (**254, 267, 280, 292, 294**). Later clerks of the works also bought and sold materials (**311, 452, 538**), paid foreign workmen (**474, 520, 526**), and at times supervised both work and materials,[35] as well as writing the accounts.

32. The figures on which these statements are based have been recalculated from component elements in the accounts, and do not rely on the sums given by the accountants.
33. Stow, *Survey*, ii, pp. 65–6; below, *passim*. See M.Carlin, 'The urban development of Southwark, c. 1200–1550' (unpublished Ph.D. thesis, Centre for Medieval Studies, University of Toronto, 1983), pp. 354–9 and fig. 9, p. 621.
34. Barron, 'Government of London', p. 593.
35. Christianson, *Memorials of the London book trade*, p. 9.

Silkeston was paid the weekly stipend of the cook of the Bridge masons and carpenters, and also the allowance for the Bridge dogs, apparently guard dogs or mastiffs.[36] The cook subsequently disappears from the accounts, but a janitor or porter of the Bridge House gate, paid the same weekly wage and allowance for the dogs, appears, and it seems likely that he fulfilled the role of house manager (**243–94**; cf. **2–54, 349, 395**). In 1537–8 it was the Bridge's boatkeeper who kept the dogs, still at 10d. a week (**487**). The Bridge House employed a boatman or keeper of boats and shouts at a low weekly wage (2s. 6d.), but paid him year round. Part of his job must have been transporting materials, normally unrecorded except in special cases (**535, 538, 541, 544, 551**), but he also employed and supervised labourers working with boats and at the starlings of the bridge (**346, 528, 531, 534, 538**), and supplied the tide-masons with cement (**480, 532–3, 536**). In 1350 the Bridge House had three boats, a great one, a small one, and a shout or barge;[37] the accounts printed here record the building of two new boats (**74–9, 346**) and the purchase of two (**252, 382**). In 1538 there were seven boats, including one known as the cement boat (**473, 484**).

At the beginning of the period covered by these accounts the Bridge House employed a carter, paid like the boatman a low weekly wage throughout the year, with at least one cart and a team of cart-horses. However, these could not do all the Bridge's carting, and were quite expensive to maintain (**56–107, 243–94**). Evidently the advantages of buying materials delivered to the store or site, and of hiring carters as the occasion warranted, prevailed. In 1462, halfway through the accounting year, the wardens sold the six carthorses and two carts, together with all the harness and some of the store of hay, and ceased to employ a carter (**311, 338**). They kept the riding-horses for the wardens until c.1470,[38] but thereafter the wardens received an allowance for horsehire (**338, 382, 487**).

The building workforce

The best-known name among medieval Bridge Wardens must be that of Henry Yevele, architect and mason, who may have served from 1365 to 1395, though he asked to be allowed to resign in 1383. As a result of his experience and skill gained in London, he also contributed to the new building of Rochester Bridge in the 1390s.[39] He appears to be the only warden within the period covered by this volume who had a specialist knowledge of architecture and construction. At other times the wardens must have depended on the skills of the master masons and carpenters employed by the Bridge and perhaps also of the clerk of

36. Carlin, 'Southwark', p. 356.
37. H.T.Riley, *Memorials of London and London life in the XIIIth, XIVth and XVth centuries, A.D. 1276–1419* (London, 1868), p. 262.
38. Bridge House Rental 3, f. 144v, cited in Christianson, *Memorials of the London book trade*, p. 9.
39. Harvey, *Yevele*, pp. 28–9; *CLBH*, p. 213.

the works.[40] Throughout the period covered by this volume at least one chief or master mason and one chief or master carpenter were paid an extra allowance in respect of their supervisory activities. In 1381–2 they received a weekly wage at the same rate as the other skilled workmen, a quarterly reward of 5s. each, and offerings totalling 2s. each (**67, 82, 93, 107**). In 1420–1 they received a wage and an annual reward of 20s. (**294**), but they may also have profited from the supply of materials.[41] In 1461–2 the chief mason and carpenter were rewarded by full employment, that is they were paid wages for a six-day week throughout the year, and each also had an apprentice, for whom he received a wage for all or most of the year, but no extra reward seems to have been paid (**340–1**). In 1501–2 there was a chief mason, paid a yearly fee, and both a master carpenter of the Bridge works, and a warden carpenter. The former was clearly in overall charge, receiving a yearly fee for 'overseeing and putting-to his helping hand at all times needful', while the latter, appointed during the year, was paid for a six-day week from the time of his appointment (**386–7, 390**). By 1537–8 the chief mason was also credited with supervising work and buying materials, while there was now a chief carpenter and under him two warden carpenters, one for the waterworks, that is work on and under the bridge, and one for the land works, presumably mostly house-carpentry. The chief mason and chief carpenter each received an annual fee of £10, while the warden carpenters were paid wages for a six-day week throughout the year whether or not they worked the whole week (**478–9**).

The other building workmen employed by the bridge included a team of masons, usually four to six not counting the master, and a larger number of carpenters, depending on the amount of work in hand. In the fourteenth century they were paid by the week throughout the year, for a six-day week except in the weeks following Christmas, Easter and Whitsun (**68, 83, 90**). Two sawyers, a dauber, and a paviour were also paid for a six-day week throughout the year, with the same exceptions. One of the notable features of these accounts, however, is the progressive casualisation of the Bridge's workforce during the fifteenth century. By 1461–2 there had been a noticeable shift away from reliance on a permanent workforce, paid for the whole week, to day labour, while by 1501, day labour was dominant. By that time all the masons, carpenters, labourers, dauber, paviour, and tilers, apart from the chief masons and carpenters, were paid by the day. None of them worked for the Bridge for more than 260 days, and most worked for less than 200 days. One sawyer 'and his fellows', now paid by the hundred-foot sawn, did all the Bridge's sawing, but they probably did not get more than half a year's work; similarly, the Bridge gave almost all

40. John Normavyle, clerk of the works 1488–1502, was rewarded in 1496 for overseeing the workmen and labourers in the bridge works in the absence of the wardens: Bridge House Rental 4, f. 180, cited in Christianson, *Memorials of the London book trade*, p. 9.
41. See index under Beek, Richard (chief mason), and Clerk, William (chief carpenter).

its tiling, paving and daubing work to one craftsman in each case, who brought servants and others, but none worked for a full year.

It does not appear that workmen moved from weekly work into daily labour for the sake of higher pay in the short term, since where weekly and daily wages were paid, the rates were equivalent, and few of the men employed by the day worked for as many days a year. The Bridge wardens did not actually save money by employing fewer people: though there were obvious variations from year to year, the number of days worked did not change significantly, but is possible that they gained flexibility, and were able to meet changing needs with a greater short-term variation in the number of workmen employed.

One area where there was little change was the work at the ram or gins. Work here was as continuous as tides and weather would allow: it seems to have stopped overwinter. It evidently needed a team of about 20 to 25 for the great ram, and 8 to 11 working on the lesser rams or gins, and the impression gained is of a coherent group of men working regularly together. The actual wage paid – 3d. a tide – changed not at all, while the extra benefits in ale were reduced over the period. Men very rarely worked more than 5 tides in one week, so it is not clear if those who worked in this way also had other employment; it seems likely that they would have needed it. But unless the Bridge was able to coerce labour (and there is no indication that this was the case) it appears that tidework (despite being part-time, irregular, wet and perhaps dangerous) was nevertheless sufficently attractive without an increasing financial reward.

The chapel

A further part of the Bridge Wardens' charge was the maintenance of services in the chapel on the bridge. The wages of the chaplains and clerks, and the other expenses of the chapel, formed quite a significant part of the wardens' annual outlay, around £40 a year in the fourteenth and fifteenth centuries, rising to £60 in the sixteenth. These services appear to have comprised a daily mass and the seasonal observances of the church, together with *placebo*, *dirige* and requiem mass for the benefactors of the bridge four times a year, and celebration of the feasts of St Thomas the Martyr and other saints.[42]

The establishment was intended to be four chaplains, but in fact the number of chaplains and clerks varied. In 1381–2 there were at different times three, four, or five chaplains, and one clerk; in 1420–1 four chaplains and two clerks; in 1460–1 four chaplains and three clerks; in 1501–2 two chaplains and four clerks; and in 1537–8 three chaplains and six clerks. The chaplains, who were nominated by the mayor, aldermen, and commonalty, received a salary of 10 marks (£6 13s. 4d.) from the early fifteenth century, slightly better than the weekly wage of 2s. 3½d. with 2s. offerings they had had in 1381–2; they also

42. Unless otherwise stated, the sources for this section are **56–107, 254, 267, 280, 294, 337, 385, 477**.

had free accommodation and fuel, and paid none of the running costs of the chapel.[43] The clerks contributed to the chapel services, and must have been in minor orders, but one at least was married,[44] and several performed other tasks, including writing, gatekeeping, and keeping the chapel. John Seyntjohn, one of the clerks of the chapel in 1420–1, who also wrote the accounts, clearly served the city in other capacities as well, receiving a pension of 12d. a week for life ($\frac{2}{3}$ of his clerk's salary) after being injured in the city's service.[45] An allowance of 20s. was at one time paid for the chaplains' cook or servant, but by 1501–2 this had been translated into a payment for keeping the chapel, made to one of the clerks.

The estates and income of the Bridge

The income of the Bridge House came from three main sources: the rents and quit-rents given or devised for the upkeep of the bridge, the rents of the Stocks market, and passage-tolls. Offerings and collections in the chapel were negligible, as were most other casual fines, gifts, and legacies, while sales of materials represented a realization of assets rather than a significant net profit (**1, 188, 296–315, 355–66, 441–57**).

The estate of the Bridge at the beginning of the fifteenth century (**109–87**), like that of many other institutional landlords, comprised properties scattered across the city and suburbs, the result of piecemeal acquisition and benefaction. The main areas of concentration were around the bridge and near St Paul's cathedral. There were 138 houses or let units on the bridge and a further 30 tenements in Southwark, not counting the Bridge House itself. There were 28 shops in Old Change and a great messuage and 30 shops in Paternoster Row, while in the parishes of St Audoen and St Nicholas Shambles there were 49 shops, several tenements, a brewhouse, and eight *cabane* or booths. There was a small cluster of houses and cottages in the parish of St Dionis Fenchurch, but elsewhere in the city the Bridge's properties were isolated units. The quit-rents owed to the Bridge were even more scattered. Outside the city to the south, the Bridge held a few acres of farmland at the Lock, St Thomas Watering, and Lambeth, and the manor of Lewisham, including a mill. On the river Lea at Stratford, on the Middlesex-Essex border, it owned two watermills, Spilmans, a fulling-mill, and Saynes mill for grain, with a few acres of meadow.

The rents from this estate accounted for more than $\frac{3}{4}$ of the Bridge's income: after allowing for decreases and vacations (but not for charges on the estate in the form of obits and quit-rents due to others, or the maintenance of the properties), the net income from lands and quit-rents made up c.75% of the total in 1381–2, rising to c.87% in 1537–8. This rise is partly explained by a decline in the income from tolls and the Stocks, but much more is due to a real increase in the

---

43. *CLBK*, pp. 290, 299.
44. Barron, 'Government of London', p. 591, notes that Nicholas Holford (**254, 267, 280, 294**) was succeeded as bailiff or tollkeeper by his widow Alice.
45. *CLBK*, p. 263.

value of the estate. Between 1404 and 1537, the net income from the estate rose from £421 11s. 6d. to £796 14s. 4½d. This remarkable overall rise does not entirely confound the argument, presented elsewhere, that London rents were generally declining between the mid-fifteenth and mid-sixteenth century.[46] Rather, it suggests that through judicious investment and maintenance, and in this case thanks also to benefactions, a landlord could improve the value of an urban estate even against the trend.

The earliest surviving rental of the estate, from 1358,[47] has been so much amended and erased that it is not possible to arrive at a total for any one date, but it is clear from the 1381–2 account (**1, 2**) that rents, or at least occupancy rates, had fallen from earlier totals: £45 2s. 1d. had to be allowed for vacancies of Bridge properties against the rental total of £466 13s. 7d. The rental for 1404, and its amendments, certainly indicates that rents were falling quite rapidly (cf. **139**, where the value of the London rents declined from £462 2s. in 1404 to £448 10s. in 1410). The rental also indicates that the most vulnerable area was the shop property in Old Change (**122**), but decreased rents are evident almost everywhere. The London rents received in 1420–1 came to around £410 (**241**).

At the same time, the value of the quit-rents assigned to the Bridge was also declining, evidence that other properties were vacant or unlet or their owners untraceable. In 1381–2 the quit-rents had a nominal value of £30 3s. 2d., of which £2 19s. 2d. could not be collected for the above reasons (**1, 2**). In 1404 the quit-rents due totalled £31 1s. 7d., but £5 12s. 1d. was denied or due from tenements now vacant; the rental provides graphic evidence of disarray (**144–87**). In 1461–2 the total received came to £22 1s. 11d., but another £9 19s. 7d. in quit-rents scattered across the city were deemed irrecoverable, because they had long been withheld and the wardens did not have the evidences with which to sustain a plea (**302–9**). In fact one rent of 2s., denied in the early fifteenth century (**171**) had recently been recovered, and some small rents had been added, but nearly a third of the original quit-rent roll had been permanently lost (cf. **361, 370, 450, 462**). It is possible that the accounts are not very sensitive to rent movements, since it was alleged in 1442 that many of the Bridge's tenants were making a profit from subletting at much higher rents than they were paying.[48] If this was so, and if an effort was made to prevent it happening in future, this could help to explain the recovery in rents received by the Bridge from the middle of the century. Rent income from property, rather than quit-rents, had begun to increase by 1460–1, when the rental total of London rents came to £541 18s. 8d. and of foreign rents to £53 18s. 8d. Part of this is attributable to new properties added to the estate, such as the tenements by the Stocks devised by Christian Mallyng[49] and the

---

46. D.Keene, *Cheapside before the Great Fire* (pamphlet, ESRC 1985), pp. 19–20.
47. CLRO, Bridge House, Small register.
48. *CLBK*, p. 268.
49. **331**; *Cal. Wills*, ii, p. 455.

lands in Deptford; rents and occupancy remained weak in some areas, and the wardens still had to ask allowance for £63 4s. 3d. of vacancies and decreased rents (**298–9, 319–20**). By 1501–2, however, rents were increasing year by year, vacancies were down, and more properties had been added to the estate (**360, 373**). Still fewer vacancies and decreased rents were reported in 1537, when the London and foreign rents brought in £796 14s. 4½d. (**445–6, 464–5**).

Comparison of the 1537 rental (**401–40**) with earlier evidence shows where the growth in value was concentrated: in the houses on the bridge itself, and in Southwark and outside the city. The rents on the bridge had been more buoyant than some in the early fifteenth century, but by 1537 a smaller number of units (51 on the east side and 49 on the west, compared with 68 and 70 in 1404) had nearly doubled in value. It seems probable that peripheral and suburban parts of London saw increased development and rising rents sooner than the city centre,[50] and this may be borne out by the fact that the Bridge's tenements in Southwark more than doubled in value. The Bridge's foreign rent income had increased because of new acquisitions, but the value of its Lewisham lands had risen, possibly with new building, while the rent from the mills in Lewisham and Stratford had doubled or nearly so.

Not all areas had done so well. The rents in Old Change had declined to a fraction of their earlier level; the combined rents from St Nicholas Shambles and St Audoen (Ewen), and those from Paternoster Row, had hardly changed. Significant improvement in value may have been achieved by considerable expenditure on repairs, even rebuilding, and it is not easy to compute the cost of the works done for comparison with the increase in rents. New shops built in the parish of St Dionis Fenchurch accounted for £2 10s. increased rent in 1381–2 (**1**); the £50 paid to rebuild Spilmans mill at Stratford in the same year (**107**) may have helped to raise its rent to the £6 13s. 4d. paid in 1404 (**143**).[51] The Bridge's property opposite the Standard in Cheapside, in the parish of All Hallows Honey Lane, fell vacant in 1508–9 and into ruin shortly after; the plot remained empty until the house was rebuilt from the foundations in 1536–8. The improved rent then charged was £13 6s. 8d., an increase of £4 on the rent before 1508, but it would have taken a good many years to recover the cost of rebuilding.[52]

The majority of the Bridge estate was treated as an investment, generating the income on which the work depended, but some other concerns were also met. Several houses in the city were set aside as storehouses for building materials, and others allowed rent-free

50. D. Keene, personal communication; G.Rosser, *Medieval Westminster*, pp. 74–92; M. Carlin, *Medieval Southwark* (Hambledon Press, forthcoming), chapter 2, 'Topographical development'.

51. Spilmans mill and Saynes mill were let for 12 marks (£8) together in 1354: *CLBG*, p. 27.

52. D.Keene and V.Harding, *Historical Gazetteer of London before the Great Fire*, i, *Cheapside* (Chadwyck-Healey microfiche, 1986), 11/1; **416, 439, 470, 472–4, 476, 479, 481–2, 486, 497–545** *passim*.

to Bridge officers or employees (**321, 371**). The names of workmen employed by the Bridge can also be found as tenants of Bridge property.[53] Some of the Bridge's rural property was used to make necessary materials: a tilekiln at Lewisham produced some 60,000 tiles in 1420–1 (**244–94** *passim*), while the limekiln at East Greenwich supplied 105 quarters of lime in 1461–2 (**323, 330**). Hay for the Bridge horses was a minor but useful product of Lewisham in 1420–1 (**247–8, 276, 285–6**), but in general the Bridge had to look outside its own estates for the supply of building materials.

The Bridge's sources of income other than its estate, as noted above, declined both in relative terms and absolutely. The importance of the Stocks revenue to the Bridge was asserted in the fourteenth century,[54] but in the fifteenth it was allowed to decline. The rents received from the butchers and fishmongers at the Stocks came to £59 7s. 3d. and £45 3s. 3d. (£104 10s. 6d. in all) in 1381–2, but only to £61 7s. 8d. together in 1420–1. By the middle of the century the wardens of the Butchers' company, and representatives of the fishmongers, leased the market in two parts for £40 and £27 14. 8d. respectively, a slight improvement, but by the end of the century the farms had been reduced to £36 19s. 10d. and £20, at which they remained in the sixteenth century. The overall decline in income from the Stocks was still greater, since in the fourteenth century a number of cupboards or aumbries at an upper level had been let to drapers selling cloth, though ⅔ of these were unlet in 1381–2 (**1, 2**) and thereafter the chambers over the Stocks were let for a small rent (**128**).

The Bridge received a variable amount each year in the form of tolls paid by carts crossing the bridge and ships passing through the drawbridge. The 13th-century customs of the Bridge list a range of tolls in money and in kind, mostly on the bringers of fish for sale,[55] but the accounts from the late fourteenth century list only money payments, probably at the rates of 2d. per cart and 1d. per ship.[56] Citizens of London were probably exempt from the cart-toll at least, and members of other communities claimed exemption,[57] so neither toll can be taken as a proxy for the amount of traffic passing over or under the Bridge. Nevertheless receipts were declining in the late fourteenth century, from £24 8s. 5d. in 1381–2, and were only £7 6s. 11d. in 1420–1, which must reflect some decrease in use. An ordinance in the 1420s, forbidding iron-shod carts from using the bridge, because of the damage they did, may have reduced traffic still further;[58] by

---

53. William Clerk, John Newman, John Swetman, John Bassett, and John Brys, carpenters in 1420–1 (**243**), all held Bridge property according to the previous rental; see index.
54. *CLBE*, pp. 179–80, 184–6, 189–90, 200; *CLBG*, pp. 127, 194; *CLBH*, pp. 242–3
55. *Liber Albus*, i, pp. 234–7.
56. The custom on laden carts was 2d.: CLRO, Journal 3, f. 64, cited by Barron, 'Government of London', p. 191, n.5.
57. *CLBC*, pp. 83, 85–6.
58. *CLBK*, p. 38.

1460, however, such carts were again allowed to use it, but for a much increased toll of 2s., with a marked increase in the Bridge's receipts, to £43 16s. 7d. from carts and wains (**310**). Iron-shod carts were again blamed for the decay of the bridge in 1481, and again banned; by this time too the drawbridge was in decay. By the end of the fifteenth century the toll on carts was farmed for £23 a year; in 1537–8 the farm was only £20 (**359, 448**). If the ban on iron-shod carts was sustained this would help to account for the decline in value.

The toll on ships had risen from a probable 1d. to 2d. by 1460 (**310**); this was increased to 6d. in 1463, but by 1481 the wardens petitioned that the bridge should only be raised for the defence of the city.[59] The drawbridge had been raised against Fauconberg in 1471, but receipts from tolls on ships were last recorded in 1475–6. In the account for 1476–7 it was stated that the drawbridge could not be raised because the stonework needed repair,[60] and this statement was repeated thereafter (**359, 448**), so that the 1481 petition must have been after the event. Fewer ships were in any case using the upper river by this time,[61] and the income to the Bridge was almost negligible, so major expenditure on the drawbridge would only have been justified for strategic and defensive reasons.

The normal annual revenue of the Bridge could not cover all the necessary expenditure in emergencies, and accounting practice discouraged the accumulation of surpluses against possible future needs, so the major works on the bridge were at least in part funded by levies, loans and gifts. Common Council raised 500 marks for the repair of the gatehouse tower in 1439; gifts of £100, 100 marks, and £20, and a loan of 250 marks are also mentioned.[62] Given that the City drew on the Bridge revenues for other purposes, such as the building of Guildhall,[63] this was probably the most appropriate way of handling exceptional demands. As suggested above, balancing the budget, in the sense of tailoring expenditure to meet income, was not a priority.

The fabric of the bridge
The evidence for the decline of passage tolls also indicates some of the problems with the bridge structure in the fifteenth century. However, concern expressed in City Journals and Letterbooks tends to focus on the superstructure, whereas the Bridge House accounts show how much continuous work was necessary to maintain the basic framework of the bridge.

The major event of the period covered here must have been the collapse, in 1437, of the gatehouse tower and the arch or arches on which it stood. There had been anxiety over the strength of the bridge from the 1420s, and it was said to be in a ruinous condition

59. *CLBL*, pp. 24–5, 180
60. *Great Chronicle*, p. 219; CLRO, Bridge House Rental 3, for 1475–6 and 1476–7.
61. *CLBL*, p. 45.
62. Barron 'Government of London', p. 190; Stow, *Survey*, ii, p. 42; *CLBK*, p. 248.
63. Riley, *Memorials*, p. 591.

in 1435, so some disaster was perhaps expected; the severe winter may have precipitated the collapse.[64] Immediate and expensive repairs were necessary, and it is not clear how long the bridge was out of commission; 500 marks was to be raised by the City in 1439, and work was continuing in 1440. Common Council remained concerned about the bridge, appointing committees to review and report on necessary repairs in 1453, 1456, and 1462.[65]

The drawbridge tower, built or rebuilt in 1426, also had serious problems. During Cade's revolt the bridge was stormed and the ropes of the drawbridge 'hewn asunder': if the raised bridge then fell open unbraked it would have caused a violent shock to the stonework. The drawbridge is also said to have been burned in 1450, and the houses round it by Fauconberg's rebels in 1471.[66] The masons were working on 'the tower', probably the drawbridge tower, in 1461–2 (**340**), but the difficulties seem to have proved insuperable, and as noted above, the drawbridge could not be raised after 1476, 'until the stonework of the drawbridge tower be amended' (**359**). The bridge's structural problems were caused principally by the continuous assault of tide and river, and to a lesser extent by the vibration of traffic and the drawbridge; careless watermen also damaged the bridge by collision, and fishermen's nets and anchors in the gulleys below the bridge may have dragged at the foundations.[67] The many piers of the bridge formed something of a dam across the river, and the stability of the stone structure depended on the maintenance of the breastworks or starlings which surrounded each pier with a timber island packed with piles and stone. Without them, the stone piers would rapidly have been undermined, but the existence of the starlings contributed to the problem they were helping to solve, since they narrowed the course of the river still further, increasing the force and scour of both tide and river flow. They must have been awash, if not flooded, at high tide, since work there was dependent on the state of the tide.

In every account printed here, teams of men worked for several months of the year by the tide at the gins and rams, piling and packing the starlings with iron-shod piles and chalk rubble; masons and carpenters also had to work by the tide on the stonework and timbering of the bridge. By the sixteenth century there was a specialist warden carpenter of the waterworks, who supervised both the work at the gin and the carpentry of the bridge (**479, 495–6, 536–40, 542–6**). Probably not more than four to five hours' work was possible at a time, since the rate, 3d. per tide at the ram, with 4d. for masons and carpenters in 1537, was half to three-fifths of the daily wage, and some of the work was by night or 'out of due time' (**386–8, 478–9**). Several rams, gins or beetles used for pile-driving are mentioned, some needing a small team

64. *Great Chronicle*, p. 173; cf. BL MS Cotton Cleopatra C iv, printed in C.L.Kingsford, *Chronicles of London* (1905, reprinted 1977), p. 142; Stow, *Survey*, 1, p. 42; *CLBK*, pp. 38, 191.
65. Barron, 'Government of London', pp. 190–2.
66. Stow, *Survey*, i, p. 24; *Great Chronicle*, pp. 150, 183–6.
67. *CLBL*, p. 180; **312, 364**.

of men to handle them; they appear to have had wooden frames bound with iron, iron handles, and ropes, and were repaired and maintained using curried horse-hides and grease or tallow.[68]

It is not easy to separate work on the bridge from that on the Bridge's other properties: years of high overall expenditure may reflect the repair or rebuilding of tenements, not a high level of work on the bridge itself. There are often indications of the location of work, however, even if the total spent on any project is not given. Thus, the staddle (a word seemingly used to denote both starling and pier) on which the chapel stood underwent repair in 1501–2 (**386**), and one of the arches at the Southwark end in 1537–8 (**478**). The team of masons probably worked almost exclusively on the stonework of the bridge: outside men were hired to make foundations, chimneys, and paving elsewhere in 1461–2 (**340**). The carpenters worked both in the waterworks and on house-building (cf. **479**), while the other building workmen employed by the Bridge (daubers, tilers, paviours, later bricklayers and glaziers) must have concentrated on the tenanted property, including the houses on the bridge.

The materials bought for the works on the bridge give some idea of the nature of its construction.[69] They included stone, notably the fine 'Bridge ashlar', Reigate and Maidstone stone, rag, and chalk rubble for the starlings. The masons used iron crampets, lead, and a waterproof cement made with pitch and rosin, delivered hot, to fix the stonework. Much of the oak timber bought must have been used for house-building, but the elm trees bought and hewn were made into piles and probably boards for the waterworks. Smiths supplied iron pileshoes and nails, and also mended and sharpened tools (adzes, augers, axes) for masons at the waterworks. The wardens' activity in seeking and securing building materials, the prices they paid and the costs of delivery, are thoroughly documented in the accounts.

It is hard to estimate whether the bridge was in better or worse repair at the end of the period covered in this volume than at the beginning: it was nearly a century and a half older, after all, having undergone some severe traumas, but a high level of expenditure had been maintained. Despite the fall of the gatehouse tower and the problems with the drawbridge, London Bridge seems to have fared better than Rochester Bridge, built at the end of the fourteenth century, but cracking within 20 years and actually broken in 1445, 1465, and c.1490. Reconstruction after the the last event took longer and probably cost more than the original building.[70] London Bridge,

---

68. **57, 80, 87, 98, 102, 276, 280, 329–30, 348, 381, 389, 454, 467, 480, 483, 496–9, 501–3, 534–46, 549**. For pile-driving for bridge-work in the seventeenth and eighteenth centuries, see D.J.Ormrod, 'Rochester Bridge, 1660–1825' in Yates and Gibson, ed. *Traffic and politics*, pp. 188–91.

69. See index.

70. R.H.Britnell, 'Rochester Bridge, 1381–1530', in Yates and Gibson, ed., *Traffic and politics*, pp. 70–5.

patched and strengthened piecemeal, nevertheless stood for another three centuries, and served as the city's only bridge for two and a half of them.

The archive of the Bridge House
The Bridge House archive now forms part of the records of the Corporation of London, though the estates of the City and of the Bridge were and still are treated separately; the Chamberlain of London first assumed responsibility for the Bridge House accounts in 1854.[71] The records include muniments of title from the late 12th century, but these are inherited from earlier owners of property. The archive created by the operation of the enterprise dates really from the fourteenth century, when the surviving series of annual accounts begins, and when the rental now bound into the fifteenth-century Small Register or cartulary was compiled (c. 1358). The early sixteenth century may also have been a period when record-keeping received new attention, with the compilation of a second cartulary, the Large Register, and the survival of a second series of weekly account books.[72]

The accounts and rentals
The account rolls and books of the Bridge House run almost continuously from the late 14th century, but the form in which the account is made, and the detail and arrangement of the information provided, changed several times. In general, however, the accounts follow the medieval *compotus* form, and are more concerned to establish the wardens' indebtedness or otherwise than to provide a clear picture of the Bridge's financial state. For the first century they are in Latin, but the scribes used many English (or French) words for materials and items, especially of a technical nature; the first full account to be written in English is that for 1479/80.

The earliest surviving account is for the year Michaelmas 1381 to Michaelmas 1382, but this was certainly not the first written account rendered by the wardens: there is a reference in 1300 to rolls of account delivered to the Chamberlain,[73] and the sporadic audits noted in the early fourteenth century must have been based on some written material.[74] It seems likely that the accounting history of the Bridge was

---

71. B.R.Masters, *The Chamberlain of the City of London, 1237–1987* (1988), p. 14 n.14.
72. H.Deadman and E.Scudder, *An introductory guide to the Corporation of London Records Office* (1994), pp. 22–3; CLRO, typescript 'Catalogue of the ancient deeds, rolls, and manuscript books belonging to the Bridge House records', compiled by A.H. Thomas, Deputy Keeper of the City's records, in 1933; D.Keene and V.Harding, *A survey of documentary sources for property holding in London before the Great Fire* (London Record Society 24, 1985), 14. The materials, binding, handwriting, and decoration of the accounts before 1540 are discussed in Christianson, *Memorials of the book trade*, pp. 17–47 and plates I-XXVII.
73. *CLBC*, p. 70.
74. *CLBC*, pp. 2, 70; *CLBE*, pp. 52, 83, 143–4, 205; *CLBF*, p. 227.

similar to that of the Chamber: accounts were rendered at irregular intervals, often for several years at a time, in the first half of the fourteenth century, with some suggestion that practice was becoming regularised by the middle of the century.[75] In the 1350s indented inventories of Bridge House goods and a rental of the estate suggest a new enthusiasm for formal record-keeping.[76] From the mid 1370s both the Chamberlain's and the Bridge Wardens' accounts seem to have been rendered and audited annually, though it is not clear whether this was an administrative reform, related perhaps to the constitutional changes in the city at this time, or merely a more regular recording of an already established practice. From 1378 auditors of the Chamberlain's and the Bridge Wardens' accounts (normally two aldermen and four commoners) were elected at the assembly or congregation that met on 21 September to elect the sheriffs.[77]

The series of accounts now begins with 17 annual account rolls (Bridgemasters' Accounts 1–17) covering 1381–94, 1395–8, and 1404–5. The first roll (**1-108**), starts at Michaelmas 1381, but refers to 'arrears from the last account' (**1**), and it seems likely that a series of rolls dating from at least the mid 1370s once existed. Although the starting date of 1381 makes it tempting to suppose that earlier rolls were destroyed in the Peasants' Revolt, there does not appear to be any independent evidence for this, and the loss, if loss there was, could have occurred at a later date.[78]

The surviving annual rolls each begin with a charge or list of the income for which the wardens answered, then a list of vacancies and allowances, and a balance of the two. This is followed by week-by-week details of income through the year, and of expenditure likewise. It is thus relatively easy to chart the chronology or seasonal change in the Bridge's activity, but more difficult, or at least laborious, to compute totals for expenditure in different categories. The account rolls do not include a full rental of property, only a total, and it seems likely that the rental referred to in **1** ('as appears in the rental made thereof') is that in the Small Register, dating from the mid-fourteenth century.

From the early fifteenth century the style and physical presentation of the accounts changes. Two series of volumes begin in 1404, one known as 'Rentals' and the other as 'Weekly Payments Books'. The first Rental volume begins with an estate rental for 1404, subsequently amended and updated (**109-187**), and contains weekly receipts and annual receipt totals for the years 1404–21; Rental 2 contains similar receipt accounts for the years 1421–60. The Weekly Payments Books are larger and

75. Masters, *Chamberlain*, p.8.
76. *Memorials*, pp. 261–4; Small Register, ff. 64–86.
77. Ibid.; *CLBH*, pp. 102, 153, 168, 198, 219, 249, 273, 286–7, 313, 332, 344, 355, 367, 385, 399, 415, 425, 434, 440, 444, 449.
78. The rebels caused much damage in Southwark, where the centre of the Bridge House operations lay, but the accounts already rendered and audited should have been in the city, probably in the Chamberlain's care (Masters, *Chamberlain*, p. 10). The muniments of title appear undisturbed.

rougher, and detail weekly expenditure, usually listing wages and regular expenses first, followed by purchases, payment of quit-rents, and, at the quarters, those payments made quarterly especially for the chapel. Taken together, the Rentals and Weekly Payments Books give as full a picture of the Bridge's business as the account rolls, but with the same caveat, that figures for total income or expenditure by category have to be compiled from the weekly details. The present volume calendars the complementary accounts for 1420–1 from Rental 1 and Weekly Payments Book (first series) 2 (**188-241** and **242-95**).

The first series of Weekly Payments Books only continues to 1445, so that for the period 1445–60 there are no expenditure details. It is probably no coincidence that this gap in the records (which is preceded by several years of deterioration in the presentation and detail of the accounts), corresponds to the period when we know from other sources that there was concern over the wardens' account-keeping and management.[79]

Rental 3, starting in 1460, takes a new form, which henceforth becomes the standard for the rest of the period covered in this volume, comprising a fair copy of annual accounts which total income and expenditure by category. Rental 3 contains an estate rental at the beginning of the volume, and the first few accounts take that total as a benchmark and set rent increases, decreases and vacations against it; estate rentals subsequently become more frequent, until by the 1530s almost every annual account is preceded by a new estate rental. This series represents the formal audited accounts, signed by the auditors (**353, 400, 493**). A duplicate set of accounts was made, one being kept at Guildhall and the other at the Bridge House (**330, 351**); only one set now survives, apparently that from the Bridge House rather than the Chamber.[80]

The formal accounts were clearly compiled from a series of other documents, now lost: the bills and 'parcels' of individual workmen, contractors, and suppliers, and probably some kind of weekly reckoning used for the payment of workmen (cf. 331) and to keep a record for the final account. A second series of Weekly Payments Books, made up of annual paper accounts bound together, starts in 1505; possibly some earlier accounts of this kind are now lost, but it seems unlikely that there was ever a continuous run of such accounts from 1445. The Rental account for 1501–2 does not specifically refer to keeping a weekly account, but notes the payment (**381**) of 10d. for a book 'wherein is written all the remembrance of this account', which seems likely to be a paper volume of the kind in the surviving series. The Rental account for 1537–8, which is paralleled by a Weekly Payments Book, does refer to a 'weekly journal' with details of workmen's wages (**478, 480, 482**). The surviving Weekly Payments Books (second series) cover the period to 1538, with gaps 1515–16 and 1527–9; further books (classed as a

---

79. See above, p. xii.
80. ex inf. H.Deadman, CLRO.

third series) cover 1552–5, 1575–6, and 1594–1741, suggesting that the sixteenth-century sequence was once continuous but has since been broken by the chances or mischances of survival.

The formal accounts in the Rentals for 1461–2 and 1501–2 (**296-354 and 355-400**) give an overview of activity for the year as a whole, but not of the seasonal variation. When, as for 1537–8, the Rental account (**441-93**) is supplemented by an up-to-date estate rental (**401-40**) and a complete account of weekly payments (which also includes some memoranda of weekly income) (**494-536**), we have a very full picture of the Bridge's activity, which at this date was very extensive.

Further account series, including receipt books, accounts of materials sold, and 'cash books', begin in the later sixteenth or seventeenth centuries, and contain useful material, but by this time the Bridge House was no longer engaged in repairing and maintaining a large estate across the city: leasehold practice had transferred these responsibilities to tenants. It employed a much smaller workforce, for works in relation to the bridge itself, and the houses on it, so the variety of activity was reduced, and the accounts no longer seem to represent market wages and conditions of employment.

The language of the records

The Bridge House records are written in two languages: Medieval Latin before 1479/80, and Early Modern English after 1479/80. The Medieval Latin of the earlier records is of the type known as 'macaronic', that is, it contains an admixture of English words and suffixes. It was the usual custom of scribes in the Middle Ages to mix languages while keeping accounts. This was not a random practice: nouns, verb stems, and certain suffixes could be written in English, for example, but prepositions, determiners, and finite verbs would normally be in Medieval Latin. Word-order could either follow the Latin tradition (where, for example, adjectives follow nouns) or the English tradition (where adjectives precede the nouns they qualify).

In fact, the two languages overlapped somewhat, for three reasons. Firstly, English and Latin are related languages, descending from a common Indo-European ancestor, and therefore some of the word-stock is shared. Secondly, English had by the end of the Middle Ages borrowed a considerable amount of Latin vocabulary. In these records this is apparent in the vocabulary to do with the chapel on the bridge. Thirdly, medieval scribes used not only letters of the alphabet, but also a system of abbreviation and suspension signs. This enabled them to save valuable parchment space and to write and read more quickly. The signs were the same, whether the scribe was writing in Latin or English. Medieval Latin was a language which inflected more than Early Modern English. Much of its grammatical information was conveyed by suffixes attached to word-stems, where English used separate words, and a rather more fixed word order, to do the same job. The Bridge scribes frequently reduced the Medieval Latin inflexions to a sign, so that the reader could either interpret the whole word as fully-inflected Latin, or just look at the stem and not bother with the inflexion. So the use of the abbreviation and suspension system also helped to blend the two languages. Thus, although the records before 1479/80 are in Medieval Latin, they nevertheless contain many English words which have otherwise been lost to us, and many antedatings of English words known only at a later date elsewhere, or with a different meaning.

This archive is an invaluable source of fourteenth- and fifteenth-century London vocabulary to do with all aspects of life on the river Thames, from the technical terminology relating to the fabric of the bridge, to the now-lost names of the marshes, ditches, tributaries and sandbanks that went to make up the water-system it traversed.[81]

Note on editorial method
As stated above, the records have been translated from Medieval Latin or Early Modern English into modern English. No information has been omitted, but some of the phrases and expressions have been given more briefly, and in general an attempt has been made to render a modern version rather than a literal translation. The original form of some words is given, where the translation is difficult or dubious or the vocabulary particularly interesting, and there is a brief glossary at the end of the volume before the index. Christian names have been translated or modernised, but all surnames are given as in the manuscripts. Most place-names in London and elsewhere have been modernised, but unusual variants, or ones without a modern equivalent, are given in the original. Following the normal practice in this society's publications, the text has been broken down into paragraphs numbered in **bold**. In most cases these represent a paragraphed entry in the original, but where such an entry runs on for more than a page, it has been broken up here into smaller sections, each numbered individually, usually at the page-breaks. Indexing is by paragraph number.

In general the originals are very clear, and relatively little editorial interpolation is necessary. The exception to this is the rental for 1404 (**109–87**), heavily amended in succeeding years.[82] The following set of conventions has been adopted, principally for the rental, but is also applied elsewhere in the edition:

Words in *italics* are in the original language of the MS.
[ ] denotes an editorial insertion.
( ) denotes words or entries in the original hand of the MS, that have subsequently been crossed through.
{ } denotes words or entries in a hand later than the original, that have subsequently been crossed through.
< > denotes words or entries in a hand later than the original, not subsequently crossed through, representing the final state of the MS.

81. See L.C. Wright, *Sources of London English: Thames technical vocabulary* (Oxford University Press, forthcoming 1995).
82. One folio of the rental is reproduced in Christianson, *Memorials of the book trade*, plate II.

Division of labour on the volume reflected the respective interests of the editors. Laura Wright made a *litteratim* transcript of the accounts on computer, which Vanessa Harding translated, edited, and indexed; the latter also transcribed the estate rentals. Both editors checked the transcript/translation against the originals. Vanessa Harding wrote the introduction, with the exception of the section on the language of the records, which is by Laura Wright.

This project of work on the Bridge House records has taken some time to come to completion, and the editors owe many debts. Birkbeck College, University of London, has sustained Vanessa Harding's research activity since 1984, and made a research grant to both editors for a pilot project in 1988/9. Laura Wright held a British Academy fellowship at Keble College, Oxford, and is now at the University of Hertfordshire. Permission to publish this edition was kindly given by the Corporation of London, while work on the records was made possible by the helpful assistance of the staff of the Corporation of London Records Office, under the direction of James Sewell, Deputy Keeper of the Records. In particular, we would like to thank Derek Keene for his advice and comments on the text. We would like to dedicate the volume to Caroline Barron, in gratitude for her encouragement, inspiration and support over many years.

LONDON BRIDGE: SELECTED ACCOUNTS AND RENTALS, 1381–1538

BRIDGEMASTERS' ACCOUNT ROLL 1, 1381–2

1. [m.1r][1] [Account of John Hoo and Henry Yevele], Keepers of London Bridge from 29 September, Michaelmas, 5 Richard II [1381] to the same feast next year, 6 Richard II [1382].

[Arrears. The same answer for £122 15d.] received of arrears from the last account. Total £122 15d.

[Rents and] Farms. Item they answer for £389 16s. 4d. received from the rents of the Bridge's tenements in London and Southwark, lying in the parishes as appears in the rental made thereof. And for £12 received of the rent of 20 cabins [*cabani*] standing under the wall of the Friars Minor. For £30 3s. 2d. received of quit-rents in London and in Southwark, lying in various parishes as appears [by the rental made thereof]. And for £28 11s. 10d. received from the farm of the manor, lands, meadows, pastures and mill, namely at Lewisham, Stratford, and in the fields of Hatcham, Camberwell and Southwark, lying in various parishes as also appears [by the rental made thereof] Total £460 11s. 4d.

[Increase] Item they answer for 50s. increase of rent for 6 new shops built in the parish of St Dionis Fenchurch, for the terms of Easter and the Nativity of St John the Baptist. And 6s. 9d. received as increase of rent for a certain tenement at Lewisham [bought of Matilda] Bray [for the terms of] Christmas, Easter and the Nativity of St John the Baptist. Total 66s. 9d.

[Foreign receipts] Item they answer for 20s. received for the fishery under London Bridge, let at farm. Total 20s.

[Receipts by rolls attached to the account] Item they answer for £136 11s. 6d. received from the fishmongers and butchers standing at the Stocks, within and without, for the toll of ships passing under the Bridge [*de passag' navium*], for carts crossing the Bridge, for baskets on the Bridge, for legacies and fines [*gersumis*] as appears below in the roll attached to this account. Total £136 11s. 6d.

[Money received for cupboards for cloth merchants standing above the Stocks] Item they answer for £32 18s. 8d. received for 38 cupboards [*almarioli*] for drapers standing above the Stocks selling

1

cloth, for 52 weeks taking from each per week 4d. Total £32 18s. 8d.

Sum total of the receipt £755 19s. 6d.

1. Much of the editorial insertion in **1**, **2**, is from T.A.M.Bishop's translation (MS in CLRO). He could apparently read parts now illegible to the naked eye.

2. Vacancies. Item they seek allowance for vacancies of the Bridge's tenements in London and Southwark, as appears on the dorse of this roll, £15 12s. 9d. Item they seek allowance for vacancies of the cabins standing under the wall of the Friars Minor, as appears on the dorse of this roll, 33s. 4d. Item they seek allowance for vacancies of tenements which owe yearly quit-rent to London Bridge in London and Southwark, as appears on the dorse of this roll, 59s. 2d. Item they seek allowance for vacancies of land and meadow belonging to the Bridge in the fields of Hatcham and Camberwell, as appears on the dorse of this roll, 62s. 8d. And for the vacancy of 25 cupboards over the Stocks for 52 weeks at 4d. for each cupboard per week, £21 13s. 4d. Item they seek allowance for the debt of James Rameseye, fishmonger, since he is dead and has nothing whereby he could be distrained, 60s.

Total £48 15d.

Payments of rent [*resoluciones*]. Item they seek allowance for payments for the Bridge's tenements in London and Southwark, as appears by the rental made thereof, £18 18s. ¹/₄d. Item they seek allowance for 6s. 9d. paid to Matilda Bray for a certain tenement at Lewisham lately bought of her, namely for the terms of Easter and the Nativity of St John the Baptist, for each term 2s. 3d. Total £18 8s. 3¹/₄d.

Stipend of the Wardens and Renter. Item they seek allowance for the stipend of the said Wardens of London Bridge for the time of this account £20. And for the stipend of one man collecting the rents of the Bridge's tenements and the quit-rents belonging to the Bridge for the same time £10. Total £30.

Expenses according to the roll attached to this account. Item they seek allowance for various weekly expenses as appears below in the parcels of the roll attached to this account. For £3 9s. 8¹/₂d. Total £3 9s. 8¹/₂d.

Sum total of the expenses, stipends, vacancies of tenements and quit-rents of the Bridge, and the payment of rents, as appears in detail in the rental made thereof. For £99 19s. 2³/₄d.

And thus they owe on the account £656 3¹/₄d.

[m. 1d¹ Vacancies at Michaelmas term.

From the weighhouse and tollhouse on the Bridge 9s.

From a mansion in the stone gate on the Bridge 6s. 8d.

From a tenement in Tower Street, formerly belonging to Richard Albon 6s. 8d.

From a small house attached to the same tenement 3s. 9d.

From a shop outside the stone gate on the Bridge 8s. 4d.

From another shop there under the same gate 5s.

From 4 shops in Old Change 26s. 8d.
From 6 old shops, demolished, in the parish of St Dionis *Vanchurche* 45s.
From 3 cabins under the wall of the Friars Minor 7s. 6d.
From another cabin there 3s. 4d.
Sum £6 23d.

Vacancies at Christmas term.
From the weighhouse and tollhouse 9s.
From a mansion in the stone gate 6s. 8d.
From a tenement in Tower Street 6s. 8d.
From a small house attached to the same tenement 3s. 9d.
From 5 shops in Old Change 33s. 4d.
From 2 cabins under the wall of the Friars Minor 5s.
From another cabin there 3s. 4d.
From 6 old shops, demolished, at Fenchurch 45s.
From a tenement at Lewisham acquired from Matilda Bray 2s. 3d.
Sum 115s.

Vacancies at Easter term.
From the weighhouse and tollhouse 9s.
From a mansion in the stone gate 6s. 8d.
From a tenement in Tower Street 6s. 8d.
From a small house attached to the same tenement 3s. 9d.
From 3 shops in Old Change 20s.
From 2 cabins under the wall of the Friars Minor 5s.
From another cabin there 3s. 4d.
From a house in the parish of St Augustine Papey 2s. 6d.
From a tenement at Lewisham acquired from Matilda Bray 2s.3d.
Sum 59s. 2d.

Vacancies at the term of St John the Baptist.
From the weighhouse and tollhouse 9s.
From a mansion in the stone gate 6s. 8d.
From a tenement in Tower Street 6s. 8d.
From a small house attached to the same tenement 3s. 9d.
From 2 shops in Old Change 13s. 4d.
From a cabin under the wall of the Friars Minor 2s. 6d.
From another cabin there 3s. 4d.
From a house in the parish of St Augustine Papey 2s. 6d.
From a tenement at Lewisham acquired from Matilda Bray 2s. 3d.
Sum 50s.

Vacancies of quit-rent.
From the tenement where the park of Robert Little is now built, in the parish of St Margaret Bridge Street 12d.
From the tenement late of John Lovekyn, in the parish of St Michael Crooked Lane 5s.
From the tenement of Simon Mordone in the same parish 5s.
From the tenement of Sir William Henlee knight, in the parish of St Olave upon the Wall 3s. 6d.

3

From the tenement late of fiz Michel in Red Cross Street 4d.

From the tenement late of William de Basyngge, where the new cemetery is now built 4d.

From the tenement late of Hamo Lumbard, since he has received from the Mayor remission of the rent for life 13s. 4d.

From the tenement late of Matilda de Balsham, since it is now in possession of the Bridge 2s.

From the tenement of William de Blacchingleghe 12d.

From the tenement late of William de Sabrictesworthe 4d.

From the meadow at Stratford called *Russhope* 2s.

From the tenement of the Prior and Convent of the Blessed Mary of Southwark called *Exmuthe* 13s. 4d.

From the tenement of Ralph Double, late of Geoffrey Horn, called the *Mote* 8s.

From the tenement of Sir Thomas Peytevyn in the parish of St Alban Wood Street 2s.

From the tenement in Tower Street late of Richard Albon, since it is now in possession of the Bridge 2s.

Sum 59s. 2d.

Vacancies of the cupboards above the Stocks.

From 25 cupboards for cloth merchants standing above the Stocks, during the whole of the undermentioned year, at 17s. 4d. for each cupboard £21 13s. 4d.

Sum £21 13s. 4d.

Sum total of vacancies of tenements belonging to the Bridge, of quit-rents, cabins, lands, meadows, and cupboards above the Stocks, £41 18s. 7d.]

> 1. Almost the whole of this side of the membrane is now illegible to the naked eye.

3. [m.2] Receipts, Saturday after the feast of St Michael [5 October 1381].

From the rents of the Stocks [*les Stockes*], namely from the fishmongers standing within and without, 19s. From the butchers standing there, 27s. 4d. From tolls on ships [*de passag' navium*], 4s. 6d. From carts, 5s. 2d. Total 56s.

4. Receipts, Saturday before the feast of St Edward King and Confessor [12 October].

From the rents of the Stocks, namely from the fishmongers standing within and without, 19s. From the butchers standing there, 27s. 4d. From tolls on ships, 21d. From carts, 4s. 10d. From baskets [*corbell'*], 1d. Total 53s.

5. Receipts, Saturday after the feast of St Luke the Evangelist [19 October].

From the rents of the Stocks, namely from the fishmongers standing within and without, 19s. From the butchers standing there, 27s. 4d.

From tolls on ships, 7s. 8d. From carts, 6s. 4d. From baskets, 1d. Total 60s. 5d.

6. Receipts, Saturday before the feast of the Apostles Simon and Jude [26 October].
From the rents of the Stocks, namely from the fishmongers standing within and without, 19s. From the butchers standing there, 27s. 4d. From tolls on ships, 5s. 3d. From carts, 5s. 4d. Total 56s. 11d.

7. Receipts, Saturday after the feast of All Saints [2 November].
From the rents of the Stocks, namely from the fishmongers standing within and without, 19s. From the butchers standing there, 27s. 4d. From tolls on ships, 6s. 8d. From carts, 4s. 6d. Total 57s. 6d.

8. Receipts, Saturday after the feast of St Leonard Abbot [9 November].
From the rents of the Stocks, namely from the fishmongers standing within and without, 19s. From the butchers standing there, 27s. 4d. From tolls on ships, 8s. 5d. From carts, 7s. 2d. From baskets, 1d. Item received for 2 pieces of timber sold, 4s. Total 66s.

9. Receipts, Saturday the feast of St Edmund Archbishop of Canterbury [16 November].
From the rents of the Stocks, namely from the fishmongers standing within and without, 19s. From the butchers standing there, 27s. 4d. From tolls on ships, 2s. 3d. From carts, 4s. 10d. Total 53s. 5d.

10. Receipts, Saturday the feast of St Clement [23 November].
From the rents of the Stocks, namely from the fishmongers standing within and without, 19s. From the butchers standing there, 27s. 4d. From tolls on ships, 16d. From carts, 3s. 6d. Item received from a Flemish boatman to repair damage to the Bridge House boat, 6s. 8d. Total 57s. 10d.

11. Receipts, Saturday the feast of St Andrew the Apostle [30 November].
From the rents of the Stocks, namely from the fishmongers standing within and without, 19s. From the butchers standing there, 27s. 4d. From tolls on ships, 3s. 2d. From carts, 4s. Total 53s. 6d.

12. Receipts, Saturday before the feast of the Conception of the Blessed Mary [7 December].
From the rents of the Stocks, namely from the fishmongers standing within and without, 19s. From the butchers standing there, 27s. 4d. From tolls on ships, 22d. From carts, 5s. 6d. Total 53s. 8d.

13. Receipts, Saturday after the feast of St Lucy the Virgin [14 December].
From the rents of the Stocks, namely from the fishmongers standing within and without, 19s. From the butchers standing there, 27s. 4d. From tolls on ships, 4s. 11d. From carts, 5s. 4d. Total 56s. 7d.

14. Receipts, Saturday the feast of St Thomas the Apostle [21 December]. From the rents of the Stocks, namely from the fishmongers standing within and without, 19s. From the butchers standing there, 27s. 4d. From tolls on ships, nil. From carts, 3s. 4d. Total 49s. 8d.

15. Receipts, Saturday after Christmas [28 December]. From the rents of the Stocks, namely from the fishmongers standing within and without, 19s. From the butchers standing there, 27s. 4d. From tolls on ships, 8s. 2d. From carts, 14d. Total 55s. 8d.

16. Receipts, Saturday before Epiphany [4 January 1382]. From the rents of the Stocks, namely from the fishmongers standing within and without, 19s. From the butchers standing there, 27s. 4d. From tolls on ships, 9s. 3d. From carts, 2s. 4d. Total 57s. 11d.

17. Receipts, Saturday before the feast of St Hilary [11 January]. From the rents of the Stocks, namely from the fishmongers standing within and without, 19s. From the butchers standing there, 27s. 4d. From tolls on ships, 4s. 1d. From carts, 2s. 10d. Total 52s. 3d. [sic]

18. [m. 3] Receipts, Saturday before the feast of St Wulfstan the bishop [18 January]. From the rents of the Stocks, namely from the fishmongers standing within and without, 19s. From the butchers standing there, 27s. 4d. From tolls on ships, nil. From carts, 4s. 2d. Total 50s. 6d.

19. Receipts, Saturday the feast of the Conversion of St Paul [25 January]. From the rents of the Stocks, namely from the fishmongers standing within and without, 19s. From the butchers standing there, 27s. 4d. From tolls on ships, 21d. From carts, 4s. 8d. Total 52s. 9d.

20. Receipts, Saturday the eve of the Purification of the Blessed Mary [1 February]. From the rents of the Stocks, namely from the fishmongers standing within and without, 19s. From the butchers standing there, 27s. 4d. From tolls on ships, 2s. 3d. From carts, 3s. 8d. Total 52s. 3d.

21. Receipts, Saturday before the feast of St Agatha the Virgin [8 February]. From the rents of the Stocks, namely from the fishmongers standing within and without, 19s. From the butchers standing there, 27s. 4d. From tolls on ships, 11d. From carts, 5s. 2d. Total 52s. 5d.

22. Receipts, Saturday after the feast of St Valentine [15 February]. From the rents of the Stocks, namely from the fishmongers standing within and without, 19s. From the butchers standing there, 27s. 4d. From tolls on ships, 4s. 11d. From carts, 5s. Total 56s. 3d.

23. Receipts, Saturday the feast of St Peter in Cathedra [22 February].

From the rents of the Stocks, namely from the fishmongers standing within and without, 19s. From the butchers standing there, 27s. 4d. From tolls on ships, 5d. From carts, 3s. 10d. Total 50s. 7d.

24. Receipts, Saturday 1 March.
From the rents of the Stocks, namely from the fishmongers standing within and without, 19s. From the butchers, nil, it being Lent. From tolls on ships, nil. From carts, 5s. 2d. From baskets, 1d. From legacies, 2s. Total 26s. 3d.

25. Receipts, Saturday before the feast of St Gregory the Pope [8 March].
From the rents of the Stocks, namely from the fishmongers standing within, 19s. From the butchers, nil, it being Lent. From tolls on ships, 22d. From carts, 4s. 10d. From baskets, 1½d. Item received for 1000 Flemish tiles [*fflaundrishtyle*] sold, 6s. Total 31s. 9½d.

26. Receipts, Saturday after the feast of St Gregory the Pope [15 March].
From the rents of the Stocks, namely from the fishmongers standing within and without, 19s. From the butchers, nil, it being Lent. From tolls on ships, 7s. 1d. From carts, 5s. 10d. From baskets, 1d. Total 32s.

27. Receipts, Saturday after the feast of St Cuthbert [22 March].
From the rents of the Stocks, namely from the fishmongers standing within and without, 19s. From the butchers, nil, it being Lent. From tolls on ships, 3s. 2d. From carts, 4s. 4d. Total 26s. 6d.

28. Receipts, Saturday after the feast of the Annunciation of the Blessed Mary [29 March].
From the rents of the Stocks, namely from the fishmongers standing within and without, 19s. From the butchers, nil, it being Lent. From tolls on ships, 9s. 4d. From carts, 3s. 6d. Item received of the gift of John Gilbert of the parish of Lee in co. Kent, 20s. Total 51s. 10d.

29. Receipts, Saturday the eve of Easter [5 April].
From the rents of the Stocks, namely from the fishmongers standing within and without, 19s. From the butchers, nil, it being Lent. From tolls on ships, 9s. 5d. From carts, 2s. 10d. Item received of Gilbert Beauchamp, fishmonger, as a fine [*gersum'*] for a certain shop in Bridge Street [*in vico pont'*] which James Rameseye, fishmonger, lately held, 3s. 4d. Item received of the collection on the Bridge on Good Friday, 4s. 2d. Item received of the legacy of a certain man called Essex, 12d. Total 39s. 9d.

30. Receipts, Saturday in the week of Easter [12 April].
From the rents of the Stocks, namely from the fishmongers standing within and without, 19s. From the butchers, nil, it being Easter Week.

From tolls on ships, 6s. 9d. From carts, 4s. Item received for timber and stones sold, 24s. 8d. Total 54s. 5d.

31. Receipts, Saturday before the feast of St George the Martyr [19 April].
From the rents of the Stocks, namely from the fishmongers standing within and without, 19s. From the butchers standing there, 29s. From tolls on ships, 4s. 6d. From carts, 6s. 2d. Total 58s. 8d.

32. Receipts, Saturday after the feast of St Mark the Evangelist [26 April].
From the rents of the Stocks, namely from the fishmongers standing within and without, 19s. From the butchers standing there, 29s. From tolls on ships, 3s. 2d. From carts, 4s. 10d. Total 56s.

33. [m. 4] Receipts, Saturday the feast of the Invention of the Holy Cross [3 May].
From the rents of the Stocks, namely from the fishmongers standing within and without, 19s. From the butchers standing there, 29s. From tolls on ships, 11d. From carts, 2s. 8d. Item received of the legacy of John Dylewysh late carter of the Bridge House, 5s. Total 56s. 7d.

34. Receipts, Saturday after the feast of St John at the Latin Gate [10 May].
From the rents of the Stocks, namely from the fishmongers standing within and without, 19s. From the butchers standing there, 29s. From tolls on ships, nil. From carts, 4s. 4d. Item received for 2000 bricks [*waltyele*] sold, 9s. 4d. Total 61s. 8d.

35. Receipts, Saturday before the feast of St Dunstan the Archbishop [17 May].
From the rents of the Stocks, namely from the fishmongers standing within and without, 19s. From the butchers standing there, 29s. From tolls on ships, 3s. 2d. From carts, 6s. 8d. Total 57s. 6d. [sic]

36. Receipts, Saturday the eve of Pentecost [24 May].
From the rents of the Stocks, namely from the fishmongers standing within and without, 19s. From the butchers standing there, 29s. From tolls on ships, 5s. 5d. From carts, 7s. 2d. Total 60s. 7d.

37. Receipts, Saturday in the week of Pentecost [31 May].
From the rents of the Stocks, namely from the fishmongers standing within and without, 19s. From the butchers standing there, 29s. From tolls on ships, 15d. From carts, 5s. 6d. Total 54s. 9d.

38. Receipts, Saturday the feast of St Wulfstan the Archbishop [7 June].
From the rents of the Stocks, namely from the fishmongers standing within and without, 19s. From the butchers standing there, 29s. From tolls on ships, 11d. From carts, 6s. Total 54s. 11d.

39. Receipts, Saturday after the feast of St Barnabas the Apostle [14 June].
From the rents of the Stocks, namely from the fishmongers standing within and without, 19s. From the butchers standing there, 29s. From tolls on ships, 5s. From carts, 9s. 2d. Total 62s. 2d.

40. Receipts, Saturday before the feast of the Nativity of St John the Baptist [21 June].
From the rents of the Stocks, namely from the fishmongers standing within and without, 19s. From the butchers standing there, 24s. 5d. From tolls on ships, 12s. 6d. From carts, 7s. 2d. Total 63s. 1d.

41. Receipts, Saturday the eve of the Apostles Peter and Paul [28 June].
From the rents of the Stocks, namely from the fishmongers standing within and without, 19s. From the butchers standing there, 24s. 5d. From tolls on ships, 2s. 8d. From carts, 4s. 10d. Total 50s. 11d.

42. Receipts, Saturday before the feast of the Translation of St Thomas the Martyr [5 July].
From the rents of the Stocks, namely from the fishmongers standing within and without, 19s. From the butchers standing there, 24s. 5d. From tolls on ships, 2s. 8d. From carts, 6s. Item received for the wages of divers carpenters hired to Henry Yevele, and for stones and boards sold to him, 63s. 1d. Total 115s. 2d.

43. Receipts, Saturday before the feast of the Translation of St Swithin [12 July].
From the rents of the Stocks, namely from the fishmongers standing within and without, 19s. From the butchers standing there, 24s. 5d. From tolls on ships, 3s. 7d. From carts, 6s. 8d. Total 53s. 8d.

44. Receipts, Saturday before the feast of St Margaret [19 July].
From the rents of the Stocks, namely from the fishmongers standing within and without, 19s. From the butchers standing there, 24s. 5d. From tolls on ships, 6s. 3d. From carts, 9s. 2d. Item received of John Longe, butcher, as a fine for a certain place for a butcher at the Stocks, 6s. 8d. Total 65s 6d.

45. Receipts, Saturday after the feast of St James the Apostle [26 July].
From the rents of the Stocks, namely from the fishmongers standing within and without, 19s. From the butchers standing there, 24s. 5d. From tolls on ships, 5s. From carts, 12s. 6d. Total 60s. 11d.

46. Receipts, Saturday after the feast of St Peter ad Vincula [2 August].
From the rents of the Stocks, namely from the fishmongers standing within and without, 19s. From the butchers standing there, 24s. 5d. From tolls on ships, 5s. 3d. From carts, 7s. 8d. From the legacy of a certain man called Essex, 2s. Total 58s. 4d.

47. Receipts, Saturday the eve [of the feast] of St Lawrence [9 August].
From the rents of the Stocks, namely from the fishmongers standing within and without, 12s. 1½d. From the butchers standing there, 24s. 5d. From tolls on ships, nil. From carts, 6s. 2d. Total 42s. 8d. [sic]

48. Receipts, Saturday after the feast of the Assumption of the Blessed Mary [16 August].
From the rents of the Stocks, namely from the fishmongers standing within and without, 10s. 9d. From the butchers standing there, 22s. 5d. From tolls on ships, 3s. 7d. From carts, 6s. 10d. Total 43s. 7d.

49. Receipts, Saturday the eve of St Bartholomew the Apostle [23 August].
From the rents of the Stocks, namely from the fishmongers standing within and without, 6s. 7½d. From the butchers standing there, 22s. 5d. From tolls on ships, 16d. From carts, 9s. 4d. Total 39s. 8½d.

50. [m. 5] Receipts, Saturday after the feast of the Decollation of St John the Baptist [30 August].
From the rents of the Stocks, namely from the fishmongers standing within and without, 8s. 9d. From the butchers standing there, 22s. 5d. From tolls on ships, 16d. From carts, 5s. 2d. Total 37s. 8d.

51. Receipts, Saturday before the feast of the Nativity of the Blessed Mary [6 September].
From the rents of the Stocks, namely from the fishmongers standing within and without, 7s. 3d. From the butchers standing there, 22s. 5d. From tolls on ships, 4s. 6d. From carts, 4s. 8d. Total 38s. 10d.

52. Receipts, Saturday before the feast of the Exaltation of the Holy Cross [13 September].
From the rents of the Stocks, namely from the fishmongers standing within and without, 7s. 3d. From the butchers standing there, 22s. 5d. From tolls on ships, 21d. From carts, 7s. 2d. Total 38s. 7d.

53. Receipts, Saturday the eve of St Matthew the Apostle and Evangelist [20 September].
From the rents of the Stocks, namely from the fishmongers standing within and without, 7s. 3d. From the butchers standing there, 22s. 5d. From tolls on ships, 10d. From carts, 5s. 10d. Total 36s. 4d.

54. Receipts, Saturday before the feast of Michaelmas [27 September].
From the rents of the Stocks, namely from the fishmongers standing within and without, 7s. 3d. From the butchers standing there, 22s. 5d. From tolls on ships, 11d. From carts, 7s. 2d. Item received from John Leveryngton as a fine for a certain shop on the Bridge which Nicholas Braundeston lately held, 6s. 8d. Total 44s. 5d.

55. Sum of all the moneys received in the aforesaid parcels, £136 11s. 6d. [sic]

56. [m. 6] Expenses, Saturday after the feast of St Michael [5 October 1381].
In the wages of 5 chaplains celebrating in the chapel on the bridge, 11s. 5½d. Item in bread and wine, 3d. Item to the clerk of the chapel, 15d. Item to the clerk of the drawbridge [*pontis vertibil'*], 20d. Item in the wages of 6 carpenters, 22s. 1d. Item in the wages of 4 masons, 14s. 3d. Item in the wages of 2 sawyers, 7s. Item in the wages of the boatman, 2s. 6d. Item in the wages of the cook and dogs, 2s. 6d. Item in the wages of the carter, 22d. Item in the horses' fodder, 15d. Item in the wages of 1 servant [*garcionis*], 2s. Item in the wages of 1 paviour, 3s. 4d. Item in the wages of 1 dauber and his servant, 4s. 6d. Item in the wages of 21 tidemen [*tidemannorum*] working at the Ram for 6 hours, 32s. Item paid to a certain mason hired for 3 days, 12½d. Item paid for binding 3 barrels and 1 tine, 10d. Item paid for 1 boatload of ragstone [*Rag'*], 18s. Item paid for 1 boatload of chalk [*calc'*], 9s. Item paid for 1 horse hired to draw the Bridge House cart for 1 week, 12d. Total £6 18s. 7d. [sic; *recte* £6 17s. 9d.]

57. Expenses, Saturday before the feast of the Translation of St Edward King and Confessor [12 October].
In the wages of 5 chaplains, 11s. 5½d. Item in bread and wine, 3d. Item to the clerk of the chapel, 15d. Item to the clerk of the bridge, 20d. Item in the wages of 6 carpenters, 22s. 1d. Item in the wages of 5 masons, 18s. Item in the wages of 2 sawyers, 7s. Item in the wages of the boatman, 2s. 6d. Item in the wages of the cook and dogs, 2s. 6d. Item in the wages of the carter, 22d. Item in the horses' fodder, 15d. Item in the wages of 2 servants, 4s. Item in the wages of 21 tidemen working at the Ram for 5 hours, 26s. 8d. Item in the wages of 1 paviour, 3s. 4d. Item in the wages of 1 dauber and his servant, 4s. 6d. Item paid for 1 boatload of ragstone bought, 15s. Item paid to 3 tilers and their 3 servants for 6 days, taking between them 3s. the day, 18s. Item paid to another tiler for himself for 6 days, taking 7d. the day, 3s. 6d. Item paid for 1 gallon of tallow [*pinguedinis*] bought to grease the blade [*swerdo*],[1] 8d. Item paid for 1 new axe bought and for steeling another axe 4s. Item paid for 1 horse hired for 1 week, 12d. Total £7 10s. 5½d. [sic; *recte* £7 10s. 4½d.]

1. Apparently the striking part of the ram or pile-driver: cf. **80, 87**.

58. Expenses, Saturday after the feast of St Luke the Evangelist [19 October].
In the wages of 5 chaplains, 11s. 5½d. Item in bread and wine, 3d. Item to the clerk of the chapel, 15d. Item to the clerk of the bridge, 20d. Item in the wages of 6 carpenters, 22s 1d. Item in the wages of 5 masons, 18s. Item in the wages of 2 sawyers, 7s. Item in the wages of the boatman, 2s. 6d. Item in the wages of the cook and dogs, 2s. 6d. Item in the wages of the carter, 22d. Item in the wages of 2 servants, 4s. Item in the horses'

fodder, 15d. Item in the wages of 1 paviour, 3s. 4d. Item in the wages of 1 dauber and his servant, 4s. 6d. Item in the wages of 21 tidemen working at the Ram for 4 hours, 21s. 4d. Item paid for 4 tilers and their servants for 5 days, 20s. Item paid for 1 boatload of chalk, 9s. Item paid for 2½ hundred[weight] of lime [*calc' ust'*], at 6s. the hundred, 15s. Item paid for 1 horse hired for 1 week, 12d. Total £7 7s. 11½d.

59. Expenses, Saturday after the feast of the Apostles Simon and Jude [26 October].
In the wages of 5 chaplains, 11s. 5½d. Item in bread and wine, 3d. Item to the clerk of the chapel, 15d. Item to the clerk of the bridge, 20d. Item in the wages of 6 carpenters, 22s. 1d. Item in the wages of 5 masons, 18s. Item in the wages of 2 sawyers, 7s. Item in the wages of the boatman, 2s. 6d. Item in the wages of the cook and dogs, 2s. 6d. Item in the wages of the carter, 22d. Item in the horses' fodder, 15d. Item in the wages of 2 servants, 4s. Item in the wages of 1 paviour, 3s 4d. Item in the wages of 1 dauber and his servant, 4s. 6d. Item in the wages of 21 tidemen working at the Ram for 4 hours, 21s. 4d. Item paid for 8 cartloads of sand [*zabuli*] at 3½d. the cartload, 2s. 4d. Item paid for 1 horse hired for 1 week, 12d. Item paid to 4 tilers and their servants for 6 days, 24s. Item paid for 30,000 *tylepynnes* 3s. 9d. Item paid for 25 hollow [*concav'*] tiles, 20d. Item paid for straw bought for the dauber, 21d. Item paid for 5,800 tiles at 6s. 4d. the thousand, 36s. 9d. Total £8 14s. 2½d. [sic; *recte* £8 13s. 2½d.]

60. Expenses, Saturday after the feast of All Saints [2 November].
In the wages of 5 chaplains, 11s. 5½d. Item in bread and wine, 3d. Item to the clerk of the chapel, 15d. Item to the clerk of the bridge, 20d. Item in the wages of 6 carpenters, 22s. 1d. Item in the wages of 5 masons, 18s. Item in the wages of 2 sawyers, 7s. Item in the wages of the boatman, 2s. 6d. Item in the wages of the cook and dogs, 2s. 6d. Item in the wages of the carter, 22d. Item in the horses' fodder, 15d. Item in the wages of 2 servants, 4s. Item in the wages of 1 paviour, 3s. 4d. Item in the wages of 1 dauber and his servant, 4s. 6d. Item in the wages of 21 tidemen working at the Ram for 2 hours, 10s. 8d. Item paid for 2 skins of parchment, 6d. Item paid for incense bought, 2d. Item paid for 1 boatload of chalk bought, 9s. Item paid for 48 rings and 48 latches with fittings bought for doors, 14s. Item paid for 1 pr. wheels, 4s. 6d. Item paid for oil and varnish bought for the new shops built in Fenchurch Street, 11s. Item paid to 1 dauber in payment [*rowardo*] of his contract for daubing the said shops, 13s. 4d. Item paid for hollow tiles [*holwtyles*] called *Creestis*, 3s. 4d. Total £7 8s. 2d. [sic; *recte* £7 8s. 1½d.]

61. Expenses, Saturday after the feast of St Leonard Abbot [9 November].
In the wages of 5 chaplains, 11s. 5½d. Item in bread and wine, 3d. Item to the clerk of the chapel, 15d. Item to the clerk of the bridge, 20d. Item in the wages of 6 carpenters, 22s. 1d. Item in the wages of 5 masons, 18s. Item in the wages of 2 sawyers, 7s. Item in the wages of the boatman, 2s. 6d. Item in the wages of the cook and dogs, 2s. 6d.

Item in the wages of the carter, 22d. Item in the horses' fodder, 15d. Item in the wages of 2 servants, 4s. Item in the wages of 1 paviour, 3s. 4d. Item in the wages of 1 dauber and his servant, 4s. 6d. Item in the wages of 21 tidemen working at the Ram for 5 hours, 26s. 8d. Item paid for 2 boatloads of chalk, 17s. Item paid for 1 hundred[weight] of lime, 6s. Item paid to 1 tiler and his servant for 4 days, 4s. Item paid for 3,000 tilepins, 4½d. Item paid for 9 cartloads of clay [*argill*'], 22d. Item paid for various nails bought for the new houses at Fenchurch at various times, £4 13s. 10d. Total £11 11s. 4d.

62. Expenses, Saturday the feast of St Edmund Archbishop of Canterbury [16 November].
In the wages of 5 chaplains, 11s. 5½d. Item in bread and wine, 3d. Item to the clerk of the chapel, 15d. Item to the clerk of the bridge, 20d. Item in the wages of 6 carpenters, 22s. 1d. Item in the wages of 5 masons, 18s. Item in the wages of 2 sawyers, 7s. Item in the wages of the boatman, 2s. 6d. Item in the wages of the cook and dogs, 2s. 6d. Item in the wages of the carter, 22d. Item in the horses' fodder, 15d. Item in the wages of 2 servants, 4s. Item in the wages of 1 paviour, 3s. 4d. Item in the wages of 1 dauber and his servant, 4s. 6d. Item in the wages of 21 tidemen working at the Ram for 3 hours, 16s. Item paid for 10 cartloads of freestone bought from William Robekyn, at 5s. the cartload, 50s. Total £7 7s. 7½d.

63. Expenses, Saturday the feast of St Clement [23 November].
In the wages of 5 chaplains, 11s. 5½d. Item in bread and wine, 3d. Item to the clerk of the chapel, 15d. Item to the clerk of the bridge, 20d. Item in the wages of 6 carpenters, 22s. 1d. Item in the wages of 5 masons, 18s. Item in the wages of 2 sawyers, 7s. Item in the wages of the boatman, 2s. 6d. Item in the wages of the cook and dogs, 2s. 6d. Item in the wages of the carter, 22d. Item in the horses' fodder, 15d. Item in the wages of 2 servants, 4s. Item in the wages of 1 paviour, 3s. 4d. Item in the wages of 1 dauber and his servant, 4s. 6d. Item paid to 3 tilers and their 3 servants for 6 days, 18s. Item paid for 3,000 tilepins, 12d. Item paid for roofing a certain house at the Lock [*le Loke*], 3s. 11d. Item paid for 1 horse bought for the Bridge House cart, 60s. Item paid for 4 oars bought for the Bridge House boat, 4s. 8d. Item paid to a certain carpenter for making various works of carpentry in the Bridge's rents at Fenchurch, according to the contract made with him, 6s. 8d. Item paid for 1 boatload of chalk, 8s. 6d. Total £9 22½d. [*sic; recte* £9 4s. 4½d.]

64. Expenses, Saturday the feast of St Clement [*sic*, but *recte* the feast of St Andrew the Apostle, 30 November].
In the wages of 5 chaplains, 11s. 5½d. Item in bread and wine, 3d. Item to the clerk of the chapel, 15d. Item to the clerk of the bridge, 20d. Item in the wages of 6 carpenters, 22s. 1d. Item in the wages of 5 masons, 18s. Item in the wages of 2 sawyers, 7s. Item in the wages of the boatman, 2s. 6d. Item in the wages of the cook and dogs, 2s. 6d.

Item in the wages of the carter, 22d. Item in the horses' fodder, 15d. Item in the wages of 2 servants, 4s. Item in the wages of 1 paviour, 3s. 4d. Item in the wages of 1 dauber and his servant, 4s. 6d. Item paid to 2 tilers and their 2 servants for 4 days, 8s. Item paid for 4,000 tilepins, 6d. Item paid for 20 roof tiles, 20d. Total £4 11s. 9½d.

65. Expenses, Saturday before the feast of the Conception of the Blessed Mary [7 December].
In the wages of 5 chaplains, 11s. 5½d. Item in bread and wine, 3d. Item to the clerk of the chapel, 15d. Item to the clerk of the bridge, 20d. Item in the wages of 7 carpenters, 25s. 10d. Item in the wages of 6 masons, 21s. 4d. Item in the wages of 2 sawyers, 7s. Item in the wages of the boatman, 2s. 6d. Item in the wages of the cook and dogs, 2s. 6d. Item in the wages of the carter, 22d. Item in the horses' fodder, 15d. Item in the wages of 2 servants, 4s. Item in the wages of 1 paviour, 3s. 4d. Item in the wages of 1 dauber and his servant, 4s. 6d. Item paid for 1 skin of parchment, 3d. Item paid for mending the surplices of the chapel, 2d. Item in the wages of 21 tidemen working at the Ram for 4 hours, 21s. 4d. Item paid for 1 sieve [*cribro*] and 1 tray [*trey*], 9d. Item paid for a hundred[weight] of lime, 6s. Item paid for hinges, hooks, and other ironwork bought for the new houses at Fenchurch, weighing 684 lb., at 2d. the lb., 114s. Item paid for 2 new surplices bought for the chapel, including making them, 12s. Item paid to 2 tilers and their 2 servants for 4 days, 8s. Item paid for 18,000 transom-nails [*transsaynnayl*] bought for the aforesaid new houses, at 10½d. the thousand, 15s. 9d. Item paid for 4,000 other nails, 12s. Item paid for 13 cartloads of timber at 5s. 6d. the cartload, 71s. 6d. Total £17 10s. 5½d.

66. [m. 7] Expenses, Saturday [after] the feast of St Lucy the Virgin [14 December].
In the wages of 5 chaplains, 11s. 5½d. Item in bread and wine, 3d. Item to the clerk of the chapel, 15d. Item to the clerk of the bridge, 20d. Item in the wages of 7 carpenters, 27s. 10d. [sic] Item in the wages of 7 masons, 24s. 8d. Item in the wages of 2 sawyers, 7s. Item in the wages of the boatman, 2s. 6d. Item in the wages of the cook and dogs, 2s. 6d. Item in the wages of the carter, 22d. Item in the horses' fodder, 15d. Item in the wages of 3 servants, 6s. Item in the wages of 1 paviour, 3s. 4d. Item in the wages of 1 dauber and his servant, 4s. 6d. Item in the wages of 21 tidemen working at the Ram for 2 hours, 10s. 8d. Item paid for washing the surplices and towels of the chapel, 8d. Item paid for 40 cartloads of sand, at 3d. the cartload, and for 84 [sic] cartloads of loam [*Lom*] bought, at 2d. the cartload, 25s. 8d. Item paid for a hundred[weight] of lime, 6s. Item paid to 2 tilers and their 2 servants for 6 days, 12s. Item paid for 13 hollow tiles, 10d. Item paid for 2,000 tilepins, 3d. Item paid for 2 prs. wheels bought, 8s. Total £7 18s. 1½d. [sic]

67. Expenses, Saturday the feast of St Thomas the Apostle [21 December].
In the wages of 5 chaplains, 11s. 5½d. Item to them for offerings [*pro oblacionibus*], 5s. Item in bread and wine, 3d. Item to the clerk of the

chapel, 15d. Item to him for an offering [*pro oblac'*], 8d. Item to the clerk of the bridge, 20d. Item to him for an offering, 6d. Item in the wages of 7 carpenters, 25s. 10d. Item in the wages of 7 masons, 24s. 8d. Item in the wages of 2 sawyers, 7s. Item in the wages of the boatman, 2s. 6d. Item in the wages of the cook and dogs, 2s. 6d. Item in the wages of the carter, 22d. Item in the horses' fodder, 15d. Item in the wages of 3 servants, 6s. Item in the wages of another servant for 5½ days, 22d. Item in the wages of 1 mason for 3 days, 22½d. Item in the wages of 1 paviour, 3s. 4d. Item in the wages of 1 dauber and his servant, 4s. 6d. Item in the wages of 21 tidemen working at the Ram for 3 hours, 16s. Item paid for iron staples and hooks weighing 62 lb., at 2d. the lb., 10s. 4d. Item paid for straw bought for the dauber, 4d. Item paid to 1 servant for 1 day, 4d. Item paid for mats bought for the chapel, 8d. Item paid to the master carpenter and master mason for their quarterage, 10s. Item to them for an offering, 2s. Item paid to 5 carpenters after the master, for an offering, 8d. to each, 3s. 4d. Item paid to 5 masons after the master, for an offering, 8d. to each, 3s. 4d. Item paid to 2 sawyers for offerings, 16d. Item paid to the cook for an offering, 6d. Item paid to the carter for his quarterage, 10d. Item paid to the clerk writing this account, for his quarterage, 6s. 8d. Item paid to 2 tilers and their 2 servants for 5 days, 10s. Item paid to another tiler and his servant for 1 day, 12d. Item paid for 1,000 tilepins, 1½d. Item paid for 17½ hundred[weight] of lime, at 6s. the hundred, 105s. Item paid for 1 boatload of ragstone, 18s. Item paid for 16,000 sprignails [*sprig*] bought, at 9d. the thousand, 12s. Item paid for 7 cartloads of freestone, at 5s. the cartload, 35s. Item paid for battering the tools of the Bridge House masons, 2s. 11d. Total £16 12s. 7½d.

68. Expenses, Saturday after Christmas [28 December].
In the wages of 5 chaplains, 11s. 5½d. Item in bread and wine, 3d. Item to the clerk of the chapel, 15d. Item to the clerk of the bridge, 20d. Item in the wages of 7 carpenters for 1½ days, 6s 5d. Item in the wages of 6 masons for 1½ days, 5s. 6d. Item in the wages of 2 sawyers for 1½ days, 21d. Item in the wages of the boatman, 2s. 6d. Item in the wages of the cook and dogs, 2s. 6d. Item in the wages of the carter, 22d. Item in the horses' fodder, 15d. Item in the wages of 2 servants for 1½ days, 12d. Item paid to 3 tilers and their 2 servants for 1 day, 2s. 7d. Item paid for incense bought, 2d. Item paid for brooms [*scop'*] bought, 1d. Item paid for 13 hollow tiles bought, 10d. Item paid to 1 paviour for 1½ days, 10d. Item paid to 1 dauber and his servant for 1½ days, 13½d. Item paid for 1 cartload of sand, 4d. Item for 1,000 tilepins, 1½d. Total 43s. 5½d.

69. Expenses, Saturday before Epiphany [4 January 1382].
In the wages of 5 chaplains, 11s. 5½d. Item in bread and wine, 3d. Item to the clerk of the chapel, 15d. Item to the clerk of the bridge, 20d. Item in the wages of 8 carpenters, 29s. 7d. Item in the wages of 6 masons, 21s. 9d. Item in the wages of 2 sawyers, 7s. Item in the wages

of the boatman, 2s. 6d. Item in the wages of the cook and dogs, 2s. 6d. Item in the wages of the carter, 22d. Item in the horses' fodder, 15d. Item in the wages of 2 servants, 4s. Item in the wages of 1 paviour, 3s. 4d. Item in the wages of 1 dauber and his servant, 4s. 6d. Item paid for farriery for the Bridge House horses for the past quarter, 6s. 3d. Item paid for a hundred[weight] of lime bought, 6s. Total 105s. 1½d.

70. Expenses, Saturday before the feast of St Hilary the Bishop [11 January].
In the wages of 5 chaplains, 11s. 5½d. Item in bread and wine, 3d. Item to the clerk of the chapel, 15d. Item to the clerk of the bridge, 20d. Item in the wages of 8 carpenters, 29s. 7d. Item in the wages of 6 masons, 21s. 9d. Item in the wages of 1 mason by himself, 2s. Item in the wages of 2 sawyers, 7s. Item in the wages of the boatman, 2s. 6d. Item in the wages of the cook and dogs, 2s. 6d. Item in the wages of the carter, 22d. Item in the horses' fodder, 15d. Item in the wages of 3 servants, 6s. Item in the wages of 1 paviour, 3s. 4d. Item in the wages of 1 dauber and his servant, 4s. 6d. Item paid for straw bought for daubing, 4d. Item paid for 1 boatload of ragstone, 18s. Total 115s. 2½d.

71. Expenses, Saturday before the feast of St Wulfstan Bishop and Confessor [18 January].
In the wages of 5 chaplains, 11s. 5½d. Item in bread and wine, 3d. Item to the clerk of the chapel, 15d. Item to the clerk of the bridge, 20d. Item in the wages of 8 carpenters, 29s. 7d. Item in the wages of 6 masons, 21s. 9d. Item in the wages of 2 sawyers, 7s. Item in the wages of the boatman, 2s. 6d. Item in the wages of the cook and dogs, 2s. 6d. Item in the wages of the carter, 22d. Item in the horses' fodder, 15d. Item in the wages of 3 servants, 6s. Item in the wages of 1 paviour, 3s. 4d. Item in the wages of 1 dauber and his servant, 4s. 6d. Item paid for straw bought for daubing, 6d. Total £4 14s. 10½d. [sic; *recte* £4 15s. 4½d.]

72. Expenses, Saturday the feast of the Conversion of St Paul [25 January].
In the wages of 5 chaplains, 11s. 5½d. Item in bread and wine, 3d. Item to the clerk of the chapel, 15d. Item to the clerk of the bridge, 20d. Item in the wages of 8 carpenters, 29s. 7d. Item in the wages of 6 masons, 21s. 9d. Item in the wages of 2 sawyers, 7s. Item in the wages of the boatman, 2s. Item in the wages of the cook and dogs, 2s. 6d. Item in the wages of the carter, 22d. Item in the horses' fodder, 15d. Item in the wages of 3 servants, 6s. Item in the wages of 1 paviour, 3s. 4d. Item in the wages of 1 dauber and his servant, 4s. 6d. Item paid for 2 shovels without iron edges [*tribul' sine ferr'*], 4d. Item paid to 1 servant hired for 2 days, 8d. Item paid for 63 cartloads of clay at 2d. the cartload, 10s. 6d. Item paid for 13 cartloads of sand bought, at 3d. the cartload, 3s. 3d. Item paid for one new axle-tree [*Extree*] bought for the Bridge House cart, including making it, 14d. Item paid for 1 boatload of ragstone bought, 18s. Total £6 8s. 3½d.

73. Expenses, Saturday the eve of the Purification of the Blessed Mary [1 February].
In the wages of 5 chaplains, 11s. 5½d. Item in bread and wine, 3d. Item to the clerk of the chapel, 15d. Item to the clerk of the bridge, 20d. Item in the wages of 8 carpenters, 29s. 7d. Item in the wages of 6 masons, 21s. 9d. Item in the wages of 2 sawyers, 7s. Item in the wages of the boatman, 2s. Item in the wages of the cook and dogs, 2s. 6d. Item in the wages of the carter, 22d. Item in the horses' fodder, 15d. Item in the wages of 3 servants, 6s. Item in the wages of 1 paviour, 3s. 4d. Item in the wages of 1 dauber and his servant, 4s. 6d. Item in the wages of 1 tiler and his servant for 5 days, 5s. Item paid for a hundred[weight] of lime bought, 6s. Item paid for 1 boatload of ragstone, 15s. Total £6 4½d.

74. Expenses, Saturday after the feast of St Agatha the Virgin [8 February].
In the wages of 5 chaplains, 11s. 5½d. Item in bread and wine, 3d. Item to the clerk of the chapel, 15d. Item to the clerk of the bridge, 20d. Item in the wages of 8 carpenters, 29s. 7d. Item in the wages of 6 masons, 21s. 9d. Item in the wages of 2 sawyers, 7s. Item in the wages of the boatman, 2s. 6d. Item in the wages of the cook and dogs, 2s. 6d. Item in the wages of the carter, 22d. Item in the horses' fodder, 15d. Item in the wages of 5 servants, 10s. Item in the wages of 1 paviour, 3s. 4d. Item in the wages of 1 dauber and his servant, 4s. 6d. Item paid to 2 tilers and 1 servant for 4 days, 6s. 4d. Item for 1 new bowl [*bolle*], 7d. Item paid for 2 carpenters called *Shipwrightes* working on a new boat for 6 days, to each of them 8d. per day, 8s. Item for 2 other shipwrights working on the said boat for 6 days, each taking 7d. per day, 7s. Item paid for 80 ft. of Kent paving stone [*Pavemenston*] bought, 6s. 8d. Item paid for 23 ft. of steps of the same stone, at 4d. [sic] the ft., 5s. 9d. Item paid for 15,000 Flanders tiles bought, at 5s. 4d. the thousand, £4. Item paid for 3 cartloads of sand, 9d. Item paid for 3,900 Flanders tiles, at 4s. 10d. the thousand, 18s. 11d. Total £11 12s. 10½d.

75. Expenses, Saturday after the feast of St Valentine [15 February].
In the wages of 5 chaplains, 11s. 5½d. Item in bread and wine, 3d. Item to the clerk of the chapel, 15d. Item to the clerk of the bridge, 20d. Item in the wages of 8 carpenters, 29s. 7d. Item in the wages of 6 masons, 21s. 9d. Item in the wages of 2 sawyers, 7s. Item in the wages of the boatman, 2s. 6d. Item in the wages of the cook and dogs, 2s. 6d. Item in the wages of the carter, 22d. Item in the horses' fodder, 15d. Item in the wages of 4 servants, 8s. Item in the wages of 1 paviour, 3s. 4d. Item in the wages of 1 dauber and his servant, 4s. 6d. Item paid for one piece of curved timber for 2 stems [*stampnes*], to make a new boat out of, 15d. Item paid to 2 carpenters called *shipwrightes* working on the said boat for 6 days, 8s. Item to 2 other shipwrights working on the said boat for that time, 7s. Item paid for 125 ft. of hard Kent stone, at 10s. the hundred, 12s. 6d. Item paid for 5 cartloads of daub [*luto*], 15d. Item paid for the cost of 4 horses at Petersham, carrying piles to

the waterside, 5s. 4d. Item paid for wiveling [*Wyuelyngge*] bought for the aforesaid boat, 15d. Item paid to 2 tilers and their 2 servants for 6 days, 12s. Item paid for 10,000 tilepins, 15d. Total £7 6s. 8½d.

76. [m. 8] Expenses, Saturday the feast of St Peter in Cathedra [22 February].
In the wages of 5 chaplains, 11s. 5½d. Item in bread and wine, 3d. Item to the clerk of the chapel, 15d. Item to the clerk of the bridge, 20d. Item in the wages of 8 carpenters, 29s. 7d. Item in the wages of 6 masons, 21s. 9d. Item in the wages of 2 sawyers, 7s. Item in the wages of the boatman, 2s. 6d. Item in the wages of the cook and dogs, 2s. 6d. Item in the wages of the carter, 22d. Item in the horses' fodder, 15d. Item in the wages of 4 servants, 8s. Item in the wages of 1 paviour, 3s. 4d. Item in the wages of 1 dauber and his servant, 4s. 6d. Item paid to 2 tilers and their 2 servants for 6 days, 12s. Item paid for 6,000 tilepins, 9d. Item paid to 2 shipwrights working on the aforesaid boat for 4 days, to each 8d. per day, 5s. 4d. Item paid to 2 other shipwrights working on the same boat for 4 days, each taking 7d. per day, 4s. 8d. Item paid for a thousand[weight] of lime, at 6s. the hundred, 60s. Total £8 19s. 7½d.

77. Expenses, Saturday the first day of March. In the wages of 5 chaplains, 11s. 5½d. Item in bread and wine, 3d. Item to the clerk of the chapel, 15d. Item to the clerk of the bridge, 20d. Item in the wages of 8 carpenters, 29s. 7d. Item in the wages of 6 masons, 21s. 9d. Item in the wages of 2 sawyers, 7s. Item in the wages of the boatman, 2s. 6d. Item in the wages of the cook and dogs, 2s. 6d. Item in the wages of the carter, 22d. Item in the horses' fodder, 15d. Item in the wages of 3 servants, 6s. Item in the wages of 1 paviour, 3s. 4d. Item in the wages of 1 dauber and his servant, 4s. 6d. Item paid to 1 tiler and his servant for 3 days, 3s. Item paid to 4 shipwrights working on the aforesaid boat for 6 days, 15s. Total 112s. 10½d. [sic; *recte* 113s. ½d.]

78. Expenses, Saturday before the feast of St Gregory the Pope [8 March].
In the wages of 5 chaplains, 11s. 5½d. Item in bread and wine, 3d. Item to the clerk of the chapel, 15d. Item to the clerk of the bridge, 20d. Item in the wages of 8 carpenters, 29s. 7d. Item in the wages of 6 masons, 21s. 9d. Item in the wages of 2 sawyers, 7s. Item in the wages of the boatman, 2s. 6d. Item in the wages of the cook and dogs, 2s. 6d. Item in the wages of the carter, 22d. Item in the horses' fodder, 15d. Item in the wages of 2 servants, 4s. Item in the wages of 1 paviour, 3s. 4d. Item in the wages of 1 dauber and his servant, 4s. 6d. Item paid to 4 shipwrights working on the aforesaid boat for 6 days, 15s. Item paid for 60 elms bought from Chertsey Abbey, at 2s. 6d. each, £10 10s. [sic; *recte* £7 10s.]. Item paid for the carriage by water of all the said elms from Petersham to the Bridge House, 67s. 10d. Item paid for 5,000 laths bought, 31s. Item paid for various nails bought, 53s. Item paid to 2 tilers and their 2 servants for 6 days, 12s. Item paid for 400 wainscot

[*weynscot*] bought, at 18s. 6d. the hundred, 74s. Item paid for 1 barrel of pitch bought, 3s. Item paid for 4 gallons of tar, 16d. Item paid for straw bought for daubing, 2d. Item paid for nails bought of William Bys, 6s. 5d. Total £25 6s. 7½d. [sic; it is correct if the price of the elms is corrected]

79. Expenses, Saturday after the feast of St Gregory the Pope [15 March].
In the wages of 5 chaplains, 11s. 5½d. Item in bread and wine, 3d. Item to the clerk of the chapel, 15d. Item to the clerk of the bridge, 20d. Item in the wages of 8 carpenters, 29s. 7d. Item in the wages of 6 masons, 21s. 9d. Item in the wages of 2 sawyers, 7s. Item in the wages of the boatman, 2s. 6d. Item in the wages of the cook and dogs, 2s. 6d. Item in the wages of the carter, 22d. Item in the horses' fodder, 15d. Item in the wages of 3 servants, 6s. Item in the wages of 1 paviour, 3s. 4d. Item in the wages of 1 dauber and his servant, 4s. 6d. Item paid to 2 tilers and their 2 servants for 6 days, 12s. Item paid to 4 shipwrights working on the aforesaid boat for 6 days, 15s. Item paid for 2,000 laths bought, 14s. Item paid for 300 trenails [*cauill' lign'*] for the said boat, 3s. Item paid for 4 pieces of curved timber bought to make the knees [*genibus*] of the said boat, 16d. Item paid for other timber bought for the said boat, 4s. Item paid for oil and rosin bought for the said boat, 2s. 1d. Item paid for a hundred[weight] of lime, 6s. Item paid for mending 1 saddle [for the] Bridge House cart, 6d. Item paid for 1,000 clench nails [*clenchnayl*] bought for the said boat, 15s. Item paid for 300 spike nails [*spikyng'*] bought for the said boat, 2s. 3d. Item paid for 1 great iron binding tie [*nagna* [sic] *ligatur' ferri*] for the said boat, weighing 38 lb., at 2d. the lb., 6s. 4d. Item paid for one boatload of chalk, 8s. Item paid to various labourers hired to unload piles from the boat at the Bridge House, 16d. Total £9 5s. 8d. [sic; *recte* £9 5s. 8½d.]

80. Expenses, Saturday after the feast of St Cuthbert [22 March].
In the wages of 5 chaplains, 11s. 5½d. Item in bread and wine, 3d. Item to the clerk of the chapel, 15d. Item to the clerk of the bridge, 20d. Item in the wages of 8 carpenters, 29s. 7d. Item in the wages of 6 masons, 21s. 9d. Item in the wages of 2 sawyers, 7s. Item in the wages of the boatman, 2s. 6d. Item in the wages of the cook and dogs, 2s. 6d. Item in the wages of the carter, 22d. Item in the horses' fodder, 15d. Item in the wages of 3 servants, 6s. Item in the wages of 1 paviour, 3s. 4d. Item in the wages of 1 dauber and his servant, 4s. 6d. Item paid for tallow bought to grease the blade at the Ram, 12d. Item paid to 2 tilers and their 2 servants for 6 days, 12s. Item paid for 1 cartload of timber bought of John Samewell, 6s. Total 113s. 10½d.

81. Expenses, Saturday after the feast of the Annunciation of the Blessed Mary [29 March].

In the wages of 5 chaplains, 11s. 5½d. Item in bread and wine, 3d. Item to the clerk of the chapel, 15d. Item to the clerk of the bridge, 20d. Item in the wages of 8 carpenters, 29s. 7d. Item in the wages of 6 masons, 21s. 9d. Item in the wages of 2 sawyers, 7s. Item in the wages of the boatman, 2s. 6d. Item in the wages of the cook and dogs, 2s. 6d. Item in the wages of the carter, 22d. Item in the horses' fodder, 15d. Item in the wages of 3 servants, 6s. Item in the wages of 1 paviour, 3s. 4d. Item in the wages of 1 dauber and his servant, 4s. 6d. Item paid to 1 tiler and his servant for 5 days, 5s. Item paid for 136 ft. of paving stone bought, 12s. 6d. Item paid for washing the surplices of the chapel, 7d. Item paid for a hundred[weight] of lime, 6s. Item paid for 1 pr. wheels bought, 5s. Total £6 3s. 11½d.

82. Expenses, Saturday the eve of Easter [5 April].
In the wages of 5 chaplains, 11s. 5½d. Item to them for an offering, 5s. Item in bread and wine, 3d. Item to the clerk of the chapel, 15d. Item to him for an offering, 8d. Item to the clerk of the bridge, 20d. Item to him for an offering, 6d. Item in the wages of 8 carpenters, 29s. 7d. Item in the wages of 6 masons, 21s. 9d. Item in the wages of 2 sawyers, 7s. Item in the wages of the boatman, 2s. 6d. Item in the wages of the cook and dogs, 2s. 6d. Item in the wages of the carter, 22d. Item in the horses' fodder, 15d. Item in the wages of 3 servants, 6s. Item in the wages of 1 paviour, 3s. 4d. Item in the wages of 1 dauber and his servant, 4s. 6d. Item to the master carpenter and the master mason for their quarterage, 10s. Item to them for an offering, 2s. Item paid to 7 carpenters after the master for an offering, 8d. to each, 4s. 8d. Item paid to 5 masons after the master for an offering, 8d. to each, 3s. 4d. Item paid to 2 sawyers for an offering, 16d. Item paid to the cook for an offering, 6d. Item paid to the clerk writing this account, for his quarterage, 6s. 8d. Item paid for 1 skin of parchment, 3d. Item paid for incense bought for the chapel, 3d. Item paid to the carter for his quarterage, 10d. Item paid to 1 tiler and his servant for 5 days, 5s. Item paid for battering the masons' tools for the past quarter, 3s. 10d. Total £6 19s. 6½d. [sic; *recte* £6 19s. 8½d.]

83. Expenses, Saturday in the week of Easter [12 April].
In the wages of 5 chaplains, 11s. 5½d. Item in bread and wine, 3d. Item to the clerk of the chapel, 15d. Item to the clerk of the bridge, 20d. Item in the wages of 7 carpenters for 3 days, 12s. 11d. Item in the wages of 6 masons for 3 days, 10s. 10d. Item in the wages of 2 sawyers for 3 days, 3s. 6d. Item in the wages of the boatman, 2s. 6d. Item in the wages of the cook and dogs, 2s. 6d. Item in the wages of the carter, 22d. Item in the horses' fodder, 15d. Item in the wages of 3 servants for 3 days, 3s. Item paid for 12 new locks with keys bought, 4s. Item paid to 1 paviour for 3 days, 20d. Item paid to 1 dauber and his servant for 3 days, 2s. 4d. [sic]. Item paid to 1 tiler and his servant for 3 days, 3s. Item paid for 6,000 tilepins, at 1½d. the thousand, 2s. [sic]. Item paid for 1 boatload of chalk, 9s. Item paid for 3 hoops of wood bought for 1 barrel, 2d. Item paid for farriery for the Bridge House

horses for the past quarter, 6s. 9d. Item paid for 1 latten pulley [*polyne de laton'*] weighing 55 lb., bought for a portcullis in the stone gate on the bridge, at 3d. the lb., 13s. 9d. Total £4 15s. 8d.

84. Expenses, Saturday before the feast of St Gregory [sic, *recte* St George, 19 April].
In the wages of 5 chaplains, 11s. 5½d. Item in bread and wine, 3d. Item to the clerk of the chapel, 15d. Item to the clerk of the bridge, 20d. Item in the wages of 8 carpenters, 29s. 7d. Item in the wages of 5 masons, 18s. Item in the wages of 2 sawyers, 7s. Item in the wages of the boatman, 2s. 6d. Item in the wages of the cook and dogs, 2s. 6d. Item in the wages of the carter, 22d. Item in the horses' fodder, 15d. Item in the wages of 3 servants, 6s. Item in the wages of 1 paviour, 3s. 4d. Item in the wages of 1 dauber and his servant, 4s. 6d. Item in the wages of 1 tiler and his servant for 6 days, 6s. Item in the wages of 21 tidemen working at the Ram for 5 hours, 26s. 8d. Total £6 3s. 9½d.

85. [m. 9] Expenses, Saturday after the feast of St Mark the Evangelist [26 April].
In the wages of 5 chaplains, 11s. 5½d. Item in bread and wine, 3d. Item to the clerk of the chapel, 15d. Item to the clerk of the bridge, 20d. Item in the wages of 8 carpenters, 29s. 7d. Item in the wages of 6 masons, 21s. 9d. Item in the wages of 2 sawyers, 7s. Item in the wages of the boatman, 2s. 6d. Item in the wages of the cook and dogs, 2s. 6d. Item in the wages of the carter, 22d. Item in the horses' fodder, 15d. Item in the wages of 3 servants, 6s. Item in the wages of 1 paviour, 3s. 4d. Item in the wages of 1 dauber and his servant, 4s. 6d. Item in the wages of 21 tidemen working at the Ram for 6 hours, 32s. Item paid for brooms bought for cleaning the starlings [*lez Stathelynges*] under the bridge, 3d. Item paid for a hundred[weight] of lime, 6s. Item paid for 3 curried horsehides bought for making blades [*swerdes*], 5s. 8d. Item paid for mending and repairing the vines in the garden of the Bridge House, 2s. Item paid to 3 tilers and their 3 servants for 5 days, 15s. Item paid for various locks with keys to them bought for various rents of the Bridge, 38s. 1d. Total £9 13s. 10½d.

86. Expenses, Saturday the feast of the Invention of the Holy Cross [3 May].
In the wages of 5 chaplains, 11s. 5½d. Item in bread and wine, 3d. Item to the clerk of the chapel, 15d. Item to the clerk of the bridge, 20d. Item in the wages of 8 carpenters, 29s. 7d. Item in the wages of 6 masons, 21s. 9d. Item in the wages of 2 sawyers, 7s. Item in the wages of the boatman, 2s. 6d. Item in the wages of the cook and dogs, 2s. 6d. Item in the wages of the carter, 22d. Item in the horses' fodder, 15d. Item in the wages of 3 servants, 6s. Item in the wages of 21 tidemen working at the Ram for 2 hours, 10s. 8d. Item in the wages of 1 paviour, 3s. 4d. Item in the wages of 1 dauber and his servant, 4s. 6d. Item paid for 10,000 tilepins, 15d. Item paid for 4 pieces of timber bought of John Samewell, 16s. Item paid for 1,000 laths bought, 7s. Item paid for 1

boatload of chalk, 9s. Item paid to Gilbert Melchebourne and Thomas Skelton, men of law, for prosecuting a plea against John Denver for quit-rent owed to the Bridge, 13s. 4d. Item paid to 2 tilers and their 2 servants for 3 days, 6s. Total £7 18s. 1½d.

87. Expenses, Saturday after the feast of St John at the Latin Gate [10 May].
In the wages of 5 chaplains, 11s. 5½d. Item in bread and wine, 3d. Item to the clerk of the chapel, 15d. Item to the clerk of the bridge, 20d. Item in the wages of 8 carpenters, 29s. 7d. Item in the wages of 6 masons, 21s. 9d. Item in the wages of 2 sawyers, 7s. Item in the wages of the boatman, 2s. 6d. Item in the wages of the cook and dogs, 2s. 6d. Item in the wages of the carter, 22d. Item in the horses' fodder, 15d. Item in the wages of 3 servants, 6s. Item in the wages of 1 paviour, 3s. 4d. Item in the wages of 1 dauber and his servant, 4s. 6d. Item in the wages of 21 tidemen working at the Ram for 10 hours, 53s. 4d. Item paid to 1 tiler and his servant for 6 days, 6s. Item paid for 1 boatload of chalk, 8s. Item paid for 1 pr. wheels bought, 5s. Item paid for 1 curried horsehide bought to repair the blade [*swerd*] for the Ram, 2s. 4d. Total £8 9s. 6½d.

88. Expenses, Saturday before the feast of St Dunstan [17 May].
In the wages of 5 chaplains, 11s. 5½d. Item in bread and wine, 3d. Item to the clerk of the chapel, 15d. Item to the clerk of the bridge, 20d. Item in the wages of 8 carpenters, 29s. 7d. Item in the wages of 5 masons, 18s. Item in the wages of 2 sawyers, 7s. Item in the wages of the boatman, 2s. 6d. Item in the wages of the cook and dogs, 2s. 6d. Item in the wages of the carter, 22d. Item in the horses' fodder, 15d. Item in the wages of 3 servants, 6s. Item in the wages of 1 paviour, 3s. 4d. Item in the wages of 1 dauber and his servant, 4s. 6d. Item in the wages of 21 tidemen working at the Ram for 4 hours, 21s. 4d. Item paid to 2 tilers and their 2 servants for 4 days, 8s. Item paid to 1 servant hired for 1 day, 4d. Item paid for 1 boatload [sic], 8s. Total £6 8s. 9½d.

89. Expenses, Saturday the eve of Pentecost [24 May].
In the wages of 5 chaplains, 11s. 5½d. Item in bread and wine, 3d. Item to the clerk of the chapel, 15d. Item to the clerk of the bridge, 20d. Item in the wages of 8 carpenters, 29s. 7d. Item in the wages of 6 masons, 21s. 9d. Item in the wages of 2 sawyers, 7s. Item in the wages of the boatman, 2s. 6d. Item in the wages of the cook and dogs, 2s. 6d. Item in the wages of the carter, 22d. Item in the horses' fodder, 15d. Item in the wages of 3 servants, 6s. Item in the wages of 1 paviour, 3s. 4d. Item in the wages of 1 dauber and his servant, 4s. 6d. Item in the wages of 21 tidemen working at the Ram for 8 hours, 42s. 8d. Item paid to mend 1 axe of the Bridge House, 8d. Item in the wages of 1 tiler and his servant for 6 days, 6s. Item paid for 15 roof tiles [*roftyles*], 16d. Item paid for 100 elms bought of Matthew Langrich, at 22d. each, £9 3s. 4d. Total £16 8s. 10½d.

90. Expenses, Saturday in the week of Pentecost [31 May].
In the wages of 5 chaplains, 11s. 5½d. Item in bread and wine, 3d. Item
to the clerk of the chapel, 15d. Item to the clerk of the bridge, 20d.
Item in the wages of 6 carpenters for 3 days, 11s. ½d. [sic] Item in the
wages of 5 masons for 3 days, 9s. Item in the wages of 2 sawyers for
3 days, 3s. 6d. Item in the wages of the boatman, 2s. 6d. Item in the
wages of the cook and dogs, 2s. 6d. Item in the wages of the carter,
22d. Item in the horses' fodder, 15d. Item in the wages of 2 servants
for 3 days, 4s. [sic]. Item in the wages of 1 paviour for 3 days, 20d.
Item in the wages of 1 dauber and his servant, 2s. 3d. Item in the
wages of 21 tidemen working at the Ram for 2 hours, 10s. 8d. Item
paid for 1 cartload of freestone bought, 5s. Item paid for 25 large
pieces of timber called somers [*Sumeres*], bought of Richard Turner
according to the contract in gross made with him, £18 13s. 4d. Total
£22 14d.

91. Expenses, Saturday the feast of St Wulfstan [7 June].
In the wages of 5 chaplains, 11s. 5½d. Item in bread and wine, 3d. Item
to the clerk of the chapel, 15d. Item to the clerk of the bridge, 20d.
Item in the wages of 8 carpenters, 29s. 2d. [sic]. Item in the wages of 6
masons, 21s. 9d. Item in the wages of 2 sawyers, 7s. Item in the wages
of the boatman, 2s. 6d. Item in the wages of the cook and dogs, 2s. 6d.
Item in the wages of the carter, 22d. Item in the horses' fodder, 15d.
Item in the wages of 3 servants, 6s. Item in the wages of 1 paviour, 3s.
4d. Item in the wages of 1 dauber and his servant, 4s. 6d. Item in the
wages of 21 tidemen working at the Ram for 6 hours, 32s. Item paid for
incense bought for the chapel, 2d. Item paid for 48 hurdles bought to
make scaffolds, 12s. Item paid for 1 boatload of ragstone bought, 19s.
Item paid for 2 pieces of timber bought from John Samewell, 2s. Item
paid for 20,000 tiles bought from John Coy, at 6s. the thousand, £6.
Item paid for 21,000 [sic] tiles bought from John Pope of Colchester,
at 5s. 4d. the thousand, 114s. 8d. Total £19 14s 5½d. [sic; *recte* £19
14s. 3½d.]

92. Expenses, Saturday after the feast of St Barnabas the Apostle [14
June].
In the wages of 5 chaplains, 11s. 5½d. Item in bread and wine, 3d.
Item to the clerk of the chapel, 15d. Item to the clerk of the bridge,
20d. Item in the wages of 8 carpenters, 29s. 7d. Item in the wages of
6 masons, 21s. 9d. Item in the wages of 2 sawyers, 7s. Item in the wages
of the boatman, 2s. 6d. Item in the wages of the cook and dogs, 2s. 6d.
Item in the wages of the carter, 22d. Item in the horses' fodder, 15d.
Item in the wages of 3 servants, 6s. Item in the wages of 1 paviour, 3s.
4d. Item in the wages of 1 dauber and his servant, 4s. 6d. Item in the
wages of 21 tidemen working at the Ram for 5 hours, 26s. 8d. Item paid
for a hundred[weight] of lime bought, 6s. Item paid for 1 boatload of
chalk, 8s. Item paid for half a hundred withies, 4d. Item paid for 1 new
vestment bought for the chapel for holidays, 25s. 8d. Item paid for 2
new surplices, 13s. 4d. Total £8 18d. [sic; *recte* £8 14s. 10d.]

93. Expenses, Saturday before the feast of the Nativity of St John the Baptist [21 June].

In the wages of 5 chaplains, 11s. 5½d. Item in bread and wine, 3d. Item to the clerk of the chapel, 15d. Item to the clerk of the bridge, 20d. Item in the wages of 8 carpenters, 29s. 7d. Item in the wages of 6 masons, 21s. 9d. Item in the wages of 2 sawyers, 7s. Item in the wages of the boatman, 2s. 6d. Item in the wages of the cook and dogs, 2s. 6d. Item in the wages of the carter, 22d. Item in the horses' fodder, 15d. Item in the wages of 3 servants, 6s. Item in the wages of 1 paviour, 3s. 4d. Item in the wages of 1 dauber and his servant, 4s. 6d. Item in the wages of 21 tidemen working at the Ram for 7 hours, 37s. 4d. Item paid for 1 boatload of ragstone bought, 17s. Item paid to the master carpenter and master mason for their quarterage, 10s. Item paid to the clerk writing this account for his quarterage, 6s. 8d. Item paid to the carter for his quarterage, 10d. Item paid for 2 iron linch-pins and for 100 clout nails [*cloutnayl*] bought, 8d. Item paid to 6 carpenters for thighboots [*ocreis*] called *Bothes*, 4s. to each, 24s. Item paid to 2 sawyers for thighboots, 8s. Item paid to 4 masons for thighboots, 16s. Item paid for 2 other masons and one paviour for thighboots, 2s. to each, 6s. Total £11 16½d. [sic; *recte* £10 17s. 4½d.]

94. [m. 10] Expenses, Saturday the eve of the Apostles Peter and Paul [28 June].

In the wages of 4 chaplains, 9s. 2d. Item in bread and wine, 3d. Item to the clerk of the chapel, 15d. Item to the clerk of the bridge, 20d. Item in the wages of 8 carpenters, 29s. 7d. Item in the wages of 6 masons, 21s. 9d. Item in the wages of 2 sawyers, 7s. Item in the wages of the boatman, 2s. 6d. Item in the wages of the cook and dogs, 2s. 6d. Item in the wages of the carter, 22d. Item in the wages of 3 servants, 6s. Item in the wages of 1 paviour, 3s. 4d. Item in the wages of 1 dauber and his servant, 4s. 6d. Item in the wages of 21 tidemen working at the Ram for 4 hours, 21s. 4d. Item in the wages of 2 tilers and their 2 servants for 5 days, 10s. Item paid for 2,000 tilepins, 3d. Item paid for a hundred[weight] of lime, 6s. Item paid for 1 boatload of chalk, 7s. Item paid for 1 *tubbe* bought, 5d. Item paid for withies bought for tying scaffolds, 4d. Item paid for 354 lb. of cords, at 1½d. and 1¼d. the lb., 40s. 6d. Item paid for farriery for the Bridge House horses for the term of the Nativity of St John the Baptist, 5s. 11d. Item in the horses' fodder, 15d. Total £9 4s. 4d.

95. Expenses, Saturday before the feast of the Translation of St Thomas the Martyr [5 July].

In the wages of 4 chaplains, 11s. 5½d. [sic] Item in bread and wine, 3d. Item to the clerk of the chapel, 15d. Item to the clerk of the bridge, 20d. Item in the wages of 8 carpenters, 29s. 7d. Item in the wages of 6 masons, 21s. 9d. Item in the wages of 2 sawyers, 7s. Item in the wages of the boatman, 2s. 6d. Item in the wages of the cook and dogs, 2s. 6d. Item in the wages of the carter, 22d. Item in the horses' fodder, 15d. Item in the wages of 3 servants, 6s. Item in the wages of the paviour,

3s. 4d. Item in the wages of 1 dauber and his servant, 4s. 6d. Item in the wages of 21 tidemen working at the Ram for 6 hours, 32s. Item in the wages of 2 tilers and their servants for 6 days, 12s. Item paid for brooms bought to clean the starlings, 3d. Item paid to Gilbert Melchebourne for his fees for the term of the Nativity of St John the Baptist, 6s. 8d. Item paid for 29 *tunne tyght* of *Northeneston* bought from Robert Gameleston, at 9s. the tontight including freight, £13 12d. Item paid for 42 ft. of Portland stone bought, at 6d. the ft., 21s. Item paid for 2 ells of blue-dyed linen cloth to cover the counting-board, 20d. Total £21 7s. 2d. [sic; *recte* £21 9s. 5½d.]

96. Expenses, Saturday before the feast of the Translation of St Swithin [12 July].
In the wages of 4 chaplains, 9s. 2d. Item in bread and wine, 3d. Item to the clerk of the chapel, 15d. Item to the clerk of the bridge, 20d. Item in the wages of 8 carpenters, 29s. 7d. Item in the wages of 6 masons, 21s. 9d. Item in the wages of 2 sawyers, 7s. Item in the wages of the boatman, 2s. 6d. Item in the wages of the cook and dogs, 2s. 6d. Item in the wages of the carter, 22d. Item in the horses' fodder, 15d. Item in the wages of 3 servants, 6s. Item in the wages of 1 paviour, 3s. 4d. Item in the wages of 1 dauber and his servant, 4s. 6d. Item in the wages of 21 tidemen working at the Ram for 6 hours, 32s. Item paid for 1 skin of parchment bought, 3d. Item paid for 2 cartloads of timber bought for the works of the Bridge, 12s. Item paid to 1 tiler and his servant for 4 days, 4s. Item paid for cleaning a certain latrine in the Bridge's rents in Old Change, 16s. 8d. Total £7 17s. 6d.

97. Expenses, Saturday before the feast of St Margaret [19 July].
In the wages of 4 chaplains, 9s. 2d. Item in bread and wine, 3d. Item to the clerk of the chapel, 15d. Item to the clerk of the bridge, 20d. Item in the wages of 8 carpenters, 29s. 7d. Item in the wages of 6 masons, 21s. 9d. Item in the wages of 2 sawyers, 7s. Item in the wages of the boatman, 2s. 6d. Item in the wages of the cook and dogs, 2s. 6d. Item in the wages of the carter, 22d. Item in the horses' fodder, 15d. Item in the wages of 3 servants, 6s. Item in the wages of 1 paviour, 3s. 4d. Item in the wages of 1 dauber and his servant, 4s. 6d. Item in the wages of 21 tidemen working at the Ram for 5 hours, 26s. 8d. Item paid to a certain man for 2 charters of quit-rent belonging to London Bridge, 3s. 4d. Item paid for various nails bought for the work of the Bridge, £4 13s. 10d. Item paid for 2 boatloads of chalk, 18s. Total £11 14s. 5d.

98. Expenses, Saturday after the feast of St James the Apostle [26 July].
In the wages of 3 chaplains, 6s. 10½d. Item in bread and wine, 3d. Item to the clerk of the chapel, 15d. Item to the clerk of the bridge, 20d. Item in the wages of 8 carpenters, 29s. 7d. Item in the wages of 6 masons, 21s. 9d. Item in the wages of 2 sawyers, 7s. Item in the wages of the boatman, 2s. 6d. Item in the wages of the cook and dogs, 2s. 6d. Item in the wages of the carter, 22d. Item in the horses' fodder, 15d.

Item in the wages of 3 servants, 6s. Item in the wages of 1 paviour, 3s. 4d. Item in the wages of 1 dauber and his servant, 4s. 6d. Item in the wages of 21 tidemen working at the Ram for 5 hours, 26s. 8d. Item paid for 1½ gallons of tallow bought to grease the blade [*swerdo*] of the Ram, 12d. Item paid for steeling 1 auger [*nauegore*], 4d. Item paid for various nails bought, 38s. 5½d. Item paid for 4 ells of wadmal [*Wadmol*] to cover the collars of the Bridge's horses, 2s. Item paid for 500 lb. of worked iron, at 2d. the lb., £4 3s. 4d Total £12 1d. [sic; *recte* £12 2s. 1d.]

99. Expenses, Saturday after the feast of St Peter ad Vincula [2 August].
In the wages of 3 chaplains, 6s. 10½d. Item in bread and wine, 3d. Item to the clerk of the chapel, 15d. Item to the clerk of the bridge, 22d. [sic]. Item in the wages of 8 carpenters, 29s. 7d. Item in the wages of 6 masons, 21s. 9d. Item in the wages of 2 sawyers, 7s. Item in the wages of the boatman, 2s. 6d. Item in the wages of the cook and dogs, 2s. 6d. Item in the wages of the carter, 22d. Item in the horses' fodder, 15d. Item in the wages of 3 servants, 6s. Item in the wages of 1 paviour, 3s. 4d. Item in the wages of 1 dauber and his servant, 4s. 6d. Item in the wages of 21 tidemen working at the Ram for 4 hours, 21s. 4d. Item in the wages of 1 tiler and his servant for 1 day, 12d. Item paid for 2 oars bought for the Bridge House boat, 2s. 4d. Item paid for mowing 27 acres of meadow, at 10d. the acre, 22s. 6d. Item paid for turning, gathering and taking up all the hay from the said 27 acres of meadow, 29s. 8d. Total £8 7s. 5d. [sic; *recte* £8 7s. 1½d.]

100. Expenses, Saturday the eve of St Lawrence [9 August].
In the wages of 4 chaplains, 9s. 2d. Item in bread and wine, 3d. Item to the clerk of the chapel, 15d. Item to the clerk of the bridge, 20d. Item in the wages of 8 carpenters, 29s. 7d. Item in the wages of 6 masons, 21s. 9d. Item in the wages of 2 sawyers, 7s. Item in the wages of the boatman, 2s. 6d. Item in the wages of the cook and dogs, 2s. 6d. Item in the wages of the carter, 22d. Item in the horses' fodder, 15d. Item in the wages of 3 servants, 6s. Item in the wages of 1 paviour, 3s. 4d. Item in the wages of 1 dauber and his servant, 4s. 6d. Item in the wages of 1 tiler and his servant for 2 days, 2s. Item in the wages of 21 tidemen working at the Ram for 8 hours, 42s. 8d. Item paid for 2 iron ladles [*ladelys*] bought for the masons of the Bridge House, 3s. 4d. Item paid for 6 skins of parchment bought, 18d. Item paid 1 mason for mending a well at St Nicholas Shambles, 14s. 6s. [sic]. Total £7 16s. 7d.

101. Expenses, Saturday after the feast of the Assumption of the Blessed Mary[16 August].
In the wages of 4 chaplains, 9s. 2d. Item in bread and wine, 3d. Item to the clerk of the chapel, 15d. Item to the clerk of the bridge, 20d. Item in the wages of 8 carpenters, 29s. 7d. Item in the wages of 6 masons, 21s. 9d. Item in the wages of 2 sawyers, 7s. Item in the wages of the boatman, 2s. 6d. Item in the wages of the cook and dogs, 2s. 6d. Item

in the wages of the carter, 22d. Item in the horses' fodder, 15d. Item in the wages of 3 servants, 6s. Item in the wages of 1 paviour, 3s. 4d. Item in the wages of 1 dauber and his servant, 4s. 6d. Item in the wages of 21 tidemen working at the Ram for 3 hours, 16s. Item paid for a hundred[weight] of lime bought, 6s. Item paid for 48 cartloads of timber bought from John Horn, at 7s. the cartload, £16 16s. Total £22 10s. 7d.

102. Expenses, Saturday the eve of St Bartholomew [23 August].
In the wages of 4 chaplains, 9s. 2d. Item in bread and wine, 3d. Item to the clerk of the chapel, 15d. Item to the clerk of the bridge, 20d. Item in the wages of 8 carpenters, 29s. 7d. Item in the wages of 6 masons, 21s. 9d. Item in the wages of 2 sawyers, 7s. Item in the wages of the boatman, 2s. 6d. Item in the wages of the cook and dogs, 2s. 6d. Item in the wages of the carter, 22d. Item in the horses' fodder, 15d. Item in the wages of 3 servants, 6s. Item in the wages of 1 paviour, 3s. 4d. Item in the wages of 1 dauber and his servant, 4s. 6d. Item in the wages of 21 tidemen working at the Ram for 6 hours, 32s. Item paid for tallow bought to grease the blade, 4d. Item paid for brooms bought to clean the starlings, 3d. Item paid [for] iron cart clouts [*Cartecloutes*] bought for the Bridge House cart, 11d. Item paid for 1 new tine bought, 16d. Item paid to 1 carter for taking away a large quantity of rubbish from a certain house in Old Change, according to the contract in gross made with him, 6s. Item paid to 2 labourers hired for 1 day, 10d. Item paid for a certain quantity of timber bought in gross from John Samewell, £4 3s. 4d. Item paid for 100 pieces of plankboard [*Plaunchisbord*] bought from Richard de Kent, 19s. 10d. Item paid for 200 roof tiles, 7s. Item paid for 1 last and 9 barrels of pitch bought for the work of the Bridge masons, at 28s. the last, 49s. Total £14 13s. 5d.

103. [m. 11] Expenses, Saturday after the feast of the Decollation of St John the Baptist [30 August].
In the wages of 4 chaplains, 9s. 2d. Item in bread and wine, 3d. Item to the clerk of the chapel, 15d. Item to the clerk of the bridge, 20d. Item in the wages of 8 carpenters, 29s. 7d. Item in the wages of 6 masons, 21s. 9d. Item in the wages of 2 sawyers, 7s. Item in the wages of the boatman, 2s. 6d. Item in the wages of the cook and dogs, 2s. 6d. Item in the wages of the carter, 22d. Item in the horses' fodder, 15d. Item in the wages of 3 servants, 6s. Item in the wages of 1 paviour, 3s. 4d. Item in the wages of 1 dauber and his servant, 4s. 6d. Item in the wages of 21 tidemen working at the Ram for 5 hours, 26s. 8d. Item in the wages of 1 tiler and his servant for 6 days, 6s. Item paid for 20,000 tilepins, 2s. 6d. Item paid for 20,000 tiles bought, at 5s. 6d. the thousand, 110s. Item paid for a great boatload of ragstone bought, 24s. Item paid for another boatload of ragstone, 22s. Item paid for 1 boatload of chalk, 9s. Total £14 12s. 9d.

104. Expenses, Saturday before the feast of the Nativity of the Blessed Mary [6 September].

In the wages of 4 chaplains, 9s. 2d. Item in bread and wine, 3d. Item to the clerk of the chapel, 15d. Item to the clerk of the bridge, 20d. Item in the wages of 8 carpenters, 29s. 7d. Item in the wages of 6 masons, 21s. 9d. Item in the wages of 2 sawyers, 7s. Item in the wages of the boatman, 2s. 6d. Item in the wages of the cook and dogs, 2s. 6d. Item in the wages of the carter, 22d. Item in the horses' fodder, 15d. Item in the wages of 2 servants, 4s. Item in the wages of 1 paviour, 3s. 4d. Item in the wages of 1 dauber and his servant, 4s. 6d. Item in the wages of 21 tidemen working at the Ram for 6 hours, 32s. Item paid for 1 boatload of chalk, 8s. 6d. Item paid for 1 pr. wheels bought, 5s. Total £6 16s. 1d.

105. Expenses, Saturday before the feast of the Exaltation of the Holy Cross [13 September].
In the wages of 4 chaplains, 9s. 2d. Item in bread and wine, 3d. Item to the clerk of the chapel, 15d. Item to the clerk of the bridge, 20d. Item in the wages of 8 carpenters, 29s. 7d. Item in the wages of 6 masons, 21s. 9d. Item in the wages of 2 sawyers, 7s. Item in the wages of the boatman, 2s. 6d. Item in the wages of the cook and dogs, 2s. 6d. Item in the wages of the carter, 22d. Item in the horses' fodder, 15d. Item in the wages of 2 servants, 4s. Item in the wages of 1 paviour, 3s. 4d. Item in the wages of 1 dauber and his servant, 4s. 6d. Item in the wages of 21 tidemen working at the Ram for 5 hours, 26s. 8d. Item paid for 14 shovels without iron edges, 23d. Item paid for incense bought, 2d. Item paid to a certain carter for taking away 13 cartloads of rubbish from a certain tenement in Friday Street, 22½d. Item paid for 1 new adze [*adeze*] bought for the waterworks under the bridge, 2s. 6d. Item paid for mending 1 axe [*cecuri*] for the same work, 16d. Item paid for 1 boatload of ragstone, 20s. Total £7 5s. ½d.

106. Expenses, Saturday the eve of St Matthew Apostle and Evangelist [20 September].
In the wages of 4 chaplains, 9s. 2d. Item in bread and wine, 3d. Item to the clerk of the chapel, 15d. Item to the clerk of the bridge, 20d. Item in the wages of 8 carpenters, 29s. 7d. Item in the wages of 6 masons, 21s. 9d. Item in the wages of 2 sawyers, 7s. Item in the wages of the boatman, 2s. 6d. Item in the wages of the cook and dogs, 2s. 6d. Item in the wages of the carter, 22d. Item in the wages of 2 servants, 4s. Item in the horses' fodder, 15d. Item in the wages of 1 paviour, 3s. 4d. Item in the wages of 1 dauber and his servant, 4s. 6d. Item in the wages of 21 tidemen working at the Ram for 5 hours, 26s. 8d. Item in the wages of 1 tiler and his servant for 6 days, 6s. Item in the wages of another tiler and his servant for 1 day, 12d. Item paid to 1 servant hired for 5 hours [sic] to clear [*riddand'*] stones under the bridge, 15d. Item paid for 1 boatload of ragstone, 16s. Total £7 18d.

107. Expenses, Saturday before the feast of St Michael [27 September].
In the wages of 3 chaplains, 6s. 10½d. Item in bread and wine, 3d. Item to the clerk of the chapel, 15d. Item to the clerk of the bridge, 20d. Item in the wages of 8 carpenters, 29s. 7d. Item in the wages of 6 masons, 21s. 9d. Item in the wages of 2 sawyers, 7s. Item in the wages of the

boatman, 2s. 6d. Item in the wages of the cook and dogs, 2s. 6d. Item in the wages of the carter, 22d. Item in the horses' fodder, 15d. Item in the wages of 2 servants, 4s. Item in the wages of 1 paviour, 3s. 4d. Item in the wages of 1 dauber and his servant, 4s. 6d. Item in the wages of 21 tidemen working at the Ram for 5 hours, 26s. 8d. Item paid to the master carpenter and the master mason for their quarterage, 10s. Item paid to the clerk writing this account for his quarterage, 6s. 8d. Item paid for 3½ hundreds of reeds bought, at 2s. the hundred, 7s. Item paid for 6 cartloads of freestone, at 5s. the cartload, 30s. Item paid for 1 boatload [sic], 8s. Item paid for a quantity of chalk bought from William Bys, 6s. Item paid for 6½ hundred[weight] of lime [*lym*] at 6s. the hundred, 39s. Item paid to Thomas Bryel carpenter for making a new fulling mill at Stratford called *Spylemannesmell*, and for supplying the timber for the mill, including carriage, from the contract in gross made with him, £50. Item paid to 1 tiler and his servant for 6 days, 6s. Item paid for carrying 2 cartloads of timber and 1 cartload of tiles from the Bridge House to Friday Street, 21d. Item paid to 1 carpenter hired to fell elms at Waltham for 5 days, 2s. 11d. Item paid for battering the tools of the Bridge House masons for the past 3 quarters, 9s. Item paid for 34 weys of new lead bought for the new houses in Fenchurch Street, and for other houses in the Bridge's rents at various times for the whole year past, at 13s. the wey, £22 2s. Item paid to Richard atte Moore of Stratford for cleaning the ponds of the aforesaid mill, and for digging and ramming the earthworks of the same mill, according to the contract in gross, £8. Item paid for 42 hurdles bought for weirs [*wares*] in the ponds to stop the water, 10s. 6d. Item paid for timber bought to make the same weirs, 5s. Item paid for 1 piece of curved timber bought, 4s. Item paid for 142 lb. of cords bought, at 1½d. and 1¼d. the lb., 16s. ½d. Item paid for 126½ lb. of wrought iron, at 2d. the lb., 17s. 8d. Item paid for 65½ lb. new wax bought for the chapel for the whole year past, at 6d. the lb. including making it, 32s. Item paid for 13 gallons of oil bought for the chapel, at 16d. the gallon, 17s. 4d. Item paid for 2,400 laths, at 7s. the thousand, 16s. 9½d. Item paid for farriery for the Bridge House horses for the quarter, 7s. 7d. Item paid for taking away rubbish from a certain tenement in Old Change, 3s. Item paid for 2 boatloads of ragstone, 36s. 4d. Total £100 10s. 4½d. [sic; *recte* £100 8s. 11½d.]

108. Sum total of the expenses, £603 9s. 8½d.

BRIDGE HOUSE RENTAL 1

Rental for 1404

109. [f. 1] Rental of occupied and vacant tenements belonging to the Bridge in divers parishes in London and Southwark as found at Michaelmas 1404, the last day of the 5th year of the reign of King Henry IV, by William Sevenok and John Whatele appointed Wardens of the said Bridge from that date

110. St Magnus. In the parish of St Magnus London is one house divided in length, half of which belongs to the Bridge and is occupied as appears viz:
Of <Katharine wife of the late> Roger Crouche for one shop of the said house yearly 26s. 8d.
Of (Mazera Acton) <Adam Broun> for the solar beyond the said shop yearly 10s.

111. St Leonard. In the parish of St Leonard Eastcheap are 2 shops with solars built over, of which the wardens of the said church are now tenants.
Of the same wardens for the aforesaid shops and solar yearly £4.

112. St Benedict [lost]. In the parish of St Benet Gracechurch is one tenement called *le Horn on the hoop*.
Of <Hugo> (Robert) Whappelode for the said tenement yearly £8 13s. 4d.

113. St Mary atte [lost]. In the parish of St Mary at Hill is one tenement with 2 cottages annexed to it which are let as appears viz:
Of (Richard Assheford) {Richard Kyng} {Richard Fermory} <Esmon Chelnetham> <*de cotagiis sil*> (26s. 8d.) <33s.4d. [for both entries]>
[in margin:] <Vacated at Easter 1405>
Of (the wife of) <Alice> Asketyn for the same tenement and cottage–[in margin:] <[illegible] at Michaelmas 8 Henry IV [1407] with decrease [illegible] 8d. yearly> {[illegible] at Easter 1409} <at [illegible] 13 Henry IV>
Of (the same Richard Assheford) for the said cottages yearly (13s 4d)
(Of John Wortyng for one [<d>] cottage {3s. 4d.}
[in margin:] <[illegible] at Midsummer 1405. Vacated at Midsummer 1407>

114. All Saints Barking. In the parish of All Saints Barking is one house [*mansio*] and one cottage which are let as appears viz:

Of (William Clerk) {Robert Bolton} {Henry Somer} <John Kyng woolpacker> for the said house yearly 30s.
[in margin:] <Memorandum of its hustilments on 15 February 1403>
(Of John {John} Callere) {Henry Gerard} <Cokefeld woolpacker> for the cottage yearly (13s. 4d.) 10s.
[in margin:] <Entered at Easter 1405. Vacated at Michaelmas 1405. Gerard entered at Michaelmas 1407. Which [*quiquid*] J. Cokefeld at Midsummer 1414>

Total of this page £18 (13s. 4d.) <6s. 8d.>

115. [f 1v.] St Dunstan. In the parish of St Dunstan beside the Tower in the lane called Waterlane are two cottages with gardens which are rented as appears viz:
Of Stephen atte Ponte one of the said cottages yearly 16s.
Of (Walter Lord) <John {Goldhawk} Pope> for the other cottage yearly 16s.
[in margin:] <Said Walter entered at Midsummer 1405>

116. Fenchurch. In the parish of St Dionis Fenchurch are 4 principal houses and 3 shops with solars which are let as appears viz:
Of (Edmund atte Wode) <now John Bonaunter> *tapicer* one of the said houses yearly (50s.) {46s. 8d.} <40s.>
[in margin:] <[illegible] 40d. yearly beginning at (Easter) <Christmas term> 1404>
Of (Edmund atte Wode) <John Wellyng> for another house there yearly (50s) <46s. 8d.>
[in margin:] <Entered at Midsummer 1405 with decrease of 40d. a year>
Of (Robert Spayne) <John Goodyng> for another house there yearly (50s) {46s. 8d.} <40s.>
[in margin:] <Decreased 40d. yearly beginning (Easter) <as if entered at Christmas> 1404>
Of (John Silkeston) <Thomas Wode> for another house there yearly (53s. 4d.) <50s.>
[in margin:] <Decrease 40d. yearly beginning (Easter) <as if entered at Christmas> 1404>
Of (John Stratford) {James Horn} {William Holwode} <now Thomas Drury> for one shop there yearly 20s.
[in margin:] <Vacated at Midsummer 1406>
Of (Richard Chaundeller) {Thomas Hawkyn} {Robert Carpenter} <William Colchester> for one shop there yearly 20s.
[in margin:] <Entered at Easter 1405. Vacated at Christmas 1405>
Of (John Hamersham) {William Baron} <Walter Brewere> for 1 shop there yearly 20s.
[in margin:] <Entered at Christmas 1404. Vacated at Midsummer 1406>

In a certain alley there are 7 cottages which are let as appears below viz:

Of (John Panter) <Edmund atte Wode> <now the aforesaid John Bonaunt' not in addition to but included with the aforesaid sum of 40s.> (6s. 8d.) {4s.}
[in margin:] <Entered the morrow of Michaelmas 1405. Vacated. Wode entered at Midsummer 1409 with decrease of 2s. 8d. a year>
Of Robert Tropynell for one cottage there yearly 8s.
Of (John Lambheth) {Henry Taillour} {John {Stanes} Braynford} {Alexander Stacy} <Robert Bekett'> for another cottage there yearly 8s.
Of (Thomas Wade) {William Stowt} {Henry Taillour} { Robert Saltford} {William Stoute} <Sir Thomas chaplain> for another cottage there yearly 8s.
Of (Thomas Hankyn) {William {Stowt} Fawcon} {Robert Carpenter} <John Everyngham> for another cottage there yearly 10s.
Of (Bartholomew Peyntour) {Thomas Miles} {Thomas Hankyn} {Henry Gerard} {Richard Wrestlyngton} <John Felya> for another cottage there yearly 10s.
Of (John Wellyng) <Thomas {Miles} Hawkyn> for another cottage there yearly 10s

(Sum of the page £17 16s. at Michaelmas 5 Henry IV [1404])
{Decrease 5s. 10d. Thus sum of the page at Michaelmas 6 Henry IV [1405] £17 10s. 2d. nl}
<Sum of the page (7) <6> Henry IV £17 (2s. 8d.)>

117. [f. 2] All Saints in the Wall. In the parish of All Saints in the Wall are 4 cottages with gardens which are let etc.
Of (John Whitbred) {Clement Smyth} <John Sunneman> for one cottage there 13s. 4d.
Of (Thomas Rewe *di*) {Clement Smyth}{*fre* John} <John Sonneman> 13s. 4d.
Of (Thomas Culworth) <John Botiller> 13s. 4d.
Of John (Soneman) {Stoor} <Sonneman> 13s. 4d.

118. Augustine Papey. In the parish of St Augustine Papey are 3 cottages which are let as appears.
Of John Bruer 8s.
Of (Geoffrey Taillour) {John Bell} {John Laborer} 8s.
Of (Henry Bruer) {Richard Gardyner} {Agnes Copuldyke} <Roger Sawer> 8s.
[in margin:] <Vacated at Easter 1405 and entered at Midsummer then next. Vacated at Midsummer 1407. Entered at Midsummer 1407>

119. All Saints Hon[lost]. In the parish of All Saints in Honey Lane are 2 houses which are let as appears.
Of (John Pope) {William Grene} <Robert Kyngston grocer> (£7 6s. 8d.) {£5 6s. 8d.} <£6 [lost]>
[in margin:] <Vacated at Michaelmas 1405 and the said (William) <Robert> entered at ([illegible]) Midsummer 1412 (with decrease of

40s) <with increase of 2 marks> a year. {for the entry [illegible] before Christmas he gave 10s}>
Of (William Burton) <John Tapelegh> £4 13s. 4d.

120. St Margaret Moy[lost]. In the parish of St Margaret Moses in Friday Street is one inn [*hospitium*] called *le Cheker on the Hoop* which is let as appears.
Of (Thomas Broun) <Gy Bakere> for the said tenement 106s. 8d.

121. In the Old Fishmarket. In the parish of St Mary Magdalen beside the Old Fishmarket is one inn with 2 shops annexed which are let as appears.
Of Robert Chesterton £4.
Of (William Burton) {Russell} <Joan Shept' 5s. and Alice Mockyng 5s.> 10s.

122. Old Change. In Old Change are 28 shops with solars built over which begin at Cheap on the west side and extend to the gate of St Augustine and are let as appears.
1. Of John (Bernes) <Swafham> 66s. 8d.
2. Of (Richard Halle) <John Swafham> (66s. 8d.) <40s.>

Sum of the page (£32 7s. 4d.) <at Michaelmas 7 Henry IV [1406]> {£30 7s. 4d.}

[f. 2v.] 3. Of John Strete (16s.) <13s. 4d.>
4. Of (Thomas Wolwych) <John Strete> (16s.) <13s. 4d.>
5. Of (John Sherston) {Kirketon} {Elyne} <the storehouse> (16s.) <13s. 4d.>
[in margin:] <Entered at Easter 1405. Vacated at Michaelmas 1405>
6. Of (Isabella Shepster) {Elyne Spaldyng and her husband} {John Middilmas} <John Barley (16s.) <13s. 4d.>
[in margin:] <Entered at Easter 1405>
7. Of (Hubert Leger) <John Hewe> (16s.) <13s. 4d.>
8. Of (Cristiana Frowe) {Parker} {Agnes Coteler} {Th. Eidard} <John Hewe> (16s.) <13s. 4d.>
[in margin:] <Vacated by Cristiana Frowe Michaelmas 6 Henry IV [1405]. Entered at Midsummer 1405. Entered Parker at ([illegible]) Easter 1407. Vacated at Christmas 1408>
9. Of (Thomas Dunston) <Richard Blake> (16s.) <13s. 4d.>
10. Of (John Halle) <Emota Rede> (16s.) <13s. 4d.>
11. Of (Thomas Molton) {and Agnes Brok} <John Ewhurst> (16s.) <13s. 4d.>
12. Of Thomas Wemme (16s.) <13s. 4d.>
13. Of (Margaret de Bery) {William Fifhede} <Isabell Blakewelle> (16s.) <13s. 4d.>
14. Of (Joan Lytster) {William Skete} {Edward Alderbury} {Robert Roue} <John Rowe> (16s.) <13s. 4d.>
[in margin:] <Vacated at Christmas 1404. Entered Skete at Michaelmas. 7 Henry IV [1406]>

15. Of John Colour (16s.) <13s. 4d.>
16. Of (Margery Boteler) {William Smyth} {Th Mason} <William Fifede> (16s.) <13s. 4d.>
[in margin:] <Entered at Christmas 1404. Entered (Smyth at Midsummer 1408)>
17. Of (William Joynour *ducheman*) (16s.) <13s. 4d.>
18. Of (William Skete) <storehouse> (16s.) <13s. 4d.>
[in margin:] <Vacated at Michaelmas 7 Henry IV [1406]>
19. Of (Agnes Rodbourne) {Katharine Whappelod and Wat' Hervy} {James Sergeant} (16s.) <13s. 4d.>
20. Of (John Harle) <Vacated> (16s.) <13s. 4d.>
21. Of (John Steven) {John Lee} (16s.) <13s. 4d.>
22. Of (John Fox) {John Nicholl} {Giles Armourar} <John Tuck> (16s.) <13s. 4d.>
[in margin:] <[lost] Easter 1405>

Sum of the page £16.

[f. 3] 23. Of (William Buxton) {Henry Colworth} <John {Webbe} Sherwode> (16s.) <13s. 4d.>
[in margin:] <Entered at Michaelmas [illegible]>
24. Of (John Mapulton) {Fox} {Henry Colworth} {Emma Goldsmyth} (16s.) <13s. 4d.>
[in margin:] <Mapulton left at Midsummer 1405. Fox at Easter 1407. Vacated at Christmas 1407>
25. Of (John Prat) {Pryk} {Katherine Tapster} (16s.) <13s. 4d.>
[in margin:] <Entered at Easter 1405>
26. Of (John Herberger) {Robert Ladde} <Henry Nedeler> (16s.) <13s. 4d.>
[in margin:] <Vacated at Easter 1405>
27. Of (John Dufle) {Robert Taillour} <Nicholas Skulton> (16s.) <13s. 4d.>
[in margin:] <Entered at Michaelmas at the end of 12 Henry IV [1411] with decrease of 2s. 8d.>
28. Of Nicholas Skulton 40s.
[in margin:] <Entered {at the feast} <on the morrow> of Michaelmas 6 Henry IV [1405]>

123. Paternoster Row. In Paternoster Row is one great messuage and 30 shops with solars which are let as appears.
Of (James Hukvale) <Simon Prentoft> waxchandler, (£10) <10 marks>
[in margin:] <Vacated at Michaelmas 6 Henry IV [1405] and Simon Prentoft entered at Easter 1406 with decrease of 5 marks a year>
Of (Nicholas Copursmyth) {Roger Wodecok} {John Rede} 26s. 8d.
Of (John Yonge) {Nicholas Est} 26s. 8d.
Of (Nicholas Copursmyth) {the wife of John Yonge} {John Boys} <Peter Bilton> 26s. 8d.
<Of Peter Bylton for 1 shop 26s. 8d.>
Of (Salamon Oxneye for (3) {2} shops) <Peter Bilton> (£4) <53s. 4d.>

Of John (Roulond) <Robert> 26s. 8d.
Of Thomas (Denlond) <Fissh> 26s. 8d.
Of Richard More 26s. 8d.
Of Thomas (Hyeline) <Boweland> 26s. 8d.
Of Thomas Marleburgh for 2 shops, 53s. 4d.
Of (Richard) <Roger> Ibot 26s. 8d.
Of {the wife of} Thomas (Charleton) <Broke> 26s. 8d.
Of Maurice Wether 26s. 8d.

Sum total of the page <at Michaelmas 7 Henry IV [1406]> (£36) {£32 13s. 4d.}

[f. 3v.] Of (Nicholas Sprot) {Edmund Cook} <Edmund Cok> 26s. 8d.
Of (John Hun) <Herman Skereueyn> 26s. 8d.
Of Roger Dune 26s. 8d.
Of (Thomas Glade) {atte Wode} <John Broun> 40s.
Of (the same Thomas) <Peter Fulborn> 26s. 8d.
Of (Thomas Eynesham) 26s. 8d.
[in margin:] <Vacant because he left at Midsummer 1409>
Of (Thomas Glym) {John Lymynour} {Barbour} <William Wodehows barber> 26s. 8d.
[in margin:] <Glym left at Christmas 1407. Lymynour entered at Midsummer 1408>
Of (the same Thomas) {William Kyngeston} <Richard Martyn> 26s. 8d.
[in margin:] <Glym left at Christmas 1407>
Of (Gregory Sompnour) {William Rillesthorp} {Thomas Enysham} {John Elmham} <John Benett> 26s. 8d.
Of (John Anys) {Roger Cornewell} 26s. 8d.
[in margin:] <[illegible] at Easter 1405>
Of (William Durham) {John Brys} 26s. 8d.
Of <John Langele over the shop, and he pays 20s a year> 26s. 8d.
[in margin:] {Vacant for [illegible] beginning} <Langele entered at Christmas 1405>. {[illegible] Langele [illegible] the shop at Easter 1406}
Of (John Colmakere) {William Bilesthorp} {Richard Pryour} Thomas Byllesthorp 26s. 8d.
[in margin:] <Bilesthorp left at Easter 1409>
Of (Margaret Broun widow) {vacant} 26s. 8d.
[in margin:] <Vacated at Christmas 1404>
Of (Morice Steynour) {John White} <Roger Cornwaille>

124. Michael *atte Corn*. In the parish of St Michael le Quern is a tavern with the sign of *le Raven* which is let as appears.
Of (John Brok taverner) {Robert Bastewyk} <Bernard Roy> (£8) {£8} {£6 13s. 4d.} <£6 13s. 4d.>
[in margin:] <Entered the morrow of Michaelmas 6 Henry IV [1405]. Decreased beginning at Easter 1406 by 26s. 8d. Vacated by the said John Brok at Michaelmas 1406. Bastewik entered at Christmas 1406 with increase [lost] a year>

125. At the Shambles. In the parish of St Nicholas Shambles are divers houses which etc.

Of (Nicholas Wyght) <J. Merssh> 50s.

<Of Henry Fouler for the tenement late of Laurence Sely 20s>

Of (John Shoppe) <Robert Fynch> butcher for the tenement called *le Ball* £6 13s. 4d.

Of (Nicholas Osbarn) <William Reed> for 2 shops (£6 13s. 4d.) <£5 6s. 8d.>

[in margin:] <Decrease beginning {at Michaelmas} <on entry at Midsummer> 6 Henry IV [1405] 26s. 8d. a year>

Sum total of the page (£44 10s) <at Michaelmas 8 Henry IV [1407]> {£43 16s. 8d.} <£43 3s. 4d.>

[f. 4] Of Thomas Sompnour for 2 shops 106s 8d.

Of (John Reynes for 1 shop and 2 chambers) {John Symson} {Philip Wheler} {vacant} <Walter Drope> (£3) <£4 {6s. 8d.}> [probably refers to this and the next entry]

[in margin:] <Said Symson entered at Christmas 1404, vacated at Easter 1406. Wheler entered at Easter 1408>

Of (John Mormore for 1 shop 20s.)

[in margin:] <Vacated at Christmas 1404>

Of John Maister (£9 6s. 8d.) {£8 6s. 8d.} <£6 13s. 4d.>

[in margin:] <Decreased 26s. 8d, beginning at Christmas 1404. Item decreased 13s. 4d. at Midsummer 1411>

Of John Denge for a certain brewhouse [*domo bras'*] £4.

126. At the Shambles and St Audoen [Ewen]. In the parishes of St Nicholas Shambles and St Ewen are 17 shops and one house over the gate of the Friars Minor which are let etc.

Of (William Gyllowe) <Simon Roughhed> 33s. 4d.

Of (Geoffrey Adam) {Robert Somerton} <William Giles> 46s. 8d.

Of William (Glovere) <Giles> 40s.

Of (Simon Roughhed) <William Torold> 40s.

Of (Henry Horntoft) {William Giles} <Reginald Barbour> 40s.

Of (Robert Somerton) <John Boor> 40s.

Of (Richard Coventre) <John Brigge> 40s.

Of (William Whelpele) {William} <Richard Botle> 40s.

Of (Thomas Haberdassher) <William Loder> 40s.

[in margin:] <Vacated at Midsummer 1405. Botle entered at Michaelmas 6 Henry IV [1405]>

127. In the said parish are 8 cabins [*cabane*] which are let as appears.

Of (the wife of Thomas Taillour) {John Austyn} <Is. Huxst'> 6s. 8d.

Of (Joan Haberdassher) {Peter Cotiller} {Alice Pesecod} 5s.

Of (the same Joan) {Peter} {William Wotton} <Ralph Hill> 6s. 8d.

Of (Joan Frampton) {Agnes Brown} <Peter Coteler> 6s. 8d.

Of (John Brauncestre) {[John] More & William Wade} <Walter Holand> for (two cabins) <one cabin> (13s. 4d.) <6s. 8d.>

Of (John Spenser for another) 6s. 8d.

Of (Laurence Pynner) {Thomas Belymaker for one} (13s. 4d.) <6s. 8d.>
{Of Robert Clerk for another} 6s. 8d.
Of (John Cappe) {William Edward} 4s.

128. [in margin:] <The Stocks [*Les stokkes*]> <Of John Morion for a house over the Stocks £4.
Of the schoolmaster for another house there 66s. 8d.>

Sum total of the page (£43 9s.) <at Michaelmas 7 Henry IV [1406]> {£42 [illegible]} <9s.>

129. [f. 4v] In the parish of St Nicholas Shambles and St Ewen there are 27 shops and one house over the gate of the Friars Minor which are let as appears.
Of (Walter Blawe for 5 shops £16 13s. 4d.)
[in margin:] <Decreased 13s. 4d. yearly beginning at Easter 1405>
<Of <the wife of> John Hode for {2} <1> shop{s} <and Philip Wheler for the other shop> £6 13s. 4d.>
<Of John Lyncoln for 1 shop <now of John Goodhewe <and John Frensh> £4>
<Of John Baxstere for 1 shop <now of William Stichemersh> 53s. 4d.>
<Of John Vale for 1 shop <William Reed> 53s. 4d.>
Of William Bull 70s.
Of John (Fauconer) <Asshewell> 66s. 8d.
Of (John Rower) for the house [*mansio*] over the gate of the said Robert Huwet (26s. 8d.) <20s.>
[in margin:] <Rower vacated at Easter 1405. Huwet entered at Michaelmas next>
Of Robert Huwet 66s. 8d.
[in margin:] <Decrease of the house over the gate 6s. 8d. yearly beginning from {Midsummer} <Michaelmas> 6 Henry IV [1405]>
Of Thomas Leycestre (63s. 4d.)
Of (Marion Kyrkeby) Thomas Leycestr' (53s. 4d.) <£6 [for this and preceding property, bracketed together]>
[in margin:] <Thomas Leycestr' holds by deed for 20 years beginning at Easter 1405 and gives an increment for both of 40d. a year>
Of (John Wawe) {John Howhe} {Philip Percell} <John Bokenell> 56s. 8d.
Of (Peter Kyrkeby) <the same John Bokenell> (53s. 4d.)
[in margin:] <[lost] Peter Kirkeby at Michaelmas 6 Henry IV [1405] with {decrease} {increase} <decrease> of 10s. a year. Beginning at Michaelmas 9 Henry IV [1408] of 10s. a year.>
Of (Laurence Est) <the same John Bokenell> (40s.) {£4 3s. 4d.} <£4 13s. 4d.> [for this and preceding property, bracketed together]
Of (Robert Huwet) {Thomas Leycestr'} {John Bokenell} <Philip Porcell> 40s.
Of the same (Robert) {Thomas} {John} <Philip> 40s.

37

Of (William Wyxton) <Robert Marchale> (40s.) {53s. 4d. [for this and following entry]} <33s. 4d.>
[in margin:] <Entered the morrow of Michaelmas 6 Henry IV [1405]. with decrease of 26s. 8d in those tenements {beginning at Christmas 1404} [he] holds by deed>
Of (the same William) <John Lyndesey> (40s.) <20s.>

130. On the Bridge. On the east of the bridge beginning at the Staples [*Stulpas*][1] towards London there are divers shops which are worth yearly as appears.
Of (the wife of Abraham Seyntfeyth) {Thomas Paxon grocer} <Robert Oteleye> 53s. 4d.
Of (Thomas Kyng) <Robert Oteleye> 53s. 4d.
Of (Thomas Naunby) {Richard Burgeys} <Thomas Kyng> 53s. 4d.
Of (Simon Warle) <Thomas Kyng> 40s.
Of (Peter Blak) <James Grene> 36s. 8d.

(Sum total of the page £61 6s. 8d.) {Michaelmas 6 Henry IV [1405] £59 10s.} {£58 13s. 4d at Michaelmas 7 Henry IV [1406]} <Sum total £59 3s. 4d.>

[f. 5] Of John (Hyde) <Westowe> £3 6s.
[in margin:] <2 tenements>
Of Roger Gylot and Avice his wife 36s.
Of (Michael Mordon) <John Soler> and Agnes his wife 30s.
Of (Gilbert Peryman) <Richard Osgood> 32s.
Of (John Goldesburgh) {Walter Laurence} <William Waryn> 26s. 8d.
Of Thomas Foule spurrier <and others licensed there by t'> 26s. 8d.
Of (John Chymbeham) {Richard Clyf} <John Welys cutler> and Joan his wife 32s.
[in margin:] <Entered about 30 September 11 Henry IV [1410] [illegible] Memorandum of glazed windows bought [lost] and benches in the hall, wooden wall [lost] <and 1 lattice> shelves, partitions, chests [lost] hall and glazed windows in the shop>
Of John (Vylere) <Gilot> 26s. 8d.
Of (Thomas Bromley) {William Kynton} <Thomas Robelard> 26s. 8d.
Of Walter Peryman 32s.
Of (Margery Lynne) {Walter Weddesbury} <Thomas Hamond cutler> 23s. 4d.
Of (Peter Frenssh) <Walter Holme and Isabella his wife> 33s. 4d.
Of (William Fouche) <John Chapman haberdasher and Agnes his wife> 31s. 8d.
Of (Richard Burgeys) {Thomas Jolyf} <Robert Darcok armourer and Geliana his wife> 21s.
Of (Thomas Jolyf) <the same Robert and Geliana> 43s.
[in margin:] <2 tenements>
Of (Richard Tabelmaker) {Alice Blak, late his wife} {John Trot} <William Rotour and Cristiana his wife> 21s.

38

Of (Matilda Gerars) <Richard Brydbrook> 21s.

[in margin:] <Memorandum of the necessaries of the said house bought, as appears in the purchases in the 52nd week of [the account for the year] 8 Henry IV [1406–7]>

Of (John Reynold) <Thomas Moger> 23s

Of {the wife of} (Thomas Gaudre) <John Legat and Joan [his] wife> 21s.

Of (John Shordyche) {William Weddesbury} <John Palmere and Joan his wife> 21s.

Of (John Webbe) {[John] Hughe and Agnes his wife} {Ralph Cleef} <Thomas Fermery> 21s.

Sum total of the page £3 5s.

1. The bollards protecting the entry to the Bridge.

131. [f. 5v.] Of John Wodelond 23s.

Of John (Coman) <Swettecok> 20s.

Of <the wife of> Ralph Sporyer 20s.

Of (Robert Whitway) <Walter Pelham> 20s.

Of (John Style) {Wellys cutler} {in the hands of the Wardens for a fine} <Roger Wymmerse and Katherine his wife> 20s.

Of (Ralph Cook) <John Drewry> and Katherine his wife 22s.

Of (William Hasulden) {the wife of Hasulden} <the wife of Geoffrey Doon> 33s. 4d.

Of William Clerk 20s.

Of (Matilda Foulhardy) <Walter Takeneswell> 16s.

Of (William Moger) {for 2 Katherine Moger} (36s.) <46s 8d.>

[in margin:] <Increase 10s. 8d. beginning from Midsummer 1408>

Of (John Hert) {Richard Whityngton} {Andrew Rede} {John {Grene} Yerde} <John Spene *brochemaker*> 40s.

Of (John Verne) <William Dyngewyk} 16s.

Of (Robert White) <Bartholomew Bownde purser> <and Margaret his wife> 16s.

Of <the wife of> (John Page) <now {Thomas Waleys} his wife> 20s.

Of <the wife of> (John Page) <now {Thomas Waleys} his wife> 16s.

Of <the wife of> (Walter) Eggelof 20s.

Of (John Bury) {Drury} <Robert Breton bowyer> <and Felice his wife> 13s. 4d.

Of (John Charryng) {Agnes Babyngton {*art' de*} linendraper} <Robert Breton bowyer {and Felice his wife}> 13s. 4d.

Of (William Barton) {Robert Percyvall} {William Gilmyn} {[William] Moger} <Richard Grene cutler> 13s. 4d.

Of Thomas Edmere [name altered] 26s. 8d.

Of John Chaumbr' 20s.

Of (John Hallary) {Ralph Heriott stringer} <Stephen Sampton and Joan his wife> 16s. 8d.

Sum total of the page £24 (11s. 8d.) <2s. 4d.>

132. [f.6; heading *Pons*]

Of (Simon Aston) <John Hale> 40s.
Of (William Serteyn) <Stephen Santon> 26s. 8d.
Of (Richard Lambard) <Henry Stryngere} 20s.
Of Henry <Yoonge> Stryngere and Joan his wife 26s. 8d.
Of (John {Peter} Frenssh) <Richard Millyng> <and Anne his wife> 26s. 8d.
Of (William {Philip} Alblast') {Richard Millyng} {W Warewik fletcher} <Alexander atte Wode bowyer and Joan his wife> 13s. 4d.
Of (Agnes Mordon) {John Shadewell} {the same Richard Millyng} <Of W Warewyk> 13s. 4d.
Of (John {Roger} Cotys) {John Shadewell} <Sampson Longe> 13s. 4d.
Of (John Barbour) {Thomas Haket} {Walter Bury} <Thomas Edward> 16s.
Of (the same John) {Thomas Hille} {Alice Hill} 10s.
Of Henry Roulond 10s.
Of (the same Henry) <Alexander atte Wode bowyer> 26s. 8d.
Of (John Broun) {[John] Wellys barber} <William Shene *botelmaker*> 26s. 8d.
Of (John Knyf) {Alexander Wode} {William Clerk} <Thomas Salman> 26s. 8d.
Of Richard Peryman 26s. 8d.
Of (John Goldfynch) <Richard Phelipp grocer> 33s. 4d.
Of (Robert Man) {John Deken} <Richard Philipp grocer> 26s. 8d.
Of (John Mokkyng) {William Skot} <John Doune> (26s. 8d.) <30s>
[in margin:] <Vacated at Michaelmas 7 Henry IV [1406]>

133. On the west part of the Bridge. On the west part of the Bridge beginning at the Staples [*Stulpas*] towards Southwark are divers shops which are worth as appears.
Of (Thomas Lydeyard cook for the first shop) {Richard Abraham} {John Doke} <John Esgaston for both houses> (53s. 4d.) <£4 13s. 4d.> [for both this and next entry] <Memorandum of necessaries bought 29 [rest of date lost]>
Of the same (Thomas for the second shop) {Richard} <John> (53s. 4d.)
[in margin:] <Decreased 13s. 4d. yearly beginning {at Michaelmas} <at previous Midsummer> 6 Henry IV [1405]>
Of (Joan Foster) <Richard Peryman> (40s.) <33s. 4d.>
[in margin:] <Vacated at Christmas 1406. Entered at Michaelmas 8 Henry IV [1407]. Decreased from Midsummer 1408 6s. 8d. a year>

(Sum total appears £27 16s.) <at Michaelmas 7 Henry IV [1406]> {£27 6s. 8d.} [illegible]
<Sum appears £26 19s. 4d.>

134. [f.6v.] Of (William Stekeney) {Mokkyng} <John {Dekene} Joye> (53s. 4d.) <46s. 8d.>
[in margin:] <Vacated at Midsummer 1406. Entered {at Christmas 1406 Mokkyng} Dekene at Midsummer 1408 with decrease 6s. 8d. a year>

Of John Marchall (40s) 33s. 4d.

[in margin:] <Decrease beginning Midsummer 1408 6s. 8d. a year>

Of (William Banastre) {John Sherman} {Edward Uphewe} {John Tornour} <John Ruston (40s.) <33s. 4d.>

[in margin:] <Banastre vacated at Easter 1406 and the said Sherman entered at Midsummer 1405 [sic] with decrease 6s. 8d. yearly beginning at Midsummer 1408>

Of (Joan Blount) {John Esgaston} <Robert Fairford> (60s.) <53s. 4d.>

[in margin:] <Decrease of 6s. 8d. yearly beginning at Christmas 1404>

Of (John atte Wode) <the same Robert> (40s.) 33s.4d.

[in margin:] <Decrease 6s. 8d. beginning at Midsummer 1408>

Of (John Hethe) {Clement Bisshop} {John Doncastre} <Alexander Prior> (40s.) <33s. 4d.>

[in margin:] <Vacated at Christmas 1406. Bisshop entered at Michaelmas 11 Henry IV [1410] with decrease of 6s. [sic] a year>

Of (John Skyllere) <Clement Bisshop> (40s.) <33s. 4d.>

[in margin:] <Decrease beginning Midsummer 1408>

Of the Stone Gate 20s. <delivered to William Est paying nothing>

Of (John Tournour for 2 shops) {Ralph Strynger} {William Est} <Alice wife of the said William> 26s. 8d.

[in margin:] <2 tenements>

Of (John Delley) {Reilley} {the same Ralph} {William} <and the wife of the said William> 13s. 4d.

Of (Geoffrey Coupere) <Thomas Welbourne> 26s. 8d.

Of Richard Chaumberleyn 20s.

Of John Volantyn 20s.

Of Robert Crull 26s. 8d.

Of (Nicholas Neffold) <the same Robert Crull> 20s.

[in margin:] <[illegible] 5 March 1408 the same Nicholas voluntarily surrendered the house in the countinghouse>

Of (Ralph Heryot) {[Ralph] Blakelowe} <William Shene and Alice his wife> 26s. 8d.

Of (John Hyllary) {Roger Hillary} <John Symmes> 26s. 8d.

Of Nicholas Holford 16s.

Of (Hugh More) <the same Nicholas> 16s.

Of (John Gaudre) {John Beneyt} <Thomas Namby and Alice his wife> 13s. 4d.

Of (John Heywode) <Matilda Heywode> 13s. 4d.

Sum total appears (£39 18s. 8d.) <at Michaelmas 6 Henry IV [1405]> {£29 12s.} <£27 12s.>

135. [f. 7] Of (Laurence Sely) {Joan Whetear} {Walter Horneby draper} {John Legat and Joan his wife} <Of John Tanner barber> <and Katherine his wife> 13s. 4d.

Of {the wife of} (Thomas Rous) <Walter Horneby draper> {and Agnes his wife} 26s. 8d.

Of (William Burton) {Agnes Burton} {Andrew Reed draper} <Of Robert Miles spurrier and Agnes his wife>

Of (Thomas Cardemaker) {William Estwyk} <Richard Davy> 16s.
Of <the wife of> Thomas Prudant 20s.
Of (John Derneford) <Richard Serteyn> (16s.) <20s.>
Of Thomas Katerham 16s.
[in margin:] <by the mayor>
Of (Henry Prat) <Emote Prat> 16s.
Of (Richard Appulton) <Nicholas Deye> 16s.
Of (John Chambre haberdasher) <William Erle> 20s.
Of (Christiana Trippyng) {Thomas Flete} <John Longevile and Isabella his wife> 16s.
Of (John Bourne) <Agnes Bourne> 36s.
Of (Richard) <John> Clerk <chaplain> <holds at will> 16s.
Of (Thomas Clyfton) <John Tournour> <for 2 tenements> 66s.
[in margin:] <2 tenements>
Of (John Merston) {William Hore horner} <Henry Warde and Joan his wife> 22s.
Of (Robert Percyvale) <William Barton> 20s.
Of Thomas Mount 20s.
Of (Richard Gray) {Alice his daughter} <John Hille> 20s.
Of (Peter Bonde) <John Hille> {girdler} <hosier and Alice his wife> 20s.
Of (Henry Lydesey) {Stephen Bertelot} <John (Sandon) Santon spurrier and Agnes his wife (33s.) <30s.>
Of John Scot 21s.

Sum total appears £23 7s.

136. [f. 7v.; heading *Pons*] Of (John Stafford) <Joan> {Stafford} <Coman> 21s.
Of (John Byle) <John Goldisburgh and Joan his wife> (46s. 8d.) <21s.>
[in margin:] <This John Byle twice paid a fine for his tenement in the time of William Chicheley, then warden of the Bridge, for putting in a tenant without licence>
<Of John Johnsone 26s. 8d.>
Of John Poudere 21s.
Of (John Hert) <Thomas Leget> 43s.
Of (Thomas Robelard) <Hynton's wife> 21s.
Of John Beuers 22s.
Of (Thomas Daniell) <Nicholas Holford> 31s. 8d.
Of Thomas (Goldesburgh) <Robelard> 26s. 8d.
Of (Robert Bray) <Alice Bray> 32s.
Of (Thomas Pencryche) {Leticia Pencryche} <John Swan> 26s.
Of John Leche 26s.
Of (Robert Tot) <Andrew Hunte girdler etc> <and Denise his wife> 32s.
Of (Walter Crane) {Thomas Sawyer} <Alan Brymmesgrove> <and Alice his wife> 26s.
[in margin:] <2 October 1406 it was granted to the same T. that he might have his kitchen in the said house by licence of the masters>

Of (Thomas Sawyer) <John Sergeaunt> 26s.
Of John Sergeaunt 32s.
Of (William Gylmyn) {by the wife of T. Regnold} {Thomas Balle}
<John Farnham glover> 30s.
Of (John Brode) {Stephen Sedere} {Thomas Legat} {Guy [illegible]}
<John Paddesle 36s.
Of John Bysshop 30s.
Of (John Clyfford) <Andrew Hunte> <and Denise his wife> 36s.
Of (William Ayston) <John Hale fletcher <and Anne his wife> for 1
<new> house with a stone pit [*putt' petr'*] over the cellar of Andrew
Hunte there> (46s. 8d.) <£3>
Of John Chyld <junior and Alice his wife and John Child senior and
Matilda his wife> (36s.) <£3>
[in margin:] <2 tenements>

Sum total appears £33 10s. 4d.

[f. 8; heading *Suthwerk*]
Of (Edmund Chaumberleyn) <John Child barber> 30s.
[in margin:] <Entered at Easter 1407>

137. Southwark. In Southwark is a certain brewhouse with the sign of
le Crowne.
Of John (Wysbech for the same house) <Salford> £4.
Of (William Toche) <[blank] Clampart> (30s.) <46s. 8d.>
Of (John Lokyer) {Lambel' Lokyer} <Robert Devyt> 12s.
Of Walter Eggelof 10s.
Of <the wife of> John Pegrom 8s.
Of (John atte Mere) {Walter Pygrom} <John Hoddesdon> 8s.
Of (Arnald Savage knight) <Est's wife> (68s.) <£3 6s. 8d.>
Of (William Fuller) <John Barker fuller> 22s.
Of (Thomas Wanstall) {Nicholas Bury} {Thomas Russell} <Andrew
Taillour> 10s.
Of (Ralph Heryot) <John White fletcher> 10s.
Of (John Flecher) <John Conscience> 10s.
Of John Brys 10s.
[in margin:] <By indenture from the Annunciation [25 March] in the
same year for a term of 20 years>
Of(William Samwell) <John Dove> 10s.
Of (Geoffrey Coupere) {John Dekene} <and Robert Crull> 10s.
Of (William Trot) {Thomas Clerk} <Richard [deletion] Reek> 10s.
Of (John atte Gate) {Simon Sergeaunt} <Oliver Sawyer> 10s.
Of (John Warde) {Reignold Cristofre} <Robert Clerk> (10s.) {13s.
4d.} <20s.>
Of (John Brode) <William Clerk> (10s.) <13s. 4d.>
Of (John Hasteler) {Cristiana Hertford} <John Newman> 10s.
Of (Umfr' Shorbard) <Richard Giles> 10s.

Sum total appears (£19 8s.)

138. [f. 7v.; heading *Suthwerk*]

43

Of (William Profet) <Henry Hoke> 10s.
Of (Richard Samwell) {Gybon Bakere cutler} <John Basset> 10s.
Of (William Freman) <Henry Lord> 10s.
Of (the same William) <the same> 10s.
Of (Juliana Fuleslove) <John Welles> 10s.
Of John Swetman (10s.) <13s. 4d.>
Of <the wife of> (John Erlam) <John Toche> 10s.
Of <the wife of> (Stephen) Parker 10s.
Of (John Wellys) <Roger Reynold> (10s.) <6s. 8d.>
{Of a certain Frenchwoman [*francigena quad'*]} <William Hoore>
<5s.>

Sum total appears. £4 10s.

139. Sum total of all the aforewritten tenements at Michaelmas 5 Henry
IV [1404], at which time this book was begun. (£462 2s.)
Sum total of all tenements viz. the morrow of Michaelmas 10 Henry IV
[1409]. (£450 19s. 4d.)
Sum total of all tenements viz. the morrow of Michaelmas 11 Henry IV
[1410] (£448 10s.)

140. [f. 9] Names of the tenants of the mills, tenements, lands and
meadows belonging to the Bridge beyond the bars of Southwark in
the fields of Lambeth, at the Lock, Hatcham, Camberwell, Lewisham,
and Stratford at Michaelmas A.D. 1404 at the end of the 5th year of
Henry IV.

141. (Thomas Lake) {Henry Hooke} <Thomas Bys> holds 19 acres of
land in the field of Lambeth by farm yearly 26s. 8d.
[in margin:] {John Burnham holds for all by indenture except [that
which is] retained in the hands of the Bridge}
Richard Langeford butcher for 4 acres of land and 2 pieces of meadow
with a tenement at the Lock 50s.
Item at the Lock are 2 acres of land and 2 acres meadow called
Carpentershawe and at *le Sterte* and Hatcham 1 acre of arable land in
the hands of the Bridge, nil.
[in margin:] {John Goldesburgh and John Goodchep <and Roger
Tanner butcher> holding <*Carpentershawe*> from 10 September 1412
to the Purification [2 February] next etc. for 13s. 4d.}
(John Short junior) {Henry Hooke} {John Short} {William Steente}
<Robert Standon> holds 7 acres of land and 2 acres meadow beside
Seint Thomas Wateryng and it renders yearly 20s.
(William Mareys) {John Short} {Henry Hooke} {William Steente}
{W} <Richard> <Spore> holds one piece of land called *Tenacre*
lying towards Hatcham, and it renders yearly 33s. 4d.
Thomas Trot holds the manor of Lewisham with 91 acres of land, 2
acres meadow and 5 acres wood, and it renders yearly 26s. 8d.
Robert Adcok holds one watermill at Lewisham with 2 acres pasture,
and it renders yearly (53s. 4d.) <£3 by indenture>

Thomas Trotte holds one croft at Lewisham now newly cleared [*de novo eradicat'*] rendering therof yearly 6s. 8d.

[in margin:] <Memorandum that this croft contains in total 91 acres [illegible] and now it is cleared, increased [illegible] 6s. 8d.>

142. Quit-rents at Lewisham yearly

Of Thomas Pathe for quit-rent (6s. 8d.) <20d.>
Of Mabel Payse for quit-rent (6s. 8d.) <20d.>
Of William Crokker for quit-rent (5s.) <15d.>
Of Geoffrey Coke for quit-rent (5s. 8d.) <17d.>
Of William Couper for quit-rent (2s. 6d.) <7½d.>
Of Robert atte Mylne for quit-rent (16d.) <4d.>
Of John Capper for quit-rent (8d.) <2d.>
Of Robert Totfort for quit-rent (10d.) <2½d.>
Of William Alrede for quit-rent (16d.) <4d.>
of Elena Alrede for quit-rent (8d.) <2d.>
<Total 7s. 10d.>

143. [f. 9v.; heading *Stratford*]
Of (John Smyth) <Roger Yonge> farmer of the watermill for corn <called *Saynemylle*> and 13 acres meadow there £6 13s. 4d.
Memorandum that the vicar of West Ham has one acre assigned to him for tithe of all the said meadow.

Of (William Chylde) <Laurence Fuller> farmer of the watermill for fulling called *Spylemansmylle* and 4 acres of meadow and one embankment [*walla*] in length 3 furlongs, and one *roda*,[1] which embankment and *roda* are held of the master of the Hospital of St Thomas of Acre £6 13s. 4d.
Memorandum that this mill is free of any tithes payable to any church.

1. Roadstead or landing-place?

144. [f.10] Rental of quit-rents paid and not paid belonging to the Bridge in London and Southwark, as are found at Michaelmas 1404, the last day of the 5th year of Henry IV, in the time of William Sevenok and John Whatele.

145. St Magnus. In the parish of St Magnus the Martyr are 3 shops with solars at the Staples [*Stapulas*] of the bridge, belonging to the fraternity of *Salve* in the said parish church of St Magnus, and they render yearly to London Bridge 12s.
Item in the same parish are 3 shops at the said Staples belonging to the said fraternity, and they render to the Bridge 3s. (2d.)
Item in the same parish is one tenement late of John Lovekyn and now of (Katherine Yevelee) the church of St Magnus, by the hands of the wardens thereof, and it renders yearly to the Bridge 5s. <denied>
Item in the said parish is one tenement on the corner opposite the said church belonging to a perpetual chantry in the said church, and

it renders yearly to the Bridge by the wardens of the said church of St Magnus 66s. 8d.

Item in the said parish is one tavern sometime of Richard de Essex annexed to the said tenement belonging to the chantry, and it renders yearly to the Bridge by the said wardens of St Magnus 2s. 6d.

Item in the said parish is one shop annexed to the said tavern, and it renders yearly to the Bridge by the said wardens 15s.

Item in the said parish are 2 tenements annexed to the said tavern, of which one was of John le Brewer and the other of Thomas Warle, and now of Richard Toky, and now of Robert Rose, and they render yearly to the Bridge 40s.

Item in the said parish is one tenement lately of John de Durem now of the Prior and Convent of St Mary Southwark, and it renders yearly to the Bridge 12d.

Item in the said parish is one shop in Bridge Street now of (John Rydere) <Richard Wynter> now of the rector and wardens of the said church, and it renders yearly to the Bridge 8s. 9d. <denied>

In the same parish is one shop annexed to the said shop sometime of William Stodey now of Robert Domynyk, and it renders yearly to the Bridge 8s. 9d. <denied>

146. St Botolph by Billingsgate. In the parish of St Botulph by Billingsgate is one tenement lately of Master Henry Grofhurst and now of Henry Chaumbr' and now of his wife, and it renders yearly to the Bridge 16s. <denied>

In the same parish is one tenement lately of John Wroth and now of Robert Wydyngton, now of John Beauwmond chandler, now of Simon Seman and Thomas Selowe, and it renders yearly to the Bridge 12d. <denied>

147. St Mary at H[lost].
[in margin, referring to all 3 entries:] <Not known [*ignoratur*]>
In the parish of St Mary at Hill is one tenement lately of Henry Pycard which is parcel of a tenement lately of Alexander Bedyk, and it renders yearly to the Bridge <now of John Wade called *le Lamb* on the wharf of Billingsgate> 11s. 8d.

In the said parish is one tenement of the prior of Holy Trinity [Aldgate] which is parcel of the said tenement <on *Trayerswharf*>, and it renders yearly to the Bridge 6s. 8d.

In the same parish is one tenement sometime of John Lovekyn which is parcel of the aforesaid tenement <on either side of the lane which goes to *Treyeresquarf*>, and it renders yearly to the Bridge 3s. 4d.

148. [f. 10v.] St Dunstan by the Tower. In the parish of St Dunstan by the Tower is one tenement sometime of Nigel de Hakeney called *Cokedonhalle*, now of John Wade <now of Henry Pountfret>, and it renders yearly to the Bridge 10s.

In the same parish is one tenement belonging to <the rector of> the said church <called the parsonage>, and it renders yearly to the Bridge 7s.

In the same parish is one tenement <lately> of William atte Vyne and now of John Hende, now of William Flete, on the corner of Mincing Lane at the sign of *le Cok*, and it renders yearly to the Bridge 3s. <denied>

In the same parish is one tenement belonging to the Guildhall of London <called *le Horshed*>, and it renders yearly to the Bridge 4s. 8d.

In the same parish is one tenement lately of Adam Canon and now of John Denver, now of John Tropynell, and it renders yearly to the Bridge 4s. 8d.

In the same parish is one tenement sometime of Roger atte Ponde and now of (John Vigerous) {Richard Lynne} <now of William Turnell> now of his wife married to John Pyryton, and it renders yearly to the Bridge 2s. 6d.

In the same parish is one tenement sometime of John de Bengeo and now of Walter Bewe, now of his wife married to Alan Brett, and it renders yearly to the Bridge 2s. 6d.

In the same parish is one tenement lately of Nicholas Hotot and now of John Guy by his wife, and it renders yearly to the Bridge 4s. 8d. <denied>

In the same parish is one tenement lately of Isabella Rothyng and now of John Barbour holding there of (Nicholas) <Richard> Stowell, and it renders yearly to the Bridge 2s. <denied>

149. *Berkyngchirche*. In the parish of All Saints Barking is one tenement lately of Richard Grymesby and now of Ralph Codyngton, and it renders yearly to the Bridge 3s.
[in margin:] <This rent in arrears from 1437–8 {to 1443–4}>

150. St Andrew in Eastcheap. In the parish of St Andrew in Eastcheap is one tenement <called *le Stonhous*> lately of John Coleyne and now of Margaret Bamme, and it renders yearly to the Bridge 12d.

151. St Margaret in Bridge Street. In the parish of St Margaret in Bridge Street is one tenement <in Crooked Lane> lately of John Chircheman and now of (James Billyngford) <John Wissingflete> <sometime of John Wegge>, and it renders yearly to the Bridge 3s.
[in margin:] <Charter thereof folio 14 under number 42>

152. St Leonard in Eastcheap. In the parish of St Leonard in Eastcheap is one tenement lately of John Odyern and now of Robert Edward <and now of Richard Grove>, and it renders yearly to the Bridge 26s. 8d.

In the same parish is one tenement lately of John [erasure and insertion, illegible] and now of the prior of Christchurch Canterbury <now of Thomas Sampson butcher>, and it renders yearly to the Bridge 12d. <denied>

In the same parish is one tenement belonging to the house of Bermondsey, and it renders yearly to the Bridge <tenant {Richard Edward}> <Richard Grover> 8s.

In the same parish is one tenement lately of William Doget, and it renders yearly to the Bridge <beside *le Cheker* {towards the north}> 2s. <Vacant>
[in margin:] <Not known >
[f. 11] In the same parish of St Leonard is one tenement sometime of John de Causton and now of the prioress of St Helen, <the same holds> and it renders yearly to the Bridge 13s. 4d.
In the same parish is one shop lately of John <Fraunceys> and now of Isabella Martyn, and it renders yearly to the Bridge 12d. <Vacant>

153. St Benet Gracechurch. In the parish of St Benet Gracechurch is one brewhouse <at the sign of *le Joye*> now of John Curteys, and it renders yearly to the Bridge 9s. 4d.
In the same parish is one tenement lately of William Olyver and now of Thomas fitz Nichol <now of William Waldern called *le Katerynwhele*>, and it renders yearly to the Bridge 33s. 4d.

154. All Saints Gracechurch. In the parish of All Saints Gracechurch is one tenement with a forge lately of master Henry de Grofhurst and now of (Godfrey Coost) <George Benett>, and it renders yearly to the Bridge 40s.
In the same parish is one brewhouse [*tenementum bracineum*] lately of John le Warnere and now of John Buke tailor, and it renders yearly to the Bridge 5s.

155. St Katherine Cree [*de Crychirche*]. In the parish of St Katherine Cree is one house in the corner of Billiter Lane now of (Robert Drayton) <Thomas D Brayton [*sic*]> now of Robert Percy, and it renders yearly to the Bridge 8d.

156. St Mary Axe [*atte Nax*]. In the parish of St Mary Axe are 10 shops with solars built over, lately of John de Trumpeton and now of Thomas Davy draper and now of Walter Gawtron draper, and they render yearly to the Bridge 12d.

157. St Martin Outwich. In the parish of St Martin Outwich is one tenement lately of John de Totenham, and now belongs to the fraternity of the Tailors of London, and it renders yearly to the Bridge 3s.

158. St Michael Cornhill. In the parish of St Michael Cornhill is one tenement lately of Simon de Mordon and now belonging to the church of St Michael in Crooked Lane <sometime of Roger Piere>, and it renders yearly to the Bridge 8s. <Vacant>
[in margin:] <Not known >

159. St Edmund Lombard Street. In the parish of St Edmund Lombard Street is one tenement lately of William Dykeman <at the sign of the Skimmer [*le Scomour*]> and now it belongs to the college of Shottesbrook [*Sodesbrook*], and it renders yearly to the Bridge 5s.

160. St Clement by Candlewick Street. In the parish of St Clement by Candlewick Street is one tenement of the abbot and convent of Stratford, and it renders yearly to the Bridge 2s.

In the same parish is one tenement with 4 shops sometime of Nicholas le Neve and now of Avice Tonge <now of Theobald Allut'> <now of his wife>, and they render yearly to the Bridge 2s.

In the same parish are 3 shops with solars lately of Richard le Cotiller and now of James Snowe <now of Philip Bangor> <now of John Bokenham> <now of the son and heir of the said Philip Bangor apprentice with Stane, draper>, and they render yearly to the Bridge 4s.

[Evidence that a sum total has been cropped off the bottom of the page]

161. [f. 11v.] St Michael Crooked Lane. In the parish of St Michael Crooked Lane is one tenement lately of John Lovekyn and now [left blank], and it renders yearly to the Bridge 5s. <Vacant>

[in margin:] <Not known. Charter thereof on folio 21, number 85>

In the same parish is one bakehouse [*ten' pistrinen'*] sometime of Agnes Lucas and now of Richard Radewell <now of John Sadeler>, and it renders yearly to the Bridge 5s.

162. All Saints the Less. In the parish of All Saints the Less is one tenement lately of William le Sadler and now of (John Gravesende) <Hugh Bame> <[illegible] in the corner at Conyhope Lane>, and it renders yearly to the Bridge 4s.

In the same parish is one tenement sometime of William de Leyre and now of Adam Fraunceys, now of the Chamber of the Guildhall, and it renders yearly to the Bridge 10s.

In the same parish is one tenement of the master and college of St Laurence [Pountney], and it renders yearly to the Bridge 6s.

[in margin:] <In arrears from 1435–6>

163. St Laurence by Candlewick Street. In the parish of St Laurence by Candlewick Street is one tenement lately of Roger de Depham and now of the Chamber of the Guildhall, and it renders yearly to the Bridge 19s. 8d.

164. St Mary Abchurch. In the parish of St Mary Abchurch is one tenement lately of John de Horford and now of John Creek <now of John Wodecok>, and it renders yearly to the Bridge 10s. <denied>

165. St Swithin. In the parish of St Swithin is one tenement lately of John Dunmowe and now of William Frenyngham <now of the churchwardens of St Swithin>, and it renders yearly to the Bridge 2s. 6d.

In the same parish is one tenement annexed to the said tenement now of (John Pellyng) <the rector of the church of St Swithin>, and it renders yearly to the Bridge 2s.

166. St Mary Bothaw. In the parish of St Mary Bothaw is one tenement lately of Thomas de Salesbury and now of the relict of Hugh Fastolf <now in the hands of the mayor and aldermen>, and it renders yearly to the Bridge 12d. <denied>

167. St Stephen Walbrook. In the parish of St Stephen Walbrook are two shops under one building lately of John Pecok and now one (is of John Walcote and the other) of Thomas Somersete <and Walter Gawtron and Agnes Cornehull>, and they render yearly to the Bridge 2s. <denied 12d. by Gawtron>

168. St Mary Woolnoth. In the parish of St Mary Woolnoth is one tenement lately of Hamo Lumbard and now of Margaret Bamme, and it renders yearly to the Bridge 13s. 4d.
In the same parish is one tenement lately of John Fysshe and now [left blank], and it renders yearly to the Bridge 2s. <Vacant>
[in margin:] <Not known >

169. St Bartholomew the Little. In the parish of St Bartholomew the Little is one tenement lately of Robert Litle and now of the prior of Christchurch Canterbury, and it renders yearly to the Bridge 2s. 6d. <Vacant>

170. St Pancras. In the parish of St Pancras is one seld called *le Brodeselde* now of William Norton, and it renders yearly to the Bridge 6s. 8d.
[in margin:] <Charter thereof folio 16, number [illegible]> {Not known}
[Evidence that a sum total has been cropped off the bottom of the page]

171. [f. 12] St Michael Queenhithe. In the parish of St Michael Queenhithe is one tenement lately of John de Blythe and now of (Robert Parys) {now of Richard Merlawe} <John Parker>, and it renders yearly to the Bridge 2s. <denied>

172. St Martin Ludgate. In the parish of St Martin Ludgate is one tenement with a forge lately of Gilott de Stratton and now <of John Gravesende> <and now of Nicholas Whaddon>, and it renders yearly to the Bridge 9s.
[in margin:] <The stainer's shop outside Ludgate>

173. St Bride Fleet Street. In the parish of St Bride Fleet Street is one tenement with 2 shops belonging to the church of St Paul London, the tenant of which is (Richard Pery chaplain) <tenent' hals'>, and it renders yearly to the Bridge 8s.

174. St Alban Wood Street. In the parish of St Alban Wood Street is one brewhouse lately of William Goodrych and now [left blank], and it renders yearly to the Bridge 4s. <Vacant>

[in margin:] <Not known >
In the same parish is one tenement sometime of John de Basyngstoke and now [left blank], and it renders yearly to the Bridge 2s. <Vacant>
[in margin:] <Not known >

175. St Mary Aldermanbury. In the parish of St Mary Aldermanbury is one tenement lately of William de Berkyng and now of Robert Rous, and it renders yearly to the Bridge 2s. <denied>

176. St Michael Bassishaw. In the parish of St Michael Bassishaw is one tenement lately of John de London and now [left blank], and it renders yearly to the Bridge 2s. <Vacant>
[in margin:] <Not known >
In the same parish is one tenement lately of Richard de Stotteford and now of William Norton, and it renders yearly to the Bridge 6s. 6d.

177. St Olave on the Wall [*ad murum*]. In the parish of St Olave on the Wall is one tenement of the hospital of St Mary without Bishopsgate <between *Mugwellstret* to the east>, and it renders yearly to the Bridge 3s. 6d. <Vacant>
[in margin:] <Not known >

178. St Stephen Coleman Street. In the parish of St Stephen Coleman Street is one tenement lately of Simon Dolseby <of the gift of Henry Gloucestr' to the Bridge> and now <of Margaret Fastolf>, and it renders yearly to the Bridge 2s. <Vacant>
[in margin:] <Not known >

179. Red Cross Street [*Reedcrouchestrete*]. In Red Cross Street is one tenement sometime of Richard Fitz Michel and now [left blank], and it renders yearly to the Bridge 4d. <Vacant>
[in margin:] <Not known >

180. East Smithfield. In East Smithfield is one tenement sometime of William de Basyng which is now the common cemetery,[1] and it renders yearly to the Bridge 4d.
[in margin:] <Vacant>

1. The new cemetery opened at the time of the Black Death.

181. Bletchingley [*Blecchyngle.*] In (*Blecchyngle*) <Horton> is one tenement lately of William de Blecchyngle <and now of John King>, and it renders yearly 12d.

182. Stratford. Item at Stratford is one piece of meadow lately of John Briggewright <and now>, and it renders yearly to the Bridge 2s. <Vacant>
[in margin, for this and next entry:] <Not known>

183. Sawbridgeworth. Item at Sawbridgeworth <in Essex> is one tenement lately of Adam de Sabrichesworth <and now>, and it renders yearly to the Bridge 3d. <Vacant>

184. Paternoster Row. In Paternoster Row are tenements under the palace of the bishop of London, and they render yearly to the Bridge 40s. Whereof the bishop pays 20s., the prior of Charterhouse 10s., and John Lesse 10s., total 40s.

185. St Olave in Southwark. In the parish of St Olave in Southwark is one tenement of the hospital of St Thomas of Southwark, and it renders yearly to the Bridge 8s. <denied>
In the same parish is one tenement lately of William Fott and now belonging to the chantry of St Michael Paternoster [*Paternosterchirche*], wardens of the same church, and it renders yearly to the Bridge 13s. 4d.

186. St Margaret Southwark. In the parish of St Margaret Southwark is one tenement of the hospital of St Thomas, and it renders yearly to the Bridge 4s. <denied>

187. St George Southwark. In the parish of St George Southwark is one tenement with a garden out of the tenure of the prior and convent of St Mary in Southwark, and it renders yearly to the Bridge 13s. 4d.
In the same parish is one tenement called *le Mote*, lately of Ralph Double and now of William Neel <now of his son>, and it renders yearly to the Bridge 8s. <denied>
In the same parish is one tenement sometime of Walter de Bukstede and now [left blank], and it renders yearly to the Bridge 2s. <Vacant>
[in margin:] <A Not known >

<Total appears 48s. 8d.>
<Total £31 12s. 6d.> [written in arabic figures]

BRIDGE HOUSE RENTAL 1

Account for 1420–1

188. [f.86] William Weston and Richard Stile, Wardens, in the 8th year of Henry V.

Receipts from fishmongers and butchers standing at the Stocks [*apud lestokkes*] weekly, And from proper rents, passage-tolls on carts crossing the Bridge and ships passing under it, with fines [*gersumis*], legacies, sales, alms and other things, from Michaelmas 1420 [8 Henry V] to Michaelmas 1421, for one year, by William Weston and Richard Stile, Wardens of London Bridge.

189. 5 October [1420].

From the fishmongers at the Stocks by Aunger, for the week, 7s. 1d.

From the butchers standing there weekly, 16s. 8d.

Of proper rent by W. Aunger this week £3.

Passage-tolls. From carts crossing the Bridge, 3s.

Lewisham. Item received from Thomas Trotte for the farm of the manor of Lewisham for one year last at Michaelmas last, 33s. 4d.

Item received from him for quit-rent belonging to the said manor, for the same year, 7s. 10d.

Item received from one Lambekyn for the farm of the mill demised to him, viz. for the whole year, £3.

[Total] £9.

190. 12 October.

From the fishmongers at the Stocks, 7s. 1d.

From the butchers there weekly, 16s. 8d.

Of proper rent by the hands of W. Aunger £3 13s. 4d.

Passage-tolls. From carts crossing the Bridge, 2s. 8d.

Sales. From the sale of 3,000 bricks [*Brik'*] and 1½ hundred tiles [*fyneux*] by J. Silkeston, 27s. 8d.

Stratford. From Laurence Fuller and his associate for the farm of the fulling mill of Stratford, in full payment up to and at the feast of Easter last, £6 13s. 4d.

St Thomas Watering. Item received from Katherine late the wife of Robert Staundon, for the farm of the field/s of Peckham, to and up to Michaelmas 1419, 20s.

[Total] £13 9d.

191. 19 October.

From the fishmongers at the Stocks, 7s.

From the butchers there, 16s. 8d.

Of proper rent by the hands of W. Aunger, £6 6s. 8d.

Sales. From the sale of 6,000 bricks and 1 quartern of house-tiles [*houstyll*], 35s. 3d.

Foreign rent, Stratford. From Roger Yonge, miller, in part payment of the farm of his watermill at Stratford, £3 6s. 8d.

[Total] £12 12s. 3d.

Whereof from the Stocks, £3 11s. 2d.

Item of proper [rent], £29 14d.

Item from passage-tolls, 5s. 8d.

Item from sales, £3 2s. 11d.

From foreign rent, £16 14d.

[Total] £36 11d.

192. [f. 86v] 26 October.

From the fishmongers at the Stocks, 7s. 2d.

From the butchers there, 17s. 1d.

Of proper rent by W. Aunger, £4.

Passage-tolls. From carts crossing the Bridge, 5s.

Sales. From the sale of one elm at Lewisham, 15s.

From the sale of 4,000 bricks by Silkeston, 22s. 8d.

[Total] £7 6s. 11d.

193. [2] November.

From the fishmongers at the Stocks, 8s. 9d.

From the butchers there, 17s. 3d.

Of proper rent by W. Aunger, £4 13s. 4d.

[Total] £5 19s. 4d.

194. [9] November.

From the fishmongers at the Stocks, 7s. 7d.

From the butchers there, 17s. 3d.

Of proper rent by W. Aunger, £10 6s. 8d.

Passage-tolls. From carts crossing the Bridge, 3s. 4d.

Sales. From the sale of 5,000 bricks by J. Silkeston, 28s. 4d.

Item received of Ralph Stoke by the hands of W. Aunger in part payment of a greater sum, by bond thereof, 40s.

[Total] £15 3s. 2d.

195. 16 November.

From the fishmongers at the Stocks, 7s. 3d.

From the butchers there, 17s. 3d.

Of proper rent by W. Aunger, £10

Passage-tolls. From passage-tolls, nil.

[Total] £11 3s. 2d.

196. 23 November.

From the fishmongers at the Stocks, 7s. 5d.

From the butchers there, 17s. 7d.
Of proper rent by W. Aunger, £9 13s. 4d.
Passage-tolls. From carts crossing the Bridge, 4s. 4d.
[Total] £11 2s. 8d.

197. 30 November.
From the fishmongers at the Stocks, 7s. 6d.
From the butchers there, 17s. 7d.
Of proper rent by W. Aunger, £6 13s. 4d.
Sales. From the sale of 7,000 bricks by J.Silkeston 39s. 6d.
Foreign rent. From John Dykes, chaplain, for the farm of his tenement and garden, lately of John Clifford, at Bermondsey, for half of last year, 10s.
[Total] £10 7s. 11d.

198. 7 December.
From the fishmongers at the Stocks, 4s. 1d.
From the butchers there, 17s. 7d.
Of proper rent by W. Aunger, £7 13s. 4d.
Passage-tolls. From carts crossing the Bridge, 2s. 6d.
Sales. From the sale of 4,700 bricks and 1,000 house-tiles sold, 31s. 4d.
[Total] £10 8s. 10d.

Whereof from the Stocks £8 11s. 4d.
Item of proper [rent], £50 10s.
Item from passage-tolls, 15s. 2d.
Item from sales, £6 16s. 10d.
From foreign [rent], 50s.
Total £71 13s. 4d.

199. [f. 87] Receipts 14 December.
From the fishmongers at the Stocks, 8s. 11d.
From the butchers there, 17s. 7d.
Of proper rent by W. Aunger, £6.
Passage-tolls. From ships, 16d.
Alms. Of alms to the use of the Bridge, 6d.
Sales. From the sale of half a thousand bricks, 2s. 10d.
Lambeth. From Thomas Bys, in full payment of his farm of 19 acres at Lambeth, up to last Michaelmas, 26s. 8d.
[Total] £8 17s. 10d.

200. 21 December
From the fishmongers at the Stocks, 9s. 2d.
From the butchers there, 17s. 7d.
Of proper rent by W. Aunger, £17 13s. 4d.
Passage-tolls. From carts crossing the Bridge, 3s. 8d.
From ships, 2s.

Sales. From the sale of 8,000 bricks [*Briktill*] and 6,000 house-tiles, £3 10s.

Teenacre. Item received from Richard Spore for his farm for *le Tenacre*, viz. in full payment up to last Michaelmas, 33s. 4d.

Sales. Item received from the sale of old timber at the Bridge House, 2s.

[Total] £23 [lost]

201. 28 December.
From the fishmongers at the Stocks, 8s. 8d.
From the butchers there, 17s. 7d.
Of proper rent by W. Aunger, 26s. 8d.
The Lock. Item received from Richard Langford, butcher, for his farm at the Lock, viz. in full payment at and up to last Michaelmas, 50s.
[Total] £5 2s. 10d.

202. 4 January [1421]
From the fishmongers at the Stocks, 8s. 6d.
From the butchers there, 17s. 7d.
Of proper rent by W. Aunger, £5.
Passage-tolls. From carts, 2s.
From ships, 3s. 8d.
[Total] £6 11s. 9d.

203. 11 January.
From the fishmongers at the Stocks, 8s. 6d.
From the butchers there, 17s. 7d.
Of proper rent by W. Aunger, £6.
Passage-tolls. From carts, 2s. 2d.
Sales. From the sale of 3,000 bricks [*Briketill'*], 17s.
[Total] £8 5s. 3d.

204. 18 January.
From the fishmongers at the Stocks, 8s. 4d.
From the butchers there, 17s. 7d.
Of proper rent by W. Aunger, £4 13s. 4d.
[Total] £5 19s. 3d.

Whereof the Stocks, £7 17s. 7d.
Item of proper [rent], £46 3s. 4d.
Item from passage-tolls, 14s. 10d.
Item from sales, £4 11s. 10d.
Item from alms, 6d.
From foreign [rent], £5 10s.
[Total] £69 8s. 1d.

205. [f. 87v] 25 January.
From the fishmongers at the Stocks, 8s. 3d.
From the butchers there, 17s. 7d.

Of proper rent by W. Aunger, £6.
Passage-tolls. From carts crossing the Bridge, 2s. 8d.
From ships passing under the Bridge, nil.
Sales. From the sale of 2½ thousand bricks, 13s.
[Total] £8 18d.

206. [1] February
From the fishmongers at the Stocks, 8s. 4d.
From the butchers there, 17s. 7d.
Of proper rent by W. Aunger, £10.
Passage-tolls. From carts crossing the Bridge, 2s. 4d.
From ships passing under the Bridge, 5s.
Total £11 13s. 3d.

207. 8 February
From the fishmongers at the Stocks, 14s.
From the butchers there, 17s. 3d.
Of proper rent by W. Aunger, £12
[Total] £13 10s. 3d.

208. 15 February.
From the fishmongers at the Stocks, 12s. 1d.
Of proper rent by W. Aunger, £12.
[Total] £12 12s. 1d.

209. 22 February.
From the fishmongers at the Stocks, 11s. 6d.
Of proper rent by W. Aunger, £7.
[Total] £7 11s. 6d.

210. 1 March
From the fishmongers at the Stocks, 12s. 8d.
Of proper rent by W. Aunger, £9.
Bermondsey, foreign rent. From William Langeley for his farm of one messuage, lately of J. Clifford, at Bermondsey, for the terms of Michaelmas and Christmas last, 4s.
[Total] £9 16s. 8d.

211. 8 March.
From the fishmongers at the Stocks, 12s. 4d.
Of proper rent by W. Aunger, £6 6s. 8d.
Sales. From the sale of 7½ thousand bricks [*Briktill*], 1,000 house-tiles, 48s.
[In aid] of repairs. From Robert Bretoun, bowyer, in aid of the repair of his house on the bridge, 3s. 4d.
[Total] £9 10s. 4d.

212. 15 March.
From the fishmongers at the Stocks, 11s. 6d.

Of proper rent by W. Aunger, £4.
Passage-tolls. From carts, 2s. 10d.
Fine [*gersuma*]. From Richard Philip, grocer, for the fine of a house lately of J. Goldfynch, outside the stone gate on the eastern side of the Bridge, 33s. 4d.
[Total] £6 7s. 8d.

Whereof the Stocks £7 2s. 1d.
Item of proper [rent], £66 10s. 8d.
Item from passage-tolls, 12s. 10d.
Item from sales, 61s.
Item from fines, 33s. 4d.
Item in aid of repairs, 3s. 4d.
From foreign [rent], 4s.
[Total] £79 3s. 3d.

213. [f. 88] Received [or receipts], 22 March
From the fishmongers at the Stocks, 12s. 1d.
Of proper rent by W. Aunger, £13 6s. 8d.
Stratford, foreign [rent]. From Roger Yonge, miller, for the farm of the watermill at Stratford viz. in full payment thereof up to and at Michaelmas 1420 last, and the rest is secured by bond etc., £5.
[Total] £15 [lost]

214. 29 March.
From the fishmongers at the Stocks, 10s. 4d.
Of proper rent by W. Aunger, £4 13s. 4d.
Passage-tolls. From carts crossing the bridge, 3s.
[Total] £[lost]

215. 5 April.
From the fishmongers at the Stocks, 11s. 6d.
From the butchers there, 16s. 5d.
Of proper rent by W. Aunger, £7 [lost]
Sales. From the sale of 3,000 bricks [*Briktill*] and for house-tiles, 19[lost]
For the sale of grass and hay from the meadow which Robert Staundon lately held by St Thomas Watering, 21s. [lost]
Item from the sale of 100 laths and 2 planks, 2s.
[Total: lost]

216. 12 April.
From the fishmongers at the Stocks, 9s. 6d.
From the butchers there, 17s. 1d.
Of proper rent by W. Aunger, £5.
Passage-tolls. From carts crossing the Bridge, 3s. 4d.
[Total] £6 [lost]

217. 19 April.

From the fishmongers at the Stocks, 10s. 4d.
From the butchers there, 17s. 1d.
Of proper rent by William Aunger, £4.
Sales. From the sale of 11,000 house-tiles by Silkeston, £3 9s. 11d.
From the sale of laths this week, 14d.
Passage-tolls. From carts crossing the Bridge, 3s. 8d.
Fine. From Robert Crull, bowyer, and Agnes his wife, for the fine of one house lately of Nicholas Nefold on the western side of the Bridge, 26s. 8d.
[Total] £10 [lost]

218. 26 April.
From the fishmongers at the Stocks this week, 9s. 3d.
From the butchers there, 17s. 1d.
From William Aunger for proper rent, £4.
Sales. From the sale of 10,000 house-tiles at Lewisham by Richard Bateman, tilemaker, 40s.
Fine. From Richard Grene, cutler, and [blank] his wife, the fine of one house lately of William Moger on the eastern side of the Bridge, 20s.
Bequest. Item of the bequest of the lady de Wynkefeld for the support of the Bridge, 2s.
Passage-tolls. From carts crossing the Bridge, 3s. 4d.
Sales. From Robert Crull in part payment of 46s. 4½d. for 6,700 house-tiles and 1 thousand 3½ hundred bricks and 43 roof tiles [*rooftill*] sold, 26s. 8d.
[Total] £9 [lost]

Whereof the Stocks, £6 10s. 8d.
Item of proper [rent], £43.
Item from passage-tolls, 13s. 4d.
Item from sales, £9 1d.
Item from fines, 46s. 8d.
Item from legacies, 2s.
From foreign [rent], £5.
[Total] £61 12s. 9d.

219. [f. 88v] 3 May.
From the fishmongers at the Stocks, 10s. 2d.
From the butchers there by the week, 17s. 1d.
Of proper rent by William Aunger, 40s.
Sales. From Richard Bateman for house-tiles [*tegulis domorum*] sold at Lewisham, 26s. 8d.
From Laurence Fuller and his associate in part payment of the farm of their fulling-mill at Stratford, viz. for the terms of Midsummer and Michaelmas now last, £3 6s. 8d.
[Total] £8 5s. 2d.

220. 10 May.
From the fishmongers at the Stocks this week, 10s. 1d.

From the butchers there, 17s. 1d.
Of proper rent by William Aunger, £6 6s. 8d.
From the sale of 5,000 house-tiles by Silkeston, 27s. 6d.
From a certain chaplain for the farm of the house which John Noble lately held beside Bermondsey, sometime of John Clifford, for the terms of Christmas and Easter last, 3s. 8d.
[Total] £10 5s.

221. [17] May.
From the fishmongers at the Stocks, 10s. 6d.
From the butchers there, 17s. 1d.
Of proper rent by William Aunger, £10.
Passage-tolls. From carts crossing the Bridge, 2s. 8d.
[Total] £11 10s. 3d.

222. 24 May.
From the fishmongers at the Stocks, 10s. 4d.
From the butchers there, 17s. 3d.
Of proper rent by William Aunger, £12 6s. 8d.
[Total] £13 14s. 3d.

223. 31 May.
From the fishmongers at the Stocks, 9s. 11d.
From the butchers there, 17s. 3d.
Of proper rent by William Aunger, £10.
Passage-tolls. From carts crossing the Bridge, 20d.
[Total] £11 8s. 10d.

224. 7 June.
From the fishmongers at the Stocks, 10s. 6d.
From the butchers there, 15s. 6d.
Of proper rent by Aunger, £8.
Passage-tolls. From carts crossing the Bridge, 20d.
[Total] £9 7s. 8d.

225. 14 June.
From the fishmongers at the Stocks, 9s. 6d.
From the butchers there, 15s. 11d.
Of proper rent by W. Aunger, £8.
Passage-tolls. From carts crossing the Bridge, 2s. 4d.
From ships passing under the Bridge, 16d.
West Greenwich. Item received from the wife of John Romsey [*Ro'sey*] for quit-rent of the meadow late of John Cheseman at West Greenwich, for 1 year at Michaelmas last, 27s.
[Total] £10 16s. 1d.

Whereof from the Stocks, £9 8s. 2d.
Item from proper [rent], £62 10s. 8d.
Item from passage-tolls, 9s. 8d.

Item from sales, 54s. 2d.
From foreign [rent], £4 17s. 4d.
[Total] £75 2s. 8d.

226. [f. 89] Received [or receipts], 21 June.
From the fishmongers at the Stocks, 9s. 11d.
From the butchers there, 14s. 10d.
Of proper rent by William Aunger, £13.
Sales. From the sale of 6,000 house-tiles by Silkeston, 32s.
Stratford. From Laurence Fuller and his associate, for the farm of the
fulling-mill at Stratford, viz. for the terms of Christmas and Easter last,
£3 6s. 8d.
Passage-tolls. From carts crossing the Bridge, 6s. 8d.
From ships passing under the Bridge, 4s. 7d.
[Total: lost]

227. 28 June.
From the fishmongers at the Stocks, 9s. 9d.
From the butchers there, 14s. 10d.
Of proper rent by William Aunger, £7.
Passage-tolls. From carts crossing the Bridge, 3s. 8d.
[Total: lost]

228. 5 July.
From the fishmongers at the Stocks, 10s. 3d.
From the butchers there, 14s. 10d.
Of proper rent by W. Aunger, £5 6s. 8d.
Passage-tolls. From carts crossing the Bridge, 4s.
[Total: illegible]

229. 12 July.
From the fishmongers at the Stocks, 9s. 10d.
From the butchers there, 14s. 10d.
Of proper rent, £4.
Passage-tolls. From carts and ships passing across/through the Bridge,
5s.
Alms. From alms given in the Bridge chapel the eve and day of the
Translation of St Thomas the Martyr, 15s.
[Total] £6 [lost]

230. 19 July.
From the fishmongers at the Stocks, 8s. 6d.
From the butchers there, 14s. 10d.
Of proper rent by W. Aunger, £4.
Passage-tolls. From carts crossing the Bridge, 4s.
[Total] £5 7s. 4d.

231. 26 July.
From the fishmongers at the Stocks, 9s. 1d.

From the butchers there, 14s. 10d.
Of proper rent by W. Aunger, £4 10s.
Sales. From the sale of house-tiles [*tegul' pro dom'*], 5s. 5d.
Passage-tolls. From carts crossing the Bridge, 3s. 8d.
[Total] £6 3s.

232. 2 August.
From the fishmongers at the Stocks, 6s. 10d.
From the butchers there, 15s. 6d.
Of proper rent by William Aunger, £7 13s. 4d.
Passage-tolls. From carts crossing the Bridge, 5s. 4d.
Bermondsey, foreign [rent]. From William Langelee for the farm of 1
messuage lately of John Clifford beside Bermondsey, for the terms of
Easter and Midsummer last, 4s.
[Total] £9 5s. [lost]

Whereof from the Stocks, £8 8s. 8s.
Item of proper [rent], £49 8d.
Item from passage-tolls, 36s. 11d.
Item from sales, 37s. 5d.
Item from alms, 15s.
From foreign [rent], £3 10s. 8d.
[Total] £61 18s. 8d.

233. [f. 89v] [9] August.
From the fishmongers at the Stocks, 8s. 6d.
From the butchers there, 15s. 6d.
Of proper rent by W. Aunger, renter, £14.
[Passage-tolls]. From carts crossing the Bridge, 5s.
[Sales]. From the sale of 2 timber gates at Deptford with the puncheons
[*lespounchons*] for them, 13s. 4d.
[Total] £16 2s. 4d.

234. [16] August.
From the fishmongers at the Stocks, 8s. 5d.
From the butchers there etc., 15s. 6d.
Of proper rent by the hands of William Aunger, £9.
From tolls on carts crossing the Bridge, 4s. 8d.
[Sales]. From the sale of timber this week, 12d.
[Total] £10 9s. 7d.

235. [23] August.
From the fishmongers at the Stocks, 10s. 1d.
From the butchers there, 15s. 6d.
Of proper rent by William Aunger, £6 6s. 8d.
Passage-tolls. From carts and wains [*waynes*] crossing the Bridge, 7s. 4d.
[Total] £7 19s. 7d.

236. [30] August.

From the fishmongers at the Stocks, 9s. 8d.
From the butchers there, 15s. 6d.
Of proper rent by W. Aunger, £9.
Passage-tolls. From carts crossing the Bridge, 2s. 8d.
[Total] £10 7s. 10d.

237. 6 September.
From the fishmongers at the Stocks, 4s.
From the butchers there, 17s. 4d.
Of proper rent by William Aunger, £5 13s. 4d.
Sales. From the sale of one <great> broken ladder [*scale*], 3s. 4d.
From the sale of another ladder, 12d.
From the sale of 500 bricks by John Lane mercer, 3s.
Passage-tolls. From carts crossing the Bridge, 4s. 10d.
[Total] £7 6s. 10d.

238. 13 September.
From the fishmongers at the Stocks, 7s. 1d.
From the butchers there, 18s. 8d.
Of proper rent by William Aunger, £5 6s. 8d.
Bermondsey, foreign [rent]. From Sir John the chaplain for the farm of
one house lately of John Clifford beside Bermondsey, viz. for the term
of Midsummer last, 2s.
Passage-tolls. From carts crossing the Bridge, 5s. 4d.
[Total] £6 19s. 9d.

239. 20 September.
From the fishmongers at the Stocks, 8s. 1d.
From the butchers there, 17s. 4d.
Of proper rent by W. Aunger, £6.
Passage-tolls. From carts, 5s.
Sales. From the sale of 3½ thousand bricks [*Brik till*],21s.
Stratford. Item received from Roger Yonge and Roger Larayner in part
payment of the farm of their watermill at Stratford, viz. for the terms
of Christmas 1419, Easter and Midsummer 1420, £5.
[Total] £13 11s. 5d.

Whereof from the Stocks £8 11s. 2d.
Item from proper [rent] £60 8s. 8d., whereof foreign [rent] £5 2s.
Item from passage-tolls, 33s 10d.
Item from sales, 42s. 8d.
[Total] £72 17s. 4d.

240. [f. 90; heading 'In the 9th year of Henry V']
Michaelmas. Received [or receipts] 27 September.
From the fishmongers at the Stocks, 9s. 2d.
From the butchers there, 17s. 8d.
Of proper rent by William Aunger, £38.
Passage-tolls. From carts crossing the Bridge, 3s. 8d.

From the sale of 2,000 bricks. Item for corbels [*corbeles*], stone jambs, and 3 pieces of timber [lost]

Whereof from the Stocks, 26s. 10d.
From proper [rent], £38.
From passage-tolls, 3s. 8d.
From sales, 22s. 9d.
Total £40 13s. [lost]

241. Total receipts of the past year
Total received from the Stocks, £61 7s. 8d.
Item from proper rents, £450 5s. 2d., whereof foreign rents, £42 [lost]
Item from passage-tolls as above, £7 6s. 11d.
Item from sales, £34 9s. 8d.
Item from fines, £4.
Item from alms, 15s. 6d.
Item from legacies, 2s.
Item in aid of repairs, 3s. 4d.
[Total] £558 10s. 3d.

BRIDGE HOUSE
WEEKLY PAYMENTS BOOK

First Series, Volume 2
Account for 1420–1

242. [p. 443] In the 8th year of Henry V. W Weston and R. Stile
Wardens.

Payments of all wages of masons, carpenters, boatmen, carters, sawyers, paviours, tilers, daubers, labourers, and tidemen, and the salaries
of chaplains [and] clerks of the chapel and other expenses for the
same, together with purchases and the payment of quit-rents and other
expenses weekly as appears, from Michaelmas 1420 to Michaelmas
1421, for one whole year, by William Weston and Richard Stile,
Wardens of London Bridge.

243. Wages and other expenses.

Saturday 5 October, paid to Richard Beek, John Catelyn senior, John
Catelyn junior, and John Houswif, masons, hired for the whole week,
to each 3s. 9d., total 15s.

Item to William Warde, another mason hired for the whole week for
3s.

Item to William Clerk, John Neweman, John Sweteman, and John
Bassett, carpenters, hired for the whole week, to each by the week
3s. 9d., total 15s.

Item to John Brys, another carpenter, for the whole week, 3s. 6d.

Item to Walter Loy, shoutman [*shouteman*], for the week for his salary,
2s. 6d.

Item to William Sharp, carter, for the week for his salary, 22d.

Item to him for the horses' fodder for the whole week, 2s. 1d.

Item to John Silkeston for the stipend of the cook of the Bridge masons
and carpenters, for the week, 20d. And to him for the Bridge dogs' food
[*pro pasc' canu' Pontis*], for the week, 10d. And for ale spent at the
account for this week, 2d., total 2s. 8d.

Item to Robert Horwoode and Robert Ragenell, labourers, hired for
the whole week, 4s.

Item to 1 labourer for 5½ days for the masons, 2s. 4d.

Item to John Parys, carpenter, for 6 days, for the day 8d., total 4s.

Item for mending a lock and a key for the same, 4d.

Item to 2 men for cleaning the starlings [*lestathelynges*] for 2 tides, 6d.

Item to 2 labourers for 1 day for the carpenters, 10d.

Item to 2 sawyers for 4 days, 5s. 4d.

Item to 2 daubers with 3 servants for 6 days, 13s. 6d.

Item to 1 tiler with 1 servant for 2 days, 2s.

Item for mending the apparatus of the mill cogs [*armatur' de leskogg Molend'*] at Lewisham, 2s. 4d.
Total £4 9d.

Purchases.
Item paid for 1 pr. sculls [*sculles*] bought for the boat called 'Thomas', 2s. 4d.
Item paid for horn glue [*hornglewe*] and 18 brooms bought for the carpenters, 8d.
Total 3s.

Quit-rents.
Item paid to the lord of the manor of Lewisham for rent from the same, for 1 year last, 13s. 8½d.
Item to Robert Story, knight, for quit-rent of the same, the same year, 3s.
Item paid to the heir of Thomas Squyr for quit-rent of the same manor, 23d.
Total 19s. 7½d.
Total [for the week] £5 3s. 4½d.

244. [p. 444] W. Weston and Richard Stile Wardens.
Wages and other expenses.
Saturday 12 October, paid to Richard Beek, John Catelyn senior, J. Catelyn junior, and John Houswif, masons, hired for the whole week, to each for the week as above, total 15s.
Item to William Warde, another mason, for the week as above, 3s.
Item to William Clerk, J. Neweman, J. Sweteman, and J. Bassett, carpenters, as above, 15s.
Item to John Bris, another carpenter, for the week, 3s. 6d.
Item to Walter Loy, shoutman, for the week as above, 2s. 6d.
Item to William Sharp, carter, as above, 22d.
Item to him for the horses' fodder for the week as above, 2s. 1d.
Item to John Silkeston for the cook's stipend, the dogs' food, and for ale in form and fashion as above, total 2s. 8d.
Item to William Ragenell and William Horwoode [sic], labourers, for the whole week, 4s.
Item to 1 labourer for the masons for 6 days, 2s. 6d.
Item to another labourer for 2½ days for the same, 13d.
Item to one labourer hired for 5 days to repair the garden at the Bridge House, 2s. 8d.
Item to William Clerk, carpenter, for a horse and expenses [going] to Croydon for the Bridge, 8d.
Item to John Parys, another carpenter, hired for the whole week, 4s.
Item paid for ale given to the carpenter/s by the Wardens, 3d.
Item to the said sawyers for 4 days, by the day as above, 5s. 4d.
Item to John Loveliche, tiler, with a servant for 7 days, 7s.
Item to Thomas Bys, dauber, with 2 servants for 6 days, 8s. 6d.
Item to another dauber for 5 days, 2s. 11d.
Item to a servant for the same dauber for 4 days, 20d.

Item to a very small servant [*parvulus famulus*] of the same daubers for 6 days, 18d.
Item to Richard Bateman, tilemaker, for making 10,000 house-tiles [*tegul' dom'*] at Lewisham, 21s. 8d.
Item to 1 labourer for half a day for the masons, 2½d.
Total £5 9s 2½d.

Purchases.
Item paid for brooms and candles bought for the masons as above, 5d.
Item paid for 1 pr. of great garnets with 100 nails bought, 3s. 6d.
Item paid for 2 collars of leather, 2 back-ropes [*bakroppes*], 3 belly-ropes [*womberoppes*], and 4 pipe-ropes [*pyperop'*] bought, 6s. 8d.
Item paid for parchment bought for the account roll, indentures, bills and other things used for this whole year last to the use of the Bridge, 4s.
Total 14s. 7d.
Total for the week £6 3s. 6½d.

245. [p. 445] W. Weston and Richard Stile Wardens.
Wages and other expenses.
Saturday 19 October, paid to R. Beek, J. Catelyn senior, J. Catelyn junior, and John Houswif, masons, as above, total 15s.
Item to William Warde, another mason, for the whole week, 3s.
Item to William Clerk, J. Neweman, J. Sweteman, and J. Bassett, carpenters, as above, 15s.
Item to John Brys, another carpenter, as above, 3s. 6d.
Item to Walter Loy, shoutman, for the week as above, 2s. 6d.
Item to William Sharp, carter, as above, 22d.
Item to him for the horses' fodder for the week, 2s. 1d.
Item to John Silkeston for the cook's stipend, the dogs' food, and for ale, as above, total 2s. 8d.
Item to William Ragenell and Robert Horwoode, labourers, for the whole week, 4s.
Item to 1 labourer for 5 days, by the day 5d., total 2s. 1d.
Item to the said sawyers for 5 days, by the day as above, 6s. 8d.
Item to 1 labourer for the carpenters, for 6 days, 2s. 6d.
Item to 1 man for 1 tide for the carpenters, 3d.
Item to Thomas Bys, dauber, with 1 servant for 5 days, 5s.
Item to another dauber with 1 servant for 2 days, 2s.
Item to 1 boy [*puero*] hired for them for 5 days, 3d.
Item to William Covyngton, tiler, with 1 servant for 5 days, 5s.
Total £3 14s. 4d.

Purchases.
Item paid for 2 tubs bought for the masons, 7½d.
Total 7½d.
Total for the week £3 14s. 11½d.

246. [p. 446] W. Weston and R. Stille, Wardens.
Wages and other expenses.

Saturday 26 October, paid to R. Beek, J. Catelyn senior, John Catelyn junior, and J. Houswif, masons, to each as above, 15s.

Item to William Warde, another mason, for the week, 3s.

Item to William Clerk, J. Sweteman, J. Neweman, and J. Bassett, carpenters, as above, 15s.

Item to John Brys, another carpenter, for the whole week as above, 3s. 6d.

Item to Walter Loy, shoutman, for the week as above, 2s. 6d.

Item to William Sharp, carter, for the whole week as above, 22d.

Item to him for the horses' fodder for the week as above, 2s. 1d.

Item to John Silkeston for the cook's stipend, the dogs' food, with ale and other, as above, total 2s. 8d.

Item to the said 2 labourers working continuously [*continue exist'*], for the week, 4s.

Item to the said sawyers for 4 days, by the day between them as above, 5s. 4d.

Item to 1 labourer for 6 days for the masons, 2s. 6d.

Item to another labourer at the Lock for 5½ days digging loam, 2s. 3½d.

Item to 1 labourer for 3 tides, 3d.

Item paid for fitting 1 axle-tree [*Exiltre*] in the Bridge cart, 6d.

Item for making and mending a chain [*cathene*] for the boat and 2 shavehooks [*shafhokes*], 6d.

Item in ale given to the carpenters for their diligence for work, 3d.

Item to 1 labourer for the masons for half a day, 4d.

Item paid for carriage of 17 loads of timber bought from William Shawe of Croydon, 28s. 4d.

Item paid for loading up the said 17 loads, viz. for each load 2d., total 2s. 10d.

Item paid to William Covyngton, tiler, with 1 servant for 3 days, 3s.

Item paid for divers wax candles, 2 torches, a Paschal and *holycandele* and other wax, spent for the last year in the Bridge chapel by account, total 26s. 4d.

Total £6 2s. 6½d.

Quit-rents.
Item paid to J. Stok, rent-collector of the archbishop of Canterbury for the manor of Lambeth, for quit-rent from the Bridge House of the said Bridge, viz. for one whole year to Michaelmas last etc., and for acquittance, 10s. 4d.

Total 10s. 4d.

Purchases.
Item paid to William Colston, plumber, for 1 fother of lead bought, containing 19½ hundred[weight], total £5 16s. 8d.

Total £5 16s. 8d.

Total for the week £12 9s. 6½d.

247. [p. 447] In the 8th year of Henry V.
Wages and other expenses.

Saturday 2 November, paid to R. Beek, J. Catelyn senior, J. Catelyn junior, and John Houswif, masons, for the whole week,15s.

Item to William Warde, another mason, for the week, 3s.

Item to 2 labourers hired for the whole week for the same masons, 4s.

Item to William Clerk, J. Sweteman, J. Neweman, and J. Bassett, carpenters, as above, 15s.

Item to John Brys, another carpenter, for the whole week, 3s. 6d.

Item to Walter Loy, shoutman, for the week, 2s. 6d.

Item to William Sharp, carter, for the whole week, 22d.

Item to him for the horses' fodder for the week, 2s. 1d.

Item to John Silkeston for the cook's stipend, the dogs' food, with ale, as above, 2s. 8d.

Item to 1 labourer for 2½ days for the masons, 12½d.

Item to Thomas Trotte for 4 days for carriage of fuel [*cariag' focal'*] from the manor of Lewisham to the tilehouse [*le Tilhous*] there, 4s.

Item to him for 1 day for carriage of sand [*zabul'*] for the same and there, 12d.

Item paid for expenses made for carrying and bringing of 2 loads of hay at the Bridge House, 7d.

Item paid for ale given to the masons this week, 2d.

Item for carriage of 1 load of timber from Croydon to the Bridge House, with loading, 22d.

Item to 1 man for 2 tides in the water, 6d.

Item in ale given to the carpenters, 2d.

Item to the said sawyers for 3 days, 4s.

Item to W. Covyngton, tiler, with a servant for 3 days, 3s.

Total £3 5s. 10½d.

Purchases.

Item paid for iron staples and bolts weighing 3 lb., 6d.

Item paid for 2 cartloads of hay at *Frankyngham*, 13s. 4d.

Item paid to William Shaue of *Lyngfeld* for 32 loads of timber for joists and rafters, at 5s. the load containing 60 ft., total £8.

Item paid to William Toche, smith, for 103 lb. worked iron bought for the Bridge, 14s. 4½d.

Total £9 8s. 2½d.

Total for the week £12 14s. 1d.

248. [p. 448] W. Weston and R. Stile Wardens.

Wages and other expenses.

Saturday 9 November, paid to Richard Beek, John Catelyn senior, J. Catelyn junior, and John Houswif, masons, as above, 15s.

Item to William Warde, another mason, for the week, 3s.

Item to William Clerk, John Sweteman, J. Neweman, and J. Bassett, carpenters, as above, 15s.

Item to John Brys, another carpenter, as above, 3s. 6d.

Item to Walter Loy, shoutman, by the week, 2s. 6d.

Item to William Sharp, carter, for the week, 22d.

Item to him for the horses' fodder for the week, 2s. 1d.

Item to John Silkeston for the cook's stipend, the dogs' food, with ale, as above, total 2s. 8d.

Item to 2 labourers working constantly for the masons, as above, 4s.

Item to 1 labourer for the masons for 6 days, 2s. 6d.

Item to 1 labourer for the carpenters for 6 days, 2s. 6d.

Item to 4 labourers for the same carpenters for carrying timber for half a day, 20d.

Item in ale given to the masons this week, 4d.

Item to 1 labourer for the Bridge House for 6 days at 6d. the day, total 2s. 6d.

Item for ale given to the carpenters as above, 4d.

Item paid for a certain part of the king's fifteenth for tiles at Lewisham, 8d.

Item to the said sawyers for 6 days, taking by the day between them 14d., 7s.

Item to 1 tiler with 1 servant for 3 days, 3s.

Item to 1 dauber with 1 servant for 6 days, 6s.

Item to 1 very small servant for 6 days at 3d. the day, total 18d.

Item to a servant for the same dauber for 4 days, 20d.

Item paid in expenses made for the carriage of hay this week, 6d.

Total £3 17s. 3d.

Tides.

Item paid to 11 men working at the small Ram for 3 tides, to each by the tide 3d., total 8s. 3d.

Total 8s. 3d.

Quit-rents.

Item paid to the abbot of Kirkstead in Lincolnshire for quit-rent from the Bridge's tenement/s in London, for 1 whole year, by acquittance, 4s.

Item to Richard Sele, rent-collector of Bermondsey, for quit-rent from the land/s and tenement/s of the Bridge at Lambeth, for Michaelmas term last, by acquittance, 9s. 3d.

Item paid to the earl of Arundel by the hands of William Midelton, from the Bridge House last year to Michaelmas, 16d.

Total 14s. 7d.

Purchases.

Item paid to John Esgaston for hinges, rings, latches, spike nails [*spiknaill*], transom-nails [*trannsumnail'*], cramps, catches and others bought, total 38s. 6d.

Item paid for 1 key bought for the vestry door in the chapel, 3d.

Item paid for 1 great cable [*cord'*] for 1 anchor, weighing 201 qr. 8 lb., price 22s. 6d.

Total £3 15d.

Total for the week £8 14d.

249. [p. 449] In the 8th year of Henry V.

Wages and other expenses.

Saturday 16 November, paid to R. Beek, J. Catelyn senior, J. Catelyn junior, and J. Houswif, masons, as above, 15s.

Item to William Warde, another mason, hired for the week as above, 3s.

Item to William Clerk, J. Sweteman, J. Neweman, and J. Bassett, carpenters, for the week, 15s.

Item to John Brys, another carpenter, for the week, 3s. 6d.

Item to Walter Loy, shoutman, for the week as above, 2s. 6d.

Item to William Sharp, carter, for his stipend for the week, 22d.

Item to him for the horses' fodder for the week, 2s. 1d.

Item to John Silkeston for the cook's stipend, the dogs' food, with ale, as above, 2s. 8d.

Item to Robert Ragenell and Robert Horwode, labourers, by the week as above, 4s.

Item to the said sawyers for 6 days, taking as by the 10th week above, total 7s.

Item to 1 tiler with 1 servant for 4 days, 4s.

Item to 2 labourers for 2 days for the carpenters, 20d.

Item to another labourer for the same for 6 days, at 5d. the day, total 2s. 6d.

Total £3 4s. 9d.

Tides.
Item paid to the said 11 tidemen at the small Ram, to each of them as above, total 5s. 6d.
Total 5s. 6d.

Purchases.
Item paid for 1 boat[load] of chalk bought for R. Beek, 12s.
Item for 4 staples bought for the carpenters, 4d.
Item paid for 41 ells of linen cloth bought for surplices, at 8½d. the ell, 29s.
Total 40s. 4d.

Quit-rents.
Item paid to John de Bernardescastell, rent-collector of St James' Hospital, for quit-rent from the tenement of the Bridge in the parish of St Mary Magdalen in the Fishmarket, London, for 1 year to Michaelmas last, 7s. 4d.
Total 7s. 4d.
Total for the week £5 18s. 11d.

250. [p. 450] W. Weston and R. Stile Wardens.
Wages and other expenses.
Saturday 23 November, paid to R. Beek, J. Catelyn senior, J. Catelyn junior, and John Houswif, masons [*masons*], as above, 15s.

Item to William Warde, another mason [*cementar'*], for the whole week, 3s.

Item to William Clerk, John Neweman, J. Sweteman, and J. Bassett, carpenters, 15s.

Item to J. Brys, another carpenter, as above, 3s. 6d.

Item to Walter Loy, shoutman, for the week, 2s. 6d.
Item to William Sharp, carter, for the week, 22d.
Item to him for the horses' fodder for the week, 2s. 1d.
Item to John Silkeston for the cook's stipend, the dogs' food, with ale, as above, total 2s. 8d.
Item to the said 2 labourers for the masons, for the whole week as above, 4s.
Item to the said sawyers for 6 days as above, 7s.
Item to 1 labourer for the masons for half a day, 2d.
Item to 1 labourer for 6 days for the carpenters, 2s. 6d.
Item to Richard Bateman, tilemaker, for 3 weeks for digging loam to make tiles, 6s.
Farm of Deptford. Item paid to Katherine lately the wife of Richard Furthere of Deptford for the farm of half an acre of land there beside the tilekiln [*le Tilkylne*] for last year to Michaelmas last, 2s.
Item for carriage by the said Richard Bateman of fuel to the tilekiln at Lewisham, 12d.
Item to the said tiler with 1 servant for 6 days, 6s.
Total £3 14s. 3d.

Purchases.
Item for 7½ hundred[weight] and 48 lb. of rope and cords of divers kinds bought for the Bridge, at 1¼d. the lb., and more 2s. 3d., total £4 12s. 11d.
Total £4 12s. 11d.

Quit-rents.
Item paid to Ralph Aes and John Michell, wardens of St Mary le Bow, London, for quit-rents from the tenement/s in Honey Lane for Michaelmas term last, 16s. 8d.
Item to the Chamberlain of the Guildhall by the hands of J. Stephenes for enclosures [*closes*] beside the Shambles of London for last year, 12s.
Total 28s. 8d.
Total for the week £9 15s. 10d.

251. [p. 451] In the 8th year of Henry V.
Wages and other expenses.
Saturday 30 November, paid to [Richard Beek] J. Catelyn senior, J. Catelyn junior, and John Houswif, masons, as above, 15s.
Item to William Warde, another mason, for the week as above, 3s.
Item to W. Clerk, J. Neweman, J. Sweteman, and J. Bassett,carpenters, as above, total 15s.
Item to John Brys, another carpenter, for the week, 3s. 6d.
Item to Walter Loy, shoutman, for the week, 2s. 6d.
Item to William Sharp, carter, for the week, 22d.
Item to him for the horses' fodder for the week, 2s. 1d.
Item to John Silkeston for the cook's stipend, the dogs' food, with ale, as above, total 2s. 8d.
Item to the said 2 labourers working constantly by the week, 4s.

Item to 2 sawyers for 4 days, by the day between them 14d., 4s. 8d.
Item to 1 labourer for the carpenters for 5 days, 2s. 1d.
Item for making 1 water-adze [*wateradese*], 12d.
Item for steeling 1 water-auger [*waterawger*] and others for the carpenters, 6d.
Item for mending 1 lock by W. Aunger, 3d.
Item for divers expenses had and made by the Wardens about the seneschal and other officers of the lord earl of Salisbury at Deptford for the land/s and tenement/s lately of Robert Joynour and Thomas Cheseman there belonging to the Bridge, 3s. 6d.
Total £3 19d.

Quit-rents.
Item paid to Walter Bradmer, purser, for a certain annual rent of 16s., payable at the term of the life of Robert Bakere, joiner, and Joan his wife, viz. for the terms of Easter and Midsummer last by acquittance, 8s.
Item to John Cokermouth, renter of the house of St Thomas of Acre, London, for the rent of one embankment [*wall*] leading to the fulling-mill at Stratford, viz. for 1 year last by acquittance, 3s.
Item paid to the lord earl of Salisbury for quit-rent from certain land/s and tenement/s lately of Robert Baker and Joan his wife at Deptford, and of Thomas Cheseman and others there, in full payment up to the present, by W. Weston, 13s. 11d.
Total 24s. 11d.
Total for the week £4 6s. 6d.

252. [p. 452] W. Weston and R. Stile Wardens.
Wages and other expenses.
Saturday 7 December, paid to R. Beek, J. Catelyn senior, J. Catelyn junior, and John Houswif, masons, as above, 15s.
Item to William Warde, another mason, as above, 3s.
Item to W. Clerk, J. Neweman, J. Swetman, and John Bassett, carpenters, as above, 15s.
Item to John Brys, another carpenter, by the week, 3s. 6d.
Item to Walter Loy, shoutman, as above, 2s. 6d.
Item to William Sharp, carter, by the week, 22d.
Item to him for the horses' fodder, as above, 2s. 1d.
Item to John Silkeston for the cook's stipend, the dogs' food, with ale, as above, total 2s. 8d.
Item to Robert Ragenell and Robert Horwode, labourers for the masons, 4s.
Item to 2 sawyers for 5 days, taking as above, 5s. 10d.
Item to 1 labourer for the carpenters for 5 days, 2s. 1d.
Total 57s. 6d.

Purchases.
Item paid for 2 sculls bought for the boat, 2s. 2d.
Item paid to Robert Proffoot for 1 boat bought for the Bridge's business, £3.

Item paid to William Toche, smith, for 4 hundred[weight and] 4 lb. worked iron bought, price 14s. the hundred, total 56s. 6d.
Total £5 18s. 8d.
Total for the week £8 16s. 2d.

253. [p. 453] In the 8th year of Henry V
Wages and other expenses.
Saturday 13 December, paid to Richard Beek, J. Catelyn senior, J. Catelyn junior, and J. Houswif, masons, as above, 15s.
Item to William Warde, another mason, for the week, 3s.
Item to W. Clerk, J. Neweman, J. Swetman, and J. Bassett, carpenters, as above, 15s.
Item to John Brys, another carpenter, for the week, 3s. 6d.
Item to Walter Loy, shoutman, for the week, 2s. 6d.
Item to William Sharp, carter, for the week, 22d.
Item to him for the horses' fodder for the week, 2s. 1d.
Item to J. Silkeston for the cook's stipend, the dogs' food, with ale, as above, 2s. 8d.
Item to Robert Ragenell and Robert Horwode, labourers, for the whole week, 4s.
Item to the said sawyers for 6 days as before, 7s.
Item to 1 labourer for half a day for the masons, 2d.
Item to 1 labourer for the carpenters for 6 days, 2s. 6d.
Item to 1 labourer for J. Silkeston, hired for 3 days, 15d.
Item to J. Londones, painter, for painting 1 section [*pro pictura j Pane*] in the vault of the chapel on the Bridge, taking in all 13s. 4d.
Item paid to Thomas Bys, dauber, with 1 servant for 16½ days, 16s. 6d.
Item to 1 tiler with a servant for 6 days, 6s.
Item for the portage of books at the time of making the account for last year, 12d.
Item for making 1 chain [*chathen'*] for the Bridge boat from the Bridge's iron etc., 20d.
Total £4 18s.

Purchases.
Item paid to Richard Lymbrenner for 9 hundred[weight] of lime [*lym*] bought, at 6s. the hundred, total 54s.
Item paid for 2 iron bolts bought for the vault of the chapel, 9d.
Total 54s. 9d.
Total for the week £7 12s. 9d.

254. [p. 454] W. Weston R. Stile Wardens.
Wages and other expenses.
Saturday 21 December, paid to Richard Beek, J. Catelyn senior, J. Catelyn junior, and J. Houswif, masons, as above, 15s.
Item to William Warde, another mason, as before, 3s.
Item to William Clerk, John Neweman, J. Sweteman, and J. Bassett, carpenters, 15s.

74

Item to John Brys, another carpenter, for the week, 3s. 6d.
Item to Walter Loy, shoutman, 2s. 6d.
Item to William Sharp, carter, for the week, 22d.
Item to him for the horses' fodder for the week, 2s. 1d.
Item to John Silkeston for the cook's stipend, the dogs' food, with ale, as above, 2s. 8d.
Item to Robert Ragenell and Robert Horwode, labourers, as above, 4s.
Item to the said sawyers for 5 days, at 14d. the day, 5s. 10d.
Item to 1 labourer for the carpenters for 5 days, 2s. 1d.
Item paid to Richard Bateman, tilemaker, for digging loam at Lewisham for making tiles there, for 1 month last, 8s.
Item paid him for his diligence in selling tiles, 3s. 4d.
Item to Thomas Bys, dauber, with 1 servant for 2 days, 2s.
Item for ale given to the masons and carpenters, 4d.
Item to 1 tiler with 1 servant for 5 days, 5s.
Item to 1 labourer for 5 days for repairs to the Bridge's garden, 2s. 1d.
Item paid to Nicholas Holford for keeping the passage-tolls across and under the Bridge, for 12 weeks last quarter, at 15d. for the week, total 15s.
Item to John Hethingham, as well for writing the weekly papers as for attorning for recovering debts and for making bills and indentures, for the last quarter, 13s. 4d.
Item paid for hiring a boat for the Wardens for doing the Bridge's business and other costs, 3s.
Item repaid W. Sharp, carter, for his livery [*lib'at'*] and other reward [*regard'*] for the whole feast of Pentecost last, 6s. 8d.
Total £5 16s. 3d.

Purchases.
Item paid to J. Neweman, carpenter, for leather collar/s [*de cer'*] for the cart-horses, 20d.
Item to him for Hungary leather halters [*de hunger'*] bought, 4s. 3d.
Item paid for mending and consecrating the cloth for the cross [*celebratione manuterg' j cruce*] and other for the chapel, together with cloths, cruets and 1 surplice bought for the same, 4s. 1d.
Item paid to Thomas Kelsey, ironmonger, for 16 foreshoes [*ferr' anterior'*] at 2d. each and 21 iron hindshoes [*ferr' posterior'*] at 1½d. each, total 5s. 3½d.
Total 15s. 3½d.

[p. 455] In the 8th year of Henry V.
Chapel.
Item paid to John Bureford, Thomas Cudde, Robert Tewe and Robert Leyke, chaplains celebrating in the chapel for last quarter, £6 13s. 4d.
Item to them for the salary of their cook for the quarter, 5s.
Item to them for their *O sapiencia ut moris*, 12d.

Item paid to John SeyntJohn, one of the clerks of the chapel, for his salary for 12 weeks last term, for the week 18d., total 18s.

Item to him for bread and wine for celebrating for the same weeks, for the week 3d., total 3s.

Item to Nicholas Holford, the other clerk of the chapel, for the same weeks, for the week 15d., total 15s.

Total £8 15s. 4d.

Total for the week £15 6s. 10½d.

255. Wages and other expenses.

Saturday 28 December, paid to Richard Beek, J. Catelyn senior, J. Catelyn junior, and J. Houswif, masons, as above, 15s.

Item to William Warde, another mason, as before, 3s.

Item to William Clerk, John Neweman, J. Sweteman, and John Bassett, carpenters, 15s.

Item to John Brys, another carpenter, as above, 3s. 6d.

Item to Walter Loy, shoutman, as above, 2s. 6d.

Item to William Sharp, carter, as above, 22d.

Item to him for the horses' fodder for the week, 2s. 1d.

Item to John Silkeston for the cook's stipend, the dogs' food, with ale, as above, 2s. 8d.

Item to Robert Ragenell and Robert Horwode, labourers, for the whole week, 4s.

Item to the said sawyers for 1½ days, 21d.

Item to 1 labourer for the carpenters for 1½ days, 7½d.

Item paid for carriage of 1 load of timber from Croydon to the Bridge House, 18d.

Total for this week 53s. 5½d.

256. [p. 456] W. Weston R. Stile Wardens.

Wages and other expenses.

Saturday 4 January [1421], paid to Richard Beek, J. Catelyn junior, and J. Houswif, masons, as before, 11s. 3d.

Item to William Warde, another mason, for the week, 3s.

Item to William Clerk, J. Neweman, John Sweteman, and John Bassett, carpenters, 15s.

Item to John Brys, another carpenter, for the week, 3s. 6d.

Item to Walter Loy, shoutman, as above, 2s. 6d.

Item to William Sharp, carter, as before, 22d.

Item to him for the horses' fodder, 2s. 1d.

Item to John Silkeston for the cook's stipend, the dogs' food, with ale, as above, 2s. 8d.

Item to Robert Ragenell, labourer, for the whole week, 2s.

Item to the said sawyers for 5 days, 5s. 10d.

Item to 1 labourer for the Bridge's garden at the Bridge House, for 4 days, 20d.

Item for ale given to the masons and others, 2d.

Item to 1 tiler with a servant for 4 days, 4s.

Item to 1 paviour for 1 day in the house of John Hale, 8d.

Item paid for paving the hall of that house with paving tiles [*pavyntill*], 14d.

Total 57s. 4d.

Purchases.

Item paid for 2 stone of tallow [*Talgh'e*] bought with other costs for the same, 16d.

Item for 1 horsecomb [*horsecombe*] bought, 4d.

Item for 2 keys bought for the door of the Stocks at the bottom, 8d.

Total 2s. 4d.

Total for the week 59s. 8d.

257. [p. 457] In the 8th year of Henry V.

Wages and other expenses.

Saturday 11 January, paid to R. Beek, J. Catelyn junior, and J. Houswif, masons, 11s. 3d.

Item to William Warde, another mason, for the week, 3s.

Item to William Clerk, J. Neweman, J. Sweteman, and John Bassett, carpenters, 15s.

Item to John Brys, another carpenter, for the week, 3s. 6d.

Item to Walter Loy, shoutman, for the week, 2s. 6d.

Item to William Sharp, carter, for the week, 22d.

Item to him for the horses' fodder for the week, 2s. 1d.

Item to John Silkeston for the [cook's] stipend, the dogs' food, with ale, as above, 2s. 8d.

Item to Robert Ragenell, labourer for the masons, as above, 2s.

Item to John Catelyn, mason, for 3 days this week, $22\frac{1}{2}$d.

Item to 2 labourers for 1 tide, 6d.

Item to 1 labourer for the carpenters for 3 days, 15d.

Item to 1 labourer for $1\frac{1}{2}$ days for the stone gate, $7\frac{1}{2}$d.

Item for drinking and other expenses made about the works on the painting etc. [at] the stone gate, 22d.

Item to 1 labourer for $4\frac{1}{2}$ days, $22\frac{1}{2}$d.

Item to 2 sawyers for 5 days, as before, 5s. 10d.

Item to W. Goos, carver, for making the head of the Giant for the Bridge against the king's coming, 18d.

Total 59s. $1\frac{1}{2}$d.

Purchases.

Item paid for 100 Eastland boards [*Estrichbord'*] bought from Stephen Bary for the king's coming, 36s.

Item for 1,000 ft. of elm board bought, price 28s. 8d.

Item for 24 great alder poles bought for 10s.

Item paid for 2 plain tablecloths [*bord clothes plan'*] bought for the store of the priests' hall, price 2s.

Item for 1 lock and mending the key and other things, 8d.

Total £3 17s. 4d.

Quit-rents.

Item paid to Richard Marchall, rent-collector of W. Porter and Thomas Charleton, knight/s, for quit-rent of the Bridge's tenement/s in Honey lane, for Michaelmas term last, by acquittance etc., 20s.

Item to him for quit-rent from the tenement which Nicholas Cook lately held on the Bridge last year, to Michaelmas, 7s.

Total 27s.

Total for the week £8 3s. 5½d.

258. [p. 458] W. Weston R. Stile Wardens.

Wages and other expenses.

Saturday 18 January, paid to Richard Beek, J. Catelyn senior, J. Catelyn junior, and John Houswif, masons, as above, 15s.

Item to William Warde, another mason, for the week, 3s.

Item to William Clerk, J. Neweman, J. Sweteman, and John Bassett, carpenters, as above, 15s.

Item to John Brys, another carpenter, for the week, 3s. 6d.

Item to Walter Loy, shoutman, for the week, 2s. 6d.

Item to William Sharp, carter, for the week, 22d.

Item to him for the horses' fodder for the week, 2s. 1d.

Item to John Silkeston for the cook's stipend, the dogs' food, with ale, as above, 2s. 8d.

Item to Robert Ragenell, labourer, for the whole week, 4s.

Item to John Goodeman, plasterer, for 4½ days for the stone gate, 2s. 7½d.

Item to 1 labourer for the same plasterer for 4½ days, 22½d.

Item to the said sawyers for 6 days, as before, 7s.

Item to 1 labourer for 2 days for the carpenters, 10d.

Item to Richard Bateman, tilemaker, for making fuel and digging loam for making tiles [*pro factura focal & fossur de lom' pro tegul' faciend'*] at Lewisham for 5 weeks last, 10s.

Item to 1 labourer for 2 days for the carpenters, 7½d.

Item to 2 carpenters for the whole week for the coming etc., 7s. 6d.

Item to 1 carpenter for 1½ days for the same, 12d.

Item to 1 tiler with 1 servant for 1 day, 12d.

Item to 1 labourer for the Bridge's garden for 4½ days, 22½d.

Item repaid Walter Loy for his diligent labour on the Bridge's business, 16d.

Item to William Goos, carver, for divers things worked for the king's said ordinance, for the week, 4s. 6d.

Item paid to J. Thoresby and Richard Coyford, stainers, for 5 days for the said ordinance, 8s.

Item to J. Bron, another stainer, for 6 days for grinding colour/s for the said ordinance, 4s.

Total £4 19s. 9d.

Purchases.

Item for 16 alder poles bought for the ordinance against the king's coming, 4s. 10d.

Item paid for 24,000 tacks [*taknaill*], 6,000 other nails, and for glovers' shreds [*gloveresshredes*], bristles [*brusteles*], charcoal, calf-skins, packthread and other things for the king's said ordinance etc., 24s. 5d.

Item to William Toche, smith, by his wife, for 85 lb. worked iron bought, price 10s. 8d.

Total 39s. 11d.

Total for the week £6 19s. 8d.

259. [p. 459] In the 8th year of Henry V.

Wages and other expenses.

Saturday 25 January, paid to Richard Beek, John Catelyn senior, J. Catelyn junior, and John Houswif, masons, as above, 15s.

Item to William Warde, another mason, for the week, 3s.

Item to William Clerk, J. Neweman, John Sweteman, and John Bassett, carpenters, as above, 15s.

Item to John Brys, another carpenter, for the week, 3s. 6d.

Item to Walter Loy, shoutman, for the week, 2s. 6d.

Item to William Sharp, carter, for the week, 22d.

Item to him for the horses' fodder for the week, 2s. 1d.

Item to John Silkeston for the cook's stipend, the dogs' food, with ale, as above, 2s. 8d.

Item to Robert Ragenell, labourer for the whole week, 4s.

Item to John Goodeman, plasterer, with 1 servant, for 4½ days for the aforesaid ordinance, 4s. 6d.

Item to 1 joiner for 2½ days for the same ordinance, 20d.

Item to 5 carpenters for 5 days for the same ordinance, 21s. 3d.

Item to 1 carpenter for the same for 3 days, 2s. 1½d.

Item for ale given to the carpenters, stainers, painters, and other workmen for the same, 12d.

Item to John Parys and Thomas Gerland, carpenters, hired for the week, for the same, 7s. 6d.

Item to 1 labourer for the masons for 1½ days for the same, 7½d.

Item to 3 men, stainers, hired for 6 days for the said ordinance, to each for the day 9d., total 13s. 6d.

Item to another stainer for 6 days, at 10d. the day for the same, total 5s.

Item to 2 others for 6 days for the same, 8s.

Item to another for the same for 5 days, 3s. 9d.

Item to 2 other stainers for 3½ days, 5s. 3d.

Item to W. Goos, carver, for 6 days for the same, 4s. 6d.

Item to Laurence Joynour [? the joiner] for the same for 3 days, 2s. 3d.

Item to 3 other joiners for the same, for 1 day, 2s.

Item to the said sawyers for 6 days, 7s.

Item to 1 labourer for 1 day for the same, 4d.

Item to 2 servants of Robert Cony, joiner, for 1 day for the same, 2s. 2d.

Item to 1 dauber with 1 servant for 7 days, 7s.

Total £7 7s.

79

Purchases.

Item for 8 alder poles bought for the same ordinance, 3s. 4d.

Item for 5 other alder poles for the same, 20d.

Item for 1 lb. candles for the same ordinance, 1½d.

Item for cord bought for the same, 1d.

Total 5s. 2½d.

Total for the week £7 12s. 2½d.

260. [p. 460] W. Weston R. Stile Wardens.

Wages and other expenses.

Saturday 1 February, paid to Richard Beek, J. Catelyn senior, J. Catelyn junior, and J. Houswif, masons, 15s.

Item to William Warde, another mason, for the week, 3s.

Item to William Clerk, J. Neweman, J. Sweteman, John Bassett, J. Parys, and Thomas Gerland, carpenters, to each as above, total 22s. 6d.

Item to John Brys, another carpenter, for the whole week, 3s. 6d.

Item to Walter Loy, shoutman, for the week, 2s. 6d.

Item to William Sharp, carter, for the week, 22d.

Item to him for the horses' fodder for the week, 2s. 1d.

Item to John Silkeston for the cook's stipend, the dogs' food, with ale, as above, 2s. 8d.

Item to Robert Ragenell, labourer for the masons, for the whole week, 2s.

Item to the said sawyers for 6 days, 7s.

Item paid to 12 carpenters hired for the whole week for the coming of the king and queen, and to each of them 4s. 3d., total 51s.

Item to another carpenter hired for the whole week for the same, 4s. 6d.

Item in candles and ale for the same carpenters working by night for the same, 16d.

Item to 6 men, stainers, for the ordinance [for] the coming of the king and queen for 6 days, to each 9d. for the day, total 27s.

Item to 1 other stainer, viz J. Thoresby, for 6 days, for the day 10d., total 5s.

Item to 1 other painter for the same for 6 days, for the day 8d., total 4s.

Item paid to John Wytte, painter, for painting 5 banners of gilt and silver of divers kinds for the same coming, 34s. 4d.

Item to 1 other stainer for 2½ days [working] for Hasildon, 16d.

Item to 1 other servant for the same stainers, for 6 days, 2s.

Item to William Goos, carver, for 6 days for the same coming, 4s. 6d.

Item to Laurence Joynour [? the joiner], for the same, for 6 days, 4s. 6d.

Item to William Harlowe, 1 joiner, and Andrew Hunte, joiner, for 6 days, 12s.

Item to Thomas Norton, another joiner, for the same, for 4 days, 2s. 8d.

Item for staples, rings, and other necessaries for the donjon [*le dongeon*] for the same at 9s. 10d.

Item to J. Stone, joiner, for long planks [*tabul'*] with 5 scutcheons for painting against the said coming, 10s.

Item for linch-pins [*lynces*] bought for the cart etc., 2d.

Item in ale given to the said carpenters and workmen for the same ordinance, 8d.

Total £11 9s. 11d

Purchases.

Item paid to Stephen Barry for 50 Eastland boards [*Estrichbord*] bought for the said coming, 18s.

Item paid for 1000 ft. of board [*bord'*] bought for the same ordinance, price 27s. 6d.

Item for 100 other boards bought for the same, 3s.

Item for 4 planks [*tabul'*] for the same, 4s.

Total 52s. 6d.

Total for the week £14 2s. 5d.

261. [p. 461] In the 8th year of Henry V.

Wages and other expenses.

Saturday 8 February, paid to Richard Beek, J. Catelyn senior, J. Catelyn junior, and J. Houswif, masons, 15s.

Item to William Warde, another mason, for the week, 3s.

Item to William Clerk, J. Neweman, J. Sweteman, J. Bassett, John Parys, and Thomas Gerland, carpenters, to each as above, total 22s. 6d.

Item to John Brys, another carpenter, for the whole week, 3s. 6d.

Item to Walter Loy, shoutman, for the whole week, 2s. 6d.

Item to William Sharp, carter, for the week, 22d.

Item to him for the horses' fodder for the week, 2s. 1d.

Item to John Silkeston for the cook's stipend, the dogs' food, with ale, as above, 2s. 8d.

Item to Robert Ragenell, labourer, hired for the whole week, 2s.

Item to the said sawyers for 6 days, for the day between them 16d., total 8s.

Item paid for bread, wine, and ale spent about and for the mayor, sheriffs and other aldermen etc. viewing the ordinance [*in visu ordinac'*] for the coming of the king and queen over the Bridge, 5s. 3d.

Item paid to Richard Carleton and John Cook, paviours, for 11 days for paving the pavement against the Friars Minor of London, 14s. 8d.

Item paid to 6 men, stainers, for the ordinance of the king and queen, for 6 days, to each for the day 9d., total 22s. 6d.

Item to 1 other stainer for 7 days for the same, 5s. 3d.

Item to him for 2 leaves of double tin-foil bought, 6d.

Item to 1 other stainer for half a day, 4½d.

Item to J. Thoresby, painter, for the same, for 6 days, for the days 10d., total 5s.

Item to Richard Peyntour [? the painter], for the same for 6 days, for the days 8d., total 4s.

Item to 1 other stainer for 3 days for the same, for the day 9d., total 2s. 3d.

Item to 2 other stainers for the same for 4 days, to either for the day 8d., total 5s. 3d.

Itemto W. Goos, carver, for 6 days for the same ordinance, 4s. 6d.

Item to Laurence Joynour [? the joiner], for the same, for 6 days, for the day 9d., total 4s. 6d.

Item to 3 other joiners for 6 days, to each for the day 8d., total 12s.

Item to 1 other joiner for the same, for 5 days, for the day 8d., 3s. 4d.

Item to 2 labourers for 6 days for the same ordinance, 5s.

Item paid to 9 carpenters for the said ordinance for 6 days, to each for the day 8½d., total 38s. 7½d.

Item to 1 other carpenter for 2 days for the same, 17d.

Item to 2 other carpenters for 5 days, for the day 8½d., for the same, total 7s. 1d.

Item to 1 other carpenter for 6 days, for the day 9d., total 4s. 6d.

Item to 1 labourer for 3 days and 1 tide, 18d.

Item to 1 other labourer for 1 tide, 3d.

Item for candles and ale spent in drinking about the workmen for the coming, 23½d.

Item for fitting 1 pr. wheels for the Bridge cart, 6d.

Item paid to John Londones, in part payment for gilding the image in the stone gate for the king's coming, 10s.

Total for the week £12 10s 4½d.

262. [p. 462] W. Weston Richard Stile Wardens.

Wages and other expenses.

Saturday 15 February, paid to Richard Beek, J. Catelyn senior, J. Catelyn junior, and J. Houswif, masons, 15s.

Item to William Warde, another mason, for the week, 3s.

Item to William Clerk, J. Neweman, J. Sweteman, J. Bassett, J. Parys, and Thomas Gerland, carpenters, as above, 22s. 6d.

Item to John Brys, another carpenter, for the week, 3s. 6d.

Item to Walter Loy, shoutman, for the week, 2s. 6d.

Item to William Sharp, carter, for the week, 22d.

Item to him for the horses' fodder for the week, 2s. 1d.

Item to John Silkeston for the cook's stipend, as above, 2s. 8d.

Item to Robert Ragenell for the masons, for the week, 2s.

Item to the said sawyers for 6 days, 8s.

Item paid to 12 carpenters for the ordinance of the coming of the king and queen, for 4 days, to each for the day 8½d., total 36s.

Item to 1 other carpenter for the same for the whole week, 4s. 6d.

Item for 4 lb. candles for the carpenters working by night, 6d.

Item for cord and paper for the same, 12d.

Item for bread, ale, and other costs for the carpenters and workmen working by night this week for the same, 3s.

Item for 3 men for keeping the Giant in the king's coming, 8d.

Item to 1 labourer for 9 days last, for the same, [for the] day 6d., total 4s. 6d.

Item to 1 labourer for 4 days for the same ordinance, 21d.

Item paid to one Waltham, stainer, for 4 days and 3 nights for the same ordinance, 4s. 9d.

Item to Roger Aleyn, stainer, for the same, for 4 days and 2 nights, 4s. 2d.

Item to J. Freman, stainer, for 5 days and 5 nights for the same, for the day 9d., total 6s. 8d.

Item to Michael Steynour [? the stainer], for 7 days and 2 nights, 6s. 5d.

Item to a certain Robert Steynour Shersby and Adam Steynours for 4 days and 2 nights, 12s. 1½d.

Item to Edmund Steynour [? the stainer], for 2 days and 2 nights, total 3s. ½d.

Item to a certain Clare and Hasilden, stainers, for 4 days and 2 nights, 7s. 11½d.

Item to a certain J. Heed / Stiff / Bernard / Warewike / Asshefeld / and Simond, stainers, for 4 days and 2 nights, to each for the day 9d. and for the night, total 23s.

Item to one Jaket, stainer, for 3 days and 1 night, for the same, 2s. 7d.

<void because included elsewhere> (Item to one Chapeleyn and his servant for 3 days and 1 night, 6s. 10d.)

Item to 2 other servants of the said J. Clare for 4 days, 5s. 4d.

Item to J. Thoresby, painter, for 5 days 5 nights, for the day with the night, in all 7s. 1d.

Item to R. Peyntour [? the painter] for 5 days and 5 nights, for the day with the night 15d., total 6s. 3d.

Item to William Hewgynes, stainer, for making and clothing with stuff [*pro factura et vestur' cum stuff*] one lion, 3s. 4d.

Item to W. Goos, carver, for 4 days and 1 night, 3s. 7d.

Item to Laurence Joynour [? the joiner], [for] 3 days and 2 nights, 4s. 2d.

Item to John Coffrer [? the cofferer] for 4 days and 1 night, 4s. 2d.

Item to J. Norton for 4 days and 1 night, 3s. 3d.

Item to Andrew Hunte, joiner, for 4 days 2 nights, 3s. 10d.

Item to W. Herlawe for 4 days and 1 night, 3s. 3d.

Item repaid the said carpenters for their vigils working in the said business, 3s.

Item paid to all the said workmen and their servants for their Lenten [allowance, offering] as is accustomed, 3s. 4d.

Total £11 16s. 3½d.

[p. 463] In the 8th year of Henry V.
Of the said week.
Purchases.
Item paid for 754 elm boards bought for the said ordinance, price in all 5s. 2½d.

Item for leather [*ledyr*] bought for fitting the shield by the lion, 2d.

Item for 9 gallons of russet [*elbid'*] colour bought from Asilden the stainer, 9s.

Item for 500 thorn pins [*prykkes de spinis*] for tacking for the said ordinance, 16d.

Item to Simon Slegh of Maidstone for 60 tontight of Maidstone rag, £3 15s.

Item for horse-bread for carriage of sand [*aren'*] for the Bridge, 6d.
Total £5 11s. 1½d.

Total for the week £17 7s. 5d.

263. Wages and other expenses.

Saturday 22 February, paid to R. Beek, J. Catelyn senior, J. Catelyn junior, and J. Houswif, masons, 15s.

Item to William Warde, another mason, as above, 3s.

Item to William Clerk, J. Neweman, J. Sweteman, J. Bassett, J. Parys, and Thomas Gerland, carpenters, 22s. 6d.

Item to John Brys, another carpenter, for the week, 3s. 6d.

Item to Walter Loy, shoutman, for the week, 2s. 6d.

Item to William Sharp, carter, for the week, 22d.

Item to him for the horses' fodder for the week, 2s. 1d.

Item to John Silkeston for the cook's stipend, the dogs' food, with ale, as above, 2s. 8d.

Item to Robert Ragenell, labourer, for the whole week as before, 2s.

Item to the said sawyers for 6 days as above, 8s.

Item for ale and other expenses about and for the said ordinance about the Giants [*les Geantes*], 17d.

Item paid to John Waltham, stainer, for 2 days for the said ordinance of the king and queen, 18d.

Item to J. Freman, stainer, for the same, for 3½ days , 2s. 8d.

Item to 2 other stainers for the same for 2½ days and 1 night, 3s. 8d.

Item to Laurence Joynour [? the joiner] for the same for 5 days for the same, 3s. 9d.

Item to Thomas Norton for the same for 5 days, 3s. 4d.

Item to William Herlawe for 1 day and 1 night, 12d.

Item paid to 1 tiler with 1 servant for 10 days, 10s.
Total £4 14s. 8d.

Purchases.

Item paid to J. Oliver for 3,503 half-penny nails, 3,000 patten-nails [*Patynnail*], and 26,000 lattice nails [*latysnaill*] bought for the ordinance of the said king etc., price in all 21s. 11½d.

Item for 20 dozen gold paper/leaf [*Goldpaper*] bought for the same, 40s.

Item paid for 7 plates of black iron and half a hundred of fine gold, 3s. 8½d.

Item for 250 dozen silver paper/leaf [*silverpaper*] for the same, 2s. 6d.
Total £3 8s. 2d.

Total for the week £8 2s 10d.

264. [p. 464] W. Weston & Richard Stile Wardens.
Wages and other expenses.
Saturday 1 March, paid to Richard Beek, J. Catelyn senior, J. Catelyn junior, and J. Houswif, masons, 15s.
Item to William Warde, another mason, for the week, 3s.
Item to William Clerk, J. Neweman, J. Sweteman, J. Bassett, J. Parys, and Thomas Gerland, carpenters, 22s. 6d.
Item to John Brys, another carpenter, for the week, 3s. 6d.
Item to Walter Loy, shoutman, for the week as above, 2s. 6d.
Item to William Sharp, carter, for the week, 22d.
Item to him for the horses' fodder for the week, 2s. 1d.
Item to J. Silkeston for the cook's stipend, the dogs' food, with ale, as above, 2s. 8d.
Item to Robert Ragenell and Thomas, labourers, for the whole week taking 2s.
Item to the said sawyers for 5 days, for the day as before last week, 6s. 8d.
item to 1 labourer for 1 day for the carpenters for 6d.
Item to 2 men for 1 tide for the carpenters, 6d.
Item for beer given to the carpenters in their labour by night, 2d.
Item to 1 carpenter hired for 1 day and more, 13d.
Item paid to Richard Bateman for making fuel for making tiles at Lewisham for 5 weeks, 10s.
Item to a certain Laurence and Henry, tailors, for making 19 garments of linen cloth, stained, for the virgins on the Bridge etc., 15s. 10d.
Item to them for 1 yard of blanket for the same, 12d.
item to 3 daubers for 4 days with 1 servant, 3s. 5d.
Item for hiring 1 gin hired from John Neweman for the said ordinance, 3s. 4d.
Item to Thomas Daunt, painter, for painting image/s at and over the stone gate for the king's coming, £8.
Item paid to John Marion, stainer, in part payment of his works and labour done on the Bridge against and for the coming of the king and queen etc., 20s.
Total £13 19s. 7d.

Purchases.
Item for 1 boat[load] of rag containing 30 tontight bought by Beek, 30s.
Item for 2 water-adzes bought, price 2s. 6d.
Item for 2 augers for the water bought, 12d.
Item for 1 iron for the lathe [*lathe*] for joining boards bought, 12d.
Item for 1 barrel bought for 1 tine, with other costs for the same, 8d.
Item for cord bought for the said ordinance, 12d.
Item paid to Robert Lokyere, smith, for divers bands [*bondes*], locks, and bolts bought for the auger, 8d.
Total 36s. 10d.
Total for the week £15 16s. 5d.

265. [p. 465] In the 8th year of Henry V.
Wages and other expenses.

Saturday 8 March, paid to R. Beek, J. Catelyn senior, J. Catelyn junior, and J. Houswif, masons, 15s.

Item to William Warde, another mason, for the week, 3s.

Item to W. Clerk, J. Neweman, J. Sweteman, J. Bassett, J. Parys, and Thomas Gerland, carpenters, as above, 22s. 6d.

Item to John Brys, another carpenter, for the week, 3s. 6d.

Item to Walter Loy, shoutman, for the week, 2s. 6d.

Item to William Sharp, carter, for the week, 22d.

Item to him for the horses' fodder for the week, 2s. 1d.

Item to John Silkeston for the cook's stipend, the dogs' food, with ale, as above, 2s. 8d.

Item to William Ragenell [sic] and Thomas Spaldyng, labourers for the masons, for the whole week, 4s.

Item to the said sawyers for 6 days for the day, 8s.

Item for hiring 1 barge for the Wardens to do the Bridge's business, 14d.

Item to 1 man for 5 tides for the starlings and other things, 15d.

Item to William Covyngton, tiler, with a servant for 6 days, 6s.

Item repaid Ralph Chapman, cook, for the occupation of his house at the time of the ordinance, 3s. 4d.

Item for fitting the head-armour [*Pysens*] for the Giants, 9d.

Item to Richard Carleton and his associate, paviour/s, for 1 day on the Bridge, 14d.

Item for making 2 garments for the Giants for the same ordinance, 2s.

Total £4 9d.

Four tides.

Item paid to the said tidemen for 4 tides at the great Ram, taking as above, with their drinking, total 23s. 6d.

Total 23s. 6d.

Purchases.

Item paid for patten-nails [*patynailles*], blanknaill, wooden pegs [*Trasshnaill*], white lead, vermilion, red lead, wax, rosin, wooden struts [*pounchouns*], hurdles [*crecches*], timber, silver paper, gold paper, glue, rosin [sic], colour, packthread, ropes, and many other necessaries bought for the aforesaid ordinance, £5 4s. 7d.

Item for 16 hoops for the Giants, bought for the same ordinance, 16d.

Total £5 5s. 11d.

Total for the week £10 10s. 2d.

266. [p. 466] William Weston Richard Stile Wardens.

Wages and other expenses.

Saturday 15 March, paid to Richard Beek, J. Catelyn junior, J. Catelyn senior, and John Houswif, masons, as above, 15s.

Item to William Warde, another mason, for the week, 3s.

Item to William Clerk, J. Neweman, J. Swetman, J. Bassett for the week John Parys, carpenters, [sic] 15s.

Item to John Brys, another carpenter, for the week, 3s. 6d.

Item to Walter Loy, shoutman, for the week, 2s. 6d.
Item to William Sharp, carter, for the week, 22d.
a
Item to him for the horses' fodder for the week, 2s. 1d.
Item to Thomas Spaldyng, labourer, for the week, 2s.
Item to the said sawyers for 6 days, taking as above, 8s.
Item paid to 1 labourer for the carpenters for 2½ days, 12½d.
Item to 1 man for 2 tides for the carpenters, 6d.
Item paid to W. Covyngton, tiler, with 1 servant for 6 days, 6s.
b
Item to John Silkeston for the cook's stipend, the dogs' food, with ale, as above, 2s. 8d.
Item repaid William Sharp, carter, for his labour, 12d.
Item paid for brown Westphalian linen [*Westvale*] for the said ordinance of the king and queen, 4s. 4½d.
Total £3 8s. 6d.

Five tides.
Item paid to the said tidemen at the great Ram for 5 days, Monday, Tuesday, Wednesday, Thursday, and Friday, with their drinking, but 1 was lacking for 1 tide, whereof total 28s. 1d.
Total 28s 1d.

Purchases.
Item paid for 1 iron shovel bought for the tides, 4d.
Item for 1 stone of tallow [*talgh'*] bought for the cart, 7d.
Item for 1 boat[load] of chalk bought by Beek, 13s. 4d.
Item paid for red, indigo and blue [*bloy*] tartarin and red, indigo, and blue buckram bought for the occasion of the coming of the king and queen, price in all 46s. 11½d.
Total £3 14½d.

Quit-rent.
Item paid to Ralph Serle, rent-collector of the dean and chapter of the church of St Paul London, for quit-rent from the Bridge's tenements in the parishes of St Mary Magdalen in the Fishmarket and St Nicholas at the Shambles, viz. for the terms of Easter, Midsummer, Michaelmas, and Christmas last, by acquittance, 21s. 9d.
Total 21s. 9d.
Total for the week £8 19s. 6½d.

267. [p. 467] In the 9th year of Henry V.
Easter term.
Wages and other expenses.
Saturday 22 March, paid to Richard Beek, J. Catelyn senior, J. Catelyn junior, and John Houswif, masons, for the week as before, 15s.
Item to William Warde, another mason, for the week, 3s.
Item to William Clerk, J. Sweteman, J. Bassett, J. Parys, and Thomas Gerland, carpenters, as before, 18s. 9d.
Item to John Brys, another carpenter, for the week, 3s. 6d.

Item to Walter Loy, shoutman, for the week, 2s. 6d.
Item to William Sharp, carter, for the week, 22d.
Item to him for the horses' fodder for the week, 2s. 1d.
Item to John Silkeston for the cook's stipend, the dogs' food, with ale, as above, 2s. 8d.
Item to Thomas Spaldyng, labourer for the masons, for the week, 2s.
Item for hiring 1 horse for W. Clerk [going] to Kingston, with expenses, 16d.
Item to 1 labourer for the carpenters for 3 days, 15d.
Item for steeling 2 axes for the water, 2s.
Item for carriage of 1 load of timber from Croydon to the Bridge House, earlier bought from Shawe, 20d.
Item to 1 labourer for the Bridge House for 4 days, 20d.
Item to the said sawyers for 5 days, 6s. 8d.
Item to the said tiler with 1 servant for 4 days, 4s.
Item to 1 dauber with 1 servant for 1 [day], 12d.
Item to Nicholas Holford for keeping the passage-tolls of carts and ships across/through the Bridge, for 13 weeks last, for the week 15d., total 16s. 3d.
Item to J. Hethingham, clerk, for his salary as well for writing the paper/s as for attorning as before, 13s. 4d.
Item for making the vanes for the king's coming, 10d.
Item for mending and new painting 7 banners borrowed [*mutuat'*] for the king's coming, 7s. 8d.
Item for divers costs together with hiring virgins and their apparel and costs for the said coming, 25s. 4d.
Total £6 14s. 6d.

Four tides.
Item to the said tidemen for 4 tides this week, with their drinking, but one was lacking for 1 tide, total 23s. 3d.
Total 23s. 3d.

Purchases.
Item paid for 1 boat[load] of chalk bought, 13s. 3d.
Item paid for 5 staves [*bacul'*] with varnishing thereof, for 5 banners in the chapel, 2s. 6d.
Item for 1 auger for the water bought, 12d.
Item for horn glue bought, 3d.
Item paid to Peter Ridere for 6 loads of Reigate stone bought for 28s.
Item to Thomas Kelsy, smith, for the horses' shoes and farriery [*ferris et ferrura equorum*] for the last quarter, 5s. 1d.
Item paid to Robert Lokyere, smith, for ½ hundred and 20 lb. worked iron, price the hundred 14s., total 23s. 6d.
Item for 4 locks with keys and other fittings for the same, 3s. 8d.
Item paid for fringe, fur, hides of divers colours, plankboard [*plaunche-bord*], nails, and many other necessaries bought for the coming of the king and queen, £7 16s.
Total £11 13s. 4d.
Over the page for the same week.

[p. 468] W. Weston R. Stile Wardens.

Of the said week.

Chapel.

Item paid to John Burford, Thomas Cudde, Robert Tewe, and Robert Leyke, chaplains celebrating in the Bridge chapel, for the last quarter, to each 33s. 4d., total £6 13s. 4d.

Item to them for the salary of their cook for the same quarter, 5s.

Item to them for their Maundy as is accustomed, 12d.

Item to John Seyntjohn, one of the clerks of the said chapel, for his salary for 13 weeks of the same quarter, for the week 18d., total 19s. [sic]

Item to Nicholas Holford, the other clerk of the same chapel, for the same weeks, for the week 15d., total 16s. 3d.

Item to the said John SeyntJohn for bread and wine to celebrate in the same, for the same weeks, for the week 3d., total 3s. 3d.

Item for mending albs [and] surplices, with other necessaries for the chapel, 12d.

Item in bread and drinking for and in the king's coming spent about the clerks, 12d.

Total £8 19s. 10d.

Total for the week £28 10s. 11d.

268. Wages and other expenses.

Saturday 29 March, paid to Richard Beek, J. Catelyn senior, J. Catelyn junior, and John Houswif, masons, as above, 15s.

Item to William Warde, another mason, for the week, 3s.

Item to William Clerk, John Sweteman, J. Bassett, J. Parys, and Thomas Gerland, carpenters, as before, 18s. 9d.

Item to John Brys, another carpenter, for the week, 3s. 6d.

Item to Walter Loy, shoutman, for the week, 2s. 6d.

Item to William Sharp, carter, for the week, 22d.

Item to him for the horses' fodder for the week, 2s. 1d.

Item to John Silkeston for the cook's stipend, the dogs' food, with ale, as above, 2s. 8d.

Item to 1 tiler for 1 day, 12d.

Item to John Dove, labourer for the masons, for the whole week, 2s.

Item to 1 other labourer for them for 2½ days, 12½d.

Item to Richard Carleton, paviour, and 2 other paviours for 4 days in Old Change, 8s.

Item for 9 loads of sand for the same, 3s.

Item for mending 3 axes, 11d.

Item for mending the tines and other things for the masons, 2d.

Item to 1 labourer for the carpenters for 2½ days, 12½d.

Item for 1 horse [going] to *le Lee* [? Lee, co. Kent] for the Bridge's business, with divers expenses for the same, 2s. 2d.

Item for 1 stone of tallow [*talghe*] and 3 lb. of candles for the cart and other things, 12½d.

Item to the said sawyers for 2 days, 2s. 8d.

Total £3 12s. 4½d.

Quit-rent.
Item paid to the rent-collector of Bermondsey for quit-rent from tenement/s in London and lands in the parish of St Mary Lambeth, for last Christmas term, 9s. 3d.
Total 9s. 3d.

Purchases.
Item paid to Robert Lokyere in part payment for 170 lb. worked iron for the Bridge's business, 20s.
Total 20s.
Total for the week £5 19½d.

269. [p. 469] In the 9th year of Henry V.
Wages and other expenses.
Saturday 5 April, paid to Richard Beek, J. Catelyn senior, J. Catelyn junior, and J. Houswif, masons, 15s.
Item to William Warde, another mason, for the week as above, 3s.
Item to William Clerk, John Sweteman, John Bassett, John Parys, and Thomas Gerland, carpenters, as before, 18s. 9d.
Item to John Brys, another carpenter, for the week, 3s. 6d.
Item to Walter Loy, shoutman, for the week, 2s. 6d.
Item to William Sharp, carter, for the week, 22d.
Item to him for the horses' fodder for the week, 2s. 1d.
Item to John Silkeston for the cook's stipend, the dogs' food, with ale, as above, 2s. 8d.
Item to John Dove and William the labourer, labourers for the masons, for the whole week, 4s.
Item to 1 labourer for the carpenters for 6 days this week, 2s. 6d.
Item for divers expenses by W. Clerk, carpenter, at Lewisham for the Bridge's business, 8d.
Item for ale given to the carpenters for 2d.
Item to the said sawyers for 2 days, 2s. 8d.
Item to W. Covyng', tiler, with servant, for 6 days, 6s.
Item for carriage of 1 load of timber from Croydon to London, 22d.
Total £3 7s. 2d.

Four tides.
Item to the said tidemen for 5 [sic] tides this week, as above, with drinking, total 23s. 6d.
Total 23s. 6d.

Purchases.
Item paid for 1 boat[load] of chalk bought by Richard Beek, with other expenses, 13s. 5d.
Item for linen cloth bought for the making a frontal for 1 altar of the chapel, 20d.
Item for 700 pile-shoe nails [*Pylshonaill'*] bought by Clerk, 4s. 8d.
Total 19s. 10d.

Quit-rent.

Item paid to Walter Bradmere in part payment of a certain annuity of 16s., payable during the life of Robert Bakere, joiner, and Joan his wife, as etc., viz. for last Michaelmas and Christmas terms, 8s.

Item to the chamberlain of the church of St Peter Westminster, for quit-rent in the parish of St Nicholas at the Shambles, for last Christmas term, 5s.

Item to the churchwardens of St Mary le Bow, London, for quit-rent of tenement/s in Honey Lane, London, for last Christmas term, by acquittance, 16s. 8d.

Total 29s. 8d.

Total for the week £7 2s.

270. [p. 470] W. Weston & Richard Stile Wardens.

Wages and other expenses.

Saturday 12 April, paid to Richard Beek, J. Catelyn senior, J. Catelyn junior, and J. Houswif, masons, by the week as above, 15s.

Item to William Warde, another mason, for the week, 3s.

Item to William Clerk, J. Sweteman, J. Parys, John Bassett, and Thomas Gerland, carpenters, 18s. 9d.

Item to John Brys, another carpenter, for the week as above, 3s. 6d.

Item to Walter Loy, shoutman, for the week, 2s. 6d.

Item to William Sharp, carter, for the week, 22d.

Item to him for the horses' fodder for the week, 2s. 1d.

Item to John Silkeston for the cook's stipend, the dogs' food, with ale spent as above, 2s. 8d.

Item to John Dove and William Man, labourers, for the whole week, 4s.

Item to the said sawyers for 6 days, 8s.

Item to William Covyng', tiler, with 1 servant for 6 days, 6s.

Item for ale given to the carpenters this week, 2d.

Item to 1 labourer for the garden in the Bridge House, for 4 days, 20d.

Total £3 9s. 2d.

Five tides.

Item to the said tidemen, for 5 tides this week, with drinking as above, 29s. 4d.

Total 29s. 4d.

Total for the week £4 18s. 6d.

271. [p. 471] In the 9th year of Henry V.

Wages and other expenses.

Saturday 19 April, paid to Richard Beek, J. Catelyn senior, J. Catelyn junior, and J. Houswif, masons, 15s.

Item to William Warde, another mason, 3s.

Item to William Clerk, J. Sweteman, J. Parys, J. Bassett, and Thomas Gerland, carpenters, 18s. 9d.

Item to John Brys, another carpenter, for the week as before, 3s. 6d.

Item to Walter Loy, shoutman, for the week as before, 2s. 6d.

Item to William Sharp, carter, for the week, 22d.

Item to him for the horses' fodder for the week, 2s. 1d.

Item to J. Silkeston for the cook's stipend, the dogs' food, with ale, as above, 2s. 8d.

Item to John Dove and William Man, labourers, for the whole week, 4s.

Item to the said 2 sawyers for 6 days this week, 8s.

Item to 1 labourer for half a day for the masons, 3d.

Item for hiring 1 horse with expenses [going] to Lee and Deptford, for business etc., 6d.

Item to 1 labourer for 2 tides for the starlings, 6d.

Item for ale given to the Carpenters this week, 2d.

Item paid for divers expenses and costs for the Wardens [going] to Lee and Deptford for the bridge's business, 3s. 1d.

Item paid for 1 labourer for the Bridge's garden, for 4½ days, 22½d.

Item to William Covyng', tiler, with 1 servant, for 3 days, 3s.

Item paid to J. Hawkyn, *ducheman*, in part payment for ridge-tiles [*Crestes*] for the vault of the chapel, 2s.

Total £3 12s. 8½d.

Six tides.

Item to the said tidemen at the great Ram, for 6 tides, with drinking, 35s. 2d.

Total 35s. 2d.

Purchases.

Item paid for 1 boat[load] of chalk bought by Richard Beek, 13s. 4d.

Item for 1 lock [*lokke*] bought, 4d.

Total 13s. 8d.

Total for the week £6 18½d.

272. [p. 472] W. Weston & R. Stille Wardens.

Wages and other expenses.

Saturday 26 April, paid to Richard Beek, J. Catelyn senior, J. Catelyn junior, and J. Houswif, masons, as before, 15s.

Item to William Warde, another mason, for the week as above, 3s.

Item to William Clerk, J. Sweteman, J. Parys, J. Basset, and Thomas Gerland, carpenters, 18s. 9d.

Item to John Brys, another mason [sic], for the week, 3s. 6d.

Item to Walter Loy, shoutman, for the week, 2s. 6d.

Item to William Sharp, carter, for the week as before, 22d.

Item to him for the horses' fodder for the week, 2s. 1d.

Item to John Silkeston for the cook's stipend, the dogs' food, with ale, as above, 2s. 8d.

Item to John Dove and William Man, labourers for the masons, for the week, 4s.

Item to the said sawyers for 4 days this week, 5s. 4d.

Item to William Covyng', tiler, with a servant for 1 day, 12d.

Item paid to 1 labourer for the carpenters for 4 days, 20d.

Item to 1 other labourer for 2 tides for the same carpenters, 6d.

Item to the said tiler for his expenses [going] to Lewisham, 2d.
Total £3 2s.

Three tides.
Item to the said tidemen at the great Ram, for 3 tides this week, with drinking, 17s. 8d.
Total 17s. 8d.

Quit-rent.
Item paid to William Porter and Thomas Charleton, knights, for quit-rent from the Bridge's tenement/s in Honey Lane, for last Christmas term, by aquittance, 20s.
Total 20s.
Total for the week £4 19s. 8d.

273. [p. 473] In the 9th year of Henry V.
Wages and other expenses.
Saturday 3 May, paid to R. Beek, J. Catelyn senior, J. Catelyn junior, and J. Houswif, *Masons*, as above, 15s.
Item to William Warde, another mason, for the week, 3s.
Item to William Clerk, J. Sweteman, J. Parys, John Bassett, and Thomas Gerland, carpenters, 18s. 9d.
Item to John Brys, another carpenter, for the week, 3s. 6d.
Item to Walter Loy, shoutman, for the week, 2s. 6d.
Item to William Sharp, carter, for the week, 22d.
Item to him for the horses' fodder for the week, 2s. 1d.
Item to John Silkeston for the cook's stipend, the dogs' food, with ale, as above, 2s. 8d.
Item to John Dove and William Man, labourers for the masons, for the week, 4s.
Item to the said sawyers for 3 days this week, 4s.
Item to 1 labourer for 1 tide for the carpenters, 3d.
Item to 1 labourer for the Bridge's business for 2½ days, 12½d.
Item paid for orphreys for 1 chasuble with 4 yards of blood-red buckram, and with ribbon/s for the same and linen cloth for white fringe and other apparel for making 1 vestment of green damask for the chaplain, which damask R. Stile gave to the chapel, 24s.
Item for 1 man hired for loading the Bridge's cart with timber, 8d.
Item to the said tiler with 1 servant for 4 days, 4s.
Item to Thomas Bys, dauber, with 1 small servant for 1½ days, 16d.
Total £4 8s. 6½d.

Five tides.
Item to the said tidemen for 5 tides this week, with drinking, as above, 29s. 4d.
Total 29s. 4d.

Purchases.
Item paid for 1 boat[load] of chalk bought by R. Beek, 13s. 4d.
Total 13s. 4d.
Total for the week £6 10s. 2½d.

274. [p. 474] W. Weston & R. Stile Wardens.
Wages and other expenses.
Saturday 10 May, paid to Richard Beek, J. Catelyn senior, and J. Catelyn junior, *Masons*, 11s. 3d.
Item to William Warde, another mason [*cementar'*], for the week, 3s.
Item to William Clerk, J. Sweteman, J. Parys, John Basset, and Thomas Gerland, carpenters, taking as before, 18s. 9d.
Item to John Brys, another carpenter, for the week, 3s. 6d.
Item to Walter Loy, shoutman, for the week as above, 2s. 6d.
Item to William Sharp, carter, for the week, 22d.
Item to him for the horses' fodder for the week, 2s. 1d.
Item to John Silkeston for the cook's stipend, the dogs' food, with ale, as above, 2s. 8d.
Item to John Dove and William Man, labourers, for the week, 4s.
Item to the said sawyers for 6 days, 8s.
Item to the said masons and carpenters to drink, 4d.
Item to William Covyng', tiler, with 1 servant for 2 days, 2s.
Item to William Rikmeresworthe in full payment for felling and quartering elms previously bought from the prior of Merton, 11s.
Total £3 14s. ½d.

Two tides.
Item to the said tidemen at the great Ram, for 2 tides, with drinking, 11s. 10d.
Total 11s. 10d.

Purchases.
Item paid to William Barbour of co. York, by the hands of John Bristow his servant, for 14 tontight 5 weys and 5 nails of Northern stone [*Northerenstone*] bought, price the tontight 6s. 8d., total £4 9s. 4d.
Total £4 9s. 4d.
Total for the week £8 15s. 2½d.

275. [p. 475] In the 9th year of Henry V.
Wages and other expenses.
Saturday 17 May, paid to Richard Beek, J. Catelyn senior, J. Catelyn junior, and John Houswif, *Masons*, as above, 15s.
Item to William Warde, another mason [*cementar'*], for the week, 3s.
Item to William Clerk, J. Sweteman, J. Parys, J. Basset, and Thomas Gerland, carpenters, as above, 18s. 9d.
Item to John Brys, another carpenter, for the week, 3s. 6d.
Item to Walter Loy, shoutman, for the week, 2s. 6d.
Item to William Sharp, carter, for the week, 22d.
Item to him for the horses' fodder for the week, 2s. 1d.
Item to John Sylkeston for the cook's stipend, the dogs' food, with ale, as before, 2s. 8d.
Item to John Dove and William Man, labourers for the masons, for the week, 4s.
Item to the said sawyers for 3 days, taking as before, 3s.

94

Item in ale given to the carpenters, 2d.
Item for 2 iron hooks, 4d.
Total 57s. 10d.

Four tides.
Item to the said tidemen for 4 tides this week, with drinking, as above, 23s. 6d.
Total 23s. 6d.
Total for the week £4 16d.

276. [p. 476] W. Weston & R. Style Wardens.
Wages and other expenses.
Saturday 24 May, paid to R. Beek, J. Catelyn senior, J. Catelyn junior, and John Houswif, masons [*cementar*], as above, 15s.
Item to William Warde, another mason, for the whole week, 3s.
Item to William Clerk, John Swetman, J. Parys, J. Basset, and Thomas Gerland, carpenters, as before, 18s. 9d.
Item to John Brys, another carpenter, for the week as above, 3s. 6d.
Item to Walter Loy, shoutman, for the week as above, 2s. 6d.
Item to William Sharp, carter, for the week as before, 22d.
Item to him for the horses' fodder for the week, 2s. 1d.
Item to John Silkeston for the cook's stipend, the dogs' food, with ale, as above, 2s. 8d.
Item to John Dove and William Man, labourers, for the whole week, 4s.
Item to 1 labourer for the masons for 1 day, 4d.
Item for loading 2 loads of lead at the weigh-house, 6d.
Item for ale given to the carpenters this week, 4d.
Item for the portage of lead from Clement Lane to the Bridge House, 2d.
Item to the said sawyers for 5 days this week, 6s. 8d.
Item to the said tiler with a servant for 5 days, 5s.
Total £3 6s. 4d.

Purchases.
Item paid for 2 tawed horse-hides bought for the Bridge's business, 5s. 4d.
Item for 2 brass supports [*Bolstres de Bras*], weighing 11 lb., bought for the well in the Bridge House, 3s. 8d.
Item for 1 gallon of grease [*pinguedinis*] bought, 2s.
Item for 1 ridge-tile [*Creste*] bought for the vault under the chapel, 2s.
Item paid to John Ergaston for divers hinges [*garnetts potent'*], staples, latches, sprig nails, rove nails, spike nails [*spikyng'*], seam nails [*semnayll'*], and many other nails bought etc., total £4 17s. 3d.
Item for 1 cartload of hay bought for the Bridge horses, 6s. 8d.
Item for 1 clicket lock and 2 clamps bought, 6d.
Item paid to William Barbour of co. York, by the hands of John Bristowe his servant, in part payment of a certain bargain (viz. 20

tontight 9 weys and 20 nails of stone from Marr [Yorkshire] bought, with freight, for £9 6s. 8d., and in part payment for 2 fothers, 3 hundreds, 3 quarters, and 7 lb. lead bought, with freight, at 8 marks the fother, totalling £11 13s. 9½d.), £5 5s. ½d.
Total £12 2s. 5½d.
Total for the week £15 8s. 9½d.

277. [p. 477] In the 9th year of Henry V.
Wages and other expenses.
Saturday 31 May, paid to Richard Beek, J. Catelyn senior, and J. Houswif, masons, 11s. 3d.
Item to William Warde, another mason, for the week, 3s.
Item to William Clerk, J. Swetman, J. Parys, J. Bassett, and Thomas Gerland, carpenters, 18s. 9d.
Item to John Brys, another carpenter, for the week, 3s. 6d.
Item to Walter Loy, shoutman, for the week, 2s. 6d.
Item to William Sharp, carter, as above, 22d.
Item to him for the horses' fodder for the week, 2s. 1d.
Item to John Silkeston for the cook's stipend, the dogs' food, with ale, as above, 2s. 8d.
Item to William Man, labourer for the masons, for the week, 2s.
Item to 1 labourer for loading the cart, with beer spent on the carpenters, 6d.
Item to the said sawyers for 6 days this week, 8s.
Item to 1 tiler with 1 servant for 6 days, 6s.
Item to Thomas Bys, dauber, with 1 servant for 6 days, 6s.
Total £3 8s. 1d.

Two tides.
Item to the said tidemen for 2 tides, with their drinking, by the tide as above, 11s. 10d.
Total 11s. 10d.

Purchases.
Item for 2 boat[loads] of chalk bought by R. Beek, 26s. 8d.
Item for 1 wooden bucket, not yet bound, for the well in the Bridge House, 14d.
Item for 500 nails bought for pile-shoes [*Pylshoon*], 3s. 4d.
Item for 2 plates and sockets of iron for the same well, 8d.
Item for 3 small iron crowbars [*Crowes*] bought, 3d.
Item for 1 rope [*cord'*] for the same well, weighing 12 lb., 18d.
Item for 1 bead-hook [*bydehook*] for 1 boat, 3d.
Item for 1 lb. cable-yarn [*Cabelyern*] for mending the cable, 3d.
Item paid to Richard Warbulton for ropes called hawsers [*hauusers*] weighing 117 lb. bought, 49s. 9d.
Total £4 3s. 10d.
Total for the week £8 3s. 9d.

278. [p. 478] W. Weston & R. Stile Wardens.
Wages and other expenses.

Saturday 7 June, paid to Richard Beek, John Catelyn senior, and John Houswif, masons, 11s. 3d.

Item to William Warde, another mason, for the week, 3s.

Item to William Clerk, John Bassett, J. Sweteman, J. Parys, and Thomas Gerland, carpenters, 18s. 9d.

Item to John Brys, another carpenter, for the week as above, 3s. 6d.

Item to Walter Loy, shoutman, for the week, 2s. 6d.

Item to William Sharp, carter, for the week, 22d.

Item to him for the horses' fodder for the week, 2s. 1d.

Item to John Silkeston for the cook's stipend, the dogs' food, with ale, as above, 2s. 8d.

Item to John Dove, William Man, and Robert the labourer, labourers, for the whole week, 6s.

Item to the said sawyers for 6 days, 8s.

Item in ale given to the masons this week, 2d.

Item in ale given to the carpenters this week, 2d.

Item to the said tiler with 1 servant for 6 days, 6s.

Item to 1 man for carriage of sand to the tile-kiln at Lewisham for tiles for 2 days, 2s. 8d.

Item to 1 man for carriage of fuel for the same work to make tiles on occasions, 2s.

Item repaid Richard Bateman, tilemaker, in the sale of tiles at Lewisham, 20d.

Item to Thomas Bys, dauber, with 1 servant for 6 days, 6s.

10 acres of meadow. Item paid to the rector of St George in Southwark for 10 acres of meadow at the Lock last year, 3s.4d.

Total £4 19d.

Purchases.

Item to Isabel Beauchamp for the hire of 8 prs. of wings for angels for the king's coming, 6s. 8d.

Item paid for 2 stones of tallow [*cep'*] bought for the carpenters, 16d.

Item for 1 cord bought for the same carpenters, 8d.

Item paid to Richard Bateman, tilemaker, for making 20,000 tiles at Lewisham, 43s. 4d.

Item for the livery [*liberat'*] of the said wardens of the mayor's livery against last Christmas, 26s. 8d.

Item for their livery of the mayor against the feast of Pentecost last, 20s.

Total £4 18s. 8d.

Quit-rent.

Item paid to John Michell and Ralph Aes, wardens of the work of the church of St Mary le Bow, London, for quit-rent from the Bridge's tenement/s in Honey Lane for last Easter term, by acquittance, 16s. 8d.

Item to Walter Bradmere for a certain annual rent of 16s. granted by indenture for the term of the life of Robert Bakere, joiner, and Joan his wife, and beyond, for 1 year, 4s.

Total 20s. 8d.

Total for the week £10 10d.

279. [p. 479] In the 9th year of Henry V.
Wages and other expenses.
Saturday 14 June, paid to Richard Beek, John Catelyn senior, and John Houswif, masons, 11s. 3d.
Item to William Warde, another mason, for the week, 3s.
Item to William Clerk, John Swetman, J. Basset, J. Parys, and Thomas Gerland, carpenters, 18s. 9d.
Item to John Brys, another mason [sic], for the week, 3s. 6d.
Item to Walter Loy, shoutman, for the week, 2s. 6d.
Item to William Sharp, carter, for the week, 22d.
Item to him for the horses' fodder for the week, 2s. 1d.
Item to John Silkeston for the cook's stipend, the dogs' food, with ale, as above, 2s. 8d.
Item to John Dove, William Man, and Robert the labourer, labourers, for the whole week, 6s.
Item to the said sawyers for 5 days this week, 6s. 8d.
Item to William Forthe for carriage of elms at Kingston, earlier bought of the prior of Merton etc., to the water[side] there, 13s. 4d.
Item paid to 5 carpenters and 1 labourer for 1 night under the Bridge, for the Bridge's business, 3s. 5½d.
Item to the said tiler with 1 servant for 6 days, 6s.
Item in ale given to the carpenters this week, 2d.
Item in ale given to the tidemen this week, 4d.
Item to Thomas Bys, dauber, with 1 servant for 6 days, 6s.
Total £3 7s. 6½d.

Five tides.
Item to the said tidemen for 5 tides at the great Ram, with drinking, 29s. 4d.
Total 29s. 4d.

Purchases.
Item paid for 2 lb. candles bought for the business under the bridge, 3d.
<Query the bill of Henry Sundergiltes>
Item for 2 staples bought for 1 well, 3d.
Total 6d.
Total for the week £5 17s. 4½d.

280. [p. 480] Term of Midsummer
William Weston & Richard Stile Wardens.
Wages and other expenses.
Saturday 21 June, paid to Richard Beek, John Catelyn senior, John Catelyn junior, and John Houswif, masons, as above, 15s.
Item to William Warde, another mason, for the week, 3s.
Item to William Clerk, John Swetman, J. Bassett, J. Parys, and Thomas Gerland, carpenters, 18s. 9d.
Item to John Brys, another carpenter, for the week, 3s. 6d.

Item to Walter Loy, shoutman, for the week, 2s. 6d.

Item to William Sharp, carter, for the week as above, 22d.

Item to him for the horses' fodder for the week, 2s. 1d.

Item to John Silkeston for the cook's stipend, the dogs' food, with ale, as above, 2s. 8d.

Item to John Dove and Robert Mallyng, labourers for the masons, for the whole week, 4s.

Item to 1 other labourer for 4 days making 1 sail [*seill*] for the shout, 20d.

Item to the said sawyers for 5½ days, taking as above, 7s. 4d.

Item to 4 carpenters with 1 labourer for 1 night under the Bridge for the Bridge's business, 2s. 10½d.

Item to the said tiler with 1 servant for 6 days, 6s.

Item to Richard Carleton, paviour, for paving 11 toises [*teys*] beside the Bridge House, 7s. 4d.

Item to Richard Bateman, for making 10,000 house-tiles [*houstyll'*] at Lewisham, 21s. 8d.

Item to him for carriage of fuel for making the said tiles, 12d.

Item to Nicholas Holford for keeping the passage-tolls of carts and ships across/through the Bridge, for 13 weeks last, by the week 15d., total 16s. 3d.

Item to John Hethingham for writing the weekly paper, and for attornments for the recovery of debts, writings, indentures, and bills for the Bridge's business for last quarter, 13s. 4d.

Item to 1 labourer hired for the Bridge's business for 5 days, 2s. 2d.

Item paid to Thomas Kelsey, farrier [*ferrour*], for shoes and farriery of the Bridge's horses [*pro ferris et ferrura equorum Pontis*] for the last quarter, 5s. 8d.

Item for making 1 image of St Petronilla for the Bridge in the king's coming, 2s.

Total £5 19s. 1½d.

[p. 481] One tide.
Item to the said tidemen for 1 tide this week, with drinking, as above, 6s.

Total 6s.

Purchases.
Item paid for 18 yards of canvas for 1 sail [*vela*] for the shout, 6s.

Item for 2 gallons of tallow for the drawbridge, 20d.

Item for 3 lb. tallow candles [*candel' de cep'*] bought for the workmen by night, 4½d.

Item paid to one Cok, smith, for 120 lb. worked iron for the Bridge's business, at 14s. the hundred, total 15s. 4½d.

Total 23s. 5d.

Chapel.
Item to John Burford, Thomas Cudde, Robert Tewe, and Robert Leyk, chaplains celebrating in the chapel, for the last quarter, to each 33s. 4d., total £6 13s. 4d.

Item for the salary of the said chaplains' cook for the said quarter, 5s.
Item to John Seyntjohn, one of the clerks of the chapel, for his salary
for 13 weeks of last quarter, for the week 18d., total 19s. 6d.
Item to him for bread and wine to celebrate in the chapel, for the said
quarter, by the week 3d., total 3s. 3d.
Item to Nicholas Holford, the other clerk of the same, for the same
weeks, for the week 15d., total 16s. 3d.
Item for blessing 1 new vestment for the chapel, 8d.
Total £8 18s.
Total for the week £17 7s. 6½d.

281. [p. 482] W. Weston & R. Style Wardens.
Wages and other expenses.
Saturday 28 June, paid to Richard Beek, J. Catelyn senior, John C.
junior, and John Houswif, masons, for the week as before, 15s.
Item to William Warde, another mason, for the week, 3s.
Item to William Clerk, John Sweteman, J. Basset, J. Parys, and Thomas
Gerland, carpenters, taking as above,18s. 9d.
Item to John Brys, another carpenter, for the week, 3s. 6d.
Item to Walter Loy, shoutman, for the week, 2s. 6d.
Item to William Sharp, carter, for the week, 22d.
Item to him for the horses' fodder for the week, 2s. 1d.
Item to John Silkeston for the cook's stipend, the dogs' food, with ale,
as above, 2s. 8d.
Item to John Dove and Robert Mallyng, labourers for the masons, for
the whole week, 4s.
Item to the said sawyers for 4½ days as above, total 6s.
Item to the said tilers, viz. to master and servant for 4½ days, 4s. 6d.
Item for hiring 1 horse for W. Clerk, with other expenses [going] to
Croydon, 12d.
Item to 2 men hired for the carpenters for 2 tides, 12d.
Item to one Godewyn for mowing grass at the Lock for the Bridge's
horses, on occasions, 20d.
Total £3 7s. 6d.

Purchases.
Item for 2 stone of tallow [*cep'*] for the carpenters, 16d.
Total 16d.
Total for the week £3 8s. 10d.

282. [p. 483] In the 9th year of Henry V.
Wages and other expenses.
Saturday 5 July, paid to Richard Beek, J. Catelyn senior, J. Catelyn
junior, and John Houswif, masons, for the week as above, 15s.
Item to William Warde, another mason, for the week, 3s.
Item to William Clerk, J. Swetman, J. Bassett, J. Parys, and Thomas
Gerland, carpenters, 18s. 9d.
Item to John Brys, another mason [sic], for the week, 3s. 6d.
Item to Walter Loy, shoutman, for the week, 2s. 6d.

Item to William Sharp, carter, for the week, 22d.

Item to him for the horses' fodder for the week, 2s. 1d.

Item to John Silkeston for [the cook's] stipend, the dogs' food, with ale, as above, 2s. 8d.

Item to John Dove and William [sic] Mallyng, labourers, for the week, 4s.

Item to the said sawyers for 6 days, 8s.

Item to 2 labourers for the masons for 1 night under the Bridge, 8d.

Item to them for ale given, 2d.

Item to 5 carpenters with 1 labourer working for the whole night under the Bridge, taking 3s. 5d.

Item for carriage of divers necessaries for the same work, 6d.

Item for hiring 1 horse for W. Clerk [going] to Croydon, with other expenses, 12d.

Item paid to the said tiler with 1 servant for 6 days, 6s.

Item for loading timber, 2d.

Item paid for steeling and battering the masons' tools for the year and more, 5s. 2d.

Item paid to Joan, late the wife of John Beauchamp, plumber, as well by her own hands as by the hands of William Colston, in full payment of all debts previously for lead work done by the said John, etc., £4 19s.

Total £8 17s. 5d.

Purchases.

Item paid for 1 boat[load] of chalk bought by R. Beek, 13s. 4d.

Item paid to J. Pyherst for 22 hundred ft. of plankboard [*plaunchebord*] bought, 26s. 8d.

Item for 2 lb. candles bought for the works by night, 3d.

Item for 1 great piece of oak timber bought by W. Clerk, 10s.

Total £3 3d.

Quit-rents.

Item paid to the renter of Bermondsey for quit-rent from certain tenements lately of John Clifford in the parish of St Mary Magdalen Bermondsey, for 1 year at Christmas last, by acquittance, 4s. 10d.

Item to him for quit-rent from the Bridge's lands and tenements at Lambeth, viz. for last Easter term, by acquittance, 9s. 3d.

Total 14s. 1d.

Total for the week £12 11s. 9d.

283. [p. 484] W. Weston & R. Stile Wardens.

Wages and other expenses.

Saturday 12 July, paid to Richard Beek, John Catelyn senior, J. Catelyn junior, and John Houswif, masons, as above, 15s.

Item to William Warde, another mason, for the week, 3s.

Item to William Clerk, John Sweteman, J. Bassett, J. Parys, and Thomas Gerland, carpenters, as above, 18s. 9d.

Item to John Brys, another carpenter, for the week, 3s. 6d.

Item to Walter Loy, shoutman, for the week, 2s. 6d.

Item to William Sharp, carter, for the week, 22d.

Item to him for the horses' fodder for the week, 2s. 1d.
Item to John Silkeston for the cook's stipend, the dogs' food, with ale, as above, 2s. 8d.
Item to John Dove and Robert Mallyng, labourers, for the week, 4s.
Item to the said sawyers for 5 days this week, 6s. 8d.
Item paid to divers men hired for the whole week for making hay at *Wardales* and elsewhere, 4s. 4d.
Item to 1 labourer for divers business of the Bridge for 6 days, 2s. 6d.
Item to the said tiler with 1 servant for 5 days, 5s.
Item paid to Richard Bateman for making 10,000 house-tiles [*houstyll*] at Lewisham, 21s. 8d.
Item for divers expenses by the Bridge Wardens for the business of the Bridge, 4d.
Item to J. Wytte, painter, in part payment for painting 6 images in the chapel, and cleaning of the same, 16s. 8d.
Item paid to William Wiltsshire, carpenter, in full payment of his covenant to make 1 house on the land lately of James Hope at Deptford, together with 1 shed there beyond his covenant, 15s.
Total £6 5s. 6d.

Purchases.
Item paid for 1 pyx for the chapel to put alms in, 18d.
Item paid for divers apparel [*apparat'*] for the lamps, with other works/tasks, 14d.
Total 2s. 8d.
Total for the week £6 8s. 2d.

284. [p. 485] In the 9th year of Henry V.
Wages and other expenses.
Saturday 19 July, paid to Richard Beek, J. Catelyn senior, J. Catelyn junior, and J. Houswif, masons, 15s.
Item to William Warde, another mason, for the week, 3s.
Item to William Clerk, J. Sweteman, J. Bassett, J. Parys, and Thomas Gerland, carpenters, 18s. 9d.
Item to John Brys, another carpenter, for the week, 3s. 6d.
Item to Walter Loy, shoutman, for the week, 2s. 6d.
Item to William Sharp, carter, for the whole week, 22d.
Item to him for the horses' fodder for the week, 2s. 1d.
Item to John Silkeston for the cook's stipend, the dogs' food, with ale, as above, 2s. 8d.
Item to John Dove and Robert Mallyng, labourers, for the whole week, 4s.
Item to the said sawyers for 5 days, taking as above, 6s. 8d.
Item to 1 man for 2 tides for the carpenters, 6d.
Item paid to Peter Mowere [? the mower] for mowing and tedding 19 acres of meadow at the Lock, *Stuerte*, St Thomas Watering, and elsewhere, for each acre 11d., total 17s. 5d.
Item to the said tiler with 1 servant for 6 days, 6s.
Item to divers men and women for divers days for making hay in divers meadows of the Bridge, with drinking, 18s. 9d.

Item paid for mowing grass for the Bridge horses for 3 weeks, 20d.
Item paid for divers expenses for the Wardens at Stratford and elsewhere for the Bridge's business, 3s. 11d.
Total £5 8s. 3d.

Purchases.
Item for 2 hoops bought for 1 tine for the masons, 1½d.
Item for 2 lb. candles for the carpenters, 4d.
Item paid to Peter Reynold, carpenter, on different occasions from 22 March last up till now for timber bought for making the fulling mill at Stratford, by covenant, £4.
Total £4 5½d.
Total for the week £9 8s. 8½d.

285. [p. 486] W. Weston & R. Stile Wardens.
Wages and other expenses.
Saturday 26 July, paid to Richard Beek, J. Catelyn senior, J. Catelyn junior, and J. Houswif, masons, for the week, 15s.
Item to William Warde, another mason, for the week, 3s.
Item to William Clerk, J. Swetman, John Parys, J. Bassett, and Thomas Gerland, carpenters, for the week, 18s. 9d.
Item to John Brys, another mason [sic], for the week, 3s. 6d.
Item to Walter Loy, shoutman, for the week as above, 2s. 6d.
Item to William Sharp, carter, for the week, 22d.
Item to him for the horses' fodder for the week, 2s. 1d.
Item to John Silkeston for the cook's stipend, the dogs' food, with ale, as above, 2s. 8d.
Item to John Dove and Robert Chirche, labourers, for the whole week for the masons, 4s.
Item to the said sawyers this week because at Stratford, etc.
Item to the said 2 men for 1½ tides, 8d.
Item paid to 2 men hired for 2 days for loading up the cart with hay, together with ale and other expenses. 2s. 1d.
Item paid to Roger Godewyn in part payment for mowing and making of the Bridge's meadows, 10s.
Total £3 6s. 1d.

Purchases.
Item for 1 boat[load] of chalk bought by Richard Beek, 13s. 4d.
Item paid to Richard Beek for 1 great piece of oak timber bought for the fulling-mill at Stratford, 18s.
Item for 102 lb. of worked iron for the Bridge, 14s. 3d.
Item for iron weighing 24 lb., wrought for 1 bucket, 3s. 4d.
Item paid to John Bermyngham in part payment for 9 loads of timber bought, price 5s. the load etc., 40s.
Total £4 8s. 9d.
Total for the week £7 8s. 11d.

286. [p. 487] In the 9th year of Henry V.

Wages and other expenses.

Saturday 2 August, paid to R. Beek, J. Catelyn senior, and J. Catelyn junior, , masons, 11s. 3d.

Item to William Warde, another mason, for the week, 3s.

Item to William Clerk, John Sweteman, J. Parys, J. Basset, and Thomas Gerland, carpenters, as above, 18s. 9d.

Item to John Brys, another mason [sic], for the week, 3s. 6d.

Item to Walter Loy, shoutman, for the week as above, 2s. 6d.

Item to William Sharp, carter, for the week as above, 22d.

Item to him for the horses' fodder for the week, 2s. 1d.

Item to John Silkeston for the cook's stipend, the dogs' food, with ale, as above, 2s. 8d.

Item to John Dove and Robert Chirche, labourers for the masons, as above, 4s.

Item to 3 men to lift elms from the shout onto land at the Bridge House, 9d.

Item to 5 men hired for carriage of elms from Kingston for 2 days and 2 nights by water [in] the shout, 6s. 8d.

Item in ale given to the carpenters, 2d.

Item to 1 man hired to load the Bridge cart with hay this week, 2s. 1d.

Item for carrying in hay, with ale and bread for the same, this week, 2s. 3½d.

Item to Richard Bateman, tilemaker, for making 10,000 tiles at Lewisham, 21s. 8d.

Item to the said tilers for 1 day, 12d.

Total £4 4s. 2½d.

Purchases.

Item for 1 book, with 1 calendar and 1 crucifix, newly bound [*ligat'*] and bought for the house of the accountant [*computator*] price 20½d.

Item for 12 brooms for the bridge's business bought, 3d.

Item for 500 pile-shoe nails [*Pylshonnayll'*] bought, 3s. 4d.

Total 5s. 3½d.

Total for the week £4 9s. 6d.

287. [p. 488] W. Weston & R. Stile Wardens.

Wages and other expenses.

Saturday 9 August, paid to R. Beek, J. Catelyn senior, and J. Catelyn junior, *masons*, 11s. 3d.

Item to William Warde, another mason [*cementar'*], for the week, 3s.

Item to William Clerk, J. Sweteman, J. Parys, J. Basset, and Thomas Gerland, carpenters, as above, 18s. 9d.

Item to John Brys, another carpenter, for the week, 3s. 6d.

Item to Walter Loy, shoutman, for the week, 2s. 6d.

Item to William Sharp, carter, for the week, 22d.

Item to him for the horses' fodder for the week, 2s. 1d.

Item to John Silkeston for the cook's stipend, the dogs' food, with ale, as above, 2s. 8d.

Item to John Dove and Robert Chirche, labourers, for the whole week for the masons, 4s.

Item paid for divers expenses made by the carpenters of the Bridge and others at Stratford, for the Bridge's business, 6s. 2d.

Item paid for divers expenses made by the Wardens [going] to Deptford and there for the Bridge's business, 3s. 5d.

Item for divers expenses for entering the hay at the Bridge House, 6½d.

Item to 1 labourer hired for 3 days to load the cart, 17d.

Total £3 13½d.

Three tides.

Item to the said tidemen for 3 tides this week, with drinking, as above, 17s. 8d.

Total 17s. 8d.

Purchases.

Item for 1 axle-tree [*exiltre*] bought, with apparelling and fitting thereof, 18d.

Item for 1 horseshoe bought at Stratford for 1 horse of the Bridge, 2d.

Item paid to William Godfrey for 5 long oars [*oeres*] bought for the shout, 12s.

Item to Robert Otteley for elm boards [and] 200 ells canvas bought for the king's coming, £6 15s. 5½d.

Total £7 9s. 1½d.

Total for the week £11 7s. 11d.

288. [p. 489] In the 9th year of Henry V.

Wages and other expenses.

Saturday 16 August, paid to R. Beek, J. Catelyn senior, J. Catelyn junior, and J. Houswif, masons, 15s.

Item to William Warde, another mason, for the week as above, 3s.

Item to William Clerk, J. Swetman, J. Parys, J. Bassett, and Thomas Gerland, carpenters, 18s. 9d.

Item to John Brys, another carpenter, as above, 3s. 6d.

Item to Walter Loy, shoutman, for the week as above, 2s. 6d.

Item to William Sharp, carter, for the week as above, 22d.

Item to him for the horses' fodder for the week, 2s. 1d.

Item to John Silkeston for the cook's stipend, the dogs' food, with ale, as above, 2s. 8d.

Item to John Dove and Robert Chircher, labourers, for the whole week, 4s.

Item for the carriage of 4 loads of timber from Croydon to the Bridge House, 8s. 2d.

Item to 2 men hired to load up the cart and other expenses for the Bridge's business, 20d.

Item to the said sawyers for 1½ days, 2s.

Item in ale given to the masons, 2d.

Item to 1 labourer for the entering of hay, 2½d.
Total £3 5s. 6½d.

Four tides.
Item to the said tidemen for 4 tides, with drinking, but 2 men were lacking for 1 tide, whereof total 23s.
Total 23s.

Purchases.
Item paid for 2 loads of timber bought for plankboard [*plaunchebord*] for the mill at Stratford, 12s.
Item for 2 pr. hames bought, with drink, 8d.
Total 12s. 8d.

Quit-rents.
Item paid to Richard Marchall, rent-collector for William Porter and Thomas Charleton, knights, for quit-rent from the Bridge's tenement/s in Honey Lane, for the last terms of Easter and the Nativity of St John the Baptist, 40s.
Item to Richard Sele, rent-collector of Bermondsey, for quit-rent from the Bridge's tenement/s and lands in the parish of St Mary Lambeth, for the term of Midsummer last, 9s. 3d.
Total 49s. 3d.
Total for the week £7 10s. 5½d.

289. [p. 490] W. Weston & R. Stile Wardens.
Wages and other expenses.
Saturday 23 August, paid to Richard Beek, J. Catelyn senior, J. Catelyn junior, and John Houswif, *masoons*, as above, 15s.
Item to William Warde, another mason [*cementar'*], for the week, 3s.
Item to William Clerk, J. Swetman, J. Parys, J. Bassett, and Thomas Gerland, carpenters, 18s. 9d.
Item to John Brys, another carpenter, for the week, 3s. 6d.
Item to Walter Loy, shoutman, for the week as above, 2s. 6d.
Item to William Sharp, carter, for the week, 22d.
Item to him for the horses' fodder for the week, 2s. 1d.
Item to John Silkeston for the cook's stipend, the dogs' food, with ale, as above, 2s. 8d.
Item to John Dove and Robert Chirche, other labourers, for the whole week, 4s.
Item to the said sawyers for 6 days, as above, 8s.
Item for carriage of 2 loads of timber to Stratford for the mill there, 3s. 4d.
Item for carriage of 2 loads of timber from Croydon to the Bridge House, 4s.
Ite m for steeling and mending 2 augers and 1 water-axe, 20d.
Item in divers expenses with a horse [going] to Croydon for W Clerk, 10d.
Item in ale given to the carpenters, 2d.
Item in ale given to the tidemen by the Wardens, 2d.

Item in divers expenses made by William Sharp, carter, [going] to and at Stratford in carriage of timber and other things, 2s. 8d.
Total £3 14s. 2d.

Five tides.
Item to the said tidemen for 5 tides this week, with drinking, as above, total 29s. 4d.
Total 29s. 4d.

Purchases.
Item for 2 stone tallow [*talgh*'] bought, 16d.
Item for 2 *Warelynes* bought, 8d.
Total 2s.

Quit-rents.
Item paid to the chamberlains of the church of St Peter Westminster for quit-rent from the Bridge's tenement/s in the parish of St Nicholas Shambles, for the terms of Easter and Midsummer last, by acquitttance, 5s.
Total 5s.
Total for the week £5 10s. 6d.

290. [p. 491] In the 9th year of Henry V.
Wages and other expenses.
Saturday 30 August, paid to R. Beek, J. Catelyn senior, J. Catelyn junior, and John Houswif, masons, for the week,15s.
Item to William Warde, another mason, for the week, 3s.
Item to William Clerk, J. Sweteman, J. Parys, J. Bassett, and Thomas Gerland, carpenters, 18s. 9d.
Item to John Brys, another carpenter, for the week, 3s. 6d.
Item to Walter Loy, shoutman, for the week as above, 2s. 6d.
Item to William Sharp, carter, for the week as above, 22d.
Item to him for the horses' fodder for the week, 2s. 1d.
Item to John Silkeston for the cook's stipend, the dogs' food, with ale, as above, 2s. 8d.
Item to John Dove and Robert Chirche, labourers for the masons, for the week, 4s.
Item to the said sawyers for the whole week, viz. 6 days, 8s.
Item to 2 labourers hired for 2 nights for carriage of bricks [*Briktill*] in the shout, 16d.
Item to 1 labourer hired for 1 tide for raising stones from the water, 3d.
Item paid for carriage of 2 loads of timber from Croydon to the Bridge House, 4s.
Item to 5 carpenters hired for 1 night to mend the *Trappe* on the drawbridge, 3s. ½d.
Item to 3 labourers for the carpenters, for 3½ days, 20d.
Item paid for loading timber and other expenses at Croydon, 18d.
Item given to *les Shouteman* [sic] for drinking, 2d.
Item paid for mending the paintwork [*picture*] of the image of St Thomas over the Bridge, 2s.
Total £3 15s. 3½d.

Five tides.
Item to the said tidemen at the great Ram for 5 tides, except for 1 man for 1 tide, whereof total 29s. 1d.
Total 29s. 1d.

Quit-rents.
Item paid to the wardens of the work of the church of St Mary le Bow London, for quit-rent from the Bridge's tenement/s in Honey Lane, for the term of Midsummer last, by acquittance, 16s. 8d.
Total 16s. 8d.

Purchases.
Item paid for hames and collars for the Bridge's horses, 8s.
Item paid to William Shawe in part payment for 30 loads of timber previously bought at Croydon, price the load 5s., etc., £6 10s.
Total 6 18s.
Total for the week £12 19s. ½d.

291. [p. 492] W. Weston & Richard Stile Wardens.
Wages and other expenses.
Saturday 6 September, paid to Richard Beek, John Catelyn senior, John Catelyn junior, and John Houswif, masons, for the week,15s.
Item to William Warde, another mason, for the week, 3s.
Item to William Clerk, John Swetman, John Parys, John Bassett, and Thomas Gerland, carpenters, as above, 18s. 9d.
Item to John Brys, another carpenter, for the week, 3s. 6d.
Item to Walter Loy, shoutman, for the week, 2s. 6d.
Item to William Sharp, carter, for the week, 22d.
Item to him for the horses' fodder for the week, 2s. 1d.
Item to John Silkeston for the cook's stipend, the dogs' food, with ale, as above, 2s. 8d.
Item to John Dove and Robert Chirche, labourers, for the whole week for the masons, 4s.
Item to the said sawyers for 6 days, as above, 8s.
Item for carriage of 2 loads of timber from Croydon to the Bridge House, 4s.
Item to 1 labourer for the shout for carriage of bricks for 4 days, 2s. 2d.
Item for ale given to the masons etc., 2d.
Item for horse-bread and for assistance loading the cart with timber, 22d.
Total £3 9s. 6d.

Five tides.
Item paid to the said tidemen at the great Ram for 5 tides this week, with drinking, as above, 29s. 4d.
Total 29s. 4d.

Purchases.
Item paid for 1 boat[load] of chalk bought, 12s.

Item paid for 24 brooms bought for the carpenters and tide[men], 6d.
Item for 800 nails bought, 5s. 4d.
Total 17s. 10d.
Total for the week £5 16s. 8d.

292. [p. 493] In the 9th year of Henry V.
Wages and other expenses.
Saturday 12 September, paid to R. Beek, J. Catelyn senior, John Catelyn junior, and John Houswif, masons, for the week,15s.
Item to William Warde, another mason, for the week, 3s.
Item to William Clerk, John Swetman, John Parys, John Bassett, and Thomas Gerland, carpenters, as above, total 18s. 9d.
Item to John Brys, another carpenter, for the week, 3s. 6d.
Item to Walter Loy, shoutman, for the week as above, 2s. 6d.
Item to William Sharp, carter, for the week as above, 22d.
Item to him for the horses' fodder for the week, 2s. 1d.
Item to John Silkeston for the cook's stipend, the dogs' food, with ale, as above, 2s. 8d.
Item to John Dove and Robert Chirche, labourers for the masons, for the whole week, 4s.
Item to the said sawyers for 5 days, taking as above, 6s. 8d.
Item paid for divers expenses made in and for the breakfast [*jantaclo*'] for the auditors of the account for the 8th year last preceding, £3 14s. 4½d.
Item paid for the hire of 1 horse for W. Clerk [going] to Croydon for the Bridge's business, 10d.
Item paid to 1 tiler with 1 servant for 1 day, 12d.
Item paid to John Hethingham for making and writing the rolls of account for the 8th year last, 13s. 4d.
Item paid for 1 labourer for half a day for the Bridge's business, 3½d.
Total £7 9s. 10d.

Five tides.
Item to the said tidemen at the great Ram for 5 tides, with drinking, 29s. 4d.
Total 29. 4d.

Purchases.
Item paid to John Hacche of Harefield [*Herfeld*] in part payment of 31s. 6d. for 7 loads of timber bought at Croydon, price the load 4s. 6d., 6s. 8d.
Total 6s. 8d.
Total for the week £9 5s. 10d.

293. [p. 494] W. Weston & Richard Stile Wardens.
Wages and other expenses.
Saturday 20 September, paid to Richard Beek, J. Catelyn senior, and J. Catelyn junior, ([illegible]) <*defic'*> masons, 11s. 3d.
Item to William Warde, another mason, for the week, 3s.

Item to William Clerk, John Sweteman, J. Parys, J. Bassett, and Thomas Gerland, carpenters, as before, 18s. 9d.

Item to John Brys, another carpenter, for the week, 3s. 6d.

Item to Walter Loy, shoutman, for the week, 2s. 6d.

Item to William Sharp, carter, for the week as above, 22d.

Item to him for the horses' fodder for the week, 2s. 1d.

Item to John Silkeston for the cook's stipend, the dogs' food, with ale, as above, 2s. 8d.

Item ([illegible]) <*defic'*> to John [sic] Chirche, labourer for the masons, for the whole week, 2s.

Item to the said sawyers for half a day, 8d.

Item to 1 labourer for 1 tide for the masons, 3d.

Item to 1 tiler with 1 servant for 4 days, 4s.

Item paid to Salamon Neville of Broomfield in part payment of £12 for work and making the fulling-mill at Stratford on occasions from 3 May last up till now, by covenant, £6.

Total £8 12s. 6d.

Five tides.

Item to the said tidemen at the great Ram for 5 tides this week, with drinking, as above, 29s 4d.

Total 29s. 4d.

Purchases.

Item paid for 1 boat[load] of chalk bought by Richard Beek, price 12s.

Item paid for paper and parchment bought for the rolls of account and other business, for the whole year, 4s.

Item paid to Sir [*dompno*] Thomas Stratford by the hands of John Cook, dwelling there, for a certain weir bought there, 20s.

Item paid to John Clambert, smith, in part payment for works of iron by account on the tally previously worked and bought of his own iron etc., £3.

Item to William Colston, plumber, in part payment of £5 2s. 5d., for 15 score 8½ lb. of solder [*Sowder*] bought, and for soldering thereof for 2 years last past by account, price the lb. 4d., £3.

Total £7 16s.

Total for the week £17 17s. 10d.

294. [p. 495] In the 9th year of Henry V.

Michaelmas term.

Wages and other expenses.

Saturday 27 September, paid to Richard Beek, John Catelyn senior, and John Catelyn junior, masons, as above, 11s. 3d.

Item to William Clerk, J. Sweteman, and J. [sic] and John Parys, carpenters, for the week, 11s. 3d.

Item to John Brys, another carpenter, for the week, 3s. 6d.

Item to William Warde, another mason, for the week, 3s.

Item to Walter Loy, shoutman, for the week as above, 2s. 6d.

Item to William Sharp, carter, for the week as above, 22d.

Item to John Houswif, mason, for 3 days this week, 22½d.

Item to the said William Sharp, carter, for the horses' fodder for the week, 2s. 1d.

Item to 2 labourers aforesaid for the masons for the whole week, 4s.

Item to John Silkeston for the cook's stipend, the dogs' food, with ale, as above, 2s. 8d.

Item to the said sawyers for 4 days, 5s. 4d.

Item paid for 1 dinner [*cena*] with all expenses made for/by the mayor and certain/other aldermen to their ministers and servants at the Bridge House, to view the Bridge's store, 40s. ½d.

Item paid for lodging [*lect'*] and divers expenses and victuals for the carpenters and other servants going with the mayor and aldermen to the west to destroy the weirs, 16s. ½d.

Item paid for the exchange of old pewter vessels for the priests of the Bridge, 6s. 2d.

Item to the said (2) <1> tiler(s) with 1 servant for 5 days, 5s.

Item to 1 labourer hired for 1½ days for Silkeston, 6d.

Item paid for fitting 1 axle-tree and other repairs [*emendac'*] for the Bridge cart, 6d.

Item for horse-bread spent for the Bridge horses in the carriage of timber, 6d.

Item for assistance to load up the cart with timber, 2d.

Item paid for horse-shoes and farriery for last quarter by tally, 7s. 4d.

Item paid to William Weston and Richard Stiel, Wardens of the Bridge, for their stipend for the said year, £20.

Item paid to John Hethingham, clerk of the Bridge, for his salary for writing papers weekly, for last quarter, 6s. 8d.

Item to him for acting as general attorney [*attornacione general'*] in all secular courts, with making pleadable bills for the bridge's business, for the same quarter, 6s. 8d.

Item to John Bassett, carpenter, for 1 day, 7½d.

Item paid to Nicholas Holford for keeping the passage-tolls of carts and ships across/through the Bridge, for 14 weeks, for the week 15d., total 17s. 6d.

Item paid for laundering the surplices, albs, cloths, and other ornaments for the chapel for the whole year, 5s. 4d.

Item paid to Richard Beek, master mason, for his reward [*regard'*] for last year, 20s.

Item to William Clerk, master carpenter, for his reward for the same year, 20s.

Item to William Aunger, rent-collector, for his salary for the same year, £10.

Item to the same collector for his losses [*deperdic'*], drinking and other things for the same year, £3 6s. 8d.

[p. 496] The same week.

vacat

111

Item to the same William Aunger of allowance by the auditors of the last account on the roll/s thereof, £3 6s. 8d.

Item paid by the same for mending divers locks and keys in divers tenements for the whole year, 5s. 7d.

Item paid by the same to divers servants *vicet'* and quarrels raised and other things in prosecuting the Bridge's tenants/tenements, 13s. 4d.

Item paid to John Hethingham for making and writing the account/s of the Wardens this last year, 23s. 4d.

Item paid to Henry Sundergiltes, brickman, from 7 December up to this day for making 119,000 bricks [*Briktill'*] at Deptford, finding sand and fuel and other costs, with carriage thereof in the Bridge's shout to the Bridge House, taking 4s. 4d. for each thousand, total £25 12s. 10d. [*recte* £25 15s. 8d.]

Item to William Colston in full payment of £5 2s. 10d. for 15 score 8½ lb. of solder [*sowdur*] price 4d. the lb., as previously, 42s. 10d.

Item repaid to him beyond the said price because it was otherwise sold at 6d. the lb., and in all 13s. 4d.

Item to him for working 40 hundred lb. lead for 2 years last, at 16d the hundred, total 53s. 4d.

Total £76 3s. 7d.

Chapel.

Item the said 27 September, paid to John Burford, Robert Tiewe, and Robert Leyk, chaplains celebrating in the Bridge chapel, for the last quarter, to each 33s. 4d., total £5.

Item to John Seyntjohn, one of the clerks of the said chapel, for his salary for 14 weeks of the same quarter, for the week 18d., total 21s.

Item to him for bread and wine to celebrate, for the same weeks, for the week 3d., total 3s. 6d.

Item to Nicholas Holford, the other clerk of the same chapel, for the same weeks, for the week 15d., total 17s. 6d.

Item paid to 1 chaplain celebrating in the same for 3 weeks, 7s. 6d.

Item for the salary of the said chaplains' cook for the same quarter, 5s.

[in right margin:] £7 4s. 3d.

Item paid for divers cerges, torches, and other wax candles for the feasts of All Saints and the Purification of the Virgin, together with Paschal [candle/s] for the feast of Easter, and cerges for the feast of Pentecost, with 5 torches for the chapel and the coming of the king and queen, for the whole year by account, 52s. 5d.

Total £10 6s. 11d.

[p. 497] The same week continued.

Purchases.

Item the said 27 September, paid for canvas for hames for the Bridge horses, together with making thereof, 20d.

Item paid for divers cords and ropes bought for the Bridge's business, weighing 541 lb. and more, price in all 59s. 6d.

Item paid for 1 pr. bare wheels bought, 6s.

Item paid for line and ropes bought for the shout this week, 3s. 7d.

Item paid for 7½ gallons of oil for the chapel, 8s. 9d.

Item for 23 lb. candles bought for the same in time of winter, 2s. 10½d.

Item paid for brooms, needles [*acubis*], thread, and pins [*spyntr'*] for the chapel, 9½d.

Item for counters borrowed from the chamberlain at the time of the last account and brought by 1 auditor of the said account, 6d.

Item repaid to the Bridge's carter for his reward for half a year last, 5s.

Total £4 8s. 8d.

Total this week £80 29s. [sic] 2d.

295. Total of the year

Total of wages £330 6½d.

Item of all tides/tidemen £24 13s. 2d.

Item of purchases 145 16s. 1d.

Item of resolutions [of quit-rent] £15 18s. 9½d.

Item of the chapel £37 1d.

£554 8s.8d.

[p. 498] Item for a load of faggots 10 [sic]

BRIDGE HOUSE RENTAL 3

Account for 1461–2

296. [f. 25] Account of Peter Aldfold and Peter Caldecote, Wardens of London Bridge from Michaelmas in the first year of the reign of King Edward the Fourth since the Conquest [1461], to Michaelmas in the second year of the reign of the same King [1462], for one whole year.

297. Arrears.
Item they render account for £154 9¾d. of arrears from the last account for the preceding year, as appears on the foot of that account. Item for 40s. received from John Rokesley chaplain, pledge of Robert Watson late collector of the foreign and quit-rents of the Bridge, in part payment of £13 6s. 9d. owed hitherto, as parcel of £5 6s. 9d. of arrears of the said Robert charged in the arrears of account of Thomas Cooke and Thomas Davy late wardens of the Bridge. Total £156 9¾d.

298. Proper rent.
Item for £541 18s. 8d. proper rent of the lands and tenements of proper rent of the Bridge, as appears by the rental renewed at Michaelmas in the first year of the said king, payable at the feasts of All Hallows, the Purification of the Blessed Mary, Pentecost, and St Peter ad Vincula in equal portions.
Total £541 18s. 8d.

299. Foreign rent.
Item for £53 18s. 8d. rent of lands and tenements, mills, meadows, and pastures in Stratford, Deptford, Lewisham, Southwark, and elsewhere in the country, as appears by the rental thereof renewed at Michaelmas in the said first year etc.
Total £53 18s. 8d.

300. Farm of the Stocks.
Item for £40 received from the wardens of the craft of Butchers of London, for the farm of the moiety of the lower part of the Stocks, London, viz. on the north side there to sell flesh this year, as demised by Nicholas Wyfold, late mayor of the city, and the aldermen of the same, and Thomas Cooke and Thomas Davy, late wardens of the said Bridge, to Richard Fremot and John Bowle [f. 25v] then wardens of the said craft of Butchers in the name of the company [*societatis*] of the said craft, accustomed to order [*disponere*] the sale of flesh there, as is more fully contained in the agreement made thereof between the same mayor, aldermen, and wardens of the Bridge on the one part and

the said Richard Fremot and John Bowle in the name of the company on the other; paying yearly to the said wardens of the Bridge or their attorneys each week for the 46 weeks falling outside Lent, 17s. 4½d., and more in all on Saturday the eve of Quinquagesima Sunday 9d., counting the said Saturday the eve of Quinquagesima Sunday and Saturday the eve of Easter in the said 46 weeks.

301. Item for £27 14s. 8d. received from Edmund Newman, Henry Smyth, and William Laurens, citizens and stockfishmongers of London, for the south part of the Stocks Market called *the fisshe market*, demised to them by Peter Aldfold and Peter Caldecote, wardens of the said Bridge, to have and hold the said south part or market from 27 February 38 Henry VI, lately king *de facto* and not *de jure* [1460], until the end of ten years fully completed, rendering yearly to the said wardens and their successors or their true [*certo*] attorney £27 14s. 8d., paying every week 10s. 8d., as is more fully contained in an indenture made thereof. Total £67 14s. 8d.

302. Quit-rents.
Item for 12s. received from the wardens of the fraternity of the *Salve* founded in the church of St Magnus the Martyr, issuing yearly to the support of the Bridge from 3 shops with solars built over situated at the Staples [*Stapulas*] of the said Bridge towards London on the south side.
Item for 3s. received from the same wardens for a yearly quit-rent from three other shops with solars built over belonging to the said fraternity, situated at the said Staples on the east side between the land sometime of Roger Clovyle to the north and the common latrine there to the south.
Item for 66s. 8d. received from the wardens of the same for a yearly quit-rent to the support of the said Bridge from one corner tenement opposite the said church situated between the king's street leading to Billingsgate to the south and the common street called Bridge Street to the west.
Item for 2s. 6d. received from the said wardens for a yearly quit-rent from the tavern tenement called *the Lion* annexed to the said corner tenement on the east, which was sometime of Richard Essex and now belongs to the said church.
Item for 15d. received from the said wardens for a yearly quit-rent from a certain shop annexed to the said tavern tenement on the east, and now belonging to the said church.
[right margin:] £4 5s. 5d.

303. [f. 26] Item for 40s. for a yearly quit-rent from 2 tenements annexed to the said tavern tenement to the east of the same, whereof one tenement was sometime of John Bruer and the other sometime of Thomas Warle etc.
Item for 12d. for a yearly quit-rent from the tenement sometime of Stephen Abyndon, now belonging to the priory of St Mary Overey in Southwark and situated beside Oystergate to the east.

Item for 4s. 8d. for a yearly quit-rent from one tenement of old called *the horshede*, sometime of Henry Wymond, situated in the parish of St Dunstan in the East, now belonging to the Chamber of the Guildhall of the city of London.

Item for 4s. 8d. for a yearly quit-rent from one tenement situated in the said parish of St Dunstan in the East, sometime of Adam Canon, annexed to the said tenement called *the horshede*.

Item for 2s. 6d. from one tenement situated in the same parish, sometime of Roger atte Pounde, and now belonging to the fraternity of St John the Baptist of the Tailors of London.

Item for 2s. 6d. received of the wardens of the craft or company of Grocers of London, for a yearly quit-rent from one tenement situated in the same parish and annexed to the tenement of the fraternity of the said Tailors.

Item for 26s. 8d. for a yearly quit-rent from one tenement situated in the parish of St Leonard in Eastcheap, sometime of John Odierne, afterwards of Alice Knyght.

Item for 8s. for a yearly quit-rent from one tenement of the abbot and convent of the monastery of St Saviour of Bermondsey, situated in the same parish, between the tenement of the prior and convent of Christ Church Canterbury to the north and the corner tenement to the south.

Item for 14s. 4d. for a yearly quit-rent from from one tenement situated in the same parish, sometime of John Causton, now of the prioress and convent of the house of nuns of St Helen within Bishopsgate, London.

Item for 9s. 4d. for a yearly quit-rent from one brewhouse called *the Pye*, sometime of John Courteys, now of the prior and convent of the Charterhouse by Smithfield, and situated in the parish of St Benet Gracechurch, London.

Item for 33s. 4d. for a yearly quit-rent from one tenement situated in the same parish, which was sometime of William Olyver, now of John Levyng.

Item for 40s. for a yearly quit-rent from one tenement sometime with a forge then [*detunc*] of Master Henry Grovehurst, and now without a forge, situated in the parish of All Hallows Gracechurch, London.

Item for 5s. for a yearly quit-rent from one tenement situated in the same parish called *the White lyon*, now belonging to the fraternity of Tailors of London.

Item for 8s. for a yearly quit-rent from one tenement sometime a brewhouse, situated at the corner of Billiter Lane towards Creechurch, situated in the parish of St Katherine Creechurch, which was sometime of Thomas Brayton, afterwards of John Percy, and now of Henry Jurdan, fishmonger.
[right margin:] £9 19s.

304. [f. 26v] Item for 3s. received of the wardens of the fraternity of St John the Baptist of the Tailors of London, for a yearly quit-rent from one tenement with 4 shops annexed to it on the north side, and with

5 shops annexed to it on the south side, situated in the parish of St Martin Outwich London.

Item for 5s. for a yearly quit-rent from one tenement in Birchin Lane in the parish of St Edmund in Lombard Street, at the sign of the Skimmer [*la Scomer*], which was sometime of William Dykeman, and now belongs to the college of Shottesbrook in [blank; *recte* Berks.].

Item for 2s. from one tenement with 4 shops annexed situated in the same parish, sometime of Nicholas Sleve and now belonging to the church of St Swithin in Candlewick Street.

Item for 4s. for a yearly quit-rent from 3 shops with solars built over, together with a certain void plot of land called *a wodehawe* situated in the same parish.

Item for 4s. for a yearly quit-rent from one tenement situated in the parish of All Hallows the Less, sometime of William Sadiller, afterwards of Robert Pellican, fishmonger.

Item for 10s. received from the Chamber of the Guildhall of the city of London for a yearly quit-rent from one tenement situated in the same parish, sometime of Adam Fraunceys, now belonging to the said Chamber.

Item for 19s. 8d. received from the said Chamber for a yearly quit-rent from one tenement situated in the parish of St Laurence Pountney London, sometime of Roger Depeham.

Item for 2s. 6d. for a yearly quit-rent from one tenement situated in the parish of St Swithin in Candlewick Street, sometime of John Dunmow, and now it is the vestry of the same church.

Item for 2s. for a yearly quit-rent from one tenement situated in the same parish, annexed to the said vestry, now belonging to the rector of the same church, situated between the said vestry to the south and the tenement sometime of Richard Weste to the north.

Item for 6s. 8d. for a yearly quit-rent from a certain seld called *the Brode Selde* situated in the parish of St Pancras, which was sometime of William Norton, afterwards of William Wetenhale.

Item for 9s. from one tenement sometime with a forge, situated in the parish of St Martin without Ludgate, sometime of William de Stratton, afterwards of John Gravesende etc.

Item for 8s. for a yearly quit-rent from one tenement with 2 shops situated in the parish of St Bride in Fleet Street, belonging to the church of St Paul, London.

Item for 40s. for a yearly quit-rent from divers tenements under the palace of the bishop of London, sometime built by Michael de Norhtborow, sometime [1354–61] bishop of London.

Item for 13s. 4d. for a yearly quit-rent from one tenement situated in the parish of St Olave in Southwark at the Staples of the Bridge towards Southwark, belonging to the chantry founded in the church of St Michael *in riola* [St Michael Paternoster].

Item for 13s. 4d. received from the prior and convent of St Mary Overey for a yearly quit-rent from a tenement situated in the parish of St George in Southwark called *le Exmew*.

[right margin:] £7 22d. £7 2s. 6d.

305. [f. 27] Item for 8s. for a yearly quit-rent from a certain great garden situated in Kent Street in Southwark, sometime of William Horn, and called *le Moote*.

Item for 6s. received from the abbot and convent of the abbey of St Mary Graces by the Tower of London, in full payment of all arrears of a certain yearly quit-rent of 2s. owed yearly to the Bridge from one tenement of the said abbot and convent with houses extending to the water of Thames situated in the parish of St Michael Queenhithe [*ad ripam regine*], in arrears for a long time; as adjudged by the arbitration of Thomas Brian, common serjeant of the city of London, and Thomas Rigby, under-sheriff [*sub vicec'*] of London, such that the said abbot and convent and their successors will well and faithfully pay the said quit-rent of 2s. to the wardens of the Bridge for ever.

[right side/margin:] 14s. £22 4d. 2[lost]

Total £22 3d.

306. Quit-rents not levied.

They do not answer for 2s. quit-rent sometime received from one tenement of the abbot and convent of Stratford Langthorn situated in the parish of St Clement by Candlewick Street, because it is restored by a certain yearly quit-rent of 2s. of the same abbot and convent issuing yearly from the tenements of the said Bridge in Lewisham etc.

Nor do they answer for 5s. quit-rent lately received from one tenement situated in the parish of St Michael in Crooked Lane, sometime of Agnes Lucas and afterwards of John Levynge, fishmonger, because the said tenement stands vacant and no distraint can be taken there etc.

Nor for 8s. quit-rent lately received from one tenement called *Cokdon' halle* situated in the parish of St Dunstan in the East.

Nor for 7s. from one tenement situated in the same parish called *the personage*.

Nor for 12d. quit-rent sometime received from 2 shops with solar/s built over under one structure, situated in the parish of St Stephen in Walbrook, sometime of John Pecok and lately of John Herste.

Nor for 6s. 6d. quit-rent lately received from one tenement situated in the parish of St Michael Bassishaw, sometime of William Norton, draper, and now of Hugh Wyche, mayor of London.

[right side:] 29s. 6d.

307. [f. 27v] Nor for 5s. quit-rent sometime received from one tenement in the parish of St Magnus, sometime of John Wymondham, afterwards of John Lovekyn, now belonging to the said church.

Nor for 8s. 9d. quit-rent sometime received from one shop situated in the same parish, sometime of John Ryder, afterwards of John Wynter, and now it belongs to the said church.

Nor for 8s. 9d. quit-rent from one shop annexed to the other shop on the south side thereof, which was sometime of William Stody, afterwards of Robert Domynyk.

Nor for 16s. quit-rent sometime received from one tenement situated in the parish of St Botolph by Billingsgate, which was sometime of Master Henry Grovehurste.

Nor for 12d. from one tenement with 2 shops situated in the same parish, which was sometime of John Wrothe, afterwards of Robert Wedyngton, and lately of Thomas Selowe.

Nor for 11s. 8d. sometime received from one tenement situated in the parish of St Mary at Hill, called *the Lambe*, sometime of Henry Pycard and afterwards of John Wade.

Nor for 6s. 8d. sometime received from another tenement situated in the same parish on the wharf called *Trayerswharf* on the west part there, and it belongs to the prior and convent of the church of Holy Trinity within Aldgate London.

Nor for 3s. 4d. sometime received from one tenement situated in the same parish, which sometime was of John Lovekyn and afterwards of William Walworth.

[right margin:] 21s. 8d. in the parish of St Mary at Hill. There are no evidences concerning the right and title of the same rent.

Nor for 3s. sometime received from one tenement situated in the parish of St Dunstan in the East on the corner of Mincing Lane, called *the Cokke*.

Nor for 4s. 8d. from one tenement situated in the same parish, in the corner of the churchyard of the said church on the south, sometime of Nicholas Hotot, afterwards of John Guy.

Nor for 2s. from one tenement situated in the same parish, sometime of Isabel Rothynge, afterwards [entry incomplete]

Nor for 3s. sometime received from one tenement situated in the parish of All Hallows Barking London, sometime of Richard Grymesby, afterwards of Thomas Edyngton.

Nor for 12d. sometime received from one tenement situated in the parish of St Andrew by Eastcheap called *the Stonehous*, sometime of John Coleyne, afterwards of Margaret Bamme.

Nor for 4s. sometime received from one tenement situated in Crooked Lane in the parish of St Margaret in Bridge Street, sometime of John Lutle [sic], afterwards of John Churcheman.

Nor for 12d. sometime received from one tenement situated in the parish of St Leonard in Eastcheap, sometime of John Fraunceys, afterwards of John Litley, afterwards of Christ Church Canterbury, and afterwards of Thomas Sampson.

Nor for 2s. sometime received from one tenement situated in Candle-wick Street in the same parish, called *le Cheker*, sometime of William Doget, situated beside the tenement of the prior of the New Hospital of St Mary without Bishopsgate, London.

Nor for 12d. from one shop situated in the same parish, sometime of John Litle.

Nor for 12d. from 10 shops with solars built over, situated in the parish of St Mary Axe, sometime of John Trumpeton, afterwards of Thomas Davy, draper.

[right side] £4 3s. 9d.

308. [f. 28] Nor for 8s. quit-rent sometime received from one tenement with 2 shops situated in the parish of St Michael on Cornhill, sometime of Simon Moredon, which now belong to a certain chantry founded in the said church.

Nor for 5s. sometime received from one tenement situated in Stock-fishmongers Row in the parish of St Michael in Crooked lane, which sometime was of John Lovekyn.

Nor for 6s. from one tenement situated in the parish of All Hallows the Less, and now belonging to the master of the College of St Laurence Pountney London.

Nor for 10s. from one tenement situated in the parish of St Mary Abchurch, sometime of John Herford, afterwards of John Crooke, and afterwards of John Wodcok, and now of John Langwith, tailor.

Nor for 12d. from one tenement situated in the parish of St Mary Bothaw, which sometime was of Thomas Salesbury, knight, now belonging to the Chamber of the Guildhall of London.

(Nor for 12d. from 2 shops with solar/s built over under one building, situated in the parish of St Stephen in Walbrook, sometime of John Pecok, one shop of which was lately of John Herst, skinner, and the other shop with solar/s built over was lately of John Beverley.) [left margin:] <Because earlier>

Nor for 13s. 4d. quit-rent sometime received from one tenement situated in the parish of St Mary Woolnoth, sometime of Hamo Lumbard, afterwards of Margaret Bamme.

Nor for 2s. from one tenement situated in the same parish at the corner of Sherborne Lane, which sometime was of John Fissh, afterwards [entry incomplete]

Nor for 2s. 6d. from one tenement situated in the parish of St Bartholomew the Little, London, which sometime was of John Litle, afterwards of the prior and convent of Christ Church Canterbury.

Nor for 4s. from a tenement sometime a brewhouse called *the horshede* in the parish of St Alban in Wood Street, which sometime was of John Basyngstoke.

Nor for 2s. from one tenement situated in the same parish, sometime of the said John.

Nor for 2s. from one tenement situated in the parish of St Mary Aldermanbury, at the corner there, which sometime was of Robert Rous.

Nor for 2s. from one tenement with 8 shops situated at the corner of Basinghall Street [*Bassyngeshawe*] towards London Wall, in the parish of St Michael there, sometime of John London, and now belonging to the church of St Michael Bassishaw.

Nor for 3s. 8d. from one tenement of the prior and convent of the New Hospital of St Mary without Bishopsgate, situated in the parish of St Olave on the Wall.

Nor for 2s. from one tenement situated in the parish of St Stephen in Coleman Street, opposite the said church, sometime of Simon Dolsely, afterwards of Margaret Fastolf.

Nor for 8s. from one tenement situated at the corner at the Staples of the Bridge towards Southwark, in the parish of St Olave, now of the master and brothers [*confratrum*] of the Hospital of St Thomas the Martyr in Southwark aforesaid.

Nor for 4s. from one tenement of the said master and brothers situated in the parish of St Margaret in Southwark, between the tenement sometime of Simon le Plomer to the south and the tenement sometime of William Peyntour to the north etc.

[right side:] 76s. 6d.

309. [f. 28v] Nor for 2s. from one tenement situated in the parish of St George in Southwark, which sometime was of Walter Bukstede.

Nor for 4d. from one tenement situated in the parish of St Giles without Cripplegate, which sometime was of Richard fitzMitchell.

Nor for 4d. from one tenement sometime situated in the parish of St Botolph without Aldgate, sometime of Walter Basyng, now of the abbot and convent of the monastery of St Mary Graces by the Tower of London.

Nor for 12d. from one tenement in Horton in Surrey, sometime in the tenure of John Kynge.

Nor for 2s. from one piece of meadow lying in the parish of West Ham by Stratford atte Bow, in the meadow called *Russh Hope*, sometime of John Bruggewright.

Nor for 3d. from one tenement situated in Sawbridgeworth in Essex, which sometimes was of Adam de Sabrichworth.

Nor for 4s. 10d., parcel of the sum of 7s. 10d. quit-rent lately received from divers lands and tenements in Lewisham etc.

Because the said parcels of quit-rent have for a long time been detained and unpaid, and the evidences wherewith the said wardens should claim [*postularent*] and collect the said rent are not in their keeping.

[right side:] 10s. 9d.

[centre:] £10 7d.

Total nothing.

310. Passage across/through the Bridge.

But they render [account] for £43 16s. 7d. <with 3s. 4d. for the passage of the carts of the prioress of Halywell> received from divers men for the passage of carts and loaded wains [*carectarum et carr' onerat'*] crossing the Bridge this year, taking for each cart with iron-bound wheels 2s., and for each cart with bare wheels 2d. a time, and for each wain of the beer-brewers [*Berebruers*] and others 6s. 8d. yearly. Item for 18s. 8d. received from divers men for raising the drawbridge for the passage of ships this year, taking for each raising of the drawbridge 2d.

Total £44 15s. 3d.

311. Sales.

Item [they render account] for 33s. 4d. received from William Graunt for the price of an iron-bound cart. Item for 10s. received from the same William for a cart to carry dung and mortar. Item for £10 received from the same William for 6 cart-horses. Item for 10s. received from

121

the same William for the harness [*apparat' pro tractur'*] for the same 6 horses. Item for 13s. 4d. received from the said William for a certain parcel of hay sold to him. Item for 25s. received from [name omitted], the price of 304 loads of lime [*calc' ust'*] sold. Item for 12s. 6d. received from Richard Long for the croppings and boughs of 50 elms sold to him. Item for 9s. 10d. received from [f. 29] John Copyn founder, the price of 59 lb. of old metal from the worn-out and dismantled brass bearings [*les brases perusitat' et decapt'*] of the fulling-mill beyond Stratford. Item for 3s. 4d. received from Robert Cawode for the price of one Caen stone sold to him. Item for 4s. received from John Assh for one old cart bought from the Bridge store. Item for 24s. received from John Copyn for a parcel of old timber and old doors and windows dismantled at the tenement called *the Crown* in Southwark. Item for 10d. received from Thomas Oulegreve, alderman of the city of London, for 8 lb. wrought iron sold to him. Item for 40s. received from John Theyne limeburner for 90 one-bushel sacks and 4 four-bushel sacks to put lime in, sold to him this year. Item for 15s. received from Peter Caldecote for divers parcels of timber, shingles, planks, nails and other stuff [*stuffur'*] from the Bridge store sold to him this year. Item for 16s. 8d. received from William Bouchier clerk of the works of the Bridge for divers parcels of timber, planks and other stock from the Bridge store sold to him this year. Item for 53s. 2½d. received from divers persons for similar stuff sold this year. Total £23 11s. ½d.

312. Casual receipts.
Item for 60s. received from Thomas Pykto, citizen and hatter of London, for the reversion of those 2 tenements of the Bridge situated at the north end of Old Change in the parish of St Michael le Querne [*ad bladum*], now demised by indenture to Thomas Hare, citizen and hatter of London, to have and hold to the same Thomas Pykto for 12 years from the end of Thomas Hare's term. Item for 12d. received for carriage of 1 pipe of iron from London to Croydon with the Bridge cart. Item for 12d. received from Peter Roughhede for a fine because there was a fishery [*qr piscat' fuit*] beside the staddles of the Bridge contrary to the order made. Item for 7s. received from Thomas Clarell for the wages of the carpenter/s of the Bridge hired to install a certain great brass pan [*patellam*] in the hearth [*fornacium*] in his tenement outside Bishopsgate. Item for 22s. received from divers fullers for equipment for fulling work done within the mill of Stratford in the time it stood vacant for lack of tenants. Item for 8d. received for a certain boat hired for 2 days. Item for 3s. 9d. received for stallage of divers craftsmen standing on the Bridge in the time of Southwark fairs. Item for 2s. received from Thomas Levendale of Lee for using a certain small cart of the Bridge for 12 days, taking 2d. per day. Item for 20d. received for using and hiring a carpentry gin. Item for 10s. received from the wife of [blank] Ulfe for repairs done in her tenement on the bridge. Item for [f. 29v] 3s. 4d. received from John Humfrey, bowyer, for repairs done in his tenement. Item for 2s. received from [blank] for repairs done in his/her tenement on the bridge. Item for 40s. received

from John Blaunche for the binding and filling-up [*implecionem*] of a certain staddle of his beside the staddle of the prior and convent of St Mary Overey. Item for £16 13s. 4d. received from the prior of St Mary Overey for making a certain staddle of his situated at the east part of the bridge, between a certain staddle of the said Bridge on the west part and the staddle of John Blaunche on the east part. Item for 13s. 4d. received from the wardens of the church of St Magnus for making the moiety of a certain step/stair at the water of Thames in the lane called *Stevyns lane* beside *Malteswharf*. Item for £10 received from the executors of Simon Eyre in part payment of £14 3s. 4d. from the price of 32 tuns of Caen stone and one piece of oak timber, received by him from the Bridge store in 27 Henry VI, king *de facto* and not *de iure* of England [1448–9].
Total £35 1d.

313. Gifts.
Item for £10 received of Katherine, late the wife of William Combes, citizen and alderman of the city of London, of her gift, to make the new stonework of the Bridge and not to be spent otherwise. Item for 6s. 8d. received from [blank], late the wife of John Botiller, fishmonger, given by her to the work of the Bridge.
Total £10 6s. 8d.

314. Offerings.
Item for 26s. 2d. received from the offerings of the faithful to Christ in the chapel of St Thomas the Martyr on the Bridge this year.
Total 26s. 2d.

315. Sum total of receipts and arrears £806 12s. 3¼d.

316. [f. 30] Payment of rent.
Item they account for rent paid to Sir Thomas, archbishop of Canterbury, for a certain yearly quit-rent of 10s. 4d. from divers parcels of land of the Bridge lying in the field outside the bar of St George in Southwark, payable yearly at the terms of Michaelmas and Easter, viz. for the same terms falling this year by acquittance of Thomas Grey, rent-collector of the same lord's manor of Lambeth etc., 10s. 4d.
Item to John duke of Suffolk for a certain yearly quit-rent of 10s. 2d. from the lands and tenements of the Bridge situated in West Greenwich, viz. for one year ending at Michaelmas in the first year of the present king [1461], by one acquittance of John White, rent-collector of his manor there, remaining in the hands of the said wardens, 10s. 2d.
Item to John duke of Norfolk and Edward Nevill, knight, possessors of the lands and tenements, rents and possessions which were of the earl Warenne, for a certain yearly quit-rent of 16d. from the tenement of the Bridge in the parish of St Olave in Southwark called the Bridge House [*the Brughous*], viz. for one year ending at Michaelmas in the said first year, 16d.

Item to John Randolf, citizen and mercer of London, for a certain yearly quit-rent of 20s. from the tenements of the Bridge situated at the shambles of St Nicholas, London, at the terms of Michaelmas and Easter in equal parts, viz. for the same terms falling this year, by 2 acquittances of the said John remaining in the hands of the wardens, 20s.

Item to Thomas Charleston, knight, for a certain yearly quit-rent of £4 from the tenements of the Bridge situated at the Standard in Cheap, in the parish of All Hallows Honey Lane, at the terms of Michaelmas, Christmas, Easter, and the Midsummer in equal parts, for the said terms falling this year by 4 acquittances, £4.

Item to John Penbrooke, chaplain of the chantry of the Holy Trinity in the church of St Nicholas Shambles, for a certain quit-rent of 100s. from the tenement of the Bridge situated at the end of Ivy Lane, at the 4 terms abovesaid, viz. for those terms this year, by 4 acquittances of the said John remaining in the hands of the wardens, 100s.

Item to John Botiller and William Seyntwyn, wardens of the works and ornaments of the church of St Mary le Bow, London, for a certain yearly quit-rent of 5 marks from the tenements of the Bridge situated in the parish of All Hallows Honey Lane, payable at the 4 terms abovesaid, viz. for those terms this year, 66s. 8d.

Item to William Botery, chaplain of the chantry of Ralph Dungon' in the cathedral church of St Paul, London, for a certain yearly quit-rent of 10s. from the tenement of the Bridge, sometime of Geoffrey Fynchyngfeld, in the parish of St Nicholas Shambles, at the terms of Michaelmas and Easter in the first and second years of King Edward, viz. for those terms this year by 2 acquittances, 10s.

Item to Walter Moyle, possessor of the manor of *Brettynghurste* in Surrey, for a certain yearly quit-rent of 3s. 10d. from 10 acres of land of the Bridge, lying in the parish of Camberwell and Peckham, for one whole year ending at Christmas this year, by one acquittance of the same Walter etc., 3s. 10d.

[lower right corner:] £15 2s.

317. [f. 30v] Item to Reginald, prior of the priory of St Bartholomew West Smithfield, for a certain yearly quit-rent of 3s. 4d. from the tenement of the Bridge situated in the parish of St Dionis Backchurch London, viz. for one year ending at Easter this year, 3s. 4d.

Item to Thomas Buston, monk, chamberlain of the monastery of St Peter Westminster, for a certain yearly quit-rent of 10s. from the tenements of the Bridge situated at the shambles of St Nicholas, payable yearly at the terms of Christmas and Midsummer, viz. for those terms falling this year, by 2 acquittances of the same chamberlain, 10s.

Item to William Lettres, renter of the Chamber of the Guildhall of the city of London, for a certain yearly quit-rent of 12s. from certain common soil behind the shops of the tenements of the said Bridge situtated in the parish of St Nicholas Shambles, viz. for one year ending at Michaelmas this first year, by acquittance of the same William remaining in the hands of the wardens, 12s.

Item to the prior of the priory of St Mary Overey in Southwark, for a certain yearly quit-rent of 3s. 6d. from the tenements of the Bridge situated in the parish of St Leonard Eastcheap London, viz. for one year ending at Easter this year, 3s. 6d.

Item to the prioress of the house of nuns of St Helen within Bishopsgate London, for a certain yearly quit-rent of 13s. 4d. from the tenements of the Bridge situated in the parish of St Michael le Querne [*ad bladum*], London, for one year ending at Midsummer this year, without an acquittance af the same prioress, 13s. 4d.

Item to John Dalle, chaplain of the chantry of William Est founded in the church of St Olave, for a certain yearly quit-rent of 8 marks from the tenement of the Bridge situated in the parish of St Dionis Backchurch, London, payable yearly at the terms of Christmas, Easter, Midsummer, and Michaelmas, viz. for those terms falling within the time of this account, 106s. 8d.

Item to Thomas, abbot of the monastery of St Mary Graces by the Tower of London, for a certain yearly quit-rent of 40s. from the tenements of the Bridge lately of John Sely, skinner, situated at the shambles in the parish of St Nicholas, London, viz. for 3 years ending at Michaelmas in the said first year of the present king, by acquittance of the same abbot, £6.

Item to Richard Alley, citizen and skinner of London, for a certain yearly quit-rent of 12d. from the tenements of the Bridge situated in the parish of All Hallows Barking London, viz. for one year ending at Midsummer this year, 12d.

(Item to [blank], rent-collector of the dean and chapter of the church of St Paul London, for a certain yearly quit-rent of 19s. from the tenement of the Bridge situated in the parish of St Mary Magdalen in the Old Fishmarket, London, payable yearly at the terms of Michaelmas, Christmas, Easter, and Midsummer, viz. for those terms falling this year, by acquittance of the same rent-collector remaining in the hands of the wardens, [blank]) [left margin:] <because afterwards>

Item to the master of the house of St Thomas of Acre, London, for a yearly quit-rent of 3s. a year for a certain way called *the Walle* leading to the Bridge's mill situated in the parish of West Ham by Stratford, viz. for one year ending at Michaelmas in the said first year of the present king, by acquittance of the same master, 3s.

[right margin:] £13 12s. 10d.

318. [f. 31] Item to the prior of the house of Jesus of Bethlehem of Sheen, for a quit-rent of 8d. from the tenements of the Bridge in Lewisham, sometime of Hugh Preston, viz. for one year ending at Michaelmas in the said first year, 8d.

Item to the dean and chapter of the cathedral church of St Paul, London, for a certain yearly quit-rent of 19s. from the tenement of the Bridge situated in the parish of St Mary Magdalen in the Old Fishmarket, London, viz. for one year and one quarter ending at Michaelmas in the second year of the king, as appears by 2 acquittances thereof etc., 23s. 9d.

Nothing is here allowed for 32s. for a yearly quit-rent from the mill belonging to the Bridge, situated in the parish of West Ham by Stratford atte Bow, with the meadow belonging thereto, payable to the abbot and convent of Stratford Langthorn; nor for 18s. due yearly to the prior and convent of the house of Jesus of Bethlehem of Sheen, and to the heirs of John Bakewell, kt., from the lands and tenements belonging to the Bridge in Lewisham; because it is paid by the farmer/s of the said mill and meadow and manor in Lewisham called the Bridge House [*the Brughous*], by indenture/s of taking the farms of the same, etc.
Total £29 19s. 7d.

319. Decrease of rent.

Item in the decrease of rent of one tenement situated at the western end of the Bridge, charged in the rental of proper rent at 40s., and now demised to John Brangthwayte for 33s. 4d., viz. for the term of Midsummer within the time of this account, 20d. Total 20d.

320. Vacancies of tenements.

Item in vacancies of lands and tenements of proper rent, vacant this year and bringing no profit, for lack of tenants and letting of the same, as appears particularly by the parcels made thereof, £53 4s. 3d. Item in vacancies of lands and tenements of foreign rent, vacant this year for lack of tenants, as appears particularly by the parcels made thereof and noted in the present account, £9 18s. 4d. Total £63 2s. 7d.

321. [f. 31v] Allowance of rent.

Item in allowance of rent of one tenement situated on the Bridge beside the closable gate [*iuxta portam claudend'*], charged in the rental of proper rent at 26s. 8d., because it is let to the gatekeeper of that gate without any rent on account of his office this year, as is allowed him in the preceding account, viz. for this year 26s. 8d. Item for another tenement situated on the Bridge, charged in the same rental at 8s., because it is granted to Thomas Ebmede, warden of the passage of carts and wains crossing the Bridge, without any rent on account of his office, for storing the distresses taken by him in his office, viz. for this year as allowed in the preceding account, 8s. Item for another tenement situated in the parish of St Dionis Backchurch London, charged in the rental at 5s. 4d. a year, and for another tenement situated in Carter Lane, charged in the rental at 2s. a year, because they are retained in the hands of the wardens for storing the stock of the said Bridge [*pro stauro eiusdem pontis imponend'*], viz. for this year as allowed in preceding years, 7s. 4d. Total 42s.

322. Purchase of stone.

Item in cash paid to John Ropkyn for 47 loads of stones called Reigate stone [*Reygateston*], at 20d. the load at the quarry of *Maistham* [?Merstham, co. Surrey], 78s. 4d. Item to John Lewyn for carriage of the said 47 loads of stones from the said quarry to the Bridge House in Southwark, taking 3s. for each load, £7 12d. Item to Thomas Golay of co. Kent for 15 tontight [*doliat'*] and 1 pipe of stone called ragstone [*Raggeston*], at 4d. the tontight, 5s. 2d. Item to John Norman for 10d. freight of each tontight thence from Maidstone to the Bridge House, 12s. 6d. Item to John Bernard for 15 tontight of similar stones, at 14d. the tontight at the Bridge House aforesaid 14d., 17s. 6d. And to the same John Bernard for 20 tontight of stones <23s. 4d.> called hassock [*hassok'*] delivered there, at 14d. the tontight, 40s. 10d. Item to the said Thomas Golay for 38 tontight of hassock, at 14d. the tontight at the Bridge House, 41s. 2d. Item for 500 ft. of paving stone bought this year at 9s. the hundred, less 12d. in all, 44s. Item for 13 ft. of edging stone [*Bordour'*] bought and used in the tenement of John Mowsy, tailor, 2s. 6d. Item for 3 ft. of edging stone bought and used in the tenement of William Shepparton under the wall of the Friars Minor, 8d. Item for 1 load of ragstone bought and used in paving in the parish of St Mary at Hill, 3s. Total £18 9s. 2d.

323. [f. 32] Purchase of chalk.
Item in money paid to Thomas Womewell of Northfleet in co. Kent for 14 boatloads of chalk, each boatload containing 20 tuns in weight, bought from him and used in filling-in the staddles and the gulleys [*Goleys*], at 9s. the boatload at the Bridge House, £6 6s. Item to William Granger for 306 sacks of chalk bought from him, at 7s. the hundred, 22s. Item to John Theyn for 21 hundred[weight] of lime [*calcis ust'*] bought from him, at 6s. 8d. the hundred, £7. Item to the same John Theyn for digging and piling up [*municione*] chalk and burning it, for 105 quarters of lime [or 'of chalk burnt'] at the limekiln by Charlton near Greenwich, taking 4½d. for each hundred by the task, 39s. 4½d. spent this year. Total £16 7s. 4½d.

324. Purchase of sand [*arene*].
Item to Joan Broun for 27 loads of sand [*zabuli*] bought from her and used in making mortar for tiling, daubing, and pargeting the walls of the tenement of the Castle in Wood Street, and the bakehouse in Gracechurch Street, and other tenements repaired this year, 10s. Item to Davy Taillour for 6 loads of sand bought from him and used in the Bridge's tenement in the parish of St Botolph without Aldgate, at 5d. the load, 2s. 6d. Item to Henry Walshe for 42 loads of gravel [*grauell*] bought from him and used in paving before the Bridge's tenements in the city of London this year, at 5d. the load, 17s. 6d. Item for 2 loads of gravel, nil. Item for 2 loads of sand, used in paving at the tenement of the Crown in Southwark, 12d. Item to the said Davy Taillour for 6 loads of gravel used in paving the tenements at the Shambles and St Mary at Hill, 2s. Total 33s.

325. Purchase of timber.
Item to Richard Lyon for 100 loads of quarter-cut oak timber bought from him and delivered within the Bridge House in Southwark, at 6s.

8d. the load, £33 6s. 8d. Item to the same Richard for 4 loads of similar timber at 5s. the load at Croydon, 20s. Item to John Kynge for 40 loads of oak timber, at 5s. the load at Croydon, £10. Item to John Willynghurst for 3 loads of oak timber, 20s. 8d., and for 1½ hundred of ship planks [*shipborde*] bought from him in gross, 53s. 4d. Item to William Drayton of Tottenham for 20 loads of quarter-cut oak timber bought from him and delivered within the Bridge House, at 6s. 8d. the load, £6 20d. Item to Henry Carpenter of Dorking for 23 loads and to Richard Lambale for 28 loads of quarter-cut oak timber, at 6s. the load delivered within the Bridge House, £15 6s. Item to Thomas Cappes for 4 loads of timber, at [f. 32v] 5s. the load, 20s. Item to William Carter of Croydon for 2 loads of oak timber called principal pieces bought from him, price at Croydon 13s. 4d. Item to Richard Belamy for 8 loads of oak timber bought from him, price 4s. 8d. the load, 37s. 4d. Item to Thomas Leman for 90 elms bought from him at Beddington, without branches, 40s. Item to John Barton for 52 elms bought from him at [blank], 16s. 8d. Item to [blank] Hamond for 2 ash trees bought from him at Chelsham, 5s. Item to Simon Terry for 7 curved oaks bought from him at Westwood in the parish of Lewisham, to make mill-wheels, 9s. Item to him for 4 loads of curved timber bought there to make *wranges* for boat/s, 6s. 8d. Item used of the said timber in new building the tenement of the Crown and parcel of the tenement of the Castle, and in raising up [*sursumposicione*] one tenement at the Shambles of St Nicholas in the tenure of Thomas Johnson, butcher, and in repairing and amending divers other tenements and mills at Stratford and Lewisham repaired this year, [blank] loads.
Total £75 16s. 8d.

326. Purchase of planks.
Item to Nicholas Herman of Crawley for 4 thousand 5½ hundred and 8 ft. of quarterboard, at 2s. 2d. the hundred, £4 18s. 8d. Item paid for half a hundred of ship planks bought and used in making a new boat and repairing and amending the boat called the chalkboat, 16s. 8d. Item to John Midelton, alderman, for half a hundred of wainscot bought from him, 23s. 4d. Item to Henry Carpenter of Dorking for 450 ft. and to Walter Offold for 1800 ft. of plankboard [*plancheborde*], at 2s. the hundred at the Bridge House Wharf, bought from them as well for making doors and windows and for garnishing and flowering the tenements of the Crown and the Castle and divers other tenements of the Bridge this year, 45s. Item to Richard Lyon for 6 loads of heartlaths bought from him this year and used in new tiling the aforesaid tenements and daubing the walls of the said houses and other tenements of the Bridge repaired this year, at 13s. 4d. the load, £4. Item to the said Nicholas Herman for 2,180 ft. of quarterboard and plankboard [at] 22d. the hundred, 39s. 10d. Item to him for 100 eaves-laths, 8s. Item to Thomas Leycetre for 2,600 heartlaths, price 5¼d. the hundred, 11s. 6d.
Total £16 3s.

327. Purchase of tiles.

Item to John Morgan for 12,000 flat tiles, price 4s. 8d. the thousand delivered within the Bridge House, 56s. Item to him for 4,000 similar tiles at 5s. the thousand, 20s. Item to John Morley for 4,000 flat tiles used in repairing the tenements at Deptford, at 4s. 4d. the thousand at Deptford, 17s. 4d. Item to the said John Morgan for 203 quarters of roof tiles, 13s. 6d. Item to John Goldesborow of Shingleford [f. 33] for 20,000 flat tiles, at 4s. 4d. the thousand delivered within the Bridge House, £4 6s. 8d. Item to him for [blank] roof tiles bought from him, nil. Bought from them and used as well in new tiling the aforesaid tenements of the Crown and the Castle in Wood Street as in tiling divers other tenements of the Bridge repaired this year. Item to [blank] late wife of Thomas Preston, tiler, for roof tiles bought from her and used in the aforesaid works, 3s. 6d. Item to John Caundon for 5,500 bricks bought from him and used as well in making the chimney [*camin'*] new built this year within the Bridge House as in underpinning the plates in the tenement of the Crown, at 4s. the thousand, 22s. Total £10 19s.

328. Purchase of lead.
Item to William Taillour, alderman of the city of London, for 1 fother of lead bought from him this year, £4. Item to William Luke for 4 fother 34 lb. of sheet lead [*plumbi fus' in Webbes*] bought from him this year, price £4 the fother, £16 16d. Nothing charged for 3 fother 11 hundred 3 qr. 122 lb. lead removed from divers tenements of the Bridge this year, as it is of the Bridge store. Total 8 fother 12 hundred 1 qr. Of which 825 lb. used in the tenement/s in Southwark, in gutters and cisterns and pipes; item 7 hundred 3 qr. 23 lb. used in the tenement/s on the bridge; item 5½ hundred 5 lb. used in the tenement/s in Deptford in gutters; item half a hundred and 25 lb. used in the tenement/s in Gracechurch Street; item 10½ lb. used in the tenement/s in Cheap; item 27 lb. used in the tenement/s in Paternoster Row; item 9½ hundred 3 lb. used in the tenement/s at the Shambles; item 1,723 lb. used in the tenement in Wood Street called the Castle. Item to John Stannard, plumber, for casting, working, and squaring [*cubacione*] 4 thousand 9½ hundred 3½ lb. worked in pipes, cisterns, and gutters, taking 14d. the hundred, 57s. 9d. Item to him for 162 lb. solder used in the same works there, at 4d. the hundred, 54s. Item in money paid for carriage of the same lead from the plumber's house to the said places at divers times this year, 10s. 8d. Item in lead delivered to the masons, used in joining stones with cramps [*Crampetts*] in the foundation of the new stone work on the south part/side of the same arch/ of the same/ this year, 1 thousand 4½ hundred lb. Item in lead delivered to John Stannard of lead owed to him in parcel delivered to him last year, half a hundred 25½ lb. Item there remains in the hands of the said John, of the Bridge's store, 5½ hundred 21 lb. lead.
[left margin:] <Remains 5½ hundred 21 lb. lead>
Total £26 3s. 9d.

329. [f. 33v] Purchase of ironwork.

Item to Laurence Lane, smith, for divers parcels of iron worked in hooks, hinges, latches, catches, cramps, pileshoes, and other stuff delivered to the use of the Bridge this year, worked in the forge within the Bridge House, weighing in all 3 thousand 5 hundred 1 qr. 16 lb., at 11s. 8d. the hundred <by the great hundred>, £20 12s. 11d. Item to him for 6 iron bands for binding the timber appertaining to the Rams, 17d. Item for 4 bands for the wheel of the mill at Stratford, 12d. Item for 4 bands round the sign of the Saracen's Head in Eastcheap, 8d. Item for 100 nails, 6s. Item for 300 nails, 3s. Item for 250 nails, 20d. Item for 800 nails, 2s. 8d. Item for 4 hundred 1 qr. of clench and roves [*rof*] for the boat/s, 7s. 10d. Item for 2,000 pile-shoe nails, 13s. 4d. Item for 300 scaffold-nails, 8s. Item to him for 100 spike nails [*spykengs*], 2s. 8d. Item to him for binding one bucket with iron, 4d.

[left margin:] £22 13s.

Item to William Underwode, smith, for 91 spike nails and divers other ironworks delivered by him to the use of the Bridge as appears by bills of the parcels thereof shown on this account, £7 1d., whereof for mending 1 great bar of iron at the furnace [*furnus*] of the tenement in Gracechurch Street, 8d.; and for 4 locks with keys and staples for the same tenement, 2s. 4d.; and for making 1 spindle at the grindstone within the Bridge House, weighing 21 lb. from the Bridge's store, 21d.; for nails for the dogstones of the fulling-mill of Stratford, 16d.; and for gudgeons for the poles of the said mill, weighing 30½ lb., at 3d. the lb., 7s. 7½d.; and for 4 iron plates [*hurteis*] for the same mill, weighing 12½ lb., at 2d. the lb., 2s. 1d.; and for mending 4 bolts at the said mill, 5d. Item for keys for the same, 4d.; and for 2 hooks and 2 gudgeons for 1 folding-gate weighing 7 lb., 14d.; and in divers locks, keys, bolts, clasps, staples, latches, catches, and other ironwork placed in the tenement of John Frecok on the bridge, as appears by the parcels made thereof, 3s. 2d.; and for binding 1 small chest remaining in the countinghouse, 3s.; and for wrought ironwork for binding the wheels of the masons' cart, together with 4 bands and 2 linch-pins weighing 45 lb., at 2d. the lb., 7s. 2d.; and [left margin: <remains 1 saw>] for making 1 saw for the masons to saw stones, 6d.; and [left margin: <remains 1 pick>] for 1 pick [*pycoys*] delivered to the masons, which remains in the Bridge store, 8d.; and for 1 hoop weighing 4½ lb., and for the iron pump [*pompe iron*] for raising water, weighing 26 lb., at 2d. the lb., 6s.; and for 4 crooks [*crombes*] for the same, 2d.; and for 1 winding-hook [*wyndynghooke*] for the gin, 16d.; and for the bands round the sign of the Crown, 12d.; and for ironwork [of] 2 windows in the tenement of the Crown, weighing 31 lb., and for ironwork of 2 windows within the said tenement, weighing 33½ lb., at 2d. the lb., 10s. 9d.; and for ironwork of 2 windows in the tenement of the Castle in Wood Street, weighing half a hundred, at 2d. the lb., 9s. 4d. Item in money paid to the said William for sharpening the masons' tools this year [f. 34] as appears by tallies made between him and the masons, taking 11d. for each, 46s. 8d. Item to him for 600 nails, 17s. 6d., and roves [*rof*] delivered for repair of boats, weighing 105 lb., nil because in the said total. Item to Thomas Bernard, smith, for divers parcels of locks and keys, mending locks and keys, and hasps, staples, latches, catches, and other ironwork delivered by him to the work of the Bridge as appears by the parcels made thereof and shown and examined on this account, 14s. 11d. Item to John Estgarston for 5,000 nails at 2d. the hundred and 16d. the thousand, 6s. 8d. Item to him for 10,500 nails at 3d. the hundred and 2s. the thousand, 21s. Item to him for 9,500 nails at 4d. the hundred and 2s. 8d. the thousand, 25s. 4d. Item to him for 11,000 nails at 5d. the hundred and 3s. 4d. the thousand, 36s. 8d. Item to him for 7,000 nails at 6d. the hundred and 4s. the thousand, 28s. Item to him for 5,000 nails at 10d. the hundred and 6s. 8d. the thousand, 33s. 4d. Item to him for 3½ hundred leadnails [*lednail*] at 4d. the hundred, 14d. Item to him for half a hundred leadnails, 3d. Item to him for 2½ thousand sprig nails at 7d. the thousand, 17½d. Item to Richard Lyon for 3 bags of sprig nails at 10s. the bag, 30s. Item to Henry Draper for 1 bag of sprig nails and to Henry Penhertgart for 1 bag of sprig nails, at 10s. each, 20s. Item for 1 new lock, 8d., and for mending another lock placed in the fulling-mill of Stratford, 13d. Item to John Crechard, smith, for divers new locks and keys and mending old locks and keys and for hasps, staples, latches, catches, and other ironwork delivered by him, by the order and supervision of William Grevy, rent-collector, as appears by bill made thereof, 16s. 11d. Item to Richard Lyon for 2 seams of roof-nails bought from him to the use of the Bridge, 13s. 4d. [£44 12s. 10½d. left margin] Total £44 12s. 10½d.

330. Necessary purchases.

Item to the bailiff of Bermondsey Abbey for 14 hundred tusserds [*tussard*] bought from him and used in burning chalk at the limekiln near Charlton, at 3s. the hundred, 42s. Item for 1 wicker bushel bought for measuring chalk, 6½d. Item to John Stevyn, salter, for 32 ells, and William Blakeman for 58 ells of sackcloth bought to make sacks to put lime in, at 4¾d. the ell, 35s. 6d. Item for packthread bought and used in making the said sacks, 4d. Item for 1 piece of line bought and used in binding the said sacks, 4d. Item paid for making the said sacks, 4s. 2d. Item for 4 wooden hooks bought for the carriage of chalk, 4d. Item to John Copyn, founder, for 1 brass weighing 46 lb. bought from him and put in the fulling-mill at Stratford, at 3d. the lb., 11s. 6d. Item to the said John [for] 3 new brasses put in the same mill, weighing 105 lb., at 2¾d. the lb., 22s. 11d. [f. 34v] Item for 3 short candlesticks bought and remaining in the counting-house, 13d. Item to William Love for 1½ hundred lb. of rosin, 4s. 6d. Item to the same William for 1 thousand 1 quarter of a hundred and 2 lb. of rosin, at 2s. 4d. the hundred, 24s. Item to John Coldham for 648 lb. rosin, at 2d. the hundred, 10s. 8d., bought from them and used in making cement for fixing the foundation of the new stone work at the south end of the bridge this year. Item to Richard Flemyng for 6 barrels of pitch, at 5s. 4d. the barrel, 32s. Item to Henry Nevill for 2 barrels of pitch, 9s. 4d. Item to William Corbet for 1 barrel of pitch, 5s.; bought from them and used in making the aforesaid cement. Item to Thomas Piert, carpenter, for 1 load of hurdles bought from him to make scaffolds for the masons and tidemen, 6s. 8d. Item for 3½ yards of green cloth bought to cover the counter in the Bridge's counting-house, at 2s. 10d. the yard, 9s. 11d. Item for chalkline bought for the carpenters, 1d. Item to Thomas Briteyn for 6¼ hundred 10 lb. of rope, at 9s. the hundred, 54s. Item to him for 110 lb. rope, at 10s. 6d. the hundred, 11s. 4d. Item to him for 1 cable weighing half a hundred 22 lb., at 10s. 4d., 7s. 2½d. Item to him for 2 cables weighing 1 hundred 3 qr. 17 lb., at 10s. 6d. the hundred, 19s. 6d. Item to the same Thomas for 1 hawser weighing 1½ hundred, at 10s. 4d., 15s. 6d. Item to John Oune for 1 thousand 4¼ hundred 9 lb. of rope of divers kinds, at 9s. the hundred, £6 9s., bought from them this year for the gins at the Ram. Item paid for 4 horsehides bought and used in making harness for the gins, 9s. 3d. Item for 2 doz. brooms bought for the masons, 2½d. Item for 2 wooden poles bought for the gins of the masons, 3d. Item to William Cooke of West Ham for 1000 reeds [*arundiu'*], 8s. Item for 100 reeds bought, 12d. Item to John Crosse for 1000 reeds by him of William Robert, 7s 4d. this year, used in covering the new stone work and in heating [*in cremacione in caleffaccione*] the stones fixed in the foundation of the said new stone work, within the ebb and flow of the water of Thames. Item paid for 3 gallons of cow's-foot grease (*pinguedinis de ped' bovinis*) bought to grease the gins, 3s. Item for 8½ stone of tallow [*cepo*] bought and used in greasing the said gins, at 6d. the stone, 4s. 3d. Item for 1½ bushels of oyster-shells [*tescarum ostreorum*] bought and used in the masons' works, 3d. Item to Nicholas Walter, tawyer, for 4 prs. thighboots called *Tidebotes* bought from him, and for currying 3 pairs of thighboots from the Bridge's store, 17s. Item to Reginald Latther for 1 stone bought from him and remaining in the Bridge's store, for sharpening the masons' tools, 14d. Item for 2 pulleys [*shevers*] bought for the *waterdraught* in the tenement of John Fordham on the bridge, 4d. [left margin: <remains 1 file and 1 saw>] Item for 1 file for sharpening the *Tide sawes*, bought and remaining, 12d. Item for 1 new saw bought for the tidemen and remaining in the Bridge's store, 3s. 4d. Item for 5 pails and 4 scoops bought, 20d. Item for 1 skein of packthread bought by the keeper of the boats, 7d. Item for 1 shod shovel bought, 4d. Item for 3 shovel trays bought, 6d. Item for 14 ash poles bought for making bead-hooks [*bedehokes*], 12d. Item for 6 dozen 9 lb. candles bought and used this year as well in the counting-house as among the carpenters and labourers in winter-time this year, at 1d. the lb., 6s. 9d. Item for green candles bought and used at the feast of the Nativity of St John the Baptist this year, 3d. And for 1 well-bucket. [f. 35] Item for 1 well-bucket bought and put in the tenement of Alice Purchace, widow, 10d. Item for 1 other bucket bought, 2d. Item to William Turnour for 4 wooden pulleys [*shevers*] bought from him, 4d. Item to John Dencourt for *levers* bought from him, 4d. Item to William Grevy for 6 gallons of grease bought from him for greasing the gins, 6s. Item to John Lynke for 14 bushels of tile-pins bought and used this year, 6s. 8d. Item for 1 roll of parchment bought, containing 5 dozen skins, 33 skins thereof used in making up this account and the other book duplicating the account delivered to the Chamber of the Guildhall of London, and indentures, bills, and other memoranda this year, 8s. 4d. Item for ink bought and used this year in the counting-house, 3½d. [left margin: <there remains 1 ram and 1 marking iron>] Item to Henry Bridde for 1 ram for the gibbet gin bought from him and remaining in the Bridge's store, 46s. 8d. Item for 1 marking iron bought to mark timber, 2s. 6d. Total £29 17s.

331. Necessary expenses.

Item in money paid for bread and ale used in the counting house each Saturday at the time of the payment of the workmen, 2½d., that is ½d. in bread and 2d. in ale, for the whole year 10s. 10d.

Item in the expenses of William Taillour and Thomas Oulegrove aldermen, Nicholas Marshall, John Hampton, Robert Scrayngham and William Corbet, commoners, auditors of the city of London, sitting at the determination of the account of the said Wardens for one year ended at Michaelmas in the 1st year of the said now king [1461], viz. 14 and 16 December, together with the breakfast ordained for the chaplains, clerks, carpenters, masons and other ministers and servants of the Bridge, as accustomed of old at all accountings, 77s. 1d.

Item in the anniversary of John Fekenham, held in the church of St Clement Eastcheap on 10 November this year, 2s. 6d.

Item in the anniversary of Christian Mallyng held in the church of St Mary Woolchurch London, on Sunday before Michaelmas this year, for the lands and tenements left by her to the use of the Bridge situated on the north side of the Stocks, as contained in her testament, 20s.; of which 6s. 8d. is to be spent yearly in wax and in divine services done in honest fashion by note, and in bread, cheese, and drink, to be given publicly or openly in the said church, as well between the paupers and others coming and present; and 3s. 4d. to be distributed on the day of the said anniversary among the poorest paupers dwelling within the parish of the said church, according to the discretion of the rector and wardens of the works and ornaments of the said church; and 3s. 4d. to maintain 2 ceres around the sepulchre of our lord Jesus Christ burning there in honour of Christ and his resurrection for as long as other ceres shall burn there; and 6s. 8d. among poor prisoners in [f. 35v] prison on account only of their poverty, and among the poor, decrepit, blind, lame, and others lying in hospital, and the poor keeping their houses, and in other pious uses of charity this year as appears in the said testament.

Item in the expenses of the wardens and their servants and John Forster, chief carpenter of the Bridge, riding to Croydon, Carshalton, and Norbury to provide timber and elms, together with money paid to hire 3 horses for them, staying 1½ days and 1 night, 8s. 3½d.

Item in the expenses of the said John Forster and for hiring his horse riding to Croydon and Carshalton for the provision of timber on 3 occasions, 3s. 11d.

Item in the expenses of the said Wardens and their servants riding to Carshalton and Beddington to buy elms from Thomas Leman and John Barton, 2s. 3d.

Item in the expenses of the Wardens and John Forster riding to Tottenham to buy timber there from William Drayton, 4s. 6½d.

Item in the expenses of the said Wardens and their servants and John Forster, together with 2s. paid for 3 horses hired for them, riding to Kingston to buy 53 loads of oak timber there, 4s. 2d.

Item in the expenses of John Forster and for hiring a horse for him riding to Kingston to see and mark the said timber, 12d.

Item in expenses of the said Wardens Thomas Brian and Thomas More and their servants riding to Ilford and of others there on 22 June at the sessions of the justices assigned for banks and ditches in co. Essex, on account of the exoneration of the said wardens from making or repairing broken bridges between Stratford atte Bow and Stratford Langthorn, together with 4s. paid for 5 horses hired for the same Thomas Brian and Thomas More and their servants, 13s. 4d.

Item in reward given to them, to Thomas Brian 6s. 8d. and Thomas More 3s. 4d., in the said cause, 10s.

Item to the bailiff of Barking for his goodwill in the same matter, 20d.

Item in the expenses of the said Wardens, John Crosse, and William Bouchier, clerk of the works of the Bridge, at Lewisham to oversee the manor, lands and tenements there on 2 occasions this year, 4s. 1d

Item in their expenses at Stratford there for demising at farm and overseeing the fulling-mill there, 2s. 8d.

Item in the expenses of John Bolour going to Eltham to buy elms there, 4d.

Item in the expenses of Roger Lowde going to Northfleet to carry chalk to the Bridge, 8d.

Item to Richard Long for felling 50 elms bought of Nicholas Carew at Norbury, 4s. 6d.

Item to John Isaac for felling 252 elms bought at Carshalton and Beddington and elsewhere, 21s. 8d.

Item in the expenses of John Forster going to Lewisham and Sippenham to obtain curved timber there, 8d.

Item for making a pit to saw timber at Carshalton, 9d.

Item for steeling and mending two drills [*terebrorum*] of the Bridge store, 10d.

Item to Nicholas Walter, tawyer, for soling [*pedanacionem*] 2 pairs of thighboots of the Bridge store, 2s.

[right margin: £4 12s. 6d., quire mark]

332. [f. 36] Item to him for pitching 6 pairs of thighboots of the Bridge, 2s. 4d.

Item for rushes bought and spread in the counting house against the coming of the auditors this year, 4d.

Item for steeling and mending 5 drills of the Bridge store, 8d.

Item for steeling 4 tide-axes, 8d.

Item for filing 2 new saws for the tidemen, 10d.

Item to Ralph Reynold, painter, for painting the sign of the Saracen in Eastcheap, 13s. 4d.

Item to him for painting the sign of the Crown in the brewing tenement in Southwark, 20s.

Item to John Copyn, founder, for mending a cauldron of brass for heating cement [*cementi*] for the works of the masons, 8s. 8d.

Item for mending the mill spindle of the grain mill by Stratford, 4s.

Item to Roger Yon for emptying 12 tuns of ordure from the latrine in a tenement at the shambles of St Nicholas, at 2s. 8d. the tun, 32s.

Item to him for emptying a certain latrine in a tenement in the parish of St Dionis West' [sic] containing 19 tuns, at 2s. 6d. the tun, 47s. 6d.

Item to him for emptying 3 tuns of ordure from the latrine in the tenment of Thomas Meridale at the shambles of St Nicholas, at 2s. 4d. the tun, 7s.

Item to Simon Jacob watching and supervising the filling of the tuns for 3 nights, 12d.

Item for sharpening 2 files of the Bridge's store, 4d.

Item in money paid for the expenses of the wardens and others at the Castle in Wood Street, 25 February this year, 10d.

Item for mending a stair which suddenly collapsed in John Morley's tenement, 9d.

Item for plaster of Paris bought and used in the tenement of Benedict Wheler at the shambles of St Nicholas, 2d.

Item to Thomas Pope, cooper, for divers hoops and works done by him in the Bridge's vessels [*vas*] this year, as appears by the parcels made thereof, 7s.

Item to Thomas Fermory for writing one pair of indentures for demising the south part of the Stocks called *the fisshmarket*, let to Edmund Newman, Henry Smyth, and William Laurens, citizens and fishmongers of London, and with a certain obligation with conditions for them, 16d.

Item to them [sic] for composing a note and great bill to the mayor and aldermen and the whole Common Council of the city of London concerning the great danger to the Bridge from the force of the ice and frost this year, and the remedy therefor, 20d.

Item to him for notes and bills to the same mayor and aldermen and Common Council touching the vacancies of the Bridge's tenements, and the remedy therefor, 12d.

Item in the expenses of the said Wardens at Deptford being there to oversee the lands and tenements there and the workmen there, 6½d.

Item for mending the pavement in the hall of William Parys on the bridge, 9d.

Item to John Frecock for 35 ells of linen cloth bought from him and expenses in *le hangyng* in the new chamber in the Bridge House, at 4¾d. the ell, 13s. 10½d. Item for making and sewing the same, and fitting tapes [*lyre*] and rings to the same, 2s. Item for tapes, 16d., and rings, 2d., bought for the same, 18d. Item to Ralph Reynold painter for painting the same cloth, by covenant made with him in gross, 20s.

Total £19 8s. 5d.

[right margin:] £9 13s. 2d.

333. [f. 36v] Foreign payments.

[left margin:] Payments of courts.

Item in money paid to the bailiff of the countess of Salisbury of her manor of West Ham for the king's commission directed to the justices of banks and ditches for bridges broken and not repaired in the parish of West Ham aforesaid, 6s. 8d.

Item in money paid to Richard Chokke 6s. 8d. and to William Billyng 6s. 8d. for their labour going to the abbey of Stratford Langthorn for the matter touching 3 acres of land claimed by both the wardens of the Bridge and the Abbot and convent of the same abbey lying in the parish of West Ham aforesaid, 13s. 4d.

Item to William Wilkyns, servant of John Gloucester bailiff of the lord king in the borough of Southwark, for the proclamation made of one stray horse [*ven' de extranur'*] 4 October and remaining in keeping within the Bridge House, 6d. Item to the said William for his labour, 4d. Item to him for reward given to George Bradyngley, constable within the said borough, to William Pesemede, Thomas Stile, and William Grene valuing the said horse at 6s. 8d., 8d.

Item to William Tyler, janitor of the Priory of St Mary Overey, for his labour and attendance in opening the gate of the said priory at nighttime for the carpenter/s and other workmen of the Bridge passing though for the works on the west side of the bridge this year, as allowed in the preceding account, 20d.

Item in expenses making the covenant with William Graunt for the Bridge's carriage by him and in selling the horses and carts of the Bridge to him this year, 4d.

Item in money given to Thomas Brian by mandate of the mayor of London for overseeing of the evidences of the Bridge, and his counsel had in collecting the quit-rents of the Bridge, 6s. 8d.

Item to Thomas Say, coroner of the Marshalsea [*coronatori Maresc'*], for copies of 2 bills of presentments against the said Wardens in the court of the Marshalsea aforesaid, that they and their successors should repair and amend two bridges that were broken and not repaired in the parish of West Ham, as is more fully contained in the said bills, 3s. 4d. Item in the fee of the officer/s of the same court for entering the day to imparl [*interloquendi*], 8d. Item to the said Thomas Brian being there at the the same court on 15 and 22 March this year to annul the said two bills, 13s. 4d. Item to [blank] Baldewyn being there for the said cause on 22 March, 3s. 4d. Item in the fee of the officer/s of the said court for entering the annulment and breaking of the said 2 bills, 6s. Item to Thomas Kyngesmylle, subseneschal [*subs'*] of the same court, for the said cause, 20d. Item to Henry Yngleton, seneschal of the same court, spent for his goodwill in the same matter, 1 gallon of red wine price 10d. Item in the expenses of the said Wardens and Thomas Brian the said 22 March, 6d.

Item in reward given to the mayor's serjeant to summon John Langwith, tailor, to the mayor at the request of the said Wardens to have communication with him for a certain quit-rent of 10s. sometime received from the tenement now of the said John situated in the parish of St Mary Abchurch London, 8d.

Item in expenses over Thomas Cheseman's taking the farm of the limekiln under Blackheath, 8d.

Item in money given to the clerk of the Austin Friars preaching on Monday in Easter week this year at the hospital of St Mary, declaring the bill there touching the Bridge's necessity, 4d.

[right margin:] 61s. 6d.

334. [f. 37] Item to John Aley, one of the clerks of the chamber of Guildhall of the city of London, for writing indentures of the charters and muniments of the Bridge delivered into the court of the said chamber before the mayor and aldermen, and for writing a copy of a certain bill granted by the Common Council of the said city and enrolled concerning the parcel of a vacant foundation [*fundi vacui*] at the shambles of St Nicholas granted to the Bridge for raising [*supposicione*] one tenement of the Bridge situated in the east end of the said Shambles etc., 16d.

Item in money spent between 12 jurors in the Surrey sheriff's tourn held at *Brodegate* on 4 October this year to avoid amercement for ditches within the purview of the said tourn, 8d.

Item in money paid towards the stipend of the soldiers transported to Calais in the month of September this year, for the lands and tenements of the Bridge in Deptford, by assessment of the tenants and residents there, 10d.

Item in expenses over 12 jurors in the Surrey sheriff's tourn on 26 April this year, 16d.

Item in the expenses of 12 jurors in the view of frankpledge at Lewisham at the term of Hokeday this year, to have their goodwill in presentments over the said Wardens, 9½d.

Item in the fee of [blank] Polstede, attorney of the Bridge Wardens in the shire court of Surrey, in a certain plea to be prosecuted against the same wardens by Thomas Fostall of Peckham, 20d.

Item to John Weste, mayor's serjeant, for arresting John Burton at the suit of the said Wardens in a certain plea of trespass, and removing the said plea from the sheriffs' court to the mayor's court, 20d.

Total 69s. 9½d.

[right margin:] 8s. 3½d.

335. Costs of ditching and fencing.

Item to Richard Logan, dyker, for scouring and digging 186 perches of ditch about the close called Four Crofts, taking 3d. for each perch, 46s. 6d. Item to William Marys for scouring 16 perches of the same ditch, taking 3d. for each perch, 4s.

Item to William Carter for 38 loads of thorns, price 16d. the load, 50s. 8d. Item to him for 17 loads of stakes and eddering [*ederyngs*], price 3s. the load, bought from him in making a fence [*cepis*] about the said close, 51s. Item to him for making the said fence containing 174 perches, taking 2d. for each perch, 29s. Total £9 14d. Item for scouring the fosses in the tenement of William Crooke in Lewisham in gross, 20d. Item for 1 load of thorns and rails used in the fence in the tenement of *la Cristofre* in Deptford, 16d. Item for making the said fence, 8d. Item for planks and nails used in the garden of the same tenement, 6½d. Item paid to William Scotte for 2½ loads of thorns used in making fences in the little tenements in Lewisham, price 12d. the load, 2s. 6d.

[f. 37v] [Item] to Thomas Levendale for felling [and] carriage of 3 loads of thorns for making another fence in the little tenements in Lewisham, 15d. Item in making the same fence containing 31 perches, at 1½d. for each perch, 3s. 10½d. Item to Roger Jurdan for scouring 51 perches of ditch about the close called Carpenters Haw, taking 4d. for each perch, 17s. Item to John Dyker for scouring another ditch there containing 27 perches, taking 3d. for each perch, 5s. 6d. Total £10 15s. 6d.

336. Spent in glazing.
Item paid to William Joynour for 4 wooden cases and making windows together with hooks, nails, and leather for the same, 3s. Item for linen cloth for the same, 8d., placed in the tenement of John Brangthwayte at the west end of the bridge. Item to him for 3 wooden cases placed in the said tenement, 10d. Item to Adryan Glasyer for repairing and mending various windows in the tenement of William Grevys, 5s. Item paid for 10 bunches [*bonches*] of white glass, price 5d. the bunch, 4s. 2d. Item for 1 bunch of blood-red glass, 10d., and expenses in glazing the windows of the tenement of *la Horn* in Gracechurch Street. Item to the said Adrian Glasier for working 40 ft. of glass in images and other works there, 18s. Item to him for repairing and mending the glazed windows in the tenement of [blank] Robynson on the west principal part of the bridge, 2s. Item to Laurence Lane, <10s. 6d.> for 8 iron casings [*cases ferr'*] placed in the glazed window/s in the chamber, 10s. 6d. Item to the said Adrian Glasier for glass and working of the same in the window in the chamber within the Bridge House newly glazed this year, by covenant made with him in gross, 20s. Total 65s.

337. [f. 37A (unnumbered)] Spent in the chapel.
Item in bread bought and expenses in celebrating masses in the chapel on the bridge this year, 14½d. Item for 5 gallons 1 quart and 1 pint of wine at 10d. the gallon, 4s. 10d. Item for 1 gallon of the said wine 18d., used in celebrating the said masses this year. Item to William Reynold, waxchandler, for a wax candle weighing 1 lb., 6d. Item to him for exchanging and working 6 lb. of old wax, 6d. Item to John Talbot, waxchandler, for tapers weighing 18 lb. bought from him against the feast of the Purification this year, at 6d. the lb., 9s. Item to him for a Paschal cere weighing 12 lb., taking for the working of the same 1d. per lb., 12d. Item for 3 lb. of the same wax heated and wasted [*cremat' & vastat'*], at 6d. the lb., 18d. Item to him for 2 lb. candles used at Tenebrae in the week before Easter, 12d. Item to him for making 10 ceres weighing 20 lb., burning about the Sepulchre at Easter, taking 1d. for working each lb., 20d. Item for 4 lb. of the same heated and wasted, at 6d. the lb., 2s. Item to Richard Holte, tallowchandler, for

12 gallons of oil burnt in the lamps in the said chapel and in lamps hanging outside the door of the chapel in the vigil of the translation of St Thomas the Martyr this year, at 14d. the gallon, 14s. Item to him for 12 lb. tallow candles bought from him and used at divine obsequies in the same chapel in the winter time this year, at 1d. the lb., 12d. Item for washing the surplices of the said chapel 3 times this year, 3s. Item for washing 4 altarcloths twice this year, at 4d. each time, 12d. Item for washing 3 albs and fitting the paroffs [*lez paraffs*] twice, 6d. Item for washing 2 pairs of towels twice, 2d. Item for cleaning the branches [illegible] candelabra and *holywaterstoup'*, 6d. Item for mending the broken wheel of a bell, 3s. 4d. Item for 1 pail, 2½d., and brooms, 1d., bought for the same chapel. Item in the expenses of the chaplains and clerks of the said chapel after the exequies made or celebrated for the souls of all benefactors of the Bridge in the month of December this year, 5d. Item in their expenses for the lord's supper *pro lanas altarium* in the chapel, 6d. Item in the expenses of the chaplains and clerks serving in the said chapel on the vigil and day of the translation of St Thomas the Martyr this winter, 4s. Item to William Cheyne and John Ledbury, chaplains serving in the said chapel this year, 10 marks each, £13 6s. 8d. Item to Thomas Brigges for half a year, 66s. 8d., to Richard Brayles for 3 quarters of a year, 100s., to William Mathew for 1 quarter of a year, 33s. 4d., chaplains serving in the chapel, at the rate of 10 marks a year each, £10. Item to John Beller for 31 weeks and William Colyns for 11 weeks, at 2s. a week each, £4 4s. Item to William Holford for 44 weeks at 16d. a week, 58s. 8d. Item to him for 8 weeks, to William Richard for 7 weeks, to William Reynold for 2 weeks, and to Robert Ford for 11 weeks, clerks serving in the same chapel, at 20d. a week each, 46s. 8d. Item to John Cooke, servant of the chaplains, for his stipend this year, 20s. Item to John Recock [? *recte* Frecock] for 11 ells of linen cloth bought and used in making 2 tablecloths, 4 towels, and 8 napkins remaining among the utensils of the chaplains, at 6d. the ell, 5s. Total £36 14s. 4d.

338. [f. 37Av] Expenses of the stable.
Item in money paid for 13 quarters of oats at 2s. 6d. per quarter per medium, less in all 2d., 32s 6d. Item to Richard Longe for 20 quarters of oats, at 23d. the quarter, 38s. 4d. Item to him for 10 quarters of oats, at 2s. 4d. per quarter, 23s. 4d. Item to Alice Galon for 2 quarters of oats, 4s. Item for 18 bushels of beans bought, at 9d. the bushel, 13s. 9d., this year bought and used in fodder of 6 carthorses and 2 horses for the Wardens from Michaelmas in the 1st year of the present king to 20 January then next following. Item for 1 cartload of straw bought and used in litter for the said horses, 2s. 4d. Item for *sele* and tallow [*sepo*] bought and used in medicining the horses, 2d. Item for 1 pr. traces weighing 19 lb., 2s. Item for garnishing the same, 2s. Item for 1 horse-collar bought, 20d. Item for candles bought and used in the stable, 2d. Item for whipcord bought, 5d. Item for the said horsehide, 13d. Item for 1 cartsaddle bought, 4d. Item to Robert Trotte for 1 carthorse bought from him, 30s. Item to Thomas Colyns,

farrier [*ferrour'*], for farriery of the said horses from Michaelmas to Christmas, 10s. Item to him for 30 horseshoes [*ferris equinis*] fitted to the said horses outside the said term, price 2d. each, 5s. Item for 18 removals [*remoc'*], 9d. Item to Thomas Colyns for medicines given to sick horses, 3s. 4d. Item in expenses made in letting the horses' blood on St Stephen's day, 4d. Item for 1 horse-comb [*pectine equino*] bought, 2d. [right edge:] £8 11s. 8d.

Item to Thomas Sewet, carter, for his wages for 16 weeks, taking 2s. 4d. a week, 37s. 4d. Item to him for 3 days, 12d. Item to Roger Lowde working with him for 86 days, taking 5d. a day, 35s. 10d. Item to 1 man working with him and loading the cart, 2d. Item in expenses of the said Thomas and Roger going to Croydon, Carshalton, and other places to seek timber on 61 occasions, taking 2d. each time, 10s. 2d.

[left margin:] <there remains 1 *bura*>

Item in money paid to William Boundy, wheeler, for 1 new cart bound with iron, bought and intended for carrying lime from the limekiln to the water of Thames, viz. for 1 pr. of bare wheels, 6s. 8d. Item for 1 axle-tree for the same, 12d. Item for 1 cartbody, 5s. Item for clouts, pins, and linch-pins weighing 13 lb., price 2½d. the lb., 19½d. Item for working iron for the strakes from the Bridge store, 20d. Item for fitting them on the wheels, 12d. Item for stubnails for the same, weighing a quarter of a hundred and 5 lb., at 1¼d. the lb., 3s. 7½d. Total 20s. 7d. Item to him for 1 axletree for another cart, 12d. Item for mending 1 linch-pin and 1 stave, 2d. [right edge:] 106s. 3d.

Item in money paid for 7½ quarters of oats, at 2s. 6d. the quarter per medium, less in all 2d., bought and used in fodder for two [horses of the] Wardens from 6 March this year to Michaelmas the said 2nd year of the present king, 18s. 8d. Item in horse bread bought and used for the said 2 horses, 6d. Item for 4 bushels bran bought for mixing with the oats for the same horses, 8d. Item for green grass bought and used for the said 2 months of June and July this year, 8s. 1d. Item for 5 cartloads of hay bought for the same 2 horses, at 6s. 8d. the load within the Bridge House, 33s. 4d. [right margin:] 60s. 14d.

[f. 38] Item to Laurence Lane, smith, for 30 new horseshoes fitted to the said 2 horses within the time aforesaid., at 2d. each, 5s. Item to him for 12 removals [*remocionibus*] of the said shoes, taking ½d. each time., 6d.

Total £17 4s. 7d.

339. Carriage.
Item to William Graunt for carriage of 24 loads of timber from Croydon to the Bridge House, at 20d. the load, 40s. Item to him for carriage of 107 loads of elms from Carshalton and Beddington, at 18d. the load, £8 6d. Item to him for carriage of 43 loads of elms from Norbury, at 16d. the load, 57s. 4d. Item to him for carriage of 4 loads to the mill of Lewisham, at 10d. the load, 3s. 4d. Item to him for carriage of 2 loads to Deptford, at 8d. the load, 16d. Item to him for carriage of 4 loads of ash trees from Chelsham in co. Kent, at 3s. 4d. the load, 13s. 4d. Item to him for carriage of 115 loads from the Bridge House into the

city of London, at 4d. the load, 38s. 4d. Item to him for carriage of 36 loads from the Bridge House to the bridge and in Southwark near the Bridge House, at 2d. the load, 6s. Item to him for carriage of 3 tuns of chalk from Bow Bridge by Stratford to the grain mill, 2s. Item for carriage of 1 load of straw from Tower Hill, 8d. Item for carriage of 5 loads of gravel from *Hasardesmersh* to the bridge, at 7d. the load, 2s. 11d. Item to Thomas Alford for carriage of 2 loads of elms from Norbury to the Bridge House, 2s. Item to him for carriage of 1 load of elms from Croydon to the Bridge House, 18d. Item to Thomas Batte of Lewisham for carriage of 9 loads of curved timber from the Westwood in Lewisham to Deptford Strand, taking 12d. for each load, 9s. Item to William Garlond for carriage of 52 loads of elms from Carshalton to the Bridge House, taking 18d. for each load, 78s. Item to the same William and Robert Stilgo for carriage of 52 loads of elms from Carshalton to the Bridge House in Southwark, at 18d. the load, 78s. Item for carriage of 17 loads to Stratford, at 8d. the load, 11s. 4d. Item to Patrick Kele for carriage of 15 loads of rubbish from the tenement of the Castle in Wood street, at 3d. the load, 3s. 9d. Item for carriage of 2 loads of mortar from the Bridge House to the said tenements, 8d. Item for the carriage of 2 loads of stones and sand from the Bridge House to the tenements at the Shambles of St Nicholas, 6d. Item for carriage of 1 load of lead from the Castle to the Bridge House, 4d. Item for 1 cart hired for 3 days carrying rubbish and dung [*fimum*] from the tenement of the Crown, at 2s. a day, 6s. Item for carriage of 4 fother 34 lb. lead from Fleet Street to the Bridge House, 15d. Item paid to William Grevy for carriage of 24 loads of dust and rubbish from divers tenements this year as appears by the bill of parcels made thereof, at 3d. the load, 6s. Item to John Caunton for carriage of 10 loads of brick from the Brickkilns [*Brekelylles*] outside Aldgate to the Bridge House, at 6d. the load, 5s.
Sum of carrying £26 9s. 1d.
Total £43 13s. 8d.

340. Masons' wages.
Item in money paid to Thomas Jurdan, chief mason of the Bridge, for his wages for 11 weeks at 4s. a week, 44s. Item to him for his wages for 41 weeks at 3s. 4d. a week, £6 16s. 8d. Item to him for Thomas Daniell his apprentice for 52 weeks at 2s. 6d. a week, £6 10s. Item to Richard Combe for 67 days, Richard Blanford for 18 days, Thomas Gunne for 56 days, Peter Burbage for 60 days, Reginald Latther for 55 days, John Beket for 64 days, and Thomas Hale for 47 days, among them 367 days, at 7½d. a day each, £11 9s. 4½d. Item to them Richard Combe for 204 days, Richard Blanford for 30 days, Thomas Gunne for 27 days, Peter Burbage for 270 days, Reginald Latther for 166 [days], John Beket for 171 days, Thomas Hale for 171 days, John Boyll for 80 days, John Newman and Thomas Gardyner for 149 days, John Lilly and John Fithian for 89 days, between them for 1,495 days at 8d. a day each, £49 16s. 8d., working in hewing and fitting new stonework as well in the foundation of the south arch thereof as in fitting new

stone work to the tower there this year. Item to 5 masons working and watching in the said works within [*infra*] the river Thames for 6 tides, and 4 masons for 1 tide, to each of them 2d. for the tide by night, 5s. 8d. Item to Clement Gilbert working in making and repairing divers walls and chimneys [*caminorum*] in the Bridge's tenements this year, together with making the party foundation in the tenement of the Crown in Southwark, for 40 days at 7d. a day, 23s. 4d. Item to 1 mason working in squaring [*quadrando*] paving stone used in the tenement of John Mowsy for 5 days at 7d. a day, 2s. 11d. Item to 1 mason working in the bakehouse in Gracechurch Street for 5 days at 8d. the day, 3s. 4d. [Written over erasure: <Item to another>] mason 20d., working in the tenement of the Castle in Wood Street for 2½ days at 8d. a day, 5s. Item to John Fox working in mending walls in the latrine at the tenement in the parish of St Nicholas Shambles for 13 days at 8d. a day, 8s. 8d. Item to him working in the same work and in making walls in the foundation of the tenement of the Crown for 63 days at 7d. a day, 36s. 9d. Item to Denis Lene for making one chimney in the tenement beside the grain mill beyond Stratford, by the task 10s. Item to him for making 2 chimneys in the tenement of the Castle in Wood Street this year built anew, by the task 16s. 8d. Item to the same Clement Gilbert working in mending chimneys and other works of the Bridge for 22 days at 6d. a day, 11s. Item to 1 mason working in paving of the tenement of William Reynold for 3 days, 2s.
Total £82 18s. 8½d.

341. [f. 37] Carpenters' wages.
Item to John Forster, chief carpenter of the Bridge, for his wages this year, at 4s. a week, £10 8s. Item to him for John Blome his apprentice working with him for 200 days at 5d. a day, £4 3s. 4d. Item to William Fadir for 52 weeks, Thomas Mede for 32 weeks, John Holme for 31 weeks, John Chambre for 19 weeks, at 3s. 6d. a week each, £23 9s., working as well in river works at tides as in hewing, framing, and raising [*sursumposicione*] the tenement of the Crown in Southwark, and one parcel of the tenement in Wood Street this year built anew, and also in other works of the Bridge this year. Item to the said John Chambre for 160 days, Thomas Mede for 12 days, John Holme for 99 days, Roger Payn for 248 days, William Colyn for 148 days, Stephen Betcok for 61 days, John Bolour for 66 days, Thomas Osemond for 61 days, Robert Newnton for 116 days, John Lewis for 34 days, John Styver for 124 days, John Toky for 12 days, William Petir for 20 days, William Barrey for 27 days, William Lye for 57 days, and John Wykes for 51 days working with him in the said works, between them for 1,410 days at 7d. a day each, £40 2s. 6d. Item to the said John Wykes for 154 days, Thomas Osemond for 104 days, Thomas Style for 6 days, William Talbot for 94½ days working in the same works at 6d. a day each, £8 18s. 9d. Item to Thomas Osemond for 85 days and John Bolour for 80 days working at Carshalton, Norbury and Bedington, in hewing [*dolando*] and squaring [*quadrando*] elms there this year, at 6d. a day each, £4 2s. 6d. Item to Richard Fleccher, carpenter, working

in the works of the Bridge for 6 weeks and 2 days at 2s. 8d. a week, 16s. 10d. Item to John Bury, carver, working in the same works for 37 days at 5d. a day, 15s. 5d.
Total £93 16s. 4d.

342. Sawyers' wages.
Item to Richard Belamy, sawyer, for sawing 43 thousand 1½ hundred ft. of timber in quarters, *plankes*, *tabulis* and other necessary works by the supervision and disposition of the chief carpenter, taking 12d. for sawing each hundred foot, £21 11s. 6d.
Total £21 11s. 6d.

343. [f. 39v.] Tilers' wages.
Item to Thomas Roland, tiler, working with his labourer in tiling the tenements of the Bridge this year for 186 days at 13d. a day between them, £10 18d. Item to the same Thomas and his labourer working in the same works for 36 days, at 12d. a day between them, 36s. Item to the same Thomas for 4 loads of sand bought from him and used in the same works, 20d. Item to 1 labourer working with him in the said works for 19 days at 5d. a day, 7s. 11d. Total £12 7s. 1d.

344. Daubers' wages.
Item to Patrick Kele, dauber, working with his labourer in daubing the tenements of the Bridge for 218½ days, at 12½d. a day between them, £11 7s. 6d. Item to him for 1 dauber and 1 labourer working with him in the same works for 9 days at 12d. a day between them, 9s. Item to him for 51 loads of daub at 4d. the load, 17s. Item to him for 34 loads of daub at 5d. the load, 14s. 2d. Item to him for 14 loads of sand at 6d. the load, 7s. Item for 1 cartload of straw, 2s. 4d., bought by him and used in the aforesaid works. Item to 1 labourer working with him in the same works for 3 days, 15d. Item to him for 2 sacks of chalk bought by him and used in the same works, 4d. Item for size [*coole*] 12d. Item for 5½ dozen of moty price 18d. the dozen, bought and used in the tenement of the Saracen's head in East Cheap, 8s. 3d. Item to 1 dauber and his labourer working in daubing the walls of the Bridge's tenements in Deptford for 6 days at 12d. a day between them, 6s. Item for digging and carriage of daub used there, 21d. Item for 2 loads of gravel used there, 8d. Total £14 16s.

345. Paviours' wages.
Item to John Martyn, paviour, for paving 134 toises and to Robert Boltyng for paving 15 toises, in divers places as well within the city of London as in the tenement of the Crown in Southwark, at 8d. the toise, £4 19s. 4d. Total £4 19s. 4d.

346. [f. 40] Costs of the boats.
Item to Alan Fenne, shipwright, working in mending one little boat, by the task 7s. Item to the same Alan working in mending and making one boat called *the Chalkebote* for 29½ days, and to Robert Carpenter for

18 days working with him in the same works, at 8d. a day each, 31s. 8d. Item to John Clement for 22½ days at 7d. a day, 12s. 10d. Item to William Stanley for 23½ days at 6d. a day, 11s. 9d. Item to John Benet for 3 days and Davy Bullok for 15 days, working with him in the aforesaid works, to each 4d. a day, 9s. 4d. Item to the same Alan working in making a new small boat called *a Cokke* for 17 days at 8d. a day, 11s. 4d. Item to John Clement for 10 days at 7d. a day, 5s. 6d. Item to William Stanley for 17 days at 6d. a day, 8s. 6d. Item to Davy Bullok, working with him in the aforesaid works, for 17 days at 4d. a day, 5s. 8d. Item for 10d. [of] oakum [*okome*], 1 sack of lime, 1 pair of doorposts [*Gemolles*] 1d. and 1 piece of line 18d. Total 105s. 1d. Item to John Sutton, keeper of the Bridge boats, for his wages this year at 2s. 6d. a week, £6 10s. Item to him for 1 labourer with him watching and assisting in steering/towing [*adiutant' in conducendo*] boats loaded with timber from the Bridge House to the bridge at night time, for 166 tides at 1d. the tide, 13s. 10d. Item to divers labourers throwing chalk between the Staddles, between them for 72 tides at 1½d. the tide, 8s. 11d. Total £7 12s. 9d.

347. Wages of the labourers.
Item to William Atkyn for 255 days, Alexander Herryson for 142 days, and William Tredgold for 123 days, labouring and attending on the masons in making mortar and in carrying stones, bricks, mortar and other necessaries from divers places to divers places to the hands of the workmen, and also in unloading shouts and boats loaded with chalk and rag and other necessaries for the said works this year, between them for 520 days at 5d. a day each, £10 16s. 8d. Item to the same William Atkyn and Alexander, watching and steering/towing boats loaded with stone and mortar from the Bridge House to the bridge for 39 nights this year, at 2d. a night each, 13s. Item to Simon Jacob for 267 days, Roger Lowde for 181 days, William Bowle for 94 days, William Dawys for 26 days, Thomas Roughhede for 8 days, John Morell for 21 days, John Canyng for 39 days, William Absolon for 43 days, John Fynche for 8 days, Robert Bateman for 20 days, Nicholas Asshwell for 18 [f. 40v.] days, John White for 16 days, and William Haselwoode for 18 days, labouring and attending on the carpenters in bearing and carrying timber, planks, shingles [*scindulas*], quarters and other necessaries from divers places to divers places to the hands of the workmen and in unloading carts and boats loaded with timber, planks, and other necessaries and stock for the works of the Bridge this year, between them 759 days at 5d. the day, £15 16s. 3d. Item to John Weselhede, working in the works aforesaid and attending in keeping the boats of the Bridge, for 77 days at 5d. a day, 32s. 1d. Item to John Isaac, working with the carpenter/s in shaping and squaring elms at Carshalton, Beddington and Norbury this year, for 71 days at 5d. a day, 29s. 7d. Item to John Terry working in felling oaks bought at Lewisham for 2 days, 12d. Item to Julian Arnold for stuffing [? padding, wrapping: *stuffur'*] the vine in the Bridge's garden this year, 12d. Item to James Baas working in the garden within the Bridge House for 32 days this year at 4d. a day, 10s. 8d. Item to Robert

Bateman working in the works of the Bridge for 31 weeks this year at 20d. a week, 51s. 8d. Item to divers labourers working in moving and placing [*locando*] timber within the Bridge House at the disposition of the Warden carpenter at divers times this year, between them for 112 days at 5d. the day, 46s. 8d. Item to 1 labourer working and attending on John Fox, mason, working in divers places in mending latrines and chimneys in tenements within the city of London for 18½ days at 5d. a day, 7s. 8½d. Item to German Redeman working in roofing [*coopertur'*] the lodge [*la logge*] in the tenement at Bevis Marks, for 8 days at 7d. a day, 4s. 8d. Item to his servant working with him for 15 days at 4d. a day, 20d. Item for willow rods bought for binding of the same, 13d. Item to John Canyngs working there for 7 days at 5d. a day, 2s. 11d. Item for carriage and wharfage of reeds [*la Reede*] for covering the said lodge, 3½d. Total £36 16s. 11d.

348. [f. 41] Wages of the labourers at the Ram.
[left margin: <the Ram>] Item to 20 labourers working in drawing the gibbet Ram in piling the staddles beside the bridge for 91 tides at 3d. a tide each, £22 15s. Item to 2 labourers holding the iron hooks [*hamos*] to direct the Ram on the piles for the same tides at 4d. a tide each, 60s. 8d. Item to 8 labourers working in drawing the great iron Ram for 62 tides at 3d. a tide each, £6 4s. Item to 6 labourers working in drawing the other lesser Ram for 24 tides at 3d. a tide each, 36d. Item to 11 labourers working at the other Ram called *Wilkyn* for 47 tides at 3d. a tide each, £6 9s. 3d. Item to 8 labourers working in piling beside the grain mill at Stratford for 3 days this year at 5d. a day each, 10s. Item to 8 labourers working in extending [*producendo*], raising, and dismantling the gins for 24 days at 5d. the day between them, 10s. Item to divers labourers working within the Bridge House in fitting, extending, and removing [*aptando producendo et remouendo*] the piles and other works for 41 days this year at 5d. a day, 17s. 1d. Total £42 2s.

349. Officers' wages.
Item in money allowed to the aforesaid Wardens for their salary on account of their office this year, as is allowed in the preceding account, £10 to each of them, £20. Item to them for their clothing this year as allowed in preceding years, 20s. to each of them, 40s.
(Item to them for overseeing the tenements late of John Hattefeld, that they be well and sufficiently maintained and that a chaplain celebrate for the soul of the said John in the chapel on the Bridge, found and maintained by the testament of the same John, 3s. 4d. to each of them, 6s. 8d.) [left margin: <because disallowed by the auditors>]
Item to William Corun, lawyer [*legis perito*], for his fee this year as is allowed in preceding accounts, 13s. 4d. Item to Thomas More, attorney of the Wardens at the court of Guildhall, London, for his fee this year as in preceding, 6s. 8d. Item to William Bouchier, clerk of the works of the Bridge for his fee, on account of his office aforesaid this year, as allowed in the preceding account, £6 13s. 4d. Item to William Grevy,

collector of the proper rents of the Bridge, for his fee this year, £10. Item to John Crosse, collector of the foreign and quit-rents of the Bridge and the farms of the butchers and fishmongers for the Stocks, for his fee this year, 100s. Item to Thomas Ebmede, keeper of the passage of carts and wains crossing the Bridge, for this year for his fee, 66s. 8d. Item to William Crammond, porter and gatekeeper of the Bridge House, as well for his fee on account of his office aforesaid as for keeping and feeding the dogs of the Bridge this year, viz. for his fee 20d. and for the sustenance of the dogs 10d. per week, viz. for 52 weeks this year £6 10s. Total £54 10s.

350. [f. 41v] Allowance of rent of fugitive tenants.
Item in allowance of the rent of a tenement situated in the parish of St Nicholas Shambles, London, called the Ball, late in the tenure of John Cokerham, charged in the rental of proper rents at 46s. 8d. a year, because the same John suddenly quitted the said tenement and had nothing in goods beyond 26s. 6d. valued for the same rent of 20s. 2d. Item of a tenement situated at Bevis Marks late in the tenure of John Heynes, charged in the said rental at 24s., because the tenant of the same tenement suddenly quitted it and left nothing by which he could be distrained beyond 7s. valued, etc., 17s. Total 37s. 2d.

351. Rewards of officers.
Item in money allowed to the same Wardens in reward on account of their diligent attendance given in their aforesaid office, as allowed to them in the preceding account, £10 each, £20. Item to William Bouchier, clerk of the works of the Bridge, in reward allowed to him as well for his good and diligent attendance in his aforesaid office as in making up and duplicating this account, of which one part remains in the counting-house of the Bridge and the other part of the same account is delivered to the Chamber of the Guildhall of the city of London, and as is allowed him in the preceding account, 66s. 8d. Item to William Grevy, collector of the proper rents of the Bridge, £4. Item to John Crosse, collector of the foreign and quit-rents of the Bridge, 20s., for their labour and attendance given in their aforesaid offices, and for drinking spent among the tenants in collecting the rents and in demising tenements as is allowed them in the preceding account. Item in money allowed to John Asshe, serjeant of the mayor of London, for his attendance and labour in summoning and calling together the auditors of this account and for attendance and labour in arresting fugitive tenants, *nil* by the auditors. Item in money allowed and pardoned to Everard Frere, citizen and armourer of London, of the rent of his tenement called the Castle in Wood Street by the mayor and aldermen for divers considerations on account of his diligent attendance and labour given in keeping and defending the City against the rebels in the time of disturbance this year &c., £6 13s. 4d. Total £35.

352. Sum of all allowances and liberations £856 7s. 7d.
Item they owe £90 4s. 8¼d.

[f.42] Of which a term is assigned to John Stamer, late farmer of the fulling-mill of Stratford atte Bow, to pay £8, the residue of a certain sum of £13 6s. 8d. arrears of his farm of the said mill assigned by the mayor and aldermen of the city of London last year, to be paid thereof every quarter 26s. 8d., until the said sum is fully paid, beyond 106s. 8d thereof paid last year.

Item there remains after that assignment £82 4s. 8¼d.

Item Thomas Cook and Thomas Davy, late Wardens of the Bridge, owe in arrears of their account ending at Michaelmas 36 Henry VI, late king *de facto & non de iure* of England [1457], beyond the 40s. received of John Rokesley of the said arrears charged in the Receipt of arrears in this account, £164 12s.

353. Auditors of this account.

Thomas Oulgreve, John Stokker, aldermen. Robert Scrayngham, William Corbet, William Redeknappe, Thomas Danyel, commoners.

354. [f. 42v] Memorandum.

To be charged in the next account of timber and other delivered to repair tenements [small writing, becomes faint at end of line]

[bottom left corner:] The duplicate bill of this account contains 17 written folios.

BRIDGE HOUSE RENTAL 4

Account for 1501–2

355. [f. 221v] Account of William Maryner and Christopher Eliot, wardens of London Bridge, from Michaelmas 17 Henry VII [1501] to Michaelmas then next ensuing [1502], that is to wit for one whole year.[1]

1. This account, like all from 1479/80 onwards is written in English.

356. The same wardens account for £1,088 9¾d. of arrears of William Holte and Edward Grene, the last accountants, as appears by the foot of the same account.
Total £1,088 9¾d.

357. The charge rental of the proper rent of the Bridge livelihood extends by the year to the sum of £562 18s. And the foreign rent £59 11s. 7½d., as appears in the rental thereof made in the beginning of this present book.
Total £622 9s. 7½d.

358. Farm of the fishmongers selling fish at the Stocks on that part called the fishmarket there, let to William Barker for a term of years, at £20 a year. And of butchers selling flesh in that part called the fleshmarket there, paying every week out of Lent 16s. 1d., total £36 19s. 10d.
Total together £56 19s. 10d.

359. Passage of carts and wains [*carres*] passing over the bridge, in the holding of John Hasteler, let to him for this year £23. And as for any profits of ships passing under the drawbridge, there is none charged because it may not be drawn until the stonework of the drawbridge tower be amended.
Total £23.

360. Increase of rents of divers lands, mills, and tenements for many years past, as it is charged in the last account, £47 4s. 6d. And of the rent increased within the time of this account, £10 8s. 1d., as it appears by the parcels thereof in the rental at the beginning of this present book.
Total £57 12s. 7d.

361. Quit-rents £31 12s. 6d., the parcels whereof appear in the rental; the wardens are charged with 12d. of the farm of a little close at Horton beside Ewell in co. Surrey, as in accounts of past years.
Total £31 12s. 6d.

362. Oblations in the chapel to the said Bridge, at the feast of the Translation of St Thomas of Canterbury and at other feasts in the year, and out of divers boxes within the said chapel this year.
Total 15s. 4d.

363. Sales.
From Richard Paynell for 7½ hundred 12 ft. of quarterboard at 2s. the hundred, total 15s. 6d. And from the same Richard for 21 quarters of elm, at 2½d. the quarter, 4s. 4½d. From Robert Maunsy for boards, boxes, and other stuff of the store of the Bridge House, 2s. 6d.
Total 22s. 4½d.

364. Fines from divers persons.
Of Robert Lane for the tenement in which he now dwells, for a licence to enter the same by lease made thereof to Richard Clerke, 40s. Of the same Robert towards new making the stall of the same tenement, 10s. Of Thomas Pope, bowyer, for his stall to be taken down where now Henry Pyckenam dwells, 3s. 4d. And of divers petermen and lightermen misbehaving at the bridge, contrary to divers acts thereof made, 4s.
Total 57s. 4d.

365. [f. 222] Standings on the bridge.
From divers people standing there and in a vacant tenement at the Standard in Cheap at the coming in of the princess,[1] 54s. 3d. And at Our Lady Fair in Southwark, from divers smiths and other artificers selling their wares in the empty spaces on the said bridge this year, 7s. 5d.
Total 61s. 8d.

1. The entry of Katherine of Aragon, 12 November 1501.

366. Total of all their charge with the arrears, £1887 12s. ¾d.

367. Payment of quit-rents.
Allowance made to the Wardens for money paid to the archbishop of Canterbury for a quit-rent of 10s. 4d. a year from tenements in Southwark and from a close called the Lock called Carpenters' Haw for a year ended at Michaelmas 17 Henry VII [1501], 10s. 4d.
To the earl of Derby and Lord Bergavenny for a quit-rent of 16d. a year from the Bridge House in Southwark, with appurtenances, for a year ended at Michaelmas aforesaid, 16d.
To Sir John Sha, kt., for a quit-rent of £4 a year from tenements at the Standard in Cheap, late of Sir William Vampage, kt., for a year ended at Midsummer 15 Henry VII [1500], £4.
To the churchwardens of [St Mary le] Bow, for a quit-rent of 5 marks a year from the same tenements for a year ended at the said Midsummer, 66s. 8d.
To a chantry priest in the church of St Nicholas Shambles, for the soul of Robert Husbond, for a quit-rent of 100s. a year from tenements in the same parish, for a year ended at Midsummer aforesaid, £5.

To a priest of a chantry in St Paul's church for the soul of Ralph Dungeon, for a quit-rent of 10s. a year from tenements in the same parish, for a year ended at the same Michaelmas, 10s.

To the abbot of Tower Hill, for a quit-rent of 40s. a year from tenements in the same parish, for a year ended at Midsummer aforesaid, 40s.

To Master Alwyn of London, alderman, for a quit-rent of 20s. a year from tenements in the same parish for a year ended at Midsummer aforesaid, 20s.

To the chamberlain of Westminster for a quit-rent of 10s. a year from tenements in the same parish for a year ended at the said Midsummer, 10s.

To the Chamberlain of London for a quit-rent of 12s. a year from a common ground behind the shambles for a year ended at the said Michaelmas, 12s.

To the abbot of Kirkstead in co. Lincoln, for a quit-rent of 4s. a year from tenements in the same parish, which were sometime John Lyndesey's, for a year ended at the said Michaelmas, 4s.

368. [f. 222v] To the prioress of St Helen within Bishopsgate of London, for a quit-rent of 13s. 4d. a year from tenements in the parish of St Michael le Querne [*at Corn*], for a year ended at the said Michaelmas, 13s. 4d.

To a priest singing in the church of St Olave Southwark [erasure] for a quit-rent of 8 marks a year from tenements in the parish [words erased] London for a year ended at the said Michaelmas, 106s. 8d.

To the prior of St Bartholomew in Smithfield, for a quit-rent of 3s. 4d. a year from the same tenements, for a year ended at Easter within the period of this account, 3s. 4d.

To the dean and chapter of St Paul's for a quit-rent of 19s. a year from tenements in the parish of St Mary Magdalen in Old Fish Street for a year ended at Michaelmas aforesaid, 19s.

To the abbess of the Minoresses at Tower Hill for a quit-rent of 20s. a year from tenements in *Stevynslane* in the parish of St Magnus, for a year ended at the said Michaelmas, 20s.

To the parson of Woolchurch in London, for a quit-rent of 4 marks a year as tithe for that part of the Stocks called the fish and flesh market, for a year ended at the said Michaelmas, 53s. 4d.

To the prior of St Faith of Horsham in co. Norfolk, for a quit-rent of 3s. a year from tenements in the parish of St Margaret Moses in Friday Street, for a year ended at the said Michaelmas, 3s.

To the possessioner of Saers Court for a quit-rent of 10s. 6d. a year from lands and tenements in Deptford, lately of Sir John SaynJone, kt., for a year ended at Michaelmas aforesaid, 10s. 6d.

To the marquis Dorset for a quit-rent of 3s. a year from certain lands and tenements in Lewisham, for a year ended at the said Michaelmas, 3s.

To the master of St Thomas of Acre for a quit-rent of 3s. a year from a parcel of ground in the parish of West Ham, lying by the mill there, for a year ended at the said Michaelmas, 3s.

To the abbot and convent of Stratford for a quit-rent of 32s. a year from the mill there called *Seynesmyll*, for a year ended at the said Michaelmas, 32s.

To the prior of the Charterhouse at Sheen, for a quit-rent of 14s. 9½d. from a tenement in Lewisham called the Bridge House, and lands belonging to the same place. To the same prior for a quit-rent of 8½d. a year from a tenement that was sometime Hugh Preston's. And for a quit-rent of 6d. a year from a tenement lately Thomas Pynder's in Lewisham, for a year ended at Michaelmas aforesaid, 16s.

To the prior of St Mary Overey in Southwark, for a quit-rent of 3s. 6d. a year from a tenement in Eastcheap called the Saracen's Head, in the parish of St Leonard in London, for a year ended at the said Michaelmas, 3s. 6d.

To the abbot of Bermondsey for a quit-rent of 14s. 10d. a year from lands and pastures lying in the field outside St George's bar in Southwark, for a year ended at Midsummer aforesaid. To the same abbot for quit-rent of 2s. a year from a garden in Horselydown. And for a quit-rent of 4s. 10d. a year from certain tenements in Bermondsey Street, for a year ended at Christmas within the period of this account, 21s. 8d.

To Thomas Muschamp, gentleman, for a quit-rent of 3s. 10d. a year from certain lands lying in the fields of Peckham, for a year ended at Michaelmas aforesaid, 3s. 10d.

Total £33 6s. 6d.

369. An annuity of 4s. granted by Richard Lee, mayor of the city of London, and alderman of the same, to one Thomas Piert, late carpenter, as it appears by the grant and composition thereof made and enrolled in the Guildhall of London, 12 Edward IV [1472–3], so that the said Thomas, who was tenant of the dean and chapter of St Paul's for a tenement in Wood Street adjoining to a tenement belonging to the Bridge there, shall not stop the light from the said Bridge tenement, nor none other tenants in the same wherein John Godfrey dwells, and he received the said annuity this year, 4s.

370. [f. 223] Decay of quit-rents. £9 3s. 8½d. sometime levied and gathered of divers lands and tenements within the city of London and other places, the parcels and sums of which have been fully and particularly noted and declared in many past accounts; and as the same quit-rents for so many years past have been denied and cannot be levied without plea and showing of evidence; and the evidence concerning the said rents is not in the keeping of the said Wardens; therefore as it has been allowed in years past, £9 3s. 8½d.

371. Allowance of rent of a tenement in the parish of St Dionis, charged in the rental at 5s. 4d. a year; and of a tenement in Paternoster Row, charged in the same rental at 20s. a year: because they are reserved for storehouses etc. And there is allowed to Richard Wylford for divers repairs done by him at the order of C. Eliot and E. Finckell, extending

to the sum of £11, whereof was allowed to them in their last account made in 15 Henry VII [1499], £3. And to William Holte and Edward Grene in their acount made in 16 Henry VII [1500], £4. And now here in this account in full payment, £4. To John Hylle, merchant haberdasher, for repairs done by him in the tenement at the Standard in Cheap, in which he now dwells, so determined by Master Woode and Master Hawes, aldermen, 40s. To Robert Bekyngham, grocer, whereas he asked 40s. for lack of due repairs to the tenement which he holds such that he could not bestow his merchandise within the same for the space of 2 years within the time of controlment, [there is allowed] by the discretion of the Wardens now acountants, 13s. 4d. To the said Wardens for quit-rent paid by them after the time the last account was made up, to a chantry priest singing in the cathedral church of St Paul for the soul of Ralph Dongeon, parcel of the said last account as appears in the Journal of this year, 10s.
Total £8 8s. 8d.

372. Decrease of rent.
From a tenement in Old Change, lately held by Richard Kente, 13s. 4d. From a tenement in the parish of St Nicholas Shambles that Thomas Knight holds, 10s. From a tenement where Philip Taillour dwells in the same parish, 6s. 8d. From a tenement that Anne Wales holds in the parish of St Margaret Pattens, 4s. And from a chamber at the east end of the Stocks lately held by John Freman, 16d.
Total 35s. 4d.

373. Vacations of tenements standing void and not occupied for lack of tenants, the parcels of which have been particularly entered and declared at the beginning of this present book.
Total £35 9s. 1d.

374. Buying of stone.
To William Bostone for 20 tons of rag, 21s. To Mistress Bate for 3 tons of rag, 3s. 3d. To Henry Lawson for 30 tons of rag, 30s. 4d. To Thomas Wade for 206 ft. of Bridge ashlar delivered at Maidstone, co. Kent, at 34s. 2d. the hundred, total £3 10s. 3d. To the said Thomas to 557 ft. of hard paving stone delivered at Maidstone aforesaid, at 6s. 8d. the hundred, total 37s. 1d. To the same Thomas for 5 loads of Reigate stone delivered here at the Bridge House, at 5s. the load, total 25s. To the same Thomas for 4½ ft. of border stone, 14d. To William Bostone and Henry Lawson for ship-freight of the said stone from Maidstone to the Bridge House, containing 26½ tons, taking 12d. a ton between them both, total 26s. 6d.
Total £10 14s. 5d.

375. Timber and board.
To Walter Tanworth for 32 hundred 1 qr. 12 ft. of quarterboard, and 4½ hundred 13 ft. of planks [*plauncheborde*], at 20d. the hundred, total 60s. 20d. To the same Walter for 15 hundred of planks and 4½ hundred

15 ft. of quarterboard at 21d. the hundred, total 34s. 4d. To Robert Fenrother for 12 hundred of elm board, at 18d. the hundred, total 18s. To Robert Butler of *Craneley* [?Cranleigh, Surrey] for 9 hundred of quarterboard at 20d. the hundred, total 15s. To the same Robert for a load of *sortelathe*, 9s. For boat hire and wharfage of the said timber and laths, 6d. [f. 223v] To Sir Thomas Wylson, parson of Sheffield [*Sheffeld*; ? Berks.] for 7 loads of oaken timber at 5s. the load, total 35s. To John Veyse for a load of heartlaths, 9s. 8d. To Thomas Barker for 1,034 ft. of planks and quarterboard, at 21d. the hundred, total 18s. 1d. To John Maylasshe for 3 loads of heartlaths, at 10s. 2d. the load, total 30s. 6d. To William Clement for 830 ft. of planks, at 21d. the hundred, total 14s. 6d. To Richard Asshelarks for 2,213 ft. of plankboard and 9 hundred of quarterboard at 20d. the hundred, total 36s. 4d. To the same Richard for 1½ hundred of elm timber, 2s. To Richard Frecomber for 2,214 ft. of quarterboard and planks, at 23d. the hundred, total 42s. 2d. To the archbishop of Canterbury for 20 loads of elm timber delivered here at the Bridge House, £4 4s. To Robert Asshelarks for 2 loads of oaken timber, 10s. To William Ellys of Merstham [*Maistham*] for 9½ hundred of planks at 23d. the hundred, total 22s. To Richard Kynge of Grene in Sussex for 3 loads of heartlaths, at 9s. the load, total 26s. 8d., saved in all 4d. To Richard Grenetre of Waltham for 10 loads and 24 ft. of oaken timber, at 5s. 2d. the load, total 52s. 8d. To John Dandy for 2 hundred of quarters, 20s. To the same John for 12½ hundred of plankboard, at 23d. the hundred, total 24s. To Richard Dandy for 4½ hundred of quarterboard, at 2s. the hundred, total 9s. To the said Richard Dandy for 7¾ hundred of quarterboard, price 23d. the hundred, total 12s. 10d. To Thomas Edesale for 7¼ hundred of planks at 22d. the hundred, total 13s. 3½d. To the same Thomas for a load of heartlaths, 10s. 4d. To Simon Yonge for 7 loads of oak timber at 5s. the load, total 35s. To the same Simon for 18 hundred of great oaken planks, of 2½ inches thick, at 3s. the hundred, total 55s. To the same Simon for 18 hundred of plank- and quarterboard, at 20d. the hundred, total 30s.
Total £36 11s. 6½d.

376. Tiles and bricks.
To Hugh Byrde, ironmonger, for 800 roof tiles, at 2s. 10d. the hundred, total 22s. 8d. To Christopher Eliot and William Maryner for 3¾ hundred of roof tiles, 9s. 4d. To John Bylby for 1,000 flat [*playne*] tiles, 5s. To John Jacson of Oxgate for 35,000 flat tiles at 4s. 8d. the thousand, total £8 3s. 4d. To Master Warner for 20,000 flat tiles at 4s. 8d. the thousand, total £4 13s. 4d. To William Nedewey for 6,000 flat tiles at 4s. 4d. the thousand, total 26s. 4d. To William Warner of Burges Mylle for 4,000 flat tiles at 5s. the thousand, total 20s. To John Launce of Lewisham for 1,000 flat tiles delivered there, 4s. To the said John for a quartern of corner tiles, [and] half a quartern of roof tiles, 12d. To John Kendall's wife for half a hundred and half a quartern of tiles, 20d., delivered at the storehouses within the city and to the Bridge House here in Southwark. To John Brampstede for 17,000 bricks at 4s. 5d. the thousand, total £3 15s. 1d. To the same John for 17½ thousand bricks at 4s. 4d. the

thousand, total £3 15s. 10d. To William Hughet of Lewisham for 5,000 flat tiles delivered to the storehouses there, 22s. To William Warner of Stratford at Bowe for a load of flat tiles, 4s. 8d.
Total £26 13s. 3d.

377. Chalk, lime, sand, gravel, and loam.
To John Grove for 280 tons of chalk, at 6d. the ton delivered at the Bridge House in Southwark, total £7. To Thomas Brat for 38 hundred and 2 loads of lime at 5s. 8d. the hundred, total £10 16s. 2d. To the same Thomas for 17½ hundred and 3 sacks at 5s. 6d. the hundred, total £4 16s. delivered at the storehouses within the city of London, Stratford, Deptford, and at the Bridge House here. To John Welche for 49 bushels of plaster of Paris at 8d. the bushel, total 32s. 8d. To Patrick Fendon and Philip White for 237 loads of sand at 5d. the load, total £4 18s. 9d. To the same Patrick and Philip for 160 loads of loam at 4d. the load, total 53s. 4d. And for 67 loads of gravel at 4d. the load, total 22s. 4d.
Total £32 19s. 3d.

378. [f. 224] Ironwork and nails.
To William Underwood and John Britene, smiths, for pileshoes, crampons, dogs of iron, and other plain iron works, weighing 1,647 lb., at 1½d. the lb., total £10 6s. To them for side garnets and cross garnets and other divers iron works tinned, weighing 354 lb., at 2d. the lb., total 59s. To them for latches, catches, cramps, bolts, staples both square and round for doors and windows, 22s. To them for new locks and keys, and for stocks, joints, pins, and plates, with other necessaries, 30s. 4d. To them for battering and sharpening the masons' irons, and for steeling the same, 17s. 8d. To Peter Smyth of Westminster for 17 locks and keys, 9s. To the same Peter for a stock-lock set upon Joan Gybbyns' door at the Shambles, 10d. And for mending an old bolt on the east door at the Stocks, and a new plate to the same, 12d. To Henry Burbage of Islington for steeling 3 great augers, 3 spiking augers, 2 axes, and 2 adzes, 4s. 10d. To John Bysset for 2 iron ladles, 2s. To William Lacke and John Bodiam for 19,000 twopenny nails at 10d. the thousand, total 15s. 10d. To them for 18 thousand 7½ hundred threepenny nails at 18d. the thousand, total 28s. To them for 13,000 fourpenny nails at 2s. the thousand, 26s. To them for 15¾ thousand fivepenny nails at 2s. 8d. the thousand, total 41s. 10d. To them for 8,000 sixpenny nails at 3s. 4d. the thousand, total 26s. 8d. To them for 2,750 of tenpenny nails, 16s. 7d. To John Rowley and John Welche for 6½ bags of sprig at 9s. 6d. the bag, total £3 21d. To them for roof-nails and clench [nails], 10s. To Master Stafford of the Tower for spikings, clamps, brads, plate locks, bolts, spring locks, rings, latches and handles, £5.
Total £33 19s. 4d.

379. Lead and solder.
To James Longe, plumber, for 54 lb. of new lead, 2s. 8d. To him for casting an old lead [vessel] at the Cope behind the Shambles,

weighing 28 hundred 57 lb., taking 2s. 4d. for the casting, laying and workmanship of every hundred thereof, total £3 6s. 8d. To him for 12 lb. of solder to the same lead at 4d. the lb., total 4s. To him for the wages of the porters of the plumbers taking up the old lead and setting of the new, 6s. 8d. For lead-nails for the same, 6d. Saved in all 6d.

Total £4. To Henry Neele, plumber, for 13½ hundred of new lead at 4s. 4d. the hundred, total 58s. 6d. At the last account no lead remained. And this year 69½ hundred and 10 lb. of old lead was taken down from divers and sundry tenements.

Total of the old and new lead, 72 hundred and 10 lb. Whereof 70 hundred and 10 lb. was used in making pipes, fillets, sockets, gutters, grates, cisterns and other necessaries remaining in the said tenements and others belonging to the Bridge, taking 10d. for casting and laying every hundred of the old lead, total 52s. 2d. To the same Henry for 324 lb. of solder at 4d. the lb., total £5 8s. And so there remains in store 300 lb. of lead.

Total £15 3s. 8d.

380. Costs in glazing.
To Johan Johnson for 100 quarrels of glass, 12d. To the same Johan for a bushel of whole and half quarrels, 8d. To Thomas Turnour, glazier, for 65 ft. of old glass set in new lead, set in the tenements of Master Stede, Richard Paynel, at the Red Lion, at the White Cock, and at William Banckes upon the bridge, at 3d. the ft., total 16s. 3d. And for mending and setting-in of new quarrels in the said tenements and other places, 3s. 9d.

Total 21s. 8d.

381. Necessary purchases.
To Thomas Bulle for 3 new mill brasses for Stratford and Lewisham mills, weighing 88 lb. at 3d. the lb., total 22s. Whereof the said Thomas received 54 lb. of old metal at 2d. the lb., total 9s. And so [paid] in ready money, 13s. To Robert Elynour for 8 earthen pots to put in stone colour, 4d. To Robert Peynter for size [*syse*] at the bridge gate, 17d. To William Rolf for a load of hurdles and porters, 6s. 8d. To the same William for 24 hurdles and half a load of poles and quarters, 6s. To John Welche for ochre and size [*cole*], 9d. To Simon Yonge for half a hundred *pynne* timber, 2s. 2d., [f. 224v] and for 12 quarters, 14d., total 3s. 4d. To Richard Gadde for a last of pitch, 33s. 4d. To John Laurence, cooper, for making a gyle tun and a batch [out] of the old gyle tun, 19 hoops to a woad-vat, hooping a millstone at Lewisham, with other necessaries in divers places this year, 58s. 8d. To John Hunte for a barrel of tar, 3s. 4d. To John Joynour for 2 boxes to put in bulls and evidences belonging to the Bridge, 12d. To John Carter for a load of thorn to Copped Hall, 2s. 6d. And for rails, stakes, and workmanship of the same there, 20d. Total 4s. 2d. To Roger Grove for 4½ hundred 34 lb. of rope at 10s. the hundred, total 46s. 6d. To Henry Edmund for 4 long oars and 2 long sculls ready apparelled, 5s. To Robert Huddeson, turner, for 6 pulleys

[*shyvers*], 6d., 6 shovels, 18d., 6 spades [*skoppetts*], 18d., 6 mortar trays, 2s., with a garden shovel, 2d., total 5s. 8d. To Hugh Crompe for a new bucket, 8d. To Thomas Cawstone for a rope for the rising gin [*the Risyng ghynne*], weighing 34 lb. at 1d. the lb., total 2s. 10d. To Henry Knyght of London for a pump [*plompe*, ? for *pompe*] and for furnishing the same, 3s. 4d. To the porter for rushes 8d., brooms and boughs [*bowes*] 6d., total 14d. To Thomas Donmowe for 2 stone of tow, 12d. To Thomas Gyt, cordwainer, for 6 prs. new boots at 5s. the pair, total 30s. To Walter Ayleworth for 2 haircloth awnings [*tyltes of here*], 4s. 8d. To William Eliot of Lambeth for old ropes, 20d. To Richard Graunte for 15 hundred 9 lb. of rosin, at 22d. the hundred, total 27s. 6d. To John Curlow for 2 loads of hay to stop the gulleys, 8s. 4d. To John Bylby for 39 bushels of tilepins at 5d. the bushel, total 16s. 3d. To Robert Maunsy for 20 perches of paling set at Deptford, at 4s. 6d. the perch, let to him at task finding timber and workmanship, total £4 10s. To William Eliot, shipwright, for the new boat called the carpenters' boat, finding all manner of stuff and workmanship thereto belonging, £12. To John Halmer for a roll of parchment, 13s. 4d., for a ream of fine paper, 2s. 8d., and for a book wherein is written all the remembrance of this account, 10d.
Total £32 3s. 5d.

382. Necessary expenses.
For the obits of John Fekennam, John Clyfford, and Christian Mallyng, as it is contained in their testaments, total 35s. 10d. To the archbishop of Canterbury and to the prior of the Charterhouse at Sheen for suit to their courts in Southwark and Lewisham, total 3s. To John Perpoynte, attorney of the Common Pleas, in suit of Henry Bumstede's obligations, with his fee for this present year, 13s. 11d. To John Bysset, John Saddeler, and William Marchall, for voiding 97 tuns of ordure from divers and sundry tenements this year, at 20d. the tun, total £8 20d. To the same John and John for spreading, searching, and cleansing of 3 other privies, 9s. To Robert Wakeryng and John Crowcheman, attending nightly upon the said voiders, and to number the tuns, 4s. 8d. To William Rodley of Deptford for repairs done there at the sign of the Christopher, let to him at task by the oversight of the Bridge Masters, 6s. 8d. To Thomas Preston, carpenter, for certain repairs done by him on the house he dwells in, let to him in great by the said Bridge Masters, 6s. 8d. To William Snowden for currying and repairing boots belonging to the said Bridge House, 6s. To the same William for taking down the pageant of London Bridge, at task, 10s. And for expenses upon the masons and carpenters the day of the entry of the lady princess, for their watch and diligent attendance given by them to the same, 11s. 3d. To the vicar of Burnham for the tithe of 700 elms felled within the bounds of his parish for 3 years past, total 11s. 2d. To Patrick Annes for cutting and binding the vine in the Bridge garden, 22d. To John Porter for 2 scoops and a spade [*skoppet*], 8d. For divers repasts made unto Sir William Martyn, kt., Master Chawry, and Master Wylford, aldermen, Master Welbeck, Master Nynes, Hawkyns, draper, Ralph A

Lathum, [Richard] Gough, fishmonger, with other divers commoners *avenyng* the Bridge and the Bridge livelihood at sundry times this year as appears more largely in bills thereof, £4 10s. 1½d. [f. 225] And to the said Wardens for their expenses overseeing the Bridge livelihood in the country, at divers times this year, 23s. And in rewards given to workmen and labourers working in the waterworks for giving up their nuncheons and sleep so as to speed the same works this year, at divers times, 10s. 11d. To the same Wardens for keeping their horses, as allowed in past years, 40s. each, total £4. To William Eliot for mending and repairing all the other boats belonging to the Bridge House, as appears more largely by bill, 24s. 8d. And to a servant of John Garard, scrivener, for keeping the Journal here for certain weeks, 13s. 4d.
Total £26 4s. 4½d.

383. Repairs to mills.
To Robert Norys for 2 millstones for the 2 mills at Stratford, one for each mill, £8. To John Burgeys for holing, trimming, and setting to work the said 2 millstones in the said mills, 26s. 8d. To William Warner for carriage and portage of the said 2 stones, 2s. And for carriage of the said 2 stones from Bow Bridge, one stone to each mill, 3s. 4d. To William Warner for 2 hoops and 4 staves, 22d. For money paid to a tiler and his servant for 4 days, 4s. 4d. For 2 loads of sand, 12d. For 100 nails used on the said mills, 2d. And the said William is allowed 5s. for his mill's standing still for 16 days, at the discretion of the Bridge Masters. To Thomas Preston and his servant, working in and on the mill at Lewisham for 8 days at 14d. a day, and to the same Thomas for a pair of spindles, 8d., total 10s. To the same Thomas for making and laying planks in the floodgate there, 5s., and for mending and repairing the cogwheel there, 13s. 4d., let to him at task, total 18s. 4d. To William Hughet, millwright of Lewisham, for 3 pairs of trindles, 10s., 8 loads of sand, 4s., 3 loads of loam, 12d., 2 hooks for an oven mouth, 4d., total 15s. 4d. And the said William is allowed 2s. 8d. for his mill's standing still. To John Maidcalf, miller of the same mill, for repairs done there in his time, 6s. 8d. To John Wever for winding bans [*wyndyng bannes*] of [illegible], 2s. 2d. 100 nails, 4d. To the same, 23 lb. of strips [*stripes*] at 1½d. the lb., 2s. 10½d. 100 nails, 2d. To the same strips for the mill-wheel there. Total 5s. 6½d. To Thomas Palmer of Deptford for necking the mill spindle [*for neckyng of the mylle spyndell*], 3s., and for workmanship of the same for a hoop of iron, weighing 10 lb., 12d. to the same mill binding the water-wheel, for a *rynde* to the same mill, 4d., and for mending the same, 4d. Total 4s. 4d. And there is allowed [erasure]. To John Starkey of Lewisham for sawing 500 ft. of timber planks and board for the said mill, 5s. To William Hughet for making 21 rods of wall at task, 5s. 3d. To the same William for 4 hoops for a stone at Lewisham mill, 2s. To John Smyth of Lewisham for 2 loads of timber at 6s. the load, total 12s. To the same John for 34 loads of clay, 2 loads of loam, at 4d. the load, 12s. To the same John for carriage of 2 loads of boards and

planks for the water-wheel and the floodgate there, at 2 several times, 20d. And for 2 labourers working and labouring in the waterworks of the said mill for 2 days, 12d.
Total £15 8s. 1½d.

384. Costs of carriage.
To John Hargyll for the carriage of 5 loads of timber and other stuff from the Bridge House to the mills at Stratford, at 12d. the load, 5s. To the same John for carriage of 101 loads of timber, board, and stone from the said Bridge House to divers tenements within the city of London, and of old stuff from the said tenements to the Bridge House, at 3d. the load, total 25s. 3d. To the same John for carriage of a load of rubbish, 2d. To the same John for keeping all the void places on the bridge clean this year, 8d. To John Fuller for freight and carriage of 14 loads of elm timber from Maidenhead bridge to the Bridge wharf here, 19s. To the same John for freight and carriage of 7 loads of elm timber from Maidenhead bridge hither to the Bridge Wharf, 10s. 6d. And for drawing the said timber with horses to the waterside there, 10d.
Total 61s. 5d.

385. [f. 225v] Costs of the chapel.
For singing bread and wine, spent in the same chapel in singing masses and houseling strangers at Easter this year, 5s. 10d. To 2 chaplains doing their divine service for the whole period of this account, 10 marks each, total £13 6s. 8d. To 4 clerks ministering daily in the same chapel for the whole period of this account, at 20d. each a week, total £17 6s. 8d. To Robert Rudmarige, one of the same 4 clerks, in reward for opening and shutting the chapel doors, and for keeping the organs, jewels, and ornaments there that are committed to him, 20s. To the said chaplains and clerks singing *Placebo* and *Dirige* with requiem mass for the souls of all the benefactors of the said Bridge on 4 occasions this year, 8s. For washing the albs, altarcloths, towels, and surplices this year, 4s. For apparelling 2 prs. of vestments, 3d. To John Moncke, waxchandler, for the Paschal and Sepulchre light there at Easter, and all other lights used in the said chapel this year, 28s. 11d. To John Wylcokks for oil and lamps used here at the Bridge House gate and in the branch hanging outside the chapel door at the feasts of St John the Baptist, St Peter, and the Translation of St Thomas this year, 6s. 8d. To Thomas Downe for 8 gallons of lamp oil used at the said feasts for the whole period of this account, 8s. For 15 lb. of tallow candles used for divine service there in wintertime this year, 15d.
Total £34 16s. 3d.

386. Masons' wages.
To Thomas Wade, chief mason of the Bridge works for his fee for a year for the whole period of this account, £6 13s. 4d. To John Newman, hardhewer, working in the same works for a whole year, at 2s. a week, £5 4s. To Thomas Pylchard for 18 days, John Burdon for 13

days, Robert Seton for 2 days, Robert Oliver for 22 days, John Wylkes for 19 days, Saunder Style for 168½ days, John Wodale for 2 days, James Smyth for 146 days, John Orgar for 158 days, John Bande for 4 days, and John A Dene for 4 days, masons, working apparelling Bridge ashlar, making new chimneys, paving kitchens, mending and repairing the chapel staddle, with all other defaults belonging to the said Bridge and tenements of the same, among them all for 606½ days at 8d. a day each, total £21 7d. To the abovesaid Thomas Pylcherd for 21 days, John Burdon for 16 days, Robert Seton for 3 days, Thomas Lekenore for 3 days, from All Hallows to Candlemas, working in the said works, at 7½d. a day each, total 26s. 10½d. To William Johnson, prentice, for 21 days, [and] William Geffrey, prentice, for 77 days, working apparelling stone in the said Bridge works, at 6d. a day each, total 49s. To Thomas Wade for a quarter of coals [*cooles*: ? charcoal], brushes, bread and ale spent among the masons repairing the gate of the bridge, 14d. And to the said masons watching and working in the water works as the tides have fallen, between them this year 13s. 10d.
Total £37 8s. 9½d.

387. Carpenters' wages.
To Thomas Maunsy, master carpenter of the Bridge works, for his wages and fee for the period of this account, overseeing and putting-to his helping hand at all times needful and requisite, £8 13s. 4d. And to Robert Maunsy, warden of the carpentry of the said Bridge House, for his fee and wages from 8 January to the following Michaelmas within the time of this account, working and labouring daily in the said works, at 4s. a week, total £7 4s. [To] John Tydwey for 48 days, John Harding for 123 days, John Garlond for 67 days, Richard Penythorn for 5 days, John Owenby [f. 226] 5 days, Thomas Philip for 109 days, Thomas Westende for 183½ days, William Waylot for 5 days, Roger Maunsy for 18 days, Henry Coterell for 5 days, Robert Wodesdale for 5½ days, George Maxwell for 3 days, Thomas Maunsy for 4 days, James Maunsy for 82 days, Simon Dandy for 5 days, Edward Gybson for 5 days, carpenters, working framing and making divers new buildings in divers and sundry of the Bridge tenements this year, joisting and binding the staddles under the said bridge, between them all for 634½ days at 8d. a day each, total £21 2s. 10d. John Horren for 43½ days, William Basse for 244½ days, Robert Pasmere for 173½ days, John Arnold for 170 days, John Walker 68 days, carpenters, working in the said Bridge works for 738½ days, at 6d. a day each, total £18 19s. 9d. To Henry Saward for 133 days, John Horrell for 62½ days, carpenters, working in the works of the said Bridge and tenements thereunto belonging, for 195½ days at 8d. a day each, total £5 10s. 4d. Nicholas Byrche with his servant for 86 days, at 10d. a day for him and his servant, total 68s. 9d. Robert Chawrton for 14 days, Robert Cowrton for 53½ days, John A Dene for 12 days, carpenters, working in the works of the Bridge, between them for 79½ days at 5d. a day each, total 33s. 2d. To the abovewritten Edward Gybson for 4 days, Simon Dandy for 3 days, and Thomas Dryver for 2 days, at 8d. a day each, total 6s. And

to the abovesaid carpenters watching and working in the waterworks out of due time, working as the tides have fallen, between them all this year 24s.
Total £68 2s. 6d.

388. Labourers' wages.
To William Sporiour for 246½ days, John Archer for 50½ days, Henry Tomson for 42 days, Thomas Richard for 4 days, John Crowcheman for 11 days, John Rowland for 242 days, John Thomas for a day, Robert Wakeryng for 188 days, William White for 162½ days, William Smyth for 97 days, Edward Trummy for a day, Robert Burdon for a day, John Saunder for 95 days, John Todwell for 64 days, George Newby for 69 days, John Pierson for 88 days, John Myles for 7 days, Humfrey Woddes for 4 days, William Wright for 8 days, Edward Hudson for 5 days, Thomas Badby for 5 days, Edmund Longe for 13 days, John Barde for 36 days, William Donne for 6 days, Peter Burton for a day, Robert Sam for 13½ days, Robert Snell for 13½ days, John Cobbe for 47 days, John Hankyn for 7 days, William Morrell for a day, John Swete for 5 days, labourers labouring and attending as well unto the carpenters as to the masons, in bearing all manner of stuff requisite and necessary to the same workmen's hands and in other works of the said Bridge, between them for 1,535½ days at 5d. a day each, £31 19s. 10½d. To divers other labourers attending upon the shoutman, unloading [*havyng oute*] and loading boats at the Bridge House wharf, conveying them to the bridge with stone, chalk, [and] rubbish, and there unloading and bestowing of the same into the staddles, small dams [*dammellis*] and other works of the said Bridge, as the tides have fallen, between them all for 614 tides at 3d. a tide each, saved in all 7d., total £7 12s. 11d. To workmen and labourers attending by night tides to bring out the boats laden with timber and stuff for the repair of the staddles and stopping of the gulleys at many several times this year, £3 2s. 1½d.
Total £42 14s. 11d.

389. Wages at the gins.
To 20 labourers labouring at drawing the gin called the gibbet gin of brass, driving a great number of piles in gulleys, and cross-driving the same *all hoole* the same gulleys, for 83 tides, taking between them [f. 226v] all 5s. a tide, except that there lacked one labourer at sundry times for 4 tides, total £20 14s. And to 2 holders holding the said gin for the said 83 tides, at 4d. a tide each, total 55s. 4d. To 9 labourers labouring at the iron Ram, running in driving piles outside the arches in the same works, for 36 tides, at 2s. 3d. between the 9 of them every tide, total £4 18d. To 16 labourers labouring at St Magnus' gin, driving piles for 30 tides, taking 4s. between the 16 of them every tide, except that there lacked one of the said labourers at sundry times for 8 tides, total £5 18s. To 2 holders holding the said gin for the said 30 tides, at 4d. a tide each, total 20s.
Total £34 8s. 10d.

390. Sawyers' wages.

To Richard Blakgreve and his fellows working in sawing timber of the Bridge's stuff into boards, planks, and quarters, mullions [*Maynells*], steps for stairs, joists, binders and reson pieces, by the discretion of Thomas Maunsy the master carpenter of the said Bridge, 13,500 ft. at 12d. for sawing 100 ft., total £6 15s.

391. Tilers' wages.

To John Bylby, tiler, and his labourer, working in tiling of divers and sundry tenements of the said Bridge this year, for 217½ days, at 12d. a day for himself and his labourer, total £10 17s.

392. Bricklayers.

To Peter Burton for 77 days, William Spynke for 103 days, Thomas Wright for 114 days, James Rynde for 11 days, bricklayers, in making of new chimneys, mending and repairing old chimneys and ovens in divers tenements belonging to the said Bridge, between them all for 305 days at 8d. a day each, total £10 3s. 4d.

393. Daubers' wages.

To John Michell, dauber, and his labourer, working in daubing of the said Bridge tenements this year for 170½ days, at 12d. a day for himself and his labourer, total £8 10s. 6d.

394. Paviours' wages.

To Roger Wanham, paviour, for paving 83 toises of new pavement at the Greyfriars and the north side of St Nicholas Shambles, at 7d. the toise, total 48s. 5d. To the same Roger for paving 5 toises of new pavement upon the bridge, at 7d. the toise, total 2s. 11d. To the same Roger for paving 75½ toises behind the Shambles, in Gracechurch Street and other places within the city, at 7d. the toise, total 43s. 9d. To the same Roger for 2 workmen working and amending divers defaults within the city for 2 days at 8d. a day each, total 2s. 8d. Total £4 17s. 9d.

395. Fees and wages of officers.

To the said wardens for their fees because of their office, £10 each, total £20. Also for their clothing, 20s. each, total 40s. To John More, man of law, retained of counsel with the said Wardens in matters concerning the Bridge this year, for his fee, 13s. 4d. To John Normavile, clerk of the works of the said Bridge, from Michaelmas to Midsummer within the period of this account, £10. And to Walter Smyth, now clerk of the said works from the said feast of Midsummer to the following Michaelmas within the period of this account, 50s. To Richard Paynell, receiver of the said Bridge, for his whole fee and drinking [f. 227] with the gathering of the fishmongers and butchers at the Stocks, £23 6s. 8d. To Thomas Say, serjeant of the Chamber of London, for his fee for warning the auditors of the City to hear and determine this account, 6s. 8d. To John Arnold, porter of the Bridge House gate, for his weekly

wages, for himself 20d., and for keeping and feeding of the hounds within the same place, 10d. a week within the period of this account, total £6 10s. To Thomas Donmowe, keeper of the boats and shouts belonging to the said Bridge works, for his wages at 2s. 6d. a week, total £6 10s.
Total £71 16s. 8d.

396. Rewards to officers.
To the said wardens for their attendance and good provision done in their office, £10 each as it has been allowed in past years, total £20. And to the said clerk of the works, as reward allowed him for writing and duplicating the books of this account, whereof one book remains within the Bridge House, and the other book remains within the Chamber at the Guildhall of London, as it has been allowed in past years, total 66s. 8d.
Total £23 6s. 8d.

397. Costs of the auditors in hearing and determining of this account, and for a repast made among officers and ministers of the said Bridge, as it has been allowed in times past, total 40s. And for counters delivered to the said auditors to cast this account, 2s. 8d.
Total 42s. 8d.

398. Sum of all payments and allowances £677 19s. 7½d. And there is owing £1,209 12s. 5¼d.
[in left margin: Whereof] Upon Edward Stone and Piers Calcot and their renters as in the foot of the last account is declared desperate, £53 6s. 6½d.
William Galle late one of the Wardens as is declared in the foot of the last account also, £48 6s. 1d.
Henry Bumstede and his sureties by several obligations as is also declared in the same foot of account, £69.
William Melbourne, Chamberlain of the City of London, as in money delivered to him to the use of the said Bridge, that is to say by the hands of Simon Harrys and Christopher Eliot, as appears at large in the foot of the last account, £178 3s. 5½d.; by the hands of the said Christopher, as is declared in the foot of the last account, £133 6s. 8d.; by the hands also of the said Christopher Eliot and Edward Fenkill, as appears in a bill remaining within the remembrances of this account, £197 6s. 9d.; and by the hands of William Holte and Edward Green, last accountants, as also appears by a bill by the hand of the said Chamberlain, £286 2s. 10¾d.: in all to the said Chamberlain, £794 19s. 9¼d.

399. [f. 227v] Upon Christopher Eliot and Edward Fenkil as the residue of £319 15s. 2d. so declared in the foot of the last account, £122 8s. 5d.
The which £122 8s. 5d. was allowed to the said Christopher and Edward on 19 September 19 Henry VII [1503] by the mayor and aldermen as

in money spent and paid for new making a pageant set upon London Bridge at the entry of the lady princess of Spain, and as plainly appears of record in the court of the said mayor and aldermen, and so that [is the] total.

And upon the said accountants £121 11s. 7½d.

Of the which £121 11s. 7½d. there is remitted to the said accountants on 18 July 17 Henry VII [1502] by the mayor and aldermen on a bill of petition of the same accountants as plainly appears of record in the court of the said mayor and aldermen, £4 3s. 4d.

And so the said William Maryner and Christopher Eliott, accountants, owe clearly of their arrears within the time of this account, £117 8s. 3½d.

400. Auditors of this account Sir John Sha, kt., Mr Thomas Wodde, aldermen, Ralph A Lathum, William FitzWilliam, Richard Gough, and Simon Hoggan, commoners, which auditors heard and determined this account on 19 September 19 Henry VII and A.D. 1503.

BRIDGE HOUSE RENTAL 6

Rental for 1537–8

401. [f. 237] The rental of all the proper rents belonging to London Bridge from Midsummer 29 Henry VIII [1537] to Midsummer then next [1538], by one whole year.[1]

> 1. The text is arranged in 2 columns per page.

402. Southwark
William Sharparowe 66s. 8d.
Robert Gate 33s. 4d.
James Foster £8
William Downynge 8s.
Amedwyfe 13s. 4d.
John Flynte 20s.
Thomas Haywarde 13s. 4d.
John Laurence 66s. 8d.
John Degraven 40s.
John Laurence and John de Fryse 40s.
Cornelyus Harman 28s.
Robert Dragon 33s. 4d.
John Frenche and Rychard Hyrst £3
John Frenche 76s. 8d.
Richard Hooteman 20s.
Robert Austen 40s.
Maynard's wife 40s.
Gilbert Phillypes 40s.
William James 40s.
John Fulmer 40s.
Peter Bremer 53s. 4d.
Richard Patwey 40s.
Richard Patwey 40s.
John Joce 53s. 4d.
John Fennell 40s.
Jeffrey Wolfe £5
Richard Washer 20s.
William Towell 20s.
Total £62 6s.

403. London Bridge. The principal east part.
John Layne £6
Thomas Cheverell £7 3s. 4d.
Thomas Atkynson £10

John Philpott 73s. 4d.
Roger Willowes £5
John Catchmayde 53s. 4d.
William Ebrave £4
Simon Lawe £4
Robert Hardys £6
Antony Caverley £5 6s. 8d.
Snowden's wife 66s. 8d.
Snowden's wife 66s. 8d.
John Huskyns 40s.
John Huskyns 66s. 8d.
William Johnson 46s. 8d.
John Blande £5 6s. 8d.
John Symson £4 6s. 8d.
Richard Large £4
John Wilforde £4
Henry Brayne 53s. 4d.
Henry Bucfelde 60s.
John Harpeny 63s. 4d.
George Bridgys £7
Total £101 13s. 4d.

404. The principal west part
Master Forman £4
John Trice £6
Nicholas Cosyne £6 13s. 4d.
William Lyuers £ 13s. 4d.
Richard Theklocke £5 6s. 8d.
John Catchmayde £4 6s. 8d.
Richard Abarforde 40s.
Richard Bright £5
Richard Woodhouse 73s. 4d.
John Propter 66s. 8d.
Steven Cobbe £4
Robert Hynde £5 10s.
Robert Perpelett 40s.
William Kellet 40s.
John Vyvyan £4 9s. 8d.
Charles Wolman 73s. 4d.
Harry Brayne £8
John Wheler £5 6s. 8d.
William Kelynge £5 6s. 8d.
William Garrard £8
Total £97 6s. 4d.

405. The middle east part
Richard Lambart 53s. 4d.
John Tympson for 2 tenements £5
[f. 237v] Danyson's wife 29s. 8d.

William Buckstede 33s. 4d.
John Garrarde 66s. 8d.
Kydder's wife 30s.
Bosse's wife 30s.
William Temple 30s.
William Temple £4
William Yoxley 46s. 8d.
William Yoxley 53s. 4d.
John Branche 53s. 4d.
John Branche for 2 tenements in the drawbridge tower 6s. 8d.
Total £30 13s.

406. The middle west part
George Tadlowe 76s. 8d.
George Tadlowe £4
William Shereman 66s. 8d.
William Buckstede 46s. 8d.
William Buckstede 40s.
John Bostone 33s. 4d.
Thomas Anneslowe 43s. 4d.
Thomas Anneslowe 53s. 4d.
John Redman 46s. 8d.
Henry Coke 50s.
William Hyllys £5
Nicholas Bowman £5
Thomas Pynchester 66s. 8d.
Total £40 3s. 4d.

407. The east end
William Blank £6
John Awoodde 50s.
Thomas Bruse 50s.
William Symondson £5
[margin: <incr.>] Anne Paynell 10s. <20s.>
Arnold Turner 33s. 4d.
John Roulande 33s. 4d.
Sergyaunte's wife 46s. 8d.
Richard Tonnell 43s. 4d.
William Reynolde 40s.
Robert Maye £4 6s. 8d.
George Milman 26s. 8d.
John Alenson 66s. 8d.
John Stoddarde 46s. 8d.
Total £37 13s. 4d.

408. The west end
Richard Hyllys £4 6s. 8d.
Dunstan Checheley 46s. 8d.
John Roulys 46s. 8d.

John Thomas £4
Richard Hore 26s. 8d.
John Amesbye 26s. 8d.
Harry Bekket 20s.
Thomas Armestrong 26s. 8d.
Bygrave's wife 48s. 4d.
Henry Bordvyle £4 6s. 8d.
Thomas Hemnarshe 40s.
Henry Hyll 33s. 4d.
Henry Chambley 46s. 8d.
Henry Chambley 36s. 8d.
John Arowley £4
Thomas Johnson 40s.
Total £38 11s. 8d.

409. The parish of St Magnus
John Turke £7 5s. 4d.
John Roofe 10s.
William Lyster 10s.
John Swayne 10s.
Alice Chesshyre 10s.
John Turcke 23s. 4d.
Robert Clerke 23s. 4d.
Thomas Doughty 23s. 4d.
Robert Putenham 23s. 4d.
Thomas Doughty 50s.
Total £16 8s. 8d.

410. Gracechurch Street
John Porter £8
Nicholas Barker £4
David ap Ryce 66s. 8d.
Richard Parker 66s. 8d.
Total £18 13s. 4d.

411. The Old Change
Ralph Johnson £5
William Carter 60s.
John Peakocke 40s.
John Culthorpe 40s.
John Nelthrorpe 23s. 4d.
Henry Boltys 20s.
John Angell 33s. 4d.
[f. 238] Robert Raylton 35s.
Nicholas Milgate 23s. 4d.
Nicholas Milgate 40s.
John Abbotte 20s.
William Blande 53s. 4d.
Steven Mayson 56s. 8d.

Edmund Shawe 20s.
Edmund Shawe £6 8s. 4d.
Total £34 13s. 4d.

412. Paternoster Row
Lewis Sutton £5 6s. 8d.
John Beale 23s. 4d.
John Swettynge 23s. 4d.
William Whitman 28s. 4d.
Robert Grey 23s. 4d.
William Frere 26s. 8d.
John Baron 23s. 4d.
Thomas Gurr 26s. 8d.
John Slapar 26s. 8d.
Katherine Bennett 26s. 8d.
John Turke 26s. 8d.
James White 26s. 8d.
Henry Clerke 28s. 8d.
John Redman 26s. 8d.
Roger Rogersson 26s. 8d.
John Turner 26s. 8d.
John Turner 26s. 8d.
John Greston 26s. 8d.
Richard Warner 26s. 8d.
Thomas Orgall £4
William Bull 40s.
John Cysyll 20s.
Barker's wife 26s.
The Storehouse 20s.
Thomas Davye 20s.
Henry Miller 20s.
Thomas Poynarde 20s.
Thomas Dicson 40s.
Master Rooche 53s. 4d.
Thomas Orgall 53s. 4d.
Total £48 9s. 8d.

413. St Sepulchre
Thomas Heyre 20s.
Robert Adams 10s.
Robert Ferrour 10s.
Robert Farrour 10s.
Robert Farrour 10s.
Robert Farrour 10s.
Robert Farrour 10s.
Total £4

414. St Nicholas Shambles
Laurence Pynder £6 6s. 8d.

William Bracy 73s. 4d.
Richard Jenkyn 33s. 4d.
Thomas Ebden 46s. 8d.
Andrew Rene 40s.
Nicholas Pynchyn 50s.
Nicholas Pynchyn £5
Edward Clacye 70s.
Andrew Chesham 46s. 8d.
John Gyles 46s. 8d.
John Baynton 66s. 8d.
William Urmounde 66s. 8d.
Thomas Eve 60s.
William Petur 66s. 8d.
Robert Nelson 66s. 8d.
Robert Horsely 66s. 8d.
David Sandebrake £5 6s. 8d.
Nicholas Pynchyn £4 6s. 8d.
Nicholas Pynchyn 53s. 4d.
John Dogge £5 6s. 8d.
William Woodhawe £5
John Raulyns £4 6s. 8d.
Peter Peale 66s. 8d.
Thomas Lytchfylde £4
Total £85 13s. 4d.

415. St Ewen
William Hylyarde 46s. 8d.
William Jennyn 40s.
Henry Horne 40s.
Henry Horne £4 6s. 8d.
John Walden 53s. 4d.
Richard Farrour 73s. 4d.
John Kellet 40s.
Edward Atkyns 40s.
Simon Richardson 40s.
Simon Richardson 40s.
John Marchall 40s.
John Aylwarde 40s.
William Lawys 40s.
Total £31

416. West Cheap and Wood Street
Ralph Cressye £4 3s. 4d.
[f. 238v] Henry Payne 60s.
Thomas Newys £6 6s. 8d.
Thomas Woode £6 13s. 4d.
Meddeley £6 13s. 4d.
Total £27 6s. 8d.

417. Friday Street
[margin: <incr>] Nicholas Foxe £5 6s. 9d. <11d.>

418. All Hallows in the Wall
William Wilson 33s. 4d.
John Laurence 13s. 4d.
John Laurence 8s.
George Eglysfylde £5 6s. 8d.
Total £8 16d.

419. St Dunstan in the East
Richard Hucden 23s. 4d.
Henry Tuckye 20s.
Total 43s. 4d.

420. St Ethelburga [*Alborowe*]
William Pycas £5 6s. 8d.

421. St Margaret Pattens
John Monkeys 30s.
John de Barowes 33s. 4d.
Henry Walton 30s.
Robert Millys 30s.
<Edmund Leson 30s.>
Edmund Lesson 10s.
Total £8 3s. 4d.

422. St Dionis
John Neale 16s.
Robert Robyns 16s.
Alice Foster 16s.
William Johnson 10s.
Joan Pounde 10s.
Cicely Frenche 6s. 8d.
Master Englyshe 6s. 8d.
John Pylkyngton 8s.
Simon van Newtrik 8s.
Nicholas Parrot 40s.
Elizabeth Nicholls 36s. 8d.
William Wannesworth 26s. 8d.
William Randall 40s.
John Ravyn £4 10s. 8d.
John Ravyn 26s. 8d.
William Stubbys 12s.
William Bayly 13s. 4d.
John Goddyshalfe 16s.
The storehouse 5s. 4d.
William Robynson 20s.
William Robynson 26s. 8d.
Total £22 11s. 4d.

423. All Hallows Barking
My lord Hawarde 26s. 8d.

424. St Giles without Cripplegate
John Clerke for a void ground 8s.

425. The east end of the Stocks
William Bitmanson 66s. 8d.
Robert Herne 40s.
Richard Jesson 10s.
Robert Horden 8s.
Thomas Parson 6s. 8d.
William Smythe 10s.
Thomas Grene 6s. 8d.
Edmund Moore 6s. 8d.
Total <£7 14s. 8d.>

426. The west end of the Stocks
William Bryan 10s.
Simon Daye 6s. 8d.
Richard Robertson 6s. 8d.
Ralph Webbe 6s. 8d.
William Holte 6s. 8d.
Henry Edwarde 6s. 8d.
William Davy 6s. 8d.
Oswald Snye 6s. 8d.
William Thomson 6s. 8d.
William Valiaunte 6s. 8d.
William Wilson 6s. 8d.
Total 76s. 8d.

427. Sum of all the proper rents £739 9s. 9d.
Sum of all the increase 20s. 11d.

428. [f. 239] The foreign rents
Lewisham
William Butler for the farm place called *the Brydghous* with lands and
pasture thereunto belonging 70s.
Philip Islyngton for a mill with meadow ground thereunto belonging £6
The same Philip for a tenement 6s. 8d.
The same Philip for a tenement 6s. 8d.
The same Philip for a tenement 6s. 8d.
The same Philip for a tenement 6s. 8d.
Robert Bulbek 10s.
Thomas Carnaby 10s.
John Graunger for 2 tenements with a close of meadow ground 40s.
Thomas Bankyn 10s.
Of divers persons there for quit-rents 8s. 5½d.
Total £14 15s. 1½d.

429. Deptford town
John Hill for a tenement called the Christopher 40s.
William Cock for a tenement 20s.
Hugh Provest for a wood wharf 53s. 4d.
The same Hugh for a close with a chalk wharf 5s.
Total 118s. 4d.

430. Deptford Strand
John Harryson for certain meadow ground lying in Deptford fields 53s. 4d.
John Johnson for 4½ acres in the church marsh 4½ acres and 3 roods in the Church field and *Conywall* 21s. 4d.
The same Johnson for 2 tenements 14s.
The same Johnson for a corner tenement 23s. 4d.
Thomas Baker for a tenement 26s. 4d.
Master Gonstone for a tenement 20s.
Master Gonston for a tenement 20s.
The Round House 13s. 4d.
Total £9 12s.

431. Peckham
Thomas Peryn, John Haryson and William Cocke for a meadow grounde called Wardells, a close called 4 crofts, and a certain ground called Pipers hope and 1½ acres meadow lying at Stret bridge 66s. 8d.

432. At the Lock
[margin: <incr.>] Thomas Bully for a close called Carpenters Haw 23s. 4d. <3s. 4d.>
John Clarke for a meadow called *longe lond* with a barn 60s.
Total £4 3s. 4d.

433. Horselydown
John Cocke for a close 16s.
Thomas Wade for a close 20s.
Total 36s.

434. Bermondsey Street
John Fulmer for a tenement called Copped Hall 23s. 4d.
The same John for a tenement 10s.
The same John for a tenement 10s.
The same John for a tenement 10s.
Total 53s. 4d.

435. St George's Field
Robert Wilson for 19½ acres of land lying in several places in the said field 40s.

436. The Minories
John Slouthe 26s. 8d.

Steven Tofte 12s.
John Slouthe 12s.
John Hauteley 20s,
Thomas Pynder 46s. 8d.
Total 117s. 4d.

437. At Stratford
John Thomson for Spilmans mill and land belonging to the same £10
3s.
Robert Boote for Saynes mill, 9 acres of meadow and two hoops of
osiers £13 6s. 8d.
<Robert Duke for 4 hoops of osyers 4s.>
Total £23 13s. 4d.

438. Sum of all the foreign rents £73 10s. 9½d.
Sum of all the increase 3s. 4d.

439. [f. 239v] Vacations of tenements for the time of this present
account

	Michaelmas	Christmas	Easter	Midsummer
Cheapside				
Henry Payne a year –	15s.	15s.	15s.	15s.
Thomas Newys a year –	31s. 8d.	31s. 8d.	31s. 8d.	31s. 8d.
The east end of the Stocks				
Robert Horden –				
Thomas Parson –				
William Smythe –	2s. 6d.	2s. 6d.	2s. 6d.	
Romsen –	20d.	20d.	20d.	20d.
Edmund Moore –	20d.	20d.	20d.	20d.
The west end of the Stocks				
Francis Bryan –	20d.	20d.	20d.	
William Valyaunte –	20d.	20d.	20d.	20d.
Harry Edwardes –	20d.			
John Hunte –	20d.	20d.		
Humphrey Skynner –	20d.	20d.	20d.	20d.
St Nicholas Shambles				
Lewisham				
Walter Gadson –	2s. 6d.			
James Atlyffe –	2s. 6d.			
Thomas Bankyn –	2s. 6d.			

John Knowe for a standing at the Stocks for 8 weeks 19s. 6d.

440. Sum total of vacations £12 17s. 10d.

BRIDGE HOUSE RENTAL 6

Account for 1537–8

441. [f. 240] The account of Thomas Crull and Robert Draper, wardens of London Bridge from Michaelmas 29 Henry VIII [1537] to Michaelmas then next [1538], that is for one whole year.

442. The same wardens account for the arrears of their last account, as appears at the foot of the same, 74s.

443. The same wardens account also for money received from the duke of Suffolk in part payment for wheat, £10.
Also they account for money owed by the said duke and others for wheat, £17 6½d.
Total £27 6½d.

444. The same wardens also account for money received of Anne Panell, widow, by the hands of John Cathmayde, in full payment of the whole debt owed by the said Anne, as appears in the foot of the last account, £6 13s. 4d.
Total [blank].

445. The charge rental of the proper rents of the Bridge livelihood extends yearly according to the rental entered at the beginning of this account to the sum of £739 9s. 9d.

446. And the foreign rents of the same Bridge livelihood extend yearly according to the same rental to the sum of £73 15s. 9½d.

447. Farm of the fishmongers selling fish at the Stocks in the part called the fishmarket there, let to farm to Robert <Tippyng>, citizen and [erased] of London for a term of years, paying yearly at Michaelmas £20.
Also butchers selling flesh in the part called the fleshmarket there, paying weekly every week [out] of Lent 16s. 1d., from Michaelmas to Michaelmas within this present account, £36 19s. 10d.
Total £56 19s. 10d.

448. [f. 240v] Passage of carts and wains [*carres*] passing over London Bridge, in the tenure of John Woode, let to him for the whole time of this present account. No profits of ships passing under the drawbridge are charged because it cannot be raised until the stonework of the drawbridge tower is amended.
Total £20.

174

449. Increase of rents of divers lands and tenements within the time of this present account, as appears particularly by the parcels declared in the rental at the beginning of this account.
Total 24s. 3d.

450. Quit-rents yearly charged, the parcels whereof appear in sundry rentals made heretofore, with 16d. for the farm of a little close at Horton by Ewell in co. Surrey, as charged in previous years' accounts.
Total £31 12s. 6d.

451. Oblations in the chapel on the bridge.
Received on St George's day, 2s. 1½d. Of oblations from the chapel on the bridge, 5s. 2d.
Total 7s. 3¾d.

452. Sales.
Received of Laurence Awen for 16 ft. of oak timber at 2d. the foot, 2s. 8d. And for 52 ft. of elm board, 16d. Total 4s. Of Christopher Payne for 1 load of elm timber, 6s. Of him for 30 ft. of oak timber, 5s. 6d., for 1 load of oak for the earl's sluice, 8s., for 6 ft. of oak, 12d., and for half a hundred of oak planks, 2s. 6d. Total 17s. Received of William Jacson, the queen's bailiff of Southwark, for 16 ft. of small shells of oak, 2s. Of William Madye, the king's footman, for 10 ft. of oak, 20d. And for 6 small shells, 2s. 3s. 8d. Of William Parker, wheelwright, for 1 load of oak timber, 9s. Of William Buckmaster, merchant of the Steelyard, for 1 load of elm timber, 8s. Of John Tollow for 20 ft. of elm timber, 2s. 8d. Of my lady Peakocke for 3½ hundred of bricks and 3½ hundred of tiles at 6d. the hundred, total 3s. 6d. Of a Spaniard by William [blank] for 10 ft. of elm, 2s. Of Mr Bowes, alderman, for planks and posts, 5s. 4d. Of Henry Hoke for a granary [*garner*] in Golders for 3 quarters of a year ended at Michaelmas, 22s. 6d.

453. [f. 241] Of Mr Doughty by the hands of Robert Gold, for 20 ft. of elm timber, 3s. 4d. Of Mr Castylyon for 2½ loads of elm timber, 17s. 10d. Received at 2 sundry times of John Stacye, bellwright, for 3 loads of oak timber, 25s. Of Mr Baker for the king's attorney for a hundred of planks 3s., [for] 18 ft. of oak planks 10d., and for 6 quarters of oak, 12d. Total 4s. 10d. Of William Robynson, mill-picker, for 1 elm plank, 5d. Of Mr Sympson for 2 oak quarters, 4d. Of John Smythe for 100 bricks and 3 trays of mortar, 5d. Of Davye Lenton, carpenter, for 9 ft. of elm, 21½d. Of Richard Torner by the hands of Robert Golde for a piece of elm, 6d. Of Nidygate, one of the king's servants, for 3 ends of elm planks, 2s. Of Stacye for 2 ft. of oak timber, 6d. Of Thomas Gybson for 2 oak planks, 4s. Of Thomas Hucke for 2 quarters, 2d. Of Dr Leyghe for 60 ft. of oak timber, 12s. 6d. Of a smith for a piece of old timber, 12d. Of Thomas Doughty, fishmonger, for 17 ft. of oak timber, 2s. 4d. Of John Allarye, clothworker, for 10 ft. of oak timber, 2s. 6d. Of William Kellett of London Bridge, merchant tailor, towards the making of a shed over an arch of stone on the backside of his house, 20s. Of Dalyngton by the hands of William Cockes for 16 ft. of elm, 3s. 4d. Of [a] baker of Southwark for 4 other shells of oak, 6d. Of John Carpenter of St Katherine's for 90 ft. of featherboard for millwheels, 5s. Of Harry Byrde of London Bridge for 11 ft. of oak timber at 3d. the foot, 2s. 9d. Of Mr Sympson, haberdasher, for 3 short shells of oak, 8d. Of Robert Golde for 18 ft. of ceiling [*sylynge*] timber, 6d. Of Robert Barfoote, mercer, for a load and 8 ft. of oak timber delivered at Croydon, 6s. 10d. Of William Bomsted, bowyer, for 4 small shells of oak, 12d. Of William Dockes, mercer, for a quartern of board, 16d. Of the churchwardens of St Olave's for 2 loads and 34 ft. of oak timber, 20s. 6d. Of a Dutchman [*doucheman*] for an old stone of 15 inches, 10d. Of Thomas Allen for 2 hundredweight of chalk, 12d. Of Robert Golde for 3 ft. of oak timber, 12d. Of Eglyshfylde for 4 loads of rag, 5s. Of John Flynte for 80 ft. of oak board for a chest for his wife, 2s. Of a gunpowder maker for 20 stops of elm 20 ft. long, 6s. 8d., for 4 elm planks containing 93 ft., 5s., and for 2 ft. of elm timber, 4d. Total 12s. Of Golde for 9 ft. of board, 3d. Of Modye for an end of oak of 6 ft., 12d. Of a shipwright for 12 ft. of oak timber, 2s. 9d. Of John Cockes for 17 ft. of oak timber, 5s. 6d. Of Stacye the bellwright for 69 ft. of oak timber for the church of All Hallows the Great, 17s. 3d. Of Nicholas Barker, armourer, for divers sorts of oak shells, 4s.

454. [f. 241v] Of Richard Dicbye, plumber, for 409 lb. of lead skimmings [*betts of the skomynge of lead*], 10s. 8d. Of Mr Temple, the king's fletcher, for certain old timber and shells of oak, 12s. Of Thomas Baylye, grocer, for 8 ft. of elm, 20d. Received for an old piece of ragstone, 6d. Of a stranger for making fast his ship and breaking [its] way against the wharf, 8d. Of the churchwardens of All Hallows the Great for 49 ft. of timber, 10s. Of the same churchwardens for the loan of the Robynett gin, 2s. Of Mr [blank], clerk of the king's ships, for 18 loads of oak timber taken by him from Croydon, £4 10s. Of Doctor Smythe for 4 loads and 2 ft. of oak timber, 37s. 6d. Of William Cockes for an elm board 19 ft. long, 4d., for a small piece of elm, 3d. Of Mr More in full payment for certain timber taken from Croydon, 2s.
Total £22 7s. 8½d.

455. Incomes and fines.
Received of Elizabeth Hynde, widow, for licence to assign [*set ouer*] her house, 20s.
Of Thomas Madcocke, tailor, for the grant of a tenement that John Ball, haberdasher, now holds in Old Change, 5s.
Of Richard Bradbury for coming into a tenement in Newgate market, late Kellett's, 5s.
Of John Danyell for his coming into a tenement bakehouse in Gracechurch Street, at the sign of the Horseshoe, £6 13s. 4d.
Total £8 3s. 4d.

456. Casualties.

Received of William Johnson for and towards certain repairs and translations made in the tenement he now dwells in, 40s. Of William Gascoyne of Lambeth for the rent of a granary in Golders yard for a year ended at Candlemas last, 10s. Of Mistress Beste, widow, for the rent of a granary in Golders yard, for a year ended at the Annunciation of Our Lady last past, 26. 8d. Of her for the rent of another granary for 3 quarters of a year ended at Christmas last past, 20s. Of Mr Sympson for the rent of a little granary in Golders yard for a year ended at Midsummer, 20s. Of Mistress Hylles towards the making of a stall in her house, 9s. Of the beadle of the Bridge for certain standings at the fair, 14d. Of Roland Edwardes of London, clothworker, for the rent of his house that he now dwells in in Cheapside, for the space of 1 quarter and more ended at Midsummer in this present account, £4. [f. 242] Of William Gascon of Lambeth, baker, for the rent of a granary in Golders yard for a year ended at Lammas last past, 10s.
Total £10 16s. 10d.

457. Total of all their charges with arrears, £1312 17s. 7d.

458. [Expenditure]
Payment of quit-rents.
There is allowed to the said wardens in money paid to Thomas, archbishop of Canterbury, for a quit-rent of 10s. 4d. a year from tenements in Southwark, and from a close at the Lock called Carpenters' hall [sic], for a year ended at Michaelmas in the [blank] year of King Henry VIII, 10s. 4d.
To our sovereign lord the king, for a quit-rent of 14s. 9½d. a year from lands and tenements in Lewisham, and to our sovereign lord the king for a quit-rent of 8½d. a year from tenements sometime Hugh Preston's in Lewisham, for a year ended at Michaelmas, 15s. 6d.
To our sovereign lord the king for a quit-rent of 3s. a year from the Bridge House farm and certain lands in Lewisham aforesaid, for a year ended at the same Michaelmas, 3s.
To the duke of Norfolk, the earl of Derby, and Lord Bergavenny for a quit-rent of 16d. from the Bridge House in Southwark with the appurtenances, for a year ended at Michaelmas aforesaid, 16d.
To a priest of a chantry in the cathedral church of St Paul's in London for the soul of Ralph Dongyon for a quit-rent of 10s. a year from tenements in the parish of St Nicholas Shambles in London, for a year ended at Michaelmas aforesaid, 10s.
To a chantry priest in the church of St Nicholas Shambles for the soul of Robert Husband for a quit-rent of 100s. a year from tenements in the same parish, for a year ended at Michaelmas, 100s.
To the Chamberlain of Westminster [Abbey] for a quit-rent of 10s. a year from tenements in the said parish of St Nicholas Shambles for a year ended at Michaelmas aforesaid, 10s.

To the Chamberlain of London for a quit-rent of 12s. a year from the common ground of the City of London behind St Nicholas Shambles aforesaid, that is to say for 6 back doors, 3 belonging to the Bridge, for a year ended at Michaelmas aforesaid, 12s.

459. [f. 242v] To the prioress of St Helen's within Bishopsgate, London, for a quit-rent of 13s. 4d. a year from tenements in the parish of St Michael le Querne for a year ended at Michaelmas aforesaid, 13s. 4d.

To a priest [words erased] in the parish church of St Olave in Southwark [words erased] a quit-rent of 8 marks a year from tenements in the parish [words erased] for a year ended at Michaelmas aforesaid, 106s. 8d.

To the prior of St Bartholomew's in West Smithfield, London, for a quit-rent of 3s. 4d. a year from tenements in the parish of St Dionis for a year ended at Easter within the time of this account, 3s. 4d.

To the dean and chapter of St Paul's, London, for a quit-rent of 19s. a year from tenements in the parish of St Mary Magdalen Old Fish Street, London, for a year ended at Michaelmas aforesaid, 19s.

To the abbess of the Minories at Tower Hill, London, for a quit-rent of 20s. a year from tenements in St Stephen's lane in the parish of St Magnus for a year ended at Michaelmas aforesaid, 15s.

To the parson of Woolchurch in London for a quit-rent of 53s. 4d. a year as tithe for that part of the Stocks called the fish- and fleshmarket and the inhabitants of the same places, for a year ended at Michaelmas aforesaid, 53s. 4d.

To the prior of St Faith's in Horsham, co. Norfolk, for a quit-rent of 3s. a year from a tenement in the parish of St Margaret Moses in Friday Street, London, for a year ended at Michaelmas aforesaid, 3s.

To the king's grace for a quit-rent of 10s. 6d. a year from certain tenements in Deptford town and certain lands in Deptford marsh and fields for a year ended at Michaelmas aforesaid, 10s. 6d.

To the master and brethren of St Thomas of Acre in London for a quit-rent of 3s. a year from a parcel of ground in the parish of West Ham, lying at Spilman's mill there, and to the same master and brethren for a quit-rent of 3s. 4d. a year from 4 hoops of ground within the said parish, for a year ended at Michaelmas aforesaid, 6s. 8d.

To the abbot of Stratford for a quit-rent of 32s. a year from Saynes mill at Stratford Bow, and certain meadow ground belonging to the said mill, for a year ended at Michaelmas aforesaid, 32s.

To the prior of St Mary Overey in Southwark for a quit-rent of 3s. 6d. a year from a tenement in Eastcheap called the Saracen's Head in the parish of St Leonard, for 3 years ended at Michaelmas last past, 10s. 6d.

460. [f. 243] To the abbot of Bermondsey for a quit-rent of 2s. 6d. a year from a garden in Horselydown, and for a quit-rent of 4s. 10d. a year from certain lands and tenements in Bermondsey Street for a year ended at Christmas within this account, 7s. 4d.

To the king's grace for a quit-rent of 14s. 10d. a year from certain lands and pastures in the field without St George's bar in Southwark, called St George's field, for a year ended at Michaelmas within this account, total 14s. 10d.

To Sir John Corwallys, knight, for a quit-rent of 4s. a year from a tenement at Tower Hill, London, near to the Minories/Minoresses [*Mynoras'*], late of John Higgyns, butcher, for a year ended at Michaelmas aforesaid, 4s.

To the prioress of the house of nuns at Cheshunt, co. Herts, for a quit-rent of 4s. a year from a messuage with appurtenances in Paternoster Row called the Peter and Paul [*the Pet' and Poole*] for a year ended at the Annunciation, 4s.

To a chantry priest founded in the church of St Ethelburga [*Albrighte*] within Bishopsgate, London, for the soul of Gilbert Meriot, for a quit-rent of 33s. 4d. a year from a tenement adjoining the same church called the sign of the Angel, for a year ended at Michaelmas aforesaid, 33s. 4d.

To the friars of the infirmary [*farmary*] at the Greyfriars within Newgate, London, for a quit-rent of 3s. 4d. a year from certain lands lately taken out of the said friars' infirmary garden, for a year ended at Michaelmas aforesaid, 3s. 4d.

To the parson of St Olave in Southwark for a quit-rent of 10s. a year for tithe of certain storehouses with appurtenances, late a beerhouse, and lately belonging to Mr Monoxe, alderman, within the said parish for a year ended at Easter within this account, 10s.

To Mr George Monox, alderman, by the hands of Thomas Thrower and Robert Sheparde, for a quit-rent of 10s. a year from the said storehouses, for a year ended at Michaelmas aforesaid, 10s.

To Mr William Mushampe, gentleman, for a quit-rent of 3s. 10d. a year from certain lands in the parish of Camberwell, co. Surrey, 3s. 10d.

Sum total of quit-rents £25 10s. 10d.

461. [f. 243v] Annuity granted by Richard Lee, late mayor and alderman of the City of London, to one Thomas Pert, late carpenter, as appears by the grant and composition made thereof, enrolled in the Guildhall of London in 12 Edward IV [1472–3] so that the said Thomas, who was tenant of a tenement in Wood Street adjoining a tenement of the Bridge, did not stop the light of the Bridge's tenement or any other there; John Houe, tallowchandler, received the same annuity at Christmas within this account.

Total 4s.

462. Decay of quit-rents sometime levied and collected of divers lands and tenements within the city of London and elsewhere, the parcels whereof have been particularly noted and declared in many past accounts; and as the same quit-rents have for so many years been denied and still cannot be levied or received, therefore [is] allowed as in previous accounts, £9 3s. 8½d.

463. Allowance of rents.

Of a tenement in the parish of St Dionis, because it is reserved for a storehouse to keep all manner of stuff needed for repairs in that part of the city, charged in the rental by the year at 5s. 4d.

And another tenement in Paternoster Row, also reserved as a storehouse to keep all manner of stuff needed for repairs in that part of the city, charged in the rental by the year at 20s.

Total 25s. 4d.

464. Decrease of rents.

Of a tenement in the parish of St Nicholas Shambles which Edward Clayce, surgeon, now dwells in, 10s.

Of a tenement in Wood Street that Mr George Medley, Chamberlain of London, now holds, 13s. 4d.

Of a corner tenement in Deptford Strand which John Johnson now holds, 11s. 8d.

Of a round house at the same Deptford, 6s. 8d.

Of a tenement in the parish of St Magnus which John Turk, fishmonger, now holds, 25s.

Total 73s. 4d.

465. Vacations of tenements standing void and unoccupied for lack of tenants, the parcels and sums whereof have been fully and particularly entered and declared at the beginning of this book.

Total £12 17s. 10d.

466. [f. 244] Buying of stone.

To William Modle of Reigate for 18 loads of squared Reigate stone bought of him for bases for furnaces [*furnes*], pendants, paving for ovens and mantletrees for chimneys, at 2s. the load in the quarry, 36s.

To the same William for 5½ loads of the same stuff, with 23s. for scappling it, 34s.

To the same William Modle and Richard Beste for carriage of 19 loads of the same stuff from Reigate to the Bridge House at 3s. 6d. the load, 66s. 6d. For the carriage of 2 loads of the same stuff to the Bridge House at 3s. 4d. the load, 6s. 8d. And for the carriage of 7 loads of the like stuff half the way at 18d. the load, 10s. 6d. Total 83s. 8d.

To John Orgar, chief mason of the Bridge House, for 3 hundreds and 1½ quarters of hard stone of Kent called *bridge Ashler*, bought in the quarry at 26s. 8d. the hundred, total 90s.

To the same John Orgar for 1 hundred and 1 quarter of middle ashlar, 12s. 6d.

To him for 1 thousand 7 hundred and 3 quarters of *Chepman ware pavynge* for kitchens and courts, bought in the said quarry at 5s. the hundred, total 88s. 9d.

To him for ½ hundred of apparelled paving, 10s.

To him for 1¹/₂ hundred of apparelled paving, 24s.

To him for 354 ft. of the same hard stone of Kent called ogee and voussoir [*ugye and vawser*] at 6d. the foot in the quarry, total £8 17s.

To the same John Orgar for 57 ft. of gutter stone at 4d. the foot in the quarry, total 19s.

To him for 7 great stones called springers at 4s. the stone in the quarry, total 21s.

To the same John Orgar for land carriage of the same stuff from the said quarry called Boughton quarry to Maidstone in Kent, containing in all 145 loads at 12d. the load, except that 1d. was rebated, total £7 4s. 11d.

To John Gate, Reynolde Richardson, and William Beatley for the freight or water-carriage of the same stuff from Maidstone to the Bridge House, containing 127 tons at 12d. the ton, total £6 7s.

Total £43 7s. 10d.

467. Timber, board, and laths.

To John Carter of Colchester for 80 loads of oak timber delivered by him at the Bridge House, each load containing 55 ft. of timber, at 7s. the load, total £28.

To Sir John Gaynsforde, knight, for half a hundred loads of timber delivered at Croydon, £12 14s. 2d.

To Robert Butler, carter, for carriage of 59 loads of oak timber from Croydon to the Bridge House at 2s. 4d. the load, total £6 17s. 8d.

To Mr Thomas Sybbell of Aynesford, esquire, for 50 elm trees bought at Petham Court in Kent, at 2s. the tree, total 100s.

[f. 244v] To Richard Olyvers of Dartford, co. Kent, carter, for carriage of 74 loads of great elm timber from the said Petham Court to Dartford at 18d. the load, 98s. 8d. To him for carriage of 31 loads of board, tallwood, and billets, from the said place to Dartford at 12d. the load, 31s. To him for money paid for coming over a man's ground, 2s. And for mending a gin, 16d. Total £6 13s.

To William Raulyns for hewing and squaring 47 loads of the said elm timber at 11d. the load, 43s. 1d.

To Richard Forman for felling 38 of the trees at 2d. the tree, total 6s. 4d.

To the said Forman for making tallwood and billets, 8s.

To Thomas Alen and Proveste for their charges in buying the same timber, 2s. To Laurence, Provest and Golde for their charges in going thither to measure [*meite*] the timber, 3s. 9d. And in reward to 10 of our carpenters for working the same there, 5s. Total 10s. 9d.

To the wharfinger of Deptford for wharfage of 95 loads of the same stuff at 1d. the load, total 7s. 11d.

To Thomas Allen for water-carriage of all the said timber, board, and other from Dartford to the Bridge House at 2 several times, having divers labourers with him to convey it by drove, total 51s. 2d.

To Thomas Dendye of Surrey for 1 load of heartlaths, 11s. 2s.

To Henry Hauker of Croydon for the laystall of 118 loads of timber at 1d. the load, total 9s. 10d.

To Richard Ambrosse for 22 loads and 30 ft. of timber delivered by him to the Bridge House, £7 10s.

To Thomas Dendye of Surrey for 5 thousand 8 hundred of plankboard [*planche borde*], 3 thousand 8½ hundred of quarterboard at 20d. the hundred, £8 10d. To him for 2 loads of quarters at 8s. 6d. the load, 17s. And for 3 loads of laths at 10s. 8d. the load, 32s. Total £10 9s. 10d.

To William Porter of Weybridge for 8 thousand of planks, and 3 thousand 1 hundred of quarterboard at 2s. 2d. the hundred, total £12 6d.

Total £96 13s. 5d.

468. Tiles and bricks.

To Hugh Brampson, brickmaker, for 61,000 bricks bought from him and delivered to sundry storehouses belonging to the Bridge House within the city and to the Bridge House within the time of this account, at 4s. 8d. the thousand, total £14 4s. 8d.

To Henry Knyght of Kings hill for 46,000 tiles delivered by him to sundry of the said storehouses and to the Bridge House within the time of this present account, at 4s. 8d. the thousand, total £10 14s. 8d.

To William Lynger of Surrey for 3,000 paving tiles, 42s.

To Richard Cooke of Addington for 600 corner tiles, total 16s.

Total £27 17s. 4d.

469. [f. 245] Chalk, lime, sand, gravel and loam.

To Stephen Parrot of Deptford for 53 boat[loads] of chalk, every boat containing 12 tons, in all 636 tons, delivered at the Bridge House within the time of this account, at 6d. the ton, £15 18s.

To Richard Dryver, limeburner, for 8,604 loads and 5 sacks of lime, counting 7 loads to every hundred, delivered to sundry of the said storehouses within the time of this account, at 4s. the hundred, £16 6s. 4d.

To Robert Colte of Billingsgate for 4 mounts [*moites*] of plaster, every mount containing [blank] at 6s. the mount, 24s. And for measuring the same, 16d., total 25s. 4d.

To Jeffrey Harryson for 175 loads of sand at 6d. the load, 87s. 6d., for 110 loads of gravel at 4d. the load, 36s. 8d., and for 86 loads of loam at 4d. the load, 28s. 8d., which he delivered to sundry of the said storehouses within the time of this present account. Total £7 12s. 10d.

To Philip Miller of Lewisham for 5 loads of sand delivered at Lewisham and used there, 15d.

To the wife of James Foster for 20 tons of chalk and rag delivered at the mill-dam at Stratford at 10d. the ton, total 16s. 8d.

Total £43 5d.

470. Ironworks and nails.

To William Sharparowe, blacksmith, for divers kinds of ironworks white and black, both great and small, locks and keys, together with mending sundry sorts of ironworks and tools both for the waterworks of the bridge and for sundry new and old tenements belonging to the said Bridge, as appears by his 4 several bills. Total £43 14s. 8½d.

To Nicholas Barker, armourer, for divers kinds of nails bought of him and received by the hands of Hughwet the porter, as appears by his bill. Total £13 14s. 8½d.

To Robert Terne, blacksmith, for battering 139 dozen masons' tools at 1½d. the dozen, total 17s. 4½d.

To John Peverell, blacksmith, for battering 71 dozen of the same tools at 1½d. the dozen, total 10s. 1½d.

To Rowley, blacksmith, for 2 pile-shoes, 18d.

To Gilbert the smith of *Radlyffe* [Rotherhithe] for 700 fourpenny nails, 2s. 4d., and for 300 threepenny nails, 9d., total 3s. 1d.

To Hugh Wattes, leatherseller of London, for 10 double plate-locks without keys for Cheapside, 20s.

To [blank] for 6 round rings and 6 hearts with latches and catches for the same house, 4s.

To Robert Golde for 300 fourpenny nails used at Stratford, 12d.

To Peter Carpenter of Southwark for 10 soldering irons for the plumber and 2 cutting knives, weighing 37 lb. at 3d. the lb., total 9s. 3d.

To the smith of Lambeth for 400 tenpenny nails at 10d. the hundred, 3s. 4d., for 1 thousand 8½ hundred sixpenny nails at 6d. the hundred, 9s. 3d., for 1,800 fourpenny nails at 4d. the hundred, 6s., and for 800 threepenny nails at 3d. the hundred, 2s. Total 20s. 7d.

[f. 245v] To Sclater of Mile End for 4 new tide-axes, 4s., for 5 adzes, 5s., for steeling 7 old adzes, 3s. 6d., and for steeling 3 augers, 18d., for the waterworks. Total 14s.

Total £62 10s. 4d.

471. Lead and solder.

There remained in the plumbery house [*the plomberye house*] in lead and lead ashes weighing 7 thousand 4 hundred 3 quarters 27 lb., as appears more fully in the charge of the last account. And 8 fother 14 hundred 3 quarters of bought lead was delivered to the said plumbery house. And old lead weighing 6 thousand 2 hundred 1 quarter 21 lb. was taken from divers tenements belonging to the Bridge and delivered to the plumbery house into the hands of Richard Roberts, plumber. Total 31 thousand 1½ hundred 40 lb.

Of which lead the said Richard Robert cast up in the plumbery house and wrought and laid 21 thousand 5 hundred 3 quarters 24 lb. [of lead] in gutters, pipes, paving, cisterns, fillets, sockets, grates and other necessaries within divers tenements belonging to the said Bridge, taking 6d. for casting, laying and working every hundred. Total £5 4s. 11½d.

And [lead] weighing 2 thousand 8 hundred was wasted, consumed and quite lost in melting and casting old and new lead within the said plumbery house from Michaelmas 29 Henry VII [1537] to Michaelmas 30 Henry VIII [1538].

And there remains 6 thousand 7½ hundred 24 lb. in fine lead and ashes within the plumbery house at Michaelmas 30 Henry VIII [1538].

To the said Richard Roberts for 5 hundred 70 lb. of solder, accounting 5 score lb. to the hundred, used in divers tenements belonging to the Bridge House this year, as appears by his bill, at 4d. the lb., total £9 10s.

To the said Richard Roberts for unstopping 2 pipes on the bridge, 20d.

To my lady Pargyter for 5 fother 7 hundred <16> of Peak lead at £4 6s. 8d. the fother, bought of her for the use of the Bridge House, with 3d. over, £23 4s. 7d.

To 3 labourers for carrying and conveying over of the same from Knights Key to the Bridge House, 9d.

And paid to the wharfinger for portage and wharfage of the same, 3s. 8d.

To William Leyghe, gold-finer, for 4 sows of Peak lead, weighing 1 fother 7 hundred 3 quarters at £4 6s. 8d. the fother, except that 1d. was rebated, total £6.

To John Carver of Candlewick Street, powderer, for 2 fother of lead at £4 6s. 8d. the fother, £8 13s. 4d.

Total £53 23½d.

472. [f. 246] Costs in glazing.

To Robert Nelson, glazier, for glazing 44 lights in the hall of the new house in Cheapside containing 111½ ft. of glass, at 4½d. the foot, 41s. 9½d. For 104 ft. in the chamber over the hall at 4½d. the foot, 29s. For 90¼ ft. of glass in the chamber in the highest storey, cemented, at 5d. the foot, 37s. 7d. For taking down 3 panes and setting up in 3 cases, 8d. And for 35 quarrels with the Bridge mark and the date of Our Lord at 1d. the quarrel, 2s. 11d. Total £6 23½d.

To the said Robert Nelson for glazing certain windows on the backside of the said new house: first in the parlour a window of 14 lights containing 47 ft. at 4½d. the foot, 18s. For 3 lights over the same window, containing 24 foot, 9s. For 16 ft. in the counting-house, 6s. For 7½ ft. in the buttery, 2s. 9½d. For 8 panes in the chamber over the parlour, containing 20½ ft., 7s. 8d. For 10 panes in the kitchen containing 23 ft., 2s. 7½d. For 3 panes in a little room where the Cope stands, containing 7 ft., 2s. 7½d. For 3 panes in the highest chamber containing 4½ ft., 20d. For 2 panes in the jakes containing 3 ft., 13½d. For 3 panes in the highest chamber over the parlour containing 4 ft., 18d. For 4 panes in the garret containing 6½ ft., 2s. 5d. And for 36 quarrels with the date of Our Lord and the Bridge House mark at 1d. the quarrel, rebated 12d., 2s. Total 63s. 5d.

Total £12 19s. 2d.

473. Necessary purchases.

To William Cockes, junior [*joynn'*], for 1 lb. glue, 2½d. To John Smythe, turner, for 6 trays for the masons, 2s. To Robert Golde for 1 fir pole 25 ft. long, 4d. To Ambrose Wolles for a hundred of rosin, 4s. To Richard Petwyn for 1 dozen gloves in reward for the masons, 2s. To Mr Blande for 1 ream of paper, 3s. To Thomas Monkest for a fine sieve for lime (8d.) <7d.> To Sherman for 2 baskets, 3d. Total 12s. 4½d.

To William Hewghett for 2 dozen cotton candles spent within the Bridge House, 2s. 6d. For 6 lb. at 1½d. the lb., 9d. To William Cockys, junior, for 2 dozen cotton candles spent at Cheapside, 2s. 6d. And for 1 lb. glue, 3½d. Total 6s. ½d.

[f. 246v] To Ambrose Wolloys for 1 barrel of tar for ropes and the cement boat, 4s. 8d. To Thomas Allen for 4 lb. thrums, 8d., for 10 lb. oakum, 10d. To Smythe of Eastcheap, turner, for 4 shovels for the masons 16d., for 4 spades [*scoppetts*] for the boats 8d. To Thomas Monkeste, plasterer, for 60 bushels of hair for the new house in Cheap at 3d. the bushel, 15s. To John Smythe for 2 pails, 6d. To the cordwainer at the gates for soling 2 prs. boots, 12d. And for 4 new clouts for the axle-tree of the cart for the millstone, 9d. Total 25s. 5d.

To Laurence Couper for hooping sundry sorts of tubs, pails, buckets and other for the works as appears by bill, 5s. 4d. To him for a new tun for the Crown against the Bridge House gate, 27s. Total 32s. 4d.

To Thomas Bulbroke of Lynn for 2 warps of small and great ropes, weighing 212 lb. at 12s. the hundred, 25s. To William Buckerall of Deptford for 4 warps of ropes great and small, weighing 3 hundred 1 quarter 11 lb. at 12s. the hundred, 40s. To John Moyle for 1 hundred 1 quarter of ropes for the boats, 15s. Total £4.

To Ambrose Wolleys for 1 barrel of tar, 5s. 4d., for 1 piece of tarpaulin [*bollyng*] for the cement boat, 7s. To Thomas Monkest for 4 bushels of hair, 12d. To John Smythe for 1 pail, 3d. Total 13s. 4d.

To Thomas Allen, mercer, for 1 barrel of pitch for the shout house, 4s. To John Hore, waterman, for the blade of an oar for the cement boat, 14d. To Thomas Smyth, turner, for 6 new trays, 2s. To William Hewhett for 46 lb. tallow at 1d. the lb., 3s. 10d., for 40 lb. grease at 1d. the lb., 3s. 4d. Total 14s. 4d.

To John Goose for 21 ft. of lattice for a tenement at the Minories at 2¾d. the foot, 4s. 9¾d. To Richard Buckerell of Deptford for 1 quarter and 9 ft. of rope for buckets, 4s. Total 8s. 9¾d.

To William Stevens of London for 4 barrels of pitch at 5s. 4d. the barrel, 21s. 4d., for 4 hundred 17 lb. of rosin at 4s. the hundred, 16s. 8d., for 3 oars for the boats, 3s. And for wharfage of the same ware, 1d. Total 16s. 1d.

To a parchment maker for 10 skins of vellum for the books of this account, 6s. 8d.

Total £12 7¾d.

474. Necessary expenses for the obits of Anne Fenkenham, John Clyfforde and Christian Mallynge, as is contained in their testaments, 35s. 10d.

To the masters for their expenses in viewing the lands and tenements belonging to the Bridge this year, both within the city and at Stratford, Lewisham, and Greenwich at sundry times, and for money given by them among the workmen to cause them to apply their works, total 23s. 11½d.

To Hughwette's wife for weeding in the garden this year as before accustomed, 8s.

[f. 247] To Henry Mylles, gardener, for working in the garden this year for 16½ days at 8d. the day, 11s. To his servant for 5 days at 5d. the day, 2s. 1d. To him for poles for the garden 3d., for wire for the rosemary 5d., and for seeds for the same 9d. Total 14s. 6d.

To Thomas Wulberde of Deptford for certain repairs done by him in a house in which the king's harness lies, 7s.

To Thomas Mason, ordure voider, for voiding 66 tuns of ordure from 2 tenements within the Castle in Wood Street at 18d. the tun, total £4 19s.

To him for cleansing 6 tuns from the sluice called *le braunte* at 18d. the tun, 9s. And to him and 4 of his servants for cleaning a draught at Mr Doughtye's house, 6s. 2d. Total 15s. 2d.

To John Smyth for watching with the said ordure voiders for 11 nights to control his filling [the tuns], at 4d. the night, 3s. 8d. And for watching at Mr Doughtye's house, 9d. Total 4s. 5d.

To the said John Smythe for carriage of certain cuttings of lead from the new house in Cheapside, 3d. To Alexander, a painter of Wood Street, for painting and gilding 2 vanes and the spindle of the same for the finials set at the new building in Cheap, 10s. Total 10s. 3d.

To the wardmote inquest of the bridge in reward as has been accustomed, 2s. To 5 masons for steeling their tools at 18d. each, 7s. 6d. To William Hughwet for 18 loads of dung, 4d. To Laurence and Provest going to Petham Court to measure up the sawyers' works, for their charges, 2s. 6d. To Provest for his charges another time, 8d. Total 13s.

To learned counsel for making an answer to a bill of complaint exhibited against the Bridge wardens by the abbot and convent of Tower Hill for a quit-rent at Ivy Lane end, 10s.

To the said abbot and convent for the same matter, by commandment of the bench, £42

To William Drapar of Bromley, deputy steward of Greenwich, Lewisham, Deptford, Lee, and Stratford for his retainer to make answer for the Bridge masters in these courts, at 12d. every year and this time 5s.

To Richard Patwyn, glover, for 6 prs. gloves given amongst the masons, 12d. To Richard Howsynge of Houndsditch for casting 3 old brasses weighing 66 lb. at 1d. the lb., 5s. 6d. To Robert Golde for his costs and charges in going to Croydon, and Cockes with him, to measure [*meite*] timber, 16d. Total 7s. 10d.

To William Hughwet for boughs and flowers for the gate at Midsummer, 10d. To Thomas Dowell, dyker, for casting a piece of a drain [*shwer'*] against the Crown, 20d. To the said William Hughwet for taking up 2 oars, 2d. To Arnolde, Thomson, and Fylde for steeling their tools for 3 quarters of a year, 3s. Total 5s. 8d.

To the masters for a repast made to the lord mayor and his brethren at the audit day, over and above their old allowances allowed in previous acounts, total 10s. 7d.

Total £60 2½d.

475. [f. 247v] Repairs of mills.
To Bridges, wharfinger at Mr Forman's wharf, for holing 2 millstones, 10s.
To Andrew Morres for wharfage of the same 3 stones, 2s. And for portage and carriage of the same from the wharf into the street, 2s. 8d. Total 4s. 8d.
To William Carter for carriage of the same stones to both mills in Stratford, 2s.
To Thomas Whyte of Stratford for mending a pair of wheels for the same stones, 10d.
Total 18s. 4d.

476. Costs of carriage.
To Robert Butler for carriage of 81 loads of framed timber from the Bridge House to the Standard in Cheap at 6d. the load, total 40s. 6d.
To Mistress Foster for carriage of 126 loads of framed timber, board, stone, and other stuff from the said Bridge House to the Standard and other places within the city at 4d. the load, total 42s.
To her for carriage of 45 loads of like stuff from the Bridge House to the bridge and from the bridge home, at 2d. the load, 7s. 6d. And for the carriage of 23 loads of rubbish from her own house at 2d. the load, 3s. 10d. Total 11s. 4d.
To her for carriage of 5 loads of rubbish from a joiner's house in Southwark rents at 2d. the load, 10d., for carriage of 1 load to Gracechurch, 3d., and for carriage of 1 load to Stratford, 12d., 2s. 1d.
To Jeffrey Harryson for carriage of 7 loads of timber and other stuff to divers places within the city at 4d. the load, total 2s. 4d.
To him for carriage of 31 loads of rubbish from Newgate market, Paternoster Row, and Cheapside at 2½d. the load, 6s. 5½d., and for carriage of 8 loads of rubbish at 2d. the load, 16d. Total 7s. 9½d.
To John Clerke of Southwark, carter, for carriage of 22 loads of timber, board, and other stuff to divers places within the city at 4d. the load, total 7s. 4d.
To him for carriage of 7 loads of rubbish from Cheapside in his small cart at 2d. the load, 14d.
To Thomas Mason for carriage of 17 loads of rubbish from the Castle in Wood Street and from Cheap at 2½d. the load, 3s. 6½d., and for carriage of 12 loads from the same places at 2d. the load, 2s., 5s. 6½d.
To William Bonde for carriage of 14 loads of rubbish from Cheapside at 2d. the load, total 2s. 4d.
To Philip Myller of Lewisham for carriage of 8 loads of timber, board, and other stuff from Deptford to Lewisham at 4d. the load, 2s. 8d.
Total £6 5s. 1d.

477. Costs of the chapel.

First to 3 chaplains ministering daily in the chapel on the bridge for 52 weeks within the time of the present account, to each for a whole year at £6 13s. 4d. a year, total £20. [f. 248] To 5 clerks serving and attending daily in the chapel, each for 52 weeks within the time of this present account at 2s. a week, £26. To Roger Robyns also serving in the chapel for 52 weeks at 12d. a week, 52s.

To the wife of William Tanner for washing the chapel clothes this year, 4s. To John Ferrys for keeping the chapel with all the goods and ornaments belonging to it, as has been allowed in past years, 20s. To him for singing bread for the chapel this year, 8d. To the said 3 priests and 6 clerks for singing *Placebo* and *Dirige* on 4 several occasions this year for the souls of the benefactors of the said chapel, 12s. To them for singing *Te Deum* for the birth of our prince, 12d. To John Ferrys for a dozen cotton candles, 15d. To John Hacker of London, fishmonger, for 18 lb. of Polish [*pollen*] wax for the lights of the chapel, 12s. To John Houghe, organmaker, for mending the organs this year, 12d. To Robert Gray, waxchandler, for making 43 lb. of wax new and old into divers tapers great and small and other lights for the chapel at [erasure] 1/2d. the lb., total 211/2d. To him for a Paschal of his own wax, weighing 22 lb., 3s. 31/2d. To the said John Houghe, organmaker, for mending a pair of bellows, 5s. In reward to children for singing in the chapel on Lady Day, 20d. To Ralph Wilmotte for 60 pints of Gascon wine at 1d. the pint, 5s. To Nicholas Hacker for 9 gallons and a pottle of lamp-oil at 12d. a gallon, total 9s. 6d.

To Einergeger, one of the chaplains aforesaid, by commandment of my lord mayor and his brethren, for his wages for 13 weeks which should be ended at Christmas next coming, and in recompense for the discharge of his services, at 2s. 6d. a week, total 32s. 6d. To Mitchelson, Vyncent, Breght, and Stephen Robson, clerks of the said chapel, by like commandment for wages for 13 weeks at 2s. each a week, total 104s. To Roger Robynson for 13 weeks at 12d. the week, total 13s. Total £59 19s. 8d.

478. Masons' wages.

To John Orgar, chief mason of the Bridge works for his wages and fee as well for his attendance and good oversight given to the said Bridge as for making provision for all manner of hard stones of Kent necessary and convenient for the works of the said Bridge for a whole year coming within the time of this account, £10.

[f. 248v] To Bennet for 185 days, Thomson for 203 days, Arnold for 197 days, Fylde for 177 days and Haynes for 194 days, masons working as well in apparelling sundry sorts of hard stone of Kent apt for the waterworks of the said bridge and divers other works belonging to the same, as in setting the same stones in a great arch and breasts of the said bridge next to Southwark, and in paving of sundry kitchens on the said bridge, St Nicholas Shambles, Paternoster Row, Old Change, and other places within the city, as appears by the Journal of the weekly [payments], between them for 957 days at 8d. a day, £31 18s.

To the said Bennet for 59 days, Thomson for 55 days, Arnold for 54 days, Fylde for 59 days, Heynes for 59 days working in the works aforesaid, between them for 286 days at 7½d. a day. Total £8 18s. 9d.

To the said Thomson for 9 days, Arnold for 12 days, Fylde for 12 days and Haynes for 18 days, between them for 51 days at 7d. a day. Total 29s. 9d.

To Jeffrey Orgar, mason, working in the said works amongst the said masons for 277 days at 7d. a day. Total £8 2s. 2d.

To Bennet for 12 tides, Thomson for 12 tides, Arnolde for 12 tides, Fylde for 12 tides, Heynes for 11 tides, and Jeffrey Orgar for 10 tides, masons working at the said arch and breasts of the same out of due time as the tides have fallen within the time of this account, between them for 69 tides at 4d. a tide. Total 23s.

Total £61 11s. 8d.

479. Carpenters' wages.

To Richard Ambrose, chief carpenter of the Bridge works for his fee for one whole year within the time of this present account, £10.

To Robert Golde, warden carpenter of the waterworks belonging to the said Bridge for his wages for 48 weeks within the time of this present account, taking by the week broken and whole 4s., total £9 12s.

To William Cockes the younger, warden carpenter of the land works belonging to the said Bridge for his wages for 47 weeks within the time of this present account, taking for every week broken and whole 4s., total £9 8s.

To William Cockes the elder for 260 days, Browne the elder for 260 days, Henry Godfreye for 260 days, Browne junior for 257 days, Ingledewe for 227 days, Pasmer for 243 days, Palmer for 260 days, Thomas Browne for 242 days, Thomas Broke 137 days, Walter Allen 134 days, John Proveste 237 days, Leonard Holmes 260 days, Roger Maxton 5 days, carpenters working as well in hewing and squaring elm timber within the Bridge House into sundry scantlings meet and apt for the works of the said Bridge, driving piles and stopping in and [f. 249] about certain starlings of the same, joisting and binding sundry staddles of the same, as in setting up and finishing of the new house or tenement against the Standard in Cheap, mending and making new of Simon Lowys' house, in repairs within sundry tenements upon the said bridge, St Nicholas Shambles, Paternoster Row, St Dionis, St Margaret Patten lane, Friday Street, Fenchurch Street, Lewisham, Deptford and Stratford, with divers other places belonging to the said Bridge, between them for 2,784 days at 8d. a day. Total £92 16s.

To Robert Golde for 18 days, William Cockes the younger for 18 days, William Cockes the elder for 17 days, Browne senior for 17 days, Browne junior for 17 days, Henry Godfreye for 17 days, Leonard Holmes for 17 days, Palmer for 17 days, Thomas Browne for 12 days, Inggledewe for 17 days, Pasmer for 17 days, and John Proveste for 17 days, carpenters working in the works aforesaid between them for 201 days at 7d. a day. Total 117s. 3s.

To Simon Cockes, carpenter, for 24 days at 4d. a day 7s. To him for 253 days working in the said works at 5d. a day. 105s. 5d. 113s. 5d.

To John Pasmer, carpenter, for 139 days at 5d. a day, 57s. 11d., and to him for 129 days working in the said works at 6d. a day, 64s. 6d. Total 122s. 5d.

To Nicholas Holoway, carpenter, for 125 days working in the said works at 6d. a day. Total 62s. 6d.

To William Wynter, carpenter for 44 days at 5d. a day, 18s. 4d. And to him for 180 days working in the said works at 6d. a day, 90s. Total £5 8s. 4d.

To the said Robert Golde for 9 tides, Cockes the elder for 14 tides, Browne senior for 11 tides, Henry Godfrye for 13 tides, Browne junior for 9 tides, Simon Cockes for 14 tides, Cockes for 10 tides, Ingledewe for 10 tides, Pasmer for 11 tides, Palmer for 9 tides, Thomas Browne for 10 tides, Leonard Holmes ofr 9 tides, John Provest for 9 tides, John Pasmer for 10 tides, and Wynter for 12 tides, carpenters working in the waterworks out of due time as the tides have fallen this year, between them for 160 tides at 4d. a tide. Total 53s. 4d.

Total £150 13s. 3d.

480. Labourers' wages.

To John Smythe for 277 days, Roger Whythed for 277 days, Thomas Allen for 177 days, Wynter for 34 days, Sherman for 170 days, Tanner for 187 days, John Cleworth 101 days, Roger Hood for 5 days, Thomas Johnson 5 days, John Thomson 2 days, Shypard 3 days, labourers labouring and attending as well on the aforesaid masons as [on the] carpenters in conveying necessary stuff to the same workmen's hands and in divers other places and works belonging to the waterworks of the bridge and tenements of the same, as appears by the Journal of weekly payments, between them for 1,238 days at 5d. a day. Total £25 15s. 10d.

[f. 249v] To the said Sherman for 50 days and Tanner for 65 days, labourers labouring as aforesaid, between them for 115 days at 4d. a day, total 38s. 4d.

To divers and sundry labourers labouring with the carpenters at the bridge at the five-man beetle, driving piles for the foundations and other businesses there needing to be done, between them this year for 261 tides at (4d.) <3d.> a tide, total 65s. 3d.

To Thomas Allen for heating 38 cement pots for the masons at 4d. a pot, total 12s. 8d.

To 6 labourers for removing timber in the yard for 2 days at 3d. a day each, total 3s.

To 4 labourers for gathering, loading and unloading 4 boats of chalk, 3s. 8d.

To 6 other labourers for loading 5 boats of chalk, 3s. 4d.

To 3 labourers for placing [*bestowynge*] chalk in the yard, 18d.

To Thomas Allen for money paid by him to divers labourers for helping him to convey the boats laden with timber, stones and other engines meet for the waterworks through the bridge, and for loading the same at St Mary Overey's wall on the west side of the bridge, as the tides have fallen this year out of due time, as appears by his bill and the Journal. Total 44s. 11d.

To divers labourers for loading and unloading 6 boats of chalk, 6s. 3d.

To 10 men for loading and unloading 3 boats of chalk, 2s. 6d.

To 7 men for loading 2 boats of chalk, 14d.

To 3 labourers placing chalk for 4 tides, 3s.

To 3 labourers for loading and unloading 2 boats of chalk, 18d.

To 3 men for stowing chalk at the bridge for 1 tide, 9d.

To 6 men for unloading 4 boats of stone and chalk, 2s.

To them for unloading 2 boats of chalk, 12d.

To 8 men for loading and unloading 2 boats of chalk, 22d.

To Thomas Wright for placing chalk in the starlings for 3 tides, 9d.

To 6 men for loading and unloading 6 boats of chalk, 4s. 8d.

To 2 labourers for bearing board and laths for 2 days, 2s. 2d.

To John Auston for placing chalk, 2d.

To 4 labourers for unloading 10 boats of chalk, 3s. 4d.

To 2 labourers for labouring in placing chalk for 2 tides, 12d.

To 13 labourers for taking up 18 loads of elm timber, 3s. 4d.

To 2 labourers for placing chalk in the starlings for 3 tides, 18d.

To Robert Golde for taking up 20 loads of oak timber, 5s. 8d.

To 10 labourers for taking up a score of elm planks, 2s. 6d.

To 13 labourers for taking up a score of elm timber that came from Dartford, 5s. 5d.

To 10 men for loading and unloading 5 boats of chalk and placing the same, 4s. 2d. To 6 men for unloading 3 boats of chalk, 18d. And to 3 men for 4 tides placing chalk, 3s. Total 8s. 8d.

To 10 labourers for taking up 20 loads of oak timber, 3s. 4d.

To 4 labourers for taking up 7 loads of oak timber, 8d.

To Thomas Alen for loading 3 boats of chalk in the Bridge House and unloading the same, 2s. 6d. To him for loading 4 boats of stone at the bridge, 2s. And to him for 3 men placing chalk for 4 tides, 2s. Total 6s. 6d.

[f. 250] To the said Thomas for loading and unloading 4 boats of chalk, 21d.

To 8 men for taking up 19 loads of oak timber, 4s.

To 8 labourers for placing planks in the storehouse, 4d.

To 16 labourers for taking up a fare of elm timber and planks that came from Dartford, 7s. 6d.

To 2 labourers for bringing a boat to Deptford for 1 night, 8d.

To 7 labourers in taking up 7 loads of oak timber, 14d.

To Tanner, Wynter, and Cloworth for carriage of 1 boat of timber and board to Deptford, 12d.

To 11 labourers for taking up timber that came from Deptford, 4s. 7d. Total £39 2s. 9d.

481. Bricklayers' wages.

To William Swenson for 240 days and Richard Cherlton for 213 days, working as well in laying and setting bricks and tiles and bringing up chimneys in the new house in Cheap, Simon Lewes' [house] on the bridge, St Nicholas Shambles, Paternoster Row, Friday Street, Fenchurch Street, St Margaret Pattens, Lewisham, Deptford and other places, between them for 453 days at 8d. a day. Total £15 2s.

To the said Swenson for 17 days working in the said works at 7d. a day, total 9s. 11d.

To Nevell for 212 days, Thomas Grene for 200 days, Brogett [sic; *recte* Hogett] for 212 days, Jacson 28 days, Sherman for 44 days, Tanner for 17 days, Thomas Laurence for 2 days, Roger Dome for 2 days, and Thorley for 6 days, labourers labouring and attending on the said bricklayers and tilers in conveying stuff to the workmen's hands and works aforesaid, between them for 723 days at 5d. a day. Total £15 15d.

To the said Nevell for 59 days, Hayhet [*recte* Hogett] for 59 days, Thomas Grene for 59 days, Jacson for 6 days, and Sherman for 15 days, working in the said works, between them for 198 days at 4d. a day, 66s.

Total £33 19s. 2d.

482. Daubers' wages.

To Thomas Monkest for 218 days, Bryane for 28 days, Doucat for 39 days, working in the tenements aforesaid belonging to the said Bridge, as appears by the Journal, between them for 285 days at 8d. a day. Total £9 10s.

To the said Thomas Monkest for working in the same works for 11 days at 7d. a day, 6s. 5d., total 6s. 5d.

To John Turfyt, labourer, for 190 days, Patrick Pluckney for 65 days, and William Monkest for 5 days, labourers labouring with the said plasterers, between them for 260 days at 5d. a day, 108s. 4d.

To the said John Turfyt for 39 days working in the said works at 4d. a day, total 13s.

Total £15 17s. 9d.

483. [f. 250v] Wages at the gins.

To 20 labourers labouring in drawing at the gin called the gibbet gin, driving piles in and about the starlings on the west and north side of the bridge under Lawes' house, within the time of this account, between them for 64 tides, at 5s. a tide between them, except that there lacked 1 man for 12 tides. Total £15 17s.

To 2 labourers holding and guiding the said gibbet Ram for the said 64 tides, at 8d. a tide between them, 42s. 8d.

To John Browne for 6 men for 4 tides, making scaffolds for the said gin at 3d. a tide, total 6s.

Total £18 5s. 8d.

484. Shipwrights' wages.

To Hugh Yonge for 4 days at 11d. a day, 3s. 8d. John Lewys for 10 days at 10d. a day, 8s. 4d. Richard Forde for 6 days at 10d. a day, 5s. John Cawde for 6 days at 8d. a day, 4s. William Almonte for 10 days at 8d. a day, 6s. 8d. John Fyddeler for 10 days at 10d. a day, 8s. 4d. And

William Eglesse for 5 days at 8d. a day, 3s. 4d., shipwrights working in caulking and pitching of 7 several boats belonging to the said Bridge House. Total 39s. 4d.

Total 39s. 4d.

485. Sawyers' wages.

To John Flynt, sawyer, for sawing and slitting oak and elm timber within the Bridge House into divers scantlings necessary and convenient as well for the waterworks of the bridge as for sundry new buildings belonging to the land works of the bridge, by the discretion of Robert Golde and William Cocks, carpenters of the said works, in all 1 thousand 4 hundred at 13s. the hundred, total £17 2d.

To the same Flynte for sawing 14¼ hundred [of] board at 12d. the hundred, total 14s. 3d.

To Horton the sawyer for slitting 6 thousand 6½ hundred of the same stuff into divers scantlings as aforesaid, less 2d. rebated, 71s. 10d.

To 2 sawyers of Petham Court for sawing 2,304 ft. of planks cut and half cut [*of karfe and half karfe*] at 14d. the hundred, 26s. 11d. And for sawing 1,765 ft. of board at 12d. the hundred, 17s. 8d. For making 5 sawpits 4s. 4d. For crosswise cuts [*anthwart kyrffs*] 2s. [Total] 50s. 11d.

<To the said Horton for sawing 2 hundred of board at the Bridge House, 2s.>

Total £23 19s. 2d.

486. Paviours' wages.

To Richard Ruddynge, paviour, for paving 22 toises on the backside of the sign of the Cup in St Nicholas Shambles, for paving 29 toises before the house in Cheap, for 21 toises at the Stocks, 15 toises at Old Change, 3 toises at the corner in Eastcheap, and 10 toises in Friday Street, in all 100 toises at 7d. the toise, total 58s. 4d.

[f. 251] To him for stopping up holes and *cartwheles* [? ruts] on the bridge for 3 days, with his servant with him, 3s.

To him and his said servant working on the bridge for 4 days in like work, 4s. 4d.

Total 65s. 4d.

487. Fees and wages of officers.

To the said wardens for their fees of their office, to each £16 13s. 4d., total £33 6s. 8d.

To the said wardens for their clothing, 40s.

To them for their horses, £4.

To Ralph Coldwell, learned in the law, retained as counsel with the said wardens in matters concerning the Bridge this year, for his fee 13s. 4d.

To Laurence Awen, clerk of the works of the Bridge for his fee within the time of this account, £10.

To Richard Maunsell, receiver of all the rents and tenements of the Bridge, for his whole year's fee and drinking with gathering of the fishmongers and butchers at the Stocks this year, total £23 6s. 8d.

To the said Richard in reward over and above his year's fee, as it has been allowed in the last account, 40s.

To Thomas Holydaye, serjeant of the chamber of London, for warning the Auditors of the city to hear and determine this account, 6s. 8d.

To William Hughwet, porter of the Bridge House gate, for his wages for 52 weeks within the time of this account, at 2s. a week, total 104s.

To Thomas Allen, keeper of the boats and shouts belonging to the said Bridge, for his wages for 52 weeks, that is to say 2s. 6d. weekly for himself, and 10d. weekly for keeping and finding the hounds within the Bridge House, total £8 13s. 4d.

Total £89 10s. 8d.

488. Rewards to officers.

To the said wardens for their attendance and good provision done in their office, £10 each, total £20.

To the said clerk of the works, in reward to him allowed for writing and duplicating the books of this present account, whereof one book remains at the Guildhall in London and the other at the Bridge House, £3 6s. 8d.

Total £23 6s. 8d.

489. Costs of the auditors in hearing and determining this present account, and for a repast made among officers and ministers in the works of the Bridge, as allowed in accounts in years past, total 40s.

And for counters delivered to the said auditors to cast this present account, 2s. 8d.

Total 42s. 8d.

490. [f. 251v] Allowance for money given by the mayor and bench to the duke of Suffolk for debt for wheat, £14 13s. 4d.

491. Total of all the payments [and] allowances, £1,510 17s. 2¼d.

492. And there is owing [blank]

Whereof

Upon Andrew Cooke and his surety, 74s.

Upon sundry persons debtors to the granaries, 47s. 2½d.

Total £6 14½d.

493. And so the said accountants owe clearly of this present account £345 19s. 2¼d.

By me William Forman, mayor [signature]

By me Ralph Warey [signature]

By me Walter Mersch [signature]

By me Roger Pynchester [signature]

By me Richard Rede [signature]

By me Thomas Curteys [signature]

BRIDGE HOUSE
WEEKLY PAYMENTS BOOK

Second Series, Volume 3
Account for 1537–8

494. [f. 390] Receipts and payments of Thomas Erith and Robert Draper, Wardens of London Bridge from Michaelmas 29 Henry VIII [1537] to Michaelmas then next [1538] for one whole year.

495. [f. 390v] 5 October [1537]
Receipts Fishmongers Butchers Passage tolls
Received of Laurence Awen, clerk of the house, for 16 ft. of oak timber at 2d. the foot, 2s. 8d., and for 52 ft. of oak and elm board 16d., in all 4s.
Three chaplains 7s. 6d. Five clerks 10s. Roger Robyns 12d.
Masons. Bennett 4s. Tomson 4s. Arnold 4s. Fyld 4s. Heyneys 4s. Jeffrey Orgar 3s. 6d. in apparelling hard stone of Kent and on the arch aforesaid.
Carpenters. Robert Gold pt 4s. Cocks the elder [*maius* or *maior*] 4s. Browne senior 4s. Henry Godfrey 4s. Browne junior 4s. Simon Cocks 2s. (6d.) in the waterworks.
Cocks pt 4s. (Inglydwe 4s.) Pasmer (4s.) <2s.> 8d. Palmer 4s. Thomas Browne 4s. Leonard Holmes 4s. Provest 4s. Thomas Broke 2s. Nicholas Holowaye 3s. John Pasmer 2s. (6d.) upon the new frame aforesaid.
Sawyers. Flynt slitting [at] 7d., 8s. 1d.
Porter. William Hughwett 2s.
Shoutman. Thomas Alen 3s. 4d.
Bricklayers. Swynson 4s. Chorleton 4s. Labourers. Nevell 2s. 6d. Grene 20d. Hogett 2s. 6d. William Jacson 2s. 6d.
Daubers. Thomas Mounkest 4s. Labourer. William Mounkest 2s. 6d.
[Labourers] John Smyth 2s. 6d. Sherman 2s. 6d. Whythed 2s. 6d. Alen 2s. 6d. Tanner 2s. 6d. (James Holmes 2s. 6d.) Wynter 2s. 6d.
[Total] of this page £7 7s. 10d.
[f. 391] To Robert Gold for the gibbet gin by 5 tides, driving piles at the starling aforesaid at 5s. 8d. the tide, 28s. 4d.
To John Gate of Maidstone for freight of 6 great stones for springers for the bridge, and for a quarter of bridge ashlar, containing in all 6 tons, 6s.
Paid to (Joh) William Cocks junior for 1 [lb.] of glue 2½d.
To Roger Hoode and Thomas Sheperd, labourers labouring at the five-man beetle, to each for 5 tides at 3d. the man, 2s. 6d.
To Thomas Mason, ordure voider, for cleansing a draught in Mr Doughtye's houses at the bridge end, working there by himself with 3 men for 4 tides, 6s. 2d.

To John Smith for watching with the said ordure voider, 9d.
To Thomas Alen by bill 3s. 8d.
To heating 5 cement pots for the masons, 20d. To John Smyth, turner, for 6 trays for the masons 2s.
[Total] of this page 51s. 3½d.
Total paid this week £9 19s. 1½d.

496. [f. 391v] 13 October
Renter   Fishmongers   Butchers   Passage tolls
Received of Christopher Payne by the hands of Robert Gold for one load of elm timber, 6s. Received of him for 30 ft. of oak, 5s. 6d. For one load of oak for the earl's sluice, 8s. For 6 ft. more, 12d. For half a hundred ft. of oak planks for the said sluice, 2s. 6d. In all 17s.
The chaplains 7s. 6d. Five clerks 10s. Roger Robyns 12d.
Masons. Bennett 4s. Tomson 4s. Arnold 4s. Fyld 4s. Heynes 4s. Jeffrey Orgar 3s. 6d. in apparelling hard stone of Kent and on the arch aforesaid.
Carpenters. Robert Gold 4s. Cocks the elder 4s. Browne senior 4s. Henry Godfrey 4s. Browne junior 4s. Simon Cocks 2s. (6d.) William Cocks 4s. Inglydwe [sic] Pasmer 4s. Palmer 4s. Thomas Browne 4s. Leonard Holmes 4s. John Provest 4s. Thomas Brooke [sic] Nicholas Holowaye 3s. John Pasmer 2s. (6d.) upon the new frame aforesaid.
Sawyers. Flynt slitting 7 hundred, 7s. 6d.
Porter. William Hugwett 2s.
Shoutman. Thomas Alen 3s. 4d.
Bricklayers. Swynson 4s. Chorleton 4s. Labourers. Nevell 2s. 6d. Grene 20d. Hogett 2s. 6d. William Jacson 2s. 6d.
Daubers. Thomas Monkest. Labourers. William Mounkest.
Labourers. John Smyth 2s. 6d. Sherman 2s. 6d. Whythed 2s. 6d. Thomas Alen 2s. 6d. Tanner 2s. 6d. Wynter 2s. 6d.
[Total] of this page £6 19s. 5d.
[f. 392] To Robert Gold for the gibbet gin by [blank] tides, driving of piles on and above a starling.
To Robert Corne, blacksmith, for 260 lb. of cramp irons [blank].
To Bennett, Tomson, Arnold, Fyld, Heynes and Jeffrey Orgar, masons, working in the works aforesaid out of due time by one tide, 2s.
To 6 labourers labouring at the five-man beetle, each of them for 6 tides at 3d. the tide, in all 9s.
To 6 labourers for removing timber in the yard for 2 days this week at 3d. the man, 2s.
To Robert Gold for a fir pole 25 ft. long, 4d.
To Thomas Alen for heating the cement pot for 6 tides at 4d. the tide 2s.
To Thomas Alen, John Smyth, Roger Whythed, Tanner, Sherman, and William Wynter, labourers labouring with the said masons for 1 tide at 3d. the man, 18d.
To the priests and clerks for singing *Te Deum* for the birth of our prince, 12d.
[Total] of this page 18s. 10d.
Total paid this week £7 18s. 3d.

497. [f. 392v] 20 October

Renter   Fishmongers   Butchers   Passage tolls

Three chaplains 7s. 6d. Five clerks 10s. Roger Robyns 12d.

Masons. Bennett 4s. Tomson 4s. Arnold 4s. Fyld 4s. Heynes 4s. Jeffrey Orgar 3s. 6d. in apparelling hard stone of Kent and on the arch aforesaid.

Carpenters. Robert Gold pt 4s. Cocks the elder 3s. 4d. Browne senior 3s. 4d. Henry Godfrey 3s. 4d. Browne junior 3s. 4d. Simon Cocks 20d.

In the waterworks. Cocks pt 4s. Palmer 3s. 4d. Pasmer 3s. 4d. Browne Thomas 3s. 4d. Leonard Holmes 3s. 4d. John Provest 2s. Nicholas Holowaye 2s. 6d. John Pasmer 2s. 1d. Roger Mayton 3s. 4d.

Sawyers. Flynt slitting 5½ hundred, 5s. 11d.

Porter. William Hugwett 2s.

Shoutman. Thomas Alen 3s. 4d.

Bricklayers.William Swynson 3s. 4d. Chorleton 3s. 4d. Labourers. Nevell 2s. 1d. Hogett 2s. 1d. Thomas Grene 2s. 1d. William Jacson 2s. 1d. in Paternoster Row and in Southwark.

Labourers. Smyth 2s. 1d. Sherman 2s. 1d. Whytehed 2s. 1d. Thomas Alen 2s. 1d. Wynter 2s. 1d. Tanner 2s. 1d.

[Total] of this page £6 7s. 6d.

[f. 393] To Robert (M) <Colt> of London by the assignment of [blank] Billingsgate for 4 mounts of plaster and every mount containing [blank] at 6s. the mount, and to the aforesaid [blank] Fryer for weighing the same, 4d. for every mount 16d., in all 25s. 4d.

To the shoutman by bill 3s. 6d.

To 4 labourers for loading 4 boats with stone at the Bridge House Wharf 16d. and to 7 other labourers for unloading 4 boats of chalk 2s. 4d., in all 3s. 8d.

To Bennett, Tomson, Arnold, Fyld, and Jeffrey Orgar, masons, working out of due time by one tide, 20d.

To Robert Butler for carriage of 16 loads of framed timber for the new frame in Cheapside from the Bridge House to Cheapside at 6d. the load, 8s.

To him for carriage of 3 loads of timber from Croydon to the Bridge House, parcel of 50 loads bought of Mr Gaynesford at 2s. 4d. the load, 7s.

To 5 labourers each for 5 tides at the three-man beetle, at 3d. a man per tide, 6s. 3d.

Expenses of the masters at the new frame in Cheap this week, 8d.

To Ambrose Wolley, grocer, by the hand of his servant William [blank] for a hundred of rosin, 4s.

To the shoutman for heating the cement pots 5 several times this week, 20d.

[Total] of this page 61s. 10d.

Sum total paid this week £9 9s. 4d.

498. [f. 393v] Saturday 27 October

Renter   Fishmongers   Butchers   Passage tolls

Received of William Jacson, the Queen's bailiff of Southwark, for 16 ft. of small shells, 2s.

Received of William Modye, the king's footman, for 10 ft. of oak, 20d.

Received of the said William Jacson for 6 small oak shells, 2s.

Three chaplains 7s. 6d. Five clerks 10s. Roger Robyns 12d.

Masons. Bennett 4s. Tomson 4s. Arnold 4s. Fyld 4s. Heynes 4s. Jeffrey Orgar 3s. 6d. in apparelling hard stone of Kent and on the water vault aforesaid.

Carpenters. Robert Gold pt 4s. Cocks the elder 4s. Browne senior [blank] Henry Godfrey 4s. Browne junior [blank] Simon Cocks 2s. Cocks pt 4s. Ingleydw [blank] Pasmer 4s. Palmer 4s. Thomas (Browne) 4s. Leonard Holmes 4s. John Provest 4s. Browne senior 4s. Nicholas Heynes 3s. (6d.) John Pasmer 2s. 6d. Robert Broke 4s. Walter Alen 3s. 4d. Browne junior 4s.

Sawyers. Flynt slitting 7 hundred, 6s. 7d. [blotted]

Porter. Hugwet 2s.

Shoutman. Thomas Alen 3s. 4d.

Bricklayers. William Swynson 4s. Chorleton 4s. Labourers. Nevell 2s. 6d. Hogett 2s. 6d. Thomas Grene 2s. 6d. William Jacson 2s. 6d.

Labourers. John Smyth 2s. 6d. Sherman 2s. 6d. Whythed 2s. 1d. Thomas Alen 2s. 6d. Tanner 2s. 6d. Wynter 2s. 6d. Roger Hood 20d.

Daubers. Monkest [blank] Labourer. Thomas Monkest [blank]

[Total] of this page £7 8s. 5d.

[f. 394] Paid John Ferres for a dozen white lights for the chapel, 16d.

To 2 men at the three-man beetle for 6 tides and one man by 2 tides, taking 3d. the tide, 3s. 6d.

To Thomas Alen, shoutman, by bill 16d. To him for heating the cement pot once, 4d.

To 10 labourers for loading and unloading 6 boats of chalk and rag at the Bridge House, 3s. 6d.

To Richard Patwyn for a dozen gloves given to the carpenters at the raising of the new house in Cheap, 2s.

To Robert Butler for carriage of 14 loads of framed timber from the Bridge House to Cheapside at 6d., 7s.

To the masters in expenses this week, 8d.

[Total] of this page 19s. 6d.

Sum total paid this week £8 7s. 11d.

499. [f. 394v] 3 November

From the hands of the renter £8   Fishmongers   Butchers   Passage tolls

Received of William Parker, wheelwright, for 1½ loads of elm timber, 9s.

Received of Bullmaister of the Steelyard for 33 ft. of elm timber, 8s.

Received of John Towe by the hands of William Cocks for 16 ft. of elm timber, 6s. 8d.

Received of Elizabeth Hynd, widow, for licence to set over her house and tenement, 20s.

Three chaplains [7s. 6d.] Five clerks [10s.] Roger Robyns 12d.

Masons. Bennett 4s. Arnold 4s. Tomson 4s. Fyld 4s. Heynes 4s. Jeffrey 3s. 6d. in apparelling hard stone.

Carpenters. Gold pt 4s. Cocks the elder 3s. 4d. Simon Cocks 2s. 1d. in the waterworks.

Cocks pt 4s. Inglydew 2s. 8d. Browne senior 3s. 4d. Browne junior 3s. 4d. Palmer 3s. 4d. Pasmer 3s. 4d. Thomas Browne 3s. (4d.) Leonard Holmes 3s. 4d. on the frame of the new house aforesaid and setting up the same.

John Provest 2s. Robert Broke 3s. 4d. Walter Alen 3s. 4d. Nicholas Holowaye (2s. 1d.) <18d.> John Pasmer 2s. 1d. Henry Godfrey 3s. 4d. in the same works.

Sawyers. Flint slitting 6 hundred, 6s. 6d. [blotted]

Porter. William Hugwet 2s.

Shoutman. Thomas Alen 3s. 4d.

Bricklayers. Swynson 3s. 4d. Chorleton 3s. 4d. Labourers. Nevell 2s. 1d. Hogett 2s. 1d. Thomas Grene 2s. 1d. William Jacson 2s. 1d. upon certain houses in Southwark.

Labourers. John Smyth 2s. 1d. Whythed 2s. 1d. Sherman 2s. 1d. Tanner 2s. 1d. Thomas Alen 2s. 1d. Wynter 2s. 1d. in the works aforesaid.

Daubers. Thomas Monkest 3s. 4d. Labourer. William Monkest 2s. 1d. in Paternoster Row and Newgate market.

[Total] of this page £6 17s. 1d.

[f. 395] Paid to William Lenger of Surrey for 3,000 paving tiles 9 inches thick, at 14d. the thousand, 52s.

To Thomas Wolberd of Deptford for certain repairs done by him on a house that the king's harness lies in, by bill 7s.

To 3 men at the three-man beetle, each for 3 tides, in waterworks, at 3d. the tide, 2s. 3d.

To 6 labourers for loading and unloading 5 boats of chalk, 3s. 4d.

To 3 labourers for placing [*bestowyng*] chalk in the yard, 18d.

To Robert Butteler for carriage of 8 loads of framed timber from the Bridge House to Cheapside at 6d. the load, 4s. To him for carriage of 4 loads of timber from Croydon to the Bridge House at 2s. 4d. the load, 9s. 4d.

[Total] of this page 69s. 5d.

Sum total paid this week £10 6s. 6d.

500. [f. 395v] 10 November

Renter   Fishmongers   Butchers   Passage tolls

Received of my lady Peycocke for 3½ hundred of bricks and 3 hundred tiles at 6d., 3s. 6d.

Received of a Spaniard by the hands of William Cocks senior for a 10–ft. piece of elm, 2s.

Old debts received of Mr Bows, alderman, for certain planks and posts, 5s. 4d.

Received of Henry [blank] for the rent of a granary in Golders yard over 3 quarters, 23s. 4d.

Three chaplains 7s. 6d. Five clerks 10s. Roger Robyns 12d.

Masons. Bennett 3s. 9d. Tamson 3s. 9d. Arnold 3s. 9d. Thomas Fyld 3s. 9d. Thomas Heyneys 3s. 9d. Jeffrey Orger 3s. 6d.

Carpenters. Robert Gold pt 4s. Cocks the elder 4s. Godfrey 4s. Browne senior 4s. Simon Cocks 2s. (1d.) <6d.> in the waterworks.

William Cocks pt 4s. Inglydw 4s. Browne junior 4s. Palmer 4s. Pasmer 4s. Thomas Browne (2s.) 8d. Leonard Holmes 4s. John Prevest 4s. Thomas Broke 4s. Walter Alen 4s. Nicholas Holowaye 2s. John Pasmer 2s. 6d. on the new frame.

Sawyers. Flint slitting 6 hundred, 7s.

Porter. William Hughwett 2s.

Shoutman. Thomas Alen 3s. 4d.

Tilers. William Swynson 4s. Chorleton 4s. Labourers. Nevell 2s. Hogett 2s. Thomas Grene 2s. William Jacson 2s.

Daubers. Monkest 4s. Labourers. Thomas Monkest 2s.

Labourers. John Smyth 2s. 6d. Sherman 2s. Wynter 2s. 6d. Thomas Alen 2s. 6d. Tanner 2s. Whythed 2s. 6d.

[Total] of this page £7 10s. 11d.

[f. 396] To Thomas Alen by bill 22d.

To divers labourers for loading and unloading 6 boats of chalk and placing the same at the bridge, 6s. 3d.

To Robert Buttelelere for carriage of 9 loads of framed timber to Cheapside at 6d. the load, 4s. 6d.

[Total] of this page 14s. 10d.

Sum total paid this week £8 5s. 7d.

501. [f. 396v] 17 November.

Renter £8   Fishmongers   Butchers   Passage tolls

Received of Mr Doughty [blotted] by Gold for 20 ft. of elm timber, 3s. 4d.

Received of Mr Cestylylon [blotted] for 2½ loads of elm timber, 17s. 10d.

Received of Mr [blank]

The chaplains 7s. Five clerks 10s. Roger Robyns 12d.

Masons. Bennett 3s. 9d. Tomson 3s. 9d. Arnold 3s. 9d. Thomas Fyld 3s. 9d. Thomas Heynes 3s. 9d. Jeffrey Orger 3s. 6d.

Carpenters. Robert Gold pt 4s. Cocks the elder 4s. Godfrey 4s. Browne senior 4s. Simon Cocks 2s. 6d. in the waterworks.

William Cocks pt 4s. Inglydw 4s. Browne junior 4s. Palmer 4s. <Pasmer 4s.> Thomas Browne 4s. Leonard Holmes 4s. Thomas Broke 4s. Walter Alen 4s. Nicholas Holowaye 3s. William Wynter 2s. 6d. John Provest 3s. [blotted] John Pasmer 2s. 6d. on the new frame.

Sawyers. Flint slitting 7 hundred, 7s. 6d.

Porter. William Hugwhett 2s.

Shoutman. Thomas Alen 3s. 4d.

Bricklayers. Swynson 4s. Chorleton 4s. Labourers. Nevell 2s. (1d.) Hogett 2s. (1d.) Grene 2s. (1d.)

Daubers. Thomas Monkest 4s. Labourer. William Monkest 2s.

Labourers. John Smyth 2s. 6d. Thomas Alen 2s. 6d. Whythed 2s. 6d. Tanner 2s. Sherman 2s.

200

[Total] of this page £7 11s. 8d.

[f. 397] Paid for the obit of John Fylingham kept at St Clement Eastcheap, 2s. 6d.

Paid to Rewley, smith, for 2 pile-shoes, 18d.

Paid to Stephen Parett of Deptford for 13 boat[load]s of chalk containing 12 tons each, at 6d. the ton, 6s. the boat, £3 18s.

To John Clerke of Southwark, carter, for carriage of 4 loads of stone and timber into London at 4d. the load, 16d., and for carriage of a load of rubbish from thence 2d., in all 18d.

In expenses of the masters this week to [3 words blotted] procuring a way for the tenant there, 2s. 4d.

To 10 men for loading and unloading 3 boats of chalk at 3d. the man, 2s. 6d.

Item for unloading 2 boats of chalk at the bridge, to 7 [men], 14d.

Item for 3 labourers at 4 tides each, for placing chalk at the bridge, 4 tides, 3s.

To 3 labourers at the five-man beetle, to each for 2 tides at 3d. the tide, 18d.

To Robert Butteler for carriage of 4 loads of timber from Croydon at 2s. 4d. the load, 9s. 4d.

To him for carriage of 8 loads of framed timber from Croydon to the Bridge House to Cheapside [*Chepe syde*] at 6d. the load, 4s.

[Total] of this page 107s. 4d.

Sum total paid this week £12 19s.

502. [f. 397v] 24 November

Renter £8   Fishmongers   Butchers   Passage tolls

Received at 2 sundry times of John Stacye, bellwright, for 3 loads of oak timber, 25s.

Received of Mr Baker, the king's attorney, for a hundred of plankboard [*planche borde*] 3s., for 18 ft. of oak plank 10d., and for 6 quarters of oak 12d., in all 4s. 10d.

Received of William Robynson, mill-picker, for 1 elm plank, 3ft. 5d.

Three chaplains 7s. Five clerks 10s. Roger Robyns 12d.

Masons. Bennett 3s. 9d. Tomson 3s. 9d. Arnold 3s. 9d. Thomas Fyld 3s. 9d. Heynes 3s. 9d. Jeffrey Orger 3s. 6d. in apparelling hard stone.

Carpenters. Gold pt 4s. Browne senior 4s. Cocks the elder 4s. Godfrey 4s. Simon Cocks 2s. 6d. in the waterworks.

Cocks pt 4s. Inglydwe 4s. Browne junior 4s. Palmer 4s. on the new [entry incomplete]

Pasmer 4s. Leonard Holmes 4s. Thomas Browne 4s. Thomas Brooke 4s. Walter Alen 4s. Nicholas Holowaye 3s. John Pasmer 2s. 6d. in the yard on the new [entry incomplete]

John Provest 4s. Wynter 2s. 6d.

Sawyers. Flint slitting 6 hundred, 7s. 8d.

Porter. William Hughwett 2s.

(Porter). Thomas Alen 3s. 4d.

Bricklayers. Swynson 4s. Chorleton 4s. Labourers. Nevell 2s. Hogett 2s. Grene 2s.

Daubers. Thomas Monkest 4s. Labourers. Thomas Monkest 2s.
Labourers. John Smyth 2s. 6d. Thomas Alen 2s. 6d. Whythed 2s. 6d.
Tanner 2s. Sherman 2s.
[Total] of this page £7 11s. 8d.
[f. 398] To my lady Pargit' by the hands of Thomas Eddon for 5 fother
7 hundred of Peak lead at £4 6s. 8d. the fother, £23 4s. 7d.
To Richard Roberts, plumber, in loan 60s.
To loading and unloading 2 boats of chalk, 18d.
To 3 men for placing chalk at the bridge for 1 tide, 9d.
To 3 labourers labouring in fetching out 5 fother of lead from Fresh
Wharf and for craning and placing the same in the yard, at 3d. the
man, 9d.
To 3 labourers at the five-man beetle for 1 tide, 9d.
Paid for wharfage, cranage, and portage of 5 fother 7 hundred of lead
at Smiths Key, 3s. 8d.
To John Clerke of Southwark for carriage of 3 loads of paving, rag, and
lead at 4d. the load, 12d.
To Robert Buttler for carriage of 6 loads of framed timber in Cheapside
at 6d. the load, 3s.
To John Gate, mariner, for freight of 12 tons of Bridge ashlar and 17
end stones at 12d. the ton, 12s.
[Total] of this page £27 8s.
Sum total paid this week £34 19s. 8d.

503. [f. 398v] 1 December
Renter £8 Fishmongers Butchers Passage tolls
Received of Mr Symson for 2 oak quarters, 4d.
Received of John Smyth for 100 bricks and 3 trays of mortar, 9d.
Received of William Johnson towards certain repairs done in his
tenement that he now dwells in, 40s.
Chaplains 7s. 6d. Five clerks 10s. Roger Robyns 12d.
Masons. Bennett 3s. 9d. Tomson 3s. 9d. Arnold 3s. 9d. Fyld 3s. 9d.
Heynes 3s. 9d. Jeffrey Orger 3s. 6d. in apparelling hard stone.
Carpenters. Robert Gold pt 4s. Cocks the elder 3s. 4d. Browne senior
3s. 4d. Henry Godfrey 3s. 4d. Simon Cocks 2s. 1d. in the water.
Cocks pt 4s. Inglydwe 3s. 4d. Palmer 3s. 4d. Browne junior 3s. 4d. John
Pasmer 2s. 1d. on the new [sic].
Pasmer 3s. 4d. Leonard Holmes 3s. 4d. Thomas Broke 3s. 4d. Walter
Alen 3s. 4d. upon in bows and drawing of boards for the new house
aforesaid.
John Provest 3s. 4d. William Wynter 1s. 1d. Thomas Brooke 3s. 4d.
Thomas Heynes 2s. 6d. in repairs.
Sawyers. Flint slitting 6½ hundred, 7s.
Porter. William Hughwett 2s.
Shout[man]. Thomas Alen 3s. 4d.
Bricklayers. William Swynson 3s. 4d. Chorleton 3s. 4d. Labourers.
Nevell 20d. Sherman 20d. Hogett 20d. Grene 20d. Thomas Laurence
10d. Roger Conne 10d.
Daubers. Thomas Monkest 3s. 4d. Labourer. William Monkest 20d.

Labourers. John Smyth 2s. 1d. Thomas Alen 2s. 1d. Whythed 2s. 1d. Tanner 20d.

[Total] of this page £6 17s. 9d.

[f. 399] To Thomas Dendye of Surrey for 1 load of heartlaths delivered at the new building in Cheap, 11s. 2d.

To 3 men at the three-man beetle, each for 3 tides at 3d. the tide, 2s. 3d.

To Clerke of Southwark for carriage of 7 loads of tiles and 3 loads of lead from the Bridge House to Cheapside at 4d. the load, 3s. 4d. To him for carriage of 2 [loads] from Paternoster Row to Cheapside at 2d. the load, 4d.

To Robert Butteler for carriage of 9 loads into Cheap of framed timber at 6d. the load, 4s. 6d. To him for 1 load from Croydon, 2s. 4d.

Paid for 1 ream of small paper, 2s.

[Total] of this page 26s. 11d.

Sum total paid this week £8 4s. 8d.

504. [f. 399v] 7 [*recte* 8] December

Renter £8   Fishmongers   Butchers   Passage tolls

Received [blank]

Three chaplains 7s. 6d. Five clerks 10s. Roger Robyns 12d.

Masons. Bennett 3s. 1½d. Tomson 3s. 1½d. Arnold 3s. 9d. Fyld 3s. 1½d. Heynes 3s.1½d. Jeffrey Orger 3s. 6d. in apparelling hard stone.

Carpenters. Gold pt 4s. Cocks the elder 2s. 8d. Browne senior 2s. 8d. Godfrey 2s. 8d. Simon Cocks 20d. in the waterworks.

Cocks pt 4s. Inglydwe 2s. 8d. Palmer 2s. 8d. Browne junior 2s. 8d. Pasmer 2s. 8d. John Pasmer 20d. in finishing of the new house.

Thomas Brooke 2s. 8d. Walter Alen 2s. 8d. Leonard Holmes 2s. 8d. upon in bows for the new house.

Thomas Browne 2s. 8d. Thomas Heynes 2s. at John William's.

John Provest 2s. 8d. William Wynter 20d. at the sign of the Shepherd.

Sawyers. Flint slitting 5 hundred, 5s. 5d.

Porter. Hughwett 2s.

Shoutman. Thomas Alen 3s. 4d.

[Bricklayers] Swenson 2s. 8d. Chorleton 2s. 8d. Labourers. Nevell 16d. Hogett 16d. Sherman 16d. Thomas Grene 16d.

Daubers. Monkest 2s. 8d. Labourer. William Monkest 16d.

Labourers. John Smyth 20d. Thomas Alen 10d. (Whythed) 20d. Tanner 16d. John Tamson 10d.

[Total] of this page (112s.) <117s.>

[f. 400] To Clerke of Southwark, carter, for carriage of 2 loads, one from the Bridge House 4d., and another from Paternoster Row 2d., in all 6d.

To Monkest, plasterer, for a fine sieve for [the] plasterer 7d.

To Richard Rodyng, paviour, for paving 22 toises on the backside at the sign of the Cup at St Nicholas Shambles, at 7d. the toise, 12s. 10d.

Expenses of the masters this week 10d.

To Robert Butteler for carriage of 9 loads of framed timber to Cheapside at 6d. the load, 4s. 6d.

To him for carriage of 3 loads of timber from Croydon to the Bridge House, at 2s. 4d. the load, 7s.

[Total] of this page 25s. 9d.

Sum total paid this week £7 2s. 9d.

505. [f. 400v] 15 December

Renter £8   Fishmongers   Butchers   Passage tolls

Received of Davye Lonton, carpenter, by William Cocks, for 9 ft. of elm timber, 21½d.

Received of Richard Tornour, searcher, by the hands of Robert Gold, for a piece of elm timber, 6d.

Three chaplains 7s. 6d. Five clerks 10s. Roger Robyns 12d.

Masons. Bennett 3s. 9d. Tomson 3s. 9d. Arnold 3s. 9d. Fyld 3s. 9d. Heynes 3s. 9d. Jeffrey Orger 3s. 6d. in apparelling hard stone.

[Carpenters] Gold pt 4s. Cocks the elder 4s. Godfrey 4s. Browne senior 4s. Simon Cocks 2s. 6d. in the waterworks.

Cocks pt 4s. Inglydwe 4s. Palmer 4s. Browne junior 4s. Pasmer 4s. John Pasmer 2s. 6d. in the rising of the new frame aforesaid.

Leonard Holmes 4s. Thomas Browne 4s. Thomas Brooke 2s. 8d. Nicholas Holowaye 3s. upon William's house

Provest 4s. Wynter 2s. 6d. Brooke Wat' 12d. at the sign of the Shepherd.

Sawyers. Flint slitting 7 hundred, 7s. 7d.

Porter. William Hugh[wett] 2s.

Shoutman. Thomas Alen 3s. 4d.

[Bricklayers] Swynson 3s. 4d. Chorleton 4s. Labourers. Nevell 2s. Hogett 2s. Thomas Grene 2s. Sherman 2s.

Monkest 4s., Thomas Monkest 2s. 6d., daubers in Cheap upon new [sic].

[Labourers] John Smyth 2s. 6d. Thomas Alen 2s. 6d. Tanner 2s. Whythed 2s. 6d. in the works aforesaid.

[Total] of this page £7 4s. 10d.

[f. 401] To Raynold Richardson for the freight of ½ hundred of Bridge ashlar, 2¼ hundred of middle ashlar, a hundred of Chapman ware paving and half a hundred of apparelled paving from Maidstone in Kent to the Bridge House, containing in all 20 tons at 12d. the ton, 20s.

To John Orgar for hardstone of Kent, as appears by his bill, £7 13s. 4d.

To Richard Amborous for his quarter's fee, 1s.

To Robert Butteler for carriage of 2 loads of timber from Croydon to the Bridge House, 4s. 8d.

[Total] of this page £11 8s.

Sum total paid this week £18 12s. 10d. <proved>

506. [f. 401v] 22 December

Renter £30   Fishmongers 100s.   Butchers £10   Passage-tolls.

Received of Thomas Maddocks, merchant tailor, for the grant of a tenement John Ball, haberdasher, now holds in Old Change, 5s.

Three chaplains 10s. Five clerks 10s. Roger Robyns 12d.

Masons in apparelling hard stone. Bennett 3s. 2d. (1/2d.) Tomson 3s. 2d. (1/2d.) Arnold 3s. 9d. Fyld 3s. 2d. (1/2d.) Heynes 3s. 2d. (1/2d.) Jeffrey Orger 3s. 6d. .

Carpenters. Gold pt 4s. Cocks the elder 3s. 4d. Browne senior 3s. 4d. Godfrey 3s. 4d. Simon Cocks 2s. 1d.

Cocks pt 4s. Inglydwe 2s. Browne junior 3s. 4d. Pasmer 3s. 4d. Palmer 3s. 4d. John Pasmer 2s. 1d. in finishing the new frame aforesaid.

Leonard Holmes 3s. 4d. Thomas Browne 3s. 4d. Nicholas Holowaye 3s. 4d. in repairs aforesaid.

Provest 3s. 4d. Wynter 2s. 1d. in repairs aforesaid.

Thomas Broke 3s. 4d. Walter Alen 3s. 4d. in bowing aforesaid.

Sawyers. Flint slitting 6½ hundred, 7s.

Porter. Hughwett 2s.

[Shoutman] Thomas Alen 3s. 4d.

[Bricklayers] Swynson 3s. 4d. Chorleton 2s. Labourers. Nevell 20d. Hodgett 20d. Grene 20d.

[Daubers] Thomas Monkest 3s. 4d. Labourer. Patrycke Playsterer 2s. 1d.

[Labourers] John Smyth 2s. 1d. Thomas Alen 2s. 1d. Whythed 2s. 1d. Tanner 20d. Sherman 20d. in the works aforesaid.

[Total] of this page £6 16s. 4d.

[f. 402] To Henry Hacher of Croydon for the laystall of 118 loads of timber received by him from Sir John Gaynesford knight at 1d. the load, 9s. 10d.

To the aforesaid masons for steeling their iron tools this year at 18d. to each man, 7s. 6d.

To Richard Dryver, (tile) <lime>burner, for 22 hundred and 5 loads of lime delivered to sundry storehouses at 4s. the hundred, by bill and tale, 90s. 7d.

To William Sharpharewe, blacksmith, for sundry sorts of iron works from Michaelmas to Christmas, by bill, £10 2s.

To Robert Terne, blacksmith, for battering 63 dozen of masons' tools this quarter at 1½d. the dozen argent, 7s. 10d.

To Hugh Brampstone, brickburner, for 15,000 bricks delivered to sundry places this quarter, by tale and bill, £3 10s.

To the aforesaid 3 chaplains and 6 clerks for *Placebo* and *Dirige*, 3s.

To Tanner's wife for washing the chaplains' stuff this [quarter], 12d.

To John Ferres for his quarter's fee, 5s.

To him for singing bread this quarter, 2d.

To William Hughwett's wife for weeding in the garden this [quarter] 2s.

To Robert Butteller, carter, for carriage of 3 loads of oak timber from Croydon to the Bridge House, 7s. To him for carriage of 2 loads of framed timber from the Bridge House to the Standard in Cheap, 12d.

To Jeffrey Haryson, sandman, by bill and [blank], 24s. 6d.

To Thomas Mason by Nevell for carriage of 4 loads of rubbish from Paternoster Row to the (Bridge House), 10d.

To Richard Roddyng, paviour, for stopping sundry holes and ruts [*cart welks*] on the bridge for 3 days with his labourers, 3s.

To John Smyth, labourer, for carriage of cuttings of lead from the new frame to the Bridge House, 3d.

To Hugh Bramson for 1,000 bricks, 4s. 8d.

To Richard Roberts, plumber, in part payment of a greater sum, for casting lead, 53s. 4d.

[f. 402v] To Alexander, painter of Wood Street, for painting and gilding 2 vanes and spindles of the same set on 2 finials at the new building in Cheap, 10s.

To Mr Buckmaister, parson of Woolchurch, for his tithe of the Stocks this quarter, 13s. 4d.

To Robert Nelson, glazier, by bill 15s. 4d.

To the churchwardens of St Olave's in S[outhwark] for the salary of a chantry priest in London, 26s. 8d.

To Thomas Crull for his fee this Christmas quarter, £7 13s. 4d.

[Total] of this page £40 12s. 1d.

Sum total of this week £42 8s. 5d.

507. [f. 403] 29 December
Renter £8   Fishmongers   Butchers   Passage tolls
Chaplains 7s. 6d. Five clerks 10s. Roger 12d.
[Porter] William Hug' 2s.
[Shoutman] Thomas Alen 3s. 4d.
Sum total 23s. 10d.

508. [f. 403v] 5 January [1538]
Renter £8   Fishmongers   Butchers   Passage tolls
Received of Neidigate for 3 ends of elm planks, 2s.
Three chaplains 7s. 6d. Clerks 10s. Roger Robyns 12d.
[Masons] Bennett 2s. 6d. Tomson. Arnold. Fyld. Heynes. Jeffrey Orger.
[Carpenters] Gold pt 4s. Cockes the elder 2s. 8d. Browne senior 2s. 8d. Henry Godfrey 2s. 8d. Simon Cocks 20d. in the waterworks.
Cocks pt 4s. Inglydwe 4s. Palmer 2s. 8d. Browne junior 2s. 8d. John Pasmer 20d. Thomas Broke 2s. 8d. Walter Alen 2s. 8d. Leonard Holmes 2s. 8d. upon the new frame.
Thomas Browne 2s. 8d. Nicholas Holowaye 2s. John Provest 2s. 8d. William Wynter 20d.
[Sawyers] Flint slitting 6 hundred, 6s. 7d.
[Porter] William Hugh[wett] 2s.
[Shoutman] Thomas Alen 3s. 4d.
[Bricklayers] Swynson 2s. 8d. Chorleton 2s. 8d. Labourers. Nevell 16d. Hogett 16d. Thomas Grene 16d.
[Dauber] Monkest 2s. 8d. [Labourer] Patrycke 20d.
[Labourers] John Smyth 20d. Whythed 20d. Thomas Alen 20d. Sherman 20d. Tanner 20d.
Sum total £4 18s. 6d. <proved>
[f. 404 blank]

509. [f. 404v] 12 January.
Renter £8   Fishmongers   Butchers   Passage tolls 20s.

Received of Stacye for 2 ft. of oak timber, 6d.

Received of Thomas Gybson for 2 oak planks, 4s.

Three chaplains 7s. 6d. Five clerks 10s. Roger Robyns 12d.

[Masons] Bennett 3s. 9d. Tomson 3s. 9d. Arnold 3s. 9d. Fyld 3s. 9d. Heynes 3s. 9d. Jeffrey Orger 3s. 6d. in apparelling hard stone.

[Carpenters] Gold pt 4s. Cocks the elder 4s. Browne senior 4s. Godfrey 4s. Simon Cockes 2s. 6d. in the waterworks and in repairs at Stratford.

Cocks pt 4s. Inglydwe 4s. Browne junior 4s. Palmer 3s. 4d. Pasmer 4s. John Pasmer 2s. 6d. in finishing the new house aforesaid.

Leonard Holmes 4s. Thomas Broke 4s. Walter Alen 4s. upon in bowing and drawing of boards.

Thomas Browne 4s. Nicholas Holowaye 3s. John Provest 4s. William Wynter 2s. 6d. in repairs upon the bridge.

Sawyers. Flint slitting 6 hundred, 7s. 7d.

[Porter] William Hugh[wett] 2s.

[Shoutman] Thomas Alen 3s. 4d.

Bricklayers. Swynson 2s. 8d. Chorleton 4s. Labourers. Nevell 2s. Hogett 2s. Grene 2s. in Cheap, upon the bridge, and in Southwark.

Daubers. Thomas Monk' 4s. Labourer. Patrick Placken' 2s. 6d. upon the new house in Cheap.

Labourers. John Smyth 2s. 6d. Whythed 2s. 6d. Thomas Alen 2s. 6d. Tanner 2s. Sherman 2s. in the works aforesaid.

([Total] of this page £10 11s. 10d.) <[Total] of this page £7 7s. 5d.>

[f. 405] To Henry Mylls, gardener, for 4 days work in the garden, 2s. 8d., and one bundle of binding rods and poles for the same garden, 3d., 2s. 11d.

To Laurence Awen, clerk of the house, for his fee, 1s.

To Sir Thomas Baxster, chantry priest of [blank], for a quit-rent, by quittance 2s. 6d.

To Robert Butteler, carter, for carriage of 3 loads of oak timber this week and last week from Croydon, 7s.

To the wardmote quest of Bridge ward, in reward as accustomed, 2s.

[Total] of this page £3 4s. 5d.

Sum total this week £10 11s. 10d.

510. [f. 405v] 19 January

Renter £8   Fishmongers   Butchers   Passage tolls

Received of Thomas Huske, barber, of Southwark for 2 quarters, 2d.

Three chaplains 7s. 6d. Five clerks 10s. Roger Robyns 12d.

[Masons] Bennett 15d. Tomson 15d. Arnold 3s. 9d. Thomas Pynd 3s. 9d. Fyld 3s. 9d. Jeffrey Orger 3s. 6d.

[Carpenters] Gold 4s. Godfrey 4s. William Cocks 4s. Browne senior 4s. Simon Cocks 2s. 6d. in the waterworks.

William Browne junior 4s. Inglydwe 4s. Palmer 4s. Robert Pasmer 4s. John Pasmer 2s. 6d. Leonard Holmes 4s. in the said frame.

John Provest. William Wynter. Thomas Browne. Nicholas Holowaye. in repairs.

Thomas Brooke 4s. Walter Alen 4s. upon in bows.

[Sawyers] Flint slitting 6 hundred, 7s. 7d.

207

[Porter] William Hughwett 2s.
[Shoutman] Thomas Alen 3s. 4d.
[Bricklayers] Swynson 4s. Chorleton 4s. [Labourers] Nevell 2s. Hogett 2s. T. Grene 2s.
[Daubers] Thomas Monk' 4s. [Labourer] Patrick Plackeney 2s.
[Labourers] John Smyth 2s. 6d. Thomas Alen 2s. 6d. Whythed 2s. 6d. Sherman 2s. Tanner 2s.
To Robert Butteler, carter, for carriage of 1 load of oak timber from Croydon, 2s. 4d.
Sum total of this week £6 15s. 6d.

511. [f. 406] 26 January
Renter £8   Fishmongers   Butchers   Passage tolls
Received of Doctor Leghe for 60 ft. of oak timber argent at 2½d., 12s. 6d.
Received of a smith for a piece of old timber, 12d.
Three [chaplains] 7s. 6d. Five clerks 10s. Roger Robyns 12d.
[Masons] Bennett 3s. 9d. Tomson 3s. 9d. Arnold 3s. 9d. Fyld 3s. 9d. Thomas Heynds 3s. 9d. Jeffrey Orger 3s. 6d. in apparelling hard stone and laying of a new paving in the kitchen at the sign of the Shepherd on the bridge.
[Carpenters] Gold pt 4s. Henry Godfre 4s. in repairs at Stratford.
William Cocks the elder 4s. Browne senior 4s. Simon Cocks 2s. 6d. in the waterworks.
William Cocks 4s. Inglydwe 4s. Palmer 4s. Robert Pasmer 4s. Browne junior 4s. Thomas Broke 4s. Walter Alen 4s. John Pasmer 2s. 6d. in finishing the new house in Cheap.
John Provest 2s. William Wynter 15d. in repairs at Kellet's house.
Leonard Holmes 4s. Thomas Browne 4s. Nicholas Holoway 3s. at Johnson's [illegible]
[Sawyers] Flint slitting 7½ hundred, 8s. 1d.
[Porter] William Hughwett 2s.
[Shoutman] Thomas Alen 3s. 4d.
Bricklayers. William Swenson 4s. Chorleton 4s. Labourers. Nevell 2s. Hogett 2s. Thomas Grene 2s. in bringing up flues of privies [*twells of wedraghts*]
Daubers. Thomas Monkest 4s. Labourers. Patrick Playst' 2s.
Labourers. John Smyth 2s. 6d. Thomas Alen 2s. 6d. Whythed 2s. 6d. Tanner 2s. Sherman 2s. in the works aforesaid.
<[Total] of this page £7 8s. 11d.>
To William Modyl of Reigate for carriage of a load of parrels for chimneys, 3s. 4d.
To Gilbert the smith of Rotherhithe [*Radryff*] for 700 fourpenny nails, 2s. 4d., and for 300 threepenny nails, 9d., 3s. 1d.
To John Clerke for carriage of a load of boards to Cheap and a load of scaffolds home to the Bridge House, 8d.
The masters' expenses this week, 2s. 1d.
[Total] of this page 9s. 2d.
Sum total this week £7 18s. 1d.

512. [f. 406v] 2 February
Renter £8   Fishmongers   Butchers   Passage tolls
(Received of Mr Doctor Legh for 60 ft. of oak timber by the hands of William Cocks, 12s. 6d.
Received of a smith for a piece of old timber by the hands of Robert Gold, 12d.) <cancelled because allowed above>
Three [chaplains] 7s. 6d. Five clerks 10s. Roger Robyns 12d.
[Masons] Bennett 3s. 9d. Tomson 3s. 9d. Arnold 3s. 9d. Thomas Fyld 3s. 9d. Thomas Heynes 3s. 9d. Jeffrey Orger 3s. 6d. in apparelling hard stone.
[Carpenters] Robert Gold 4s. Cocks the elder 3s. 4d. Godfrey 3s. 4d. Browne senior 3s. 4d. Simon Cocks 2s. 1d. in the waterworks.
Cocks pt 4s. Inglydwe 3s. 4d. Palmer 3s. 4d. Robert Pasmer 3s. 4d. Browne junior 3s. 4d. Thomas Broke 3s. 4d. Walter Alen 3s. 4d. Thomas Browne 3s. 4d. Nicholas Holoway 2s. 6d. John Pasmer 2s. 1d. on the new frame at the Standard in Cheap.
Leonard Holmes 3s. 4d. John Provest 3s. 4d. William Wynter 2s. 1d. on a shed over a bow upon the bridge.
[Sawyers] Flint slitting 6 hundred, 6s. 6d.
[Porter] William Hughwett 2s.
[Shoutman] Thomas Alen 3s. 4d.
[Bricklayers] William Swenson 3s. 4d. Chorleton 3s. 4d. [Labourers] Nevell 20d. Hogett 20d. Thomas Grene 20d.
[Daubers] Thomas Monkest 3s. 4d. [Labourer] Patrick Plackyng 20d.
Labourers. John Smyth (20d.) <2s. 1d.> Thomas Alen (20d.) <2s. 1d.> Whythed (20d.) <2s. 1d.> Tanner 20d. Sherman 20d.
[Total] of this page £6 15s. 7d.
[f. 407] To Modill of Reigate quarry for 1 load of Reigate stone for borders for chimneys, 3s. 4d.
To John Orgar for his quarter's fee due at Christmas last, 50s.
Of the said John Modell of Reigate by the hands of John Orgar for 1 load of squared stone and ½ load of border, 6s.
[Total] of this page 59s. 4d.
Sum total of the week £9 14s. 11d.

513. [f. 407v] 9 February
Renter £8   Fishmongers   Butchers   Passage tolls
Three [chaplains] 7s. 6d. Five clerks 10s. Roger Robyns 12d.
[Masons] Bennett 4s. Tomson 4s. Arnold 4s. Fyld 4s. Heynes 4s. Jeffrey Orger 3s. 6d. in paving of the yard and the kitchen at the Standard in Cheap.
[Carpenters] Gold 4s. Cocks the elder 4s. Browne senior 4s. Henry Godfrey 4s. Simon Cocks 2s. 6d. in the waterworks.
William Cocks pt 4s. Inglydwe 4s. John Palmer 4s. Robert Pasmer 4s. Browne junior 4s. Thomas Broke 4s. Walter Alen 4s. Thomas Browne 4s. in the works in Cheapside.
Leonard Holmes 4s. Nicholas Holoway 3s. in drawing of boards.
John Provest 4s. William Wynter 3s. John Pasmer 2s. 6d. in repairs and making of a house over an arch against Kellett's house.

[Sawyers] Flint slitting 6½ hundred, 8s. 1d.
[Porter] William Hugh' 2s.
[Shoutman] Thomas Alen 3s. 4d.
[Bricklayers] Swenson 4s. Chorleton 4s. [Labourers] Nevell 2s. 6d. Thomas Hogett 2s. 6d. Thomas Grene 2s. 6d.
Daubers. Thomas Monkest 4s. Labourer. Patrick Playnkeney 2s. 6d.
Labourers. John Smyth 2s. 6d. Thomas Alen 2s. 6d. Whythed (3s. 6d.) <2s. 6d.> Sherman 2s. 6d. Tanner 2s. 6d.
Sum total of the page £7 16s. 11d.
[f. 408] To Modyll of Reigate for carriage of 1 load of Reigate stone for returns [*Retornes*] for chimneys, 3s. 6d.
To Thomas Dendye of Surrey in part payment of a greater sum for planks, quarterboard, quarters and laths, £4.
To the said [sic] for carriage of 1 load of plain paving for ovens by the hands of Robert Gold, 3s. 6d.
To William Lee of Luddon, gold-finer, for 4 *swoses* [?sows] of Peak lead weighing 1 fother 7 hundred 3 quarters at £4 6s. 8d. the fother, sum in all with 3d. rebated, £6.
To Sherman, labourer, for 2 baskets to carry rubbish in, 3d.
To the wife of James Foster for 20 tons of rag and chalk delivered at the mill-dam at Botts Mill for reinforcing [*fforsyng*] a new wall at 10d. the ton, 16s. 8d.
To her for carriage of (20) <24> loads of sundry stuff from the Bridge House to Cheapside and Paternoster Row, and from thence to the Bridge House in old stuff, as appears by the tale at 4d. the load, 8s., and for the carriage of 15 loads to the bridge at 2d. the load, with 12d. for carriage of 1 load to Tomson's mill at Stratford [*tretffod*], and also for carriage of 11 loads of other stuff from the Bridge House into sundry places in the city at 4d. the load, 3s. 8d., in all 15s. 2d.
[Total] of this page £11 19s. 1d.
Sum total of the week £19 16s.

514. [f. 408v] 16 February
Renter £8   Fishmongers   Butchers   Passage tolls
Received of Thomas Doughty, fishmonger, for 17 ft. of elm timber, 2s. 4d.
Received of John Albery, clothworker, for 10 ft. of elm timber at 3d. the foot, 2s. 6d.
Received of William Kellet of London Bridge, merchant tailor, by the hands of his wife towards the making of a shed over an arch of stone at the backside of his house, 20s.
Three [chaplains] 7s. 6d. Five clerks 10s. Roger Robyns 12d.
[Masons] Bennett 4s. Tomson 4s. Arnold 4s. Thomas Fyld 4s. Thomas Heyneys 4s. Jeffrey Orger 3s. 6d.
[Carpenters] Robert Gold 4s. Browne senior 4s. at Stratford.
Cocks the elder 4s. Henry Godfrey 4s. Simon Cocks 2s. 6d. Cocks pt 4s. Inglydwe 4s. Palmer 4s. Pasmer 4s. Browne (junior) 4s. Thomas Broke 4s. Walter Alen 4s. Thomas Browne 4s. Nicholas Holoway 3s. John Pasmer 2s. 6d. Leonard Holmes 4s. John Provest 4s. William Wynter

3s. in making of stairs, doors, windows, and other within the said house in Cheap.

[Sawyers] Flint slitting 7 hundred, 7s. 7d.

[Porter] William Hugh' 2s.

[Shoutman] Thomas Alen 3s. 4d.

[Bricklayers] Swenson 4s. Chorleton 4s. [Labourers] Nevell 2s. 6d. Hogett 2s. 6d. Thomas Grene 2s. 6d.

Daubers. Thomas Monkest 4s. Labourers. Patrick 2s. 6d. at the new house in Cheap.

Labourer[s]. John Smyth 2s. 6d. Thomas Alen 2s. 6d. Whythed 2s. 6d. Sherman 2s. 6d. Tanner 2s. 6d. in the waterworks aforesaid.

[f. 409] To Hugh Watts, leatherseller of London, for 10 double plate-locks without keys bought of him for the new house in Cheap, 20s.

To Modyll of Reigate for carriage of 1 load of apparelled paving [*paryled pavyng*] for ovens and 1 load of borders [*burdes*] for chimneys, 7s.

To the [said] Modyll for carriage of 1 other load of *parells* for chimneys and 1 load of forge [*forge*], 3s. 6d. the load, 7s. To the same Modyll the same day for 2 loads of plain paving, 1 load of squared stone for returns of chimneys, a load of paving for chimneys, a load of forge for ovens, and a load of border for chimneys, at 2s. the load, with 4s. for scappling the border stone, 16s.

The masters' expenses this week 18d.

[Total] of this page 51s. 2d.

Sum total of the week £10 7s. 7d.

515. [f. 409v] 23 February

Renter £8   Fishmongers   Butchers   Passage tolls

Received of Daylyngton by the hands of William Cocks for 16 ft. of elm timber, 3s. 4d.

Three [chaplains] 7s. 6d. Five clerks 10s. Roger Robyns 12d.

[Masons] Bennett 4s. Tomson 4s. Arnold 4s. Fyld 4s. Heynes 4s. Jeffrey Orger 3s. 6d. in bringing up of mantles and parells for chimneys.

[Carpenters] William the elder Cocks 4s. Browne senior 4s. Simon Cocks 2s. 6d. in the waterworks.

pt William Cocks 4s. Inglydwe 4s. Palmer 4s. Pasmer 4s. Thomas Broke 4s. Walter Alen 4s. John Pasmer 2s. 6d. in Cheapside aforesaid.

Gold pt 4s. Godfrey 4s. Leonard Holmes 4s. Thomas Browne 4s. Browne junior 4s. John Provest 4s. Nicholas Holowaye 3s. William Wynter 3s. (6d.) in hewing and squaring timber bought of Mr Sybbell in Kent.

Labourers. Thomas Alen 2s. 6d. Tanner 2. 6d. with the carpenters aforesaid.

[Sawyers] Flint slitting 7 hundred, 7s. 7d.

[Porter] Hughwet 2s.

[Shoutman] Thomas Alen 3s. 4d.

[Bricklayers] Swenson 4s. Chorleton 4s. [Labourers] Nevell 2s. 6d. Hogett 2s. 6d. Grene 2s. 6d. on chimneys in Cheapside aforesaid.

Daubers. Thomas Monk' 4s. Labourers. Patrick Plackeney 2s. 6d.

[Labourers] John Smyth 2s. 6d. Whythed 2s. 6d. Sherman 2s. 6d.
[Total] of this page £7 16s. 5d.
[f. 410] To John Modill' of Reigate for carriage of 1 load of Reigate stone, 3s. 6d.
To Robert Best for carriage of a load of the same stone, 3s. 6d.
To William Hurteman and Thomas Playffoote, churchwardens of St Nicholas Shambles, for a quarter's rent due at Christmas last, 25s.
To Robert Butteler, carter, for carriage of 4 loads of timber from Croydon to the Bridge House at 2s. 4d. the load, 9s. 4d.
To Thomas Mason, ordure voider, for voiding 31 tuns [*Tonne*] of ordure out of 2 vaults in the Castle in Wood Street, at 18d. the tun, 16s. 6d.
To John Smyth, labourer, for 5 nights watching with the said ordure voider, to see him fill [the tuns], 20d.
[Total] of this page £4 9s. 6d.
Sum total of the week £12 5s. 11d.

516. [f. 410v] 2 March
Renter £8 Fishmongers Butchers Passage tolls
Received of a baker of Southwark for 4 short oak shells, 6d.
Received of William Gascoyne of Lambeth, baker, for the rent of a granary in Goldes yard for a year ended at Candlemas last past, 10s.
Three [chaplains] 7s. 6d. Five clerks 10s. Roger Robyns 12d.
[Masons] Bennett 4s. Tomson 4s. Arnold 4s. Fyld 4s. Heynes 4s. Jeffrey Orger 3s. 6d. in apparelling hard stone.
[Carpenters] Gold pt 4s. Cocks the elder 4s. Browne senior 4s. Henry Godfrey 4s. Simon Cocks 2s. 6d. in the waterworks.
William Cocks pt 4s. Inglydwe 4s. Palmer 4s. Pasmer 4s. Browne junior 4s. Thomas Broke 4s. Walter Alen 4s. Thomas Browne 4s. Nicholas Holowaye 3s. John Pasmer 2s. 6d. in the new house in Cheapside.
John Provest 4s. William Wynter 3s. Leonard Holmes 4s. in repairs.
[Sawyers] Flint slitting 8 hundred, 8s. 8d.
[Porter] Hughet 2s.
[Shoutman] Thomas Alen 3s. 4d.
[Bricklayers] Swenson 4s. Chorleton 4s. in bringing up of chimneys in Cheap.
[Daubers]. Monkest 4s. [Labourer] Patrick Plackey 2s. 6d. at the new frame in Cheapside.
Labourers. Nevell 2s. 6d. Hogett 2s. 6d. Thomas Grene 2s. 6d. Sherman 2s. 6d. with the bricklayers.
[Labourers] John Smyth 2s. 6d. Whythed 2s. 6d. Tanner 2s. 6d. Thomas Alen 2s. 6d. in the works aforesaid.
[Total] of this page £7 17s. 6d.
[f. 411] To [blank] for 6 round rings and 6 hearts [*herts*] with latches and catches for them for Cheapside, 4s.
To Richard Best, carter, for carriage of 1 load of Reigate stone for borders for chimneys, 3s. 6d.
To John Modell for (carriage) 2 loads of Reigate stone squared, and 1 load of borders for chimneys with 4s. for scappling the same, 20s.

To Robert Gold for 300 fourpenny nails used at Boot's mill at Stratford, 12d.

To Thomas Mason, ordure voider, for voiding 20 tuns of ordure out of the tenement of Thomas Woode at the Castle in Wood Street at 18d. the load, 30s.

To John Smith, labourer, for watching by the space of 3 nights argent, 12d.

To Robert Butteler, carter, for carriage of 2 loads of timber from Croydon to the Bridge House, 4s. 8d.

To John Boone for a quit-rent for 1 whole year ended at Christmas last from the tenement that Mr Medley, chamberlain of London, holds, 4s.

[Total] of this page 58s. 2d.

Sum total this week £10 15s. 8d.

517. [f. 411v] 9 March

Renter £8   Fishmongers   Butchers   Passage tolls

Three [chaplains] 7s. 6d. Five clerks 10s. Roger Robyns 12d.

[Masons] Bennet 4s. Thomson 4s. Arnold 4s. (Fyld 4s.) Heynes 4s. Jeffrey Orger 3s. 6d. in apparelling hard stone.

[Carpenters] Gold pt 4s. Cocks the elder 4s. Browne senior 4s. Godfrey 4s. Leonard Holmes 4s. Simon Cockes 2s. 6d. in the waterworks.

Cocks pt 4s. Inglydwe 4s. Palmer 4s. Pasmer (4s.) <16d.> Thomas Broke 4s. Walter Alen 4s. Thomas Browne (4s.) <2s.> Nicholas Holowaye 3s. in finishing the new house in Cheapside.

John Pasmer 2s. 6d. John Provest 4s. William Wynter 3s. in repairs.

[Sawyers] Flint slitting 7½ hundred, 8s. 1d.

[Porter] Hughwett 2s.

[Shoutman] Thomas Alen 3s. 4d.

[Bricklayers] Swenson 4s. Chorleton 4s. [Labourers] Nevell 2s. 6d. Hogett 2s. 6d. Thomas Grene 2s. 6d. Sherman 2s. 6d. making chimneys in the new house in Cheap.

Daubers. Thomas Monk' 4s. Labourer. Patrick Plackeney 2s. 6d.

Labourers. John Smyth 2s. 6d. Thomas Alen 2s. 6d. Whythed 2s. 6d. Tanner 2s. 6d.

[Total] of this page £7 8s. 3d.

[f. 412] To John Backer of London, fishmonger, for 18 lb. of Polish [*pollen*] wax for [St] Thomas' chapel, 12s.

To Peter Carpenter of Southwark, blacksmith, for making 4 soldering irons for the plumbery [*plomberye*] house, weighing 12 lb., at 3d. the lb. argent, 3s.

To Thomas Mason, ordure voider, for voiding 15 tuns of ordure out of a vault in the tenement called the Castle in Wood Street, at 18d. the tun, 22s. 6d.

To John Smith, labourer, watching 2 nights with the said Mason, 8d.

[Total] of this page 38s. 2d.

Sum total of the week, £10 6s. 5d.

518. [f. 412v] 16 March

Renter £8   Fishmongers   Butchers   Passage tolls

213

Received of John Carpenter of St Katherine's for 90 ft. of featherboard for a mill-wheel, 5s.

Chaplains 7s. 6d. Five clerks 10s. Roger Robyns 12d.

[Masons] Bennet 4s. Thomson 4s. Arnold 4s. Fyld [blank] Heynes 4s. Jeffrey Orger 3s. 6d. in apparelling hard stone.

[Carpenters] Gold pt 4s. Cockes the elder 4s. Browne senior 4s. Godfrey 4s. Leonard Holmes 4s. Simon Cockes 2s. 6d. William Wynter 3s. in the waterworks.

Cocks pt 4s. Inglydwe 4s. Palmer 4s. Pasmer 4s. Thomas Broke 4s. Walter Alen 4s. Browne junior 4s. Thomas Browne 4s. Nicholas Holowaye 3s. in finishing the new house aforesaid.

John Pasmer 2s. 6d. John Provest 4s. in repairs in Newgate market.

[Sawyers] Flint slitting 7½ hundred, 8s. 1d.

[Porter] William Hug' 2s.

[Shoutman] Thomas Alen 3s. 4d.

[Bricklayers] Swenson 4s. Chorleton 4s. [Labourers] Nevell 2s. 6d. Hogett 2s. 6d. Thomas Grene 2s. 6d. Sherman 2s. 6d.

Daubers. Thomas Monkest 4s. Labourers. Patrick Plackeneye 2s. 6d. John Terset 20d.

Labourers. John Smyth 2s. 6d. Thomas Alen 2s. 6d. Whythed 2s. 6d. Tanner 2s. 6d.

[Total] of this page £7 18s. 7d.

[f. 413] To Thomas Sybbell of Aynesford [Eynesford, co. Kent] for 57 elm trees bought of him by Provest and Thomas Alen and [paid] to him by the hands of Elizabeth his daughter, 100s.

To Richard Davye of New Hythe by Maidstone, Kent, by the hands of John Orgar, for 100 ft. of bridge ashlar, containing 12 tons, and for 7 great springers and 24 ogees [*ogys*] for arches, containing together 11 tons, and for the freight of 4 hundred of Chapman ware paving, containing 10 tons, sum total 32 tons at 12d. the ton, 32s.

To Hughwett for 2 dozen cotton candles at 1¼d the dozen, 2s. 6d., and for 6 lb. at 1½d. the lb., 9d., used among the carpenters this year, in all 3s. 3d.

To John Orgar the same day by bill, for a hundred of bridge ashlar, price at the quarry 26s. 8d., for land carriage of the same 11s., for 7 great springers price at the quarry 21s., for 24 ft. of ogees [*ogys*] for arches at 6d. the foot, 12s., for land carriage of the same stone and springers containing 11 tons, 1s., for 4 hundred of Chapman ware paving at 5s. the hundred in the quarry, 30s., for land carriage of the same containing 10 tons, 10s., in all 111s. 8d.

[Total] of this page £12 7s. 11d.

Sum total of the week £20 6s. 6d.

519. [f. 413v] 23 March

Renter £30 Butchers £10 Fishmongers (£30) <100s.> Passage-tolls. Three [chaplains] (7s. 6d.) <10s.> Five clerks 10s. Roger Robyns 11d. [sic]

[Masons] Bennet 4s. Tomson 4s. Arnold 4s. Fyld 4s. Heynes 4s. Jeffrey Orgar 3s. 6d. in apparelling hard stone.

[Carpenters] Gold pt 4s. Cockes the elder 4s. Browne senior 4s. Henry Godfrey 4s. Leonard Holmes 4s. William Wynter 3s. Simon Cockes 2s. 6d. in the waterworks.

Cockes pt 4s. Inglydwe 4s. Palmer 4s. Pasmer 4s. Thomas Brooke 4s. Walter Alen 4s. Thomas Browne 4s. Nicholas Holowaye 3s. [margin, in Latin: death of the same Nicholas] Browne junior 4s. John Pasmer 2s. 6d. upon the new house in Cheapside.

John Provest 4s. in repairs in Cheap.

[Sawyers] Flynt slitting 7 hundred, 7s. 7d.

[Porter] Hughwett 2s.

[Shoutman] Thomas Alen 3s. 4d.

Bricklayers. Swenson 4s. Chorleton 4s. Labourers. Nevell 2s. 6d. Hogett 2s. 6d. Thomas Grene 2s. 6d. Tanner 2s. 6d. in raising chimneys in Cheap.

Daubers. (Cockes) Monkest 4s. Henry Bryan 4s. Labourers. Patrick Plackeney 2s. 6d. John Tursett 2s. 6d.

Labourers. John Smyth 2s. 6d. Whythed 2s. 6d. Thomas Alen 2s. 6d. (Tanner) Sherman 2s. 6d. in the works aforesaid.

[Total] of this page £8 5s. 5d.

[f. 414] To Mistress Foster, widow, for carriage of 20 loads of timber, border stone and other from the Bridge House to the new tenement in Cheap, and for 2 loads into Newgate market, at 4d. the load, 7s. 4d., and for 1 load from Paternoster Row to Cheapside at 2d., in all 7s. 6d.

To my lord Commendatory of Bermondsey by the hands of John Byrd for a quit-rent from certain lands in Bermondsey Street for a whole year ended at Christmas last past by acquittance, 6s. 10d.

To Tanner's wife for for washing the chapel stuff this quarter, 12d.

To John Ferres for his quarter's fee, 5s. 2d.

To the said priests and clerks for *Placebo* and *Dirige*, 3s.

To the wife of William Hughwett for weeding the garden this quarter, 2s.

To (the wife of) John Orgar, master mason, for his quarter's fee, 50s.

To Hugh Brampson for a load of bricks, 4s. 8d.

To Robert Nelson, glazier, by bill 6s. 2d.

[Total] of this page £4 3s. 4d.

Sum total of the week £12 8s. 9d.

520. [f. 414v] 30 March

Renter £8   Fishmongers   Butchers   Passage tolls 20s.

Three [chaplains] 7s. 6d. Five clerks 10s. Roger Robyns [12d.]

[Masons] Bennet 4s. (4d.) Tomson 4s. (4d.) Arnold 4s. (4d.) Fyld 4s. (4d.) Heynes 4s. (4d.) Jeffrey Orgar 3s. 6d. (11d.) in apparelling hard stone.

[Carpenters] Gold pt 4s. Cockes the elder 3s. 4d. Browne senior 3s. 4d. Leonard Holmes 3s. 4d. William Wynter 2s. 6d. Simon Cockes 2s. 1d. in the waterworks.

Cockes pt 4s. Inglydwe 3s. 4d. Palmer 3s. 4d. Pasmer 3s. 4d. Browne junior 3s. 4d. in finishing the new house in Cheapside.

John Provest 3s. 4d. Henry Godfrey 3s. 4d. in repairs at the Castle in Wood Street.

[Sawyers] Flynt slitting 6½ hundred, 7s.

[Porter] Hughwet 2s.

[Shoutman] Thomas Alen 3s. 4d.

[Bricklayers] Swenson 3s. 4d. Chorleton 3s. 4d. [Labourers] Hogett 2s. 1d. Nevell 2s. 1d. Thomas Grene 2s. 1d. Tanner 2s. 1d.

Daubers. Thomas Monkest 3s. 4d. Henry Bryons 3s. 4d. Labourers. Patrick Plackeney 2s. 1d. John Tursett 2s. 1d.

Labourers. John Smyth 2s. 1d. Roger Whythed 2s. 1d. Thomas Alen 2s. 1d. Sherman 2s. 1d.

[Total] of this page £7 3s. 7d.

[f. 415] To Laurence [Awen], clerk of the Bridge House, for money paid by him and laid out to divers men for hewing timber and making wood and other expenses incident to the same, by bill £4 3s. 2d.

To John Carter of Colchester, carpenter, in part payment of [words blotted: ? four score] loads of oak timber bought of him at 7s. the load, £10.

Thomas Baxster, chantry priest of Paul's, for a quarter ended at the Annunciation last past, 2s. 6d.

To William Best of Reigate, for carriage of 2 loads of Reigate stone for pendants of the arches of the bridge, 7s.

To Jeffrey Haryson for 13 loads of loam delivered in Cheapside and 12 loads delivered at the storehouse on the bridge at 4d. the load, 8s. 4d., and for 48 loads of sand delivered at Cheapside at 6d. the load, 24s., 32s. 4d.

To William [Cockes] the younger [*Minus*] for 24 lb. of cotton candles, 2s. 6d., and for 1 lb. of glue, 3½d., in all 2s. 9½d.

To Peter Carpenter of Southwark for 6 <soldering> irons and 2 (shavehooks) cutting knives for the plumber, weighing 25 lb. at 3d. the lb., 6s. 3d.

The masters' expenses at Lewisham this week in viewing the woods and divers other things there, with divers other of the House with them at the same time, 3s. 8½d.

To Henry Mylles, gardener, for his wages for 5 days working in the garden, at 8d. the day, 3s. 4d., and to him for his man for 5 days at 5d. the day, 2s. 1d., and for seeds for the same 9d., 6s. 2d.

To William Hughwett for 18 loads of dung for the garden, 4d.

[Total] of this page £17 4s. 3d.

Sum total paid this week, £24 7s. 10d.

521. [f. 415v] 6 April.

Renter £8   Fishmongers   Butchers   Passage tolls

Received of Henry Byrd of London Bridge, grocer, for 11 ft. of timber at 3d. the foot, 2s. 9d.

Three [chaplains] 7s. 6d. Five clerks 10s. Roger Robyns 12d.

[Masons] Bennet 4s. Thomson 4s. Arnold 4s. Fyld 4s. Heynes 4s. Jeffrey Orgar 3s. 6d. in apparelling hard stone.

[Carpenters] Gold pt 4s. Cockes the elder 4s. Browne senior 4s.

Leonard Holmes 4s. William Wynter 3s. Simon Cockes 2s. 6d. in the waterworks.

Cockes pt 4s. Inglydwe 4s. Palmer 4s. Pasmer 4s. Thomas Broke 4s. Walter Alen 4s. Thomas Browne 4s. John Browne junior 4s. John Pasmer 3s. (6d.) in repairs and making the new house in Cheapside. John Provest 4s.

[Sawyers] Flynt slitting 6 hundred, 6s. 6d., board 1 hundred, 12d., 7s. 6d.

[Porter] Hughwet 2s.

[Shoutman] Thomas Alen 3s. 4d.

[Bricklayers] Swenson 4s. Chorleton 4s. [Labourers] Nevell 2s. 6d. Hogett 2s. 6d. Thomas Grene 2s. 6d. Tanner 2s. 6d. Thomas Thorneley 2s. 6d.

Daubers. Monkest 4s. Henry Bryane 4s. Labourers. Patrick Plackeney 2s. 6d. John Tursett 2s. 6d.

Labourers. John Smyth 2s. 6d. Roger Whythed 2s. 6d. Thomas Alen [blank]. Sherman 2s. 6d.

[Total] of this page £8 4d.

[f. 416] To William Charpeharowe, blacksmith, for sundry sorts of iron works by him made and delivered to the use of the House, as appears by his bill thereof, £13 12d.

To Mr Amborous, chief carpenter of the Bridge, for his quarter's fee ended at the Annunciation [last past], 50s.

To William Best, carter, for carriage of 1 load of Reigate stone for pendants for a new arch and for carriage of 1 load of border for ovens, 7s.

To John Modyll, quarryman of Reigate, for 3 loads for pendants for arches, 6s., and for 1 load of border for chimneys, with 4s. for scappling the same, 6s., 12s.

To Mistress Foster, widow, for carriage of 17 loads of timber, board, and other from the Bridge House to Cheapside and the Minories at 4d. the load, 5s. 8d., and for carriage of 1 load from Cheap to Newgate market 2d., 5s. 10d.

[Total] of this page £16 15s. 10d.

Sum total of the week £24 16s. 2d.

522. [f. 416v] 13 April

Renter £8   Fishmongers   Butchers   Passage tolls

Received of Mistress Best, widow, for rent of a granary in Golders yard (for the rent of a backhouse) for a whole year ended at (Michaelmas) <the Annunciation> last past, 26s. 8d.

Received of her the same time for rent of another granary for 3 quarters of a year ended at Christmas last past, 20s.

Received of John Cachemayd, (widow) merchant tailor, for the debt of Anne Panell, widow, in full payment of £103 15s. 3d., £6 13s. 4d.

Three [chaplains] 7s. 6d. Five clerks 10s. Roger Robyns 12d.

[Masons] Bennet 4s. Tomson 4s. Arnold 4s. Fyld 4s. Thomas Heynes 4s. Jeffrey Orgar 3s. 6d. in apparelling hard stone for an arch.

217

[Carpenters] Gold pt 4s. William Cockes 4s. Browne senior 4s. Leonard Holmes 4s. Godfrey 4s. Wynter 3s. Simon Cockes 2s. 6d. in the waterworks.

William Cockes 4s. Inglydwe 4s. Palmer 4s. Pasmer 4s. Thomas Browne 4s. Thomas Broke 4s. Walter Alen 4s. Browne junior 4s. John Provest 4s. John Pasmer 3s. on the new house in Cheapside.

[Sawyers] Flynt slitting 4 hundred, 4s. 4d., in quarterboard 3 hundred, 3s., 7s. 4d.

[Porter] William Hughet 2s.

[Shoutman] Thomas Alen 3s. 4d.

[Bricklayers] Swenson 4s. Chorleton 4s. [Labourers] Nevell 2s. 6d. Hogett 2s. 6d. Thomas Grene 2s. 6d. Sherman 2s. 6d. in paving cellars [*selers*] at the new building.

Daubers. Thomas Monkest 4s. Henry Bryan 4s. Labourers. Patrick Plackeney 2s. 6d. John Tursyt 2s. 6d.

Labourers. John Smyth 2s. 6d. Thomas Alen 2s. 6d. Whythed 2s. 6d. Tanner 2s. 6d. in the works aforesaid.

[Total] of this page £8 2d.

[f. 417] To Hugh Brampson, brickburner, for 32½ thousand bricks, of which 30½ thousand were delivered by him to the new house in Cheapside and 1 thousand to the Castle in Wood Street, and the other thousand in repairs at St Nicholas £7 11s. 8d.

To Thomas Crull for his quarter's fee for the quarter ended at the Annunciation last past, £6 13s. 4d.

To John Clerke of Southwark, carter, for the carriage of 3 loads of timber and board from the Bridge House to Cheapside at 4d. the load, 12d., and for 1 load to Johnson's house on the bridge, 2d., 14d.

To Richard Ruddyng for paving 29 toises before the new house in Cheap at 7d. the toise, 16s. 11d.

[Total] of this page £15 3s. 1d.

Sum total of the week £23 3s. 3d.

523. [f. 417v] 20 April

Renter £8   Fishmongers   Butchers   Passage tolls

Received of Robert Gold for 18 ft. of ceiling [*selyng*] timber argent 6d.

Received of Robert Barfoote, mercer, for a load and 8 ft. of oak timber delivered at Croydon, 6s. 10d.

Received of William Bomsted, bowyer, for 4 small shells of oak, 12d.

Received of William Cockes the elder for a quarter of board, 16d.

Three [chaplains] 7s. 6d. Five clerks 10s. Roger Robynson [sic] 12d.

[Masons] Bennet 4s. Tomson 4s. Thomas Fyld 3s. 4d. Thomas Heynes 3s. 4d. Jeffrey Orgar 32s. 11d. in apparelling hard stone.

[Carpenters] Robert Gold 4s. William Cockes 3s. 4d. Browne senior 3s. 4d. Leonard Holmes 3s. 4d. Henry Godfrey 3s. 4d. John Provest 3s. 4d. Wynter 2s. 6d. Simon Cockes 2s. 1d. in the waterworks.

Cockes pt 4s. Inglydwe 3s. 4d. Palmer 3s. 4d. Pasmer 3s. 4d. Thomas Broke 3s. 4d. Walter Alen 3s. 4d. Thomas Browne 3s. 4d. Browne junior 3s. 4d. John Pasmer 2s. 6d. in finishing the new house in Cheap aforesaid.

[Sawyers] Flynt slitting 5 hundred, 5s. 5d., in elm board, 12d.

[Porter] William Hugh' 2s.

[Shoutman] Thomas Alen 3s. 4d.

Bricklayers and labourers. Swenson 3s. 4d. Chorleton 3s. 4d. Nevell 2s. 1d. Hogett 2s. 1d. Thomas Grene 2s. 1d. Sherman 2s. 1d. in raising a new chimney at St Nicholas Shambles.

Daubers. Monkest 3s. 4d. Henry Bryane 3s. 4d. John Dogett 3s. 4d.

Labourers. Patrick Plackeney 2s. 1d. John Tursett 2s. 1d. Thomas Monkest 2s. 1d. in the new house in Cheap aforesaid.

Labourers. John Smyth 2s. 1d. Thomas Alen 2s. 1d. Whythed 2s. 1d. Tanner 2s. 1d. Thomas John 2s. 1d. in the works aforesaid.

[Total] of this page £7 4s. 7d.

[f. 418] To Richard Dryver, limeburner, for 30 hundred 4 loads and 4 sacks of lime, delivered by him to Cheapside and other places in London, as appears by tale and bill, at 4s. the hundred, £6 2s. 7d.

To Mistress Foster, widow, for carriage of 13 loads of stone, board and timber from the Bridge House to Cheapside, 4s. 4d.

To Robert Terne, blacksmith, for battering 76 dozen masons' tools this quarter, by tale at $1\frac{1}{2}$d. the dozen, 9s. 6d.

To Robert Nelson, glazier, in prest for making glass in Cheap for the window in Cheap, 20s.

To Henry Mill, gardener, for working in the garden for $2\frac{1}{2}$ days at 8d. the day, 20d., and for wire to bind the rosemary to the wall 5d., 2s. 1d.

[Total] of this page £7 18s. 6d.

Sum total of the week £15 3s. 1d.

524. [f. 418v] 27 April

Renter £8   Fishmongers   Butchers   Passage tolls

Three chaplains 7s. 6d. Five clerks 10s. Roger Robynson [sic] 12d.

Masons. Bennet 16d. Tomson 16d. in apparelling hard stone.

Carpenters. Gold pt 4s. Cockes the elder 16d. Browne senior 16d. Henry Godfrey 16d. Leonard Holmes 16d. Wynter 12d. Simon Cockes 10d. in the waterworks.

Cockes pt 4s. Inglydwe 16d. Palmer 16d. Pasmer [blank]. Thomas Browne 16d. Browne junior 16d. John Provest 16d. John Pasmer 12d. in the new house in Cheap.

Sawyers. Flynt slitting $2\frac{1}{2}$ hundred, 2s. 7d.

Porter. Hughwet 2s.

[Shoutman] Thomas Alen 3s. 4d.

Bricklayers. Swenson 16d. Chorleton 16d. Labourers. Nevell 10d. (Hogett 10d.) <Stet> Thomas Grene 10d. Sherman 10d. in the well at the Cup in St Nicholas.

Daubers. Monkest 16d. John Duckett 8d. Labourers. Patrick Plackeney 10d. John Turset 10d.

Labourers. John Smyth 10d. Thomas Alen 10d. Whythed 10d. Tanner 10d. John Johnson [blank]

219

[Total] of this page 65s.

[f. 419] To the parson of Woolchurch for the tithe of the Stocks for 1 quarter ended at (Michaelmas) the Annunciation last past, 13s. 4d.

To Thomas Mason for carriage of 5 loads of rubbish from the Castle in Wood Street and another 5 loads from Newgate market at 2½d. the load, 2s. 1d.

[Total] of this page 15s. 5d.

Sum total of the week 80s. 5d.

525. [f. 419v] 4 May

Renter £8 Fishmongers Butchers Passage tolls 20s.

Received in oblations for St George's time, 2s. 1½d.

Received of the churchwardens of St Olave's for 2 loads and 23 ft. of timber, 20s. 6d.

Three chaplains 7s. 6d. Five clerks 10s. Roger [sic] 12d.

Masons. Bennet 3s. 4d. Tomson 3s. 4d. Arnold 4s. Fyld 3s. 4d. Heynes 3s. 4d. Jeffrey Orgar 2s. 11d. in apparelling hard stone.

Carpenters. Gold pt 4s. Cockes the elder 2s. 8d. Browne senior 2s. 8d. Henry Godfrey 2s. 8d. Leonard Holmes 2s. 8d. William Wynter 2s. 8d. Simon Cockes 20d. in the waterworks.

Cockes pt 4s. Inglydwe 2s. 8d. Palmer 2s. 8d. Pasmer 2s. 8d. Thomas Browne 2s. 8d. Browne junior 2s. 8d. John Pasmer 2s. John Provest 2s. 8d. (Browne junior).

Sawyers. Flynt slitting 4 hundred, 4s. 4d., planks a hundred, 12d., 5s. 4d.

Porter. Hughwet 2s.

Shoutman. Thomas Alen 3s. 4d.

Bricklayers. Swenson 2s. 8d. Chorleton 2s. 8d. Labourers. Nevell 20d. Hogett 20d. Thomas Grene 20d. in the new house in Cheap.

Daubers. Thomas Monkest 2s. 8d. John Dockett 2s. 8d. Labourers. Patrick Plackeney 20d. John Tursett 20d.

Labourers. John Smyth 20d. Thomas Alen 20d. Whytehed 20d. Tanner 20d. Sherman 20d.

[Total] of this page £5 17s. 1d.

[f. 420] To John Houghe, organmaker, for mending the organs in the chapel this year as in times past, 12d.

To Ambrose Wolleis by the hands of Thomas Alen for a barrel of tar, 4s. 8d.

To Thomas Alen for 4 lb. thrums, 8d., and for 10 lb. oakum, 10d., in all 18d.

To Robert Butteler for carriage of 4 loads of timber from Croydon at 2s. 8d. the load, 9s. 4d.

To Thomas Mason for carriage of 12 loads of rubbish out of the new house in Cheap at 2d., 2s.

To William Bound for carriage of 14 loads of rubbish from the said house at 2d. the load, 2s. 4d.

To the smith of Lambeth for 200 tenpenny nails 20d., for 400 sixpenny nails 2s., 400 fourpenny nails 16d., and 500 threepenny nails, 15d., 6s. 3d.

To the chantry priest of St Olave's for his quarter ended at the Annunciation, 26s. 8d.

To the prior of St Bartholomew for a quit-rent due at the Annunciation for a whole year, 3s. 4d.

[Total] of this page 57s. 1d.

Sum total of the week, £8 14s. 2d.

526. [f. 420v] 11 May

Renter £8   Fishmongers   Butchers   Passage tolls

Received of a Dutch [*douche*] man for 1 old stone, 10d.

Three chaplains 7s. 6d. Five clerks 10s. Roger Robyns 12d.

Masons. Bennet 4s. Tomson 4s. Arnold 4s. Fyld 4s. Heynes 4s. Jeffrey Orgar 3s. 6d. in apparelling hard stone.

[Carpenters] Gold pt 4s. Cockes the elder 4s. Browne senior 4s. Henry Godfrey 4s. Leonard Holmes 4s. William Wynter 3s. Simon Cockes 2s. 6d. in the waterworks.

Carpenters. Cockes pt 4s. Inglydwe 4s. Palmer 4s. Pasmer 4s. Thomas Browne 4s. Browne junior 4s. John Pasmer 3s. John Provest 3s. 4d. in finishing the new house in Cheap.

Sawyers. Flynt slitting 7 hundred, 7s. 7d.

Porter. Hughwett 2s.

[Shoutman] Thomas Alen 3s. 4d.

Bricklayers. Swenson 4s. Chorleton 4s. Labourers. Nevell 2s. 6d. Hogett 2s. 6d. Thomas Grene 2s. 6d.

Daubers. Thomas Monk' 4s. John Duckett 4s. Labourers. Patrick 2s. 6d. John Tursett 2s. 6d.

Labourers. John Smyth 2s. 6d. Thomas Alen 10d. Whythed 2s. 6d. Tanner 2s. (6d.) <1d.> Sherman 2s. 6d.

Shipwrights. 4 [days at] 11 [d. a day] Hugh Yong 3s. 8d. (8) <10> [days at] 10 [d. a day] John Lewis 8s. 4d. 6 [days at] 10 [d. a day] Richard Ford 5s. John Cowe 4s. William Alm' 6s. 8d. 18 [days] John Fydler 8s. 4d. William Englesse 3s. 4d. in mending boats, all.

[Total] of this page £9 9s.

[f. 421] To the 2 sawyers of Petham Court for sawing 2,091 ft. of planks cut and half cut [*of kerffe and halfe kerffe*] at 14d. the hundred, 26s. 11d., and for sawing 1,765 ft. of plankboard at 12d. the hundred, 17s. 8d., and for making 6 sawpits 4s. 4d. in all, and for making 5 rolls and cutting the crosswise cuts [*anthwart kyrffes*] 2s., in all 50s. 11d.

To Laurence and Provest going to measure [*meite*] the same timber and to pay the sawyers in prest, being away 2 days, 2s. 6d.

To Provest for this charges in going to see the sawyers, 8d.

To the masters for their expenses in going to view the same timber and to pay the sawyers their full duty, being away 2 days, with the clerk and divers others with them, 6s.

To the smith of Lambeth for 200 tenpenny nails 20d., and for 400 sixpenny nails 2s. 3d., for 400 fourpenny nails 16d., and for 300 threepenny nails 9d., in all 6s.

To William Suer for carriage of 1 load of Reigate stone for pendants, 3s. 6d.

To Richard Best for carriage of 1 load of Reigate stone for pendants, 3s. 6d.

To Laurence [Awen] for his quarter's fee ended at our lord's [sic], 50s.

To the said William Suer for 1 load of board from Reigate, 3s. 6d.

To John Gate of Maidstone for carriage by water of 1¼ hundred of bridge ashlar, for 5 ft. of [blank] and for 27 ft. of gutter stone, for a hundred of parelled paving and for a hundred of Chapman ware (ashlar) paving at 12d. the hundred, in all 18 hundred, 18s.

To Mistress Foster for carriage of 5 loads to Cheapside of timber and board at 4d. the load, 20d., and for 6 loads of timber to the bridge at 2d. the load, 12d., 2s. 8d.

[Total] of this page £7 7s. 3d.

Sum total of the week £16 16s. 3d.

527. [f. 421v] 18 May

Renter £8   Fishmongers   Butchers   Passage tolls

Received of Thomas Alen for 2 hundredweight [*CCth weight*] of chalk, 12d.

Received of Robert Gold for 3 ft. of oak timber, 12d.

Received of Eglesfyld for (3) <4> loads of Rag, 5s.

Received of John Flynt by the hands of William Cockes for 80 ft. of oak boards for a chest for his wife, 2s.

Three chaplains 7s. 6d. Five clerks 10s. Roger Robyns 12d.

Masons. Bennet 4s. Thomson 4s. Arnold 4s. Fyld 4s. Heynes 4s. Jeffrey Orgar 3s. 6d. in apparelling hard stone.

[Carpenters] Gold pt 4s. Cockes the elder 4s. Browne senior 4s. Henry Godfrey 4s. Leonard Holmes 4s. Simon Cockes 2s. 6d. William Wynter 3s. in the waterworks.

Carpenters. Cockes pt 4s. Inglydwe 4s. Palmer 4s. Pasmer 4s. Thomas Browne 4s. Browne junior 4s. Simon Cockes 3s. John Provest 4s. in finishing the new house in Cheapside.

Sawyers. Flynt 6 hundred, 6s. 6d.

[Porter] Hughwett 2s.

Shoutman. Thomas Alen 3s. 4d.

Bricklayers. Swenson 4s. Chorleton 4s. Labourers. Nevell 2s. 6d. Hogett 2s. 6d. Thomas Grene 2s. 6d. in [blank].

Daubers. Thomas Monk' 4s. John Dockett 4s. Labourers. Patrick Plackene 2s. 6d. John Tursett 2s. 6d.

Labourers. John Smyth 2s. 6d. Thomas Alen 10d. Whytehed 2s. 6d. Sherman 2s. 6d. Tanner 2s. 6d.

[Total] of this page £7 11s. 4d.

[f. 422] To William Swer for carriage half the way of 2 loads of Reigate stone for pendants for [not clear; ? ovens] and the bridge, 3s.

To John Orgar by bill 90s. 4d.

To John Modill of Kent, quarryman, for 5 loads of square Reigate stone at 2s. the load, 10s., and for 1 load of borders (2s.) with 4s. for scappling the same 6s., 16s.

To the same John for carriage of the 3 loads of the same stone halfway from the quarry at 18d. the load, 4s. 6d., and to him in full payment for carriage of 4 loads at 3s. 6d. the load, 2s. 6d.

To the said John Modyll for 1 load of pendants and for carriage of the same from Reigate, 5s. 6d.

To William Suer for carriage of a load of Reigate stone half the way, 18d.

[Total] of this page £6 2s. 4d.

Sum total of the week £13 13s. 8d.

528. [f. 422v] 25 May.

Renter £8 Fishmongers Butchers Passage tolls 20s.

Received of a gunpowder maker by the hands of Robert Gold for 20 stops of elm, 20 ft. long, 6s. 8d., for 4 elm planks containing 94 ft. of timber, 5s., and for 2 ft. of elm, 11d., 12s.

Received of the said Gold for 9 ft. of board at 3 ft. for 1d., 3d.

Received of Moodye for an end of oak of 6 ft. at 2d. the foot, 12d.

Three chaplains 7s. 6d. Five clerks 10s. Roger Robyns 12d.

Masons. Bennet 4s. Tomson 4s. Arnold 4s. Fyld 4s. Heynes 4s. Jeffrey Orgar 3s. 6d. in taking down a breast of an arch.

[Carpenters] Gold pt 4s. Cockes the elder 4s. Browne senior 4s. Henry Godfrey 4s. Wynter 3s. Simon Cockes 2s. 6d. Leonard Holmes 4s.

Carpenters. Robert Pasmer 4s. Browne junior 4s. Cockes pt 4s. John Pasmer 3s. in the new house in Cheap.

Thomas Browne 4s. John Provest 4s. John Palmer 4s. in repairs in Southwark.

Sawyers. Flynt slitting 7 hundred, 7s. 7d.

Porter. Hughwet 2s.

Shoutman. Thomas Alen 3s. 4d.

Bricklayers. Swenson 4s. Chorleton 4s. Labourers. Nevell 2s. 6d. Hogett 2s. 6d. Thomas Grene 2s. 6d. at the brownbaker's house at the sign of the Horseshoe.

Daubers. Monkest 4s. John Dogett 4s. [Labourers] Patrick 2s. 6d. John Tursett 2s. 6d. in the new house in Cheap.

Labourers. John Smyth 2s. 6d. Thomas Alen 20d. Whytehed 2s. 6d. Tanner 2s. 6d. Sherman 2s. 6d. Cloworth 2s. 6d.

[Total] of this page £7 9s. 8d.

[f. 423] To my lord of Canterbury for a quit-rent due at the Annunciation last, 5s. 2d.

To the churchwardens of St Nicholas Shambles for a quarter ended at Our Lady's Day last past, 25s.

To the said Bennet, Thomson, Arnold, Fyld, Heynes, and Jeffrey Orgar for working 1 tide out of due time in the waterworks, at 3d. the man, 2s.

To Roger Hoode for 4 tides, Thomas Shepherd for 5 tides, Thomas Wright for 6 tides, labourers labouring with the masons at 3d. the tide, 3s. 9d.

To Thomas Alen for 6 men for unloading of 4 boats of rag from the bridge, 2s.

To him for 6 labourers for unloading 2 boats, 12d.

To Thomas Sheperd for 5 tides, Thomas Wryght for 8 tides, Leonard

223

Lynsey for 3 tides, Roger Hoode for 1 tide, William Tanner for 1 tide, John Roche for 1 tide, labourers labouring with the said masons at 3d. the tide, in all 5s. 3d.

To the said Thomas Alen for 4 men for helping him through the bridge at 6 several times, and to him for 3 men at 2 tides, 6d., in all 2s. 6d.

[Total] of this page 46s. 8d.

Sum total of the week, £9 16s. 4d.

529. [f. 423v] 1 June

Renter   Fishmongers   Butchers   Passage tolls

Three chaplains 7s. 6d. Five clerks 10s. Roger Robyns 12d.

Masons. Bennet 4s. Tomson 4s. Arnold 4s. Fyld 4s. Heynes 4s. Jeffrey Orgar 3s. 6d. in apparelling hard stone.

[Carpenters] Gold pt 4s. Cockes the elder 3s. 4d. Browne senior 3s. 4d. Henry Godfrey 3s. 4d. (Leonard Holmes) Pasmer 3s. 4d. Thomas Browne 3s. 4d. John Browne 3s. 4d. William Wynter 2s. 6d. Simon Cockes 2s. 1d. in the waterworks.

(Cockes pt 4s. John Pasmer 2s. 6d.) in Cheapside [margin: at the house of the owner]

Inglydwe 3s. 4d. Palmer 3s. 4d. (4s.) Leonard Holmes 3s. 4d. John Provest 3s. 4d. at a joiner's house in Southwark.

Sawyers. Flynt slitting 6 hundred, 6s. 6d.

Porter. Hughet 2s.

[Shoutman] Thomas Alen 3s. 4d.

Bricklayers. Swenson 3s. 4d. Chorleton 3s. 4d. Labourers. Nevell 2s. 1d. Hogett 2s. 1d. Thomas Grene 2s. 1d. in repairs at the sign of the Horseshoe.

Daubers. Monkest 3s. 4d. John Dogkett 3s. 4d. [Labourers] Patrick 2s. 1d. John Tursett 2s. 1d. in the works in Cheap.

Labourers. John Smyth 2s. 1d. Whythed 2s. 1d. Tanner 2s. 1d. Sherman 2s. 1d. John Cloworth 2s. 1d. in the works aforesaid.

[Total] of this page £6 9s. 11d.

[f. 424] To Robert Butteller, carter, for the carriage of 5 loads of timber from Croydon to the Bridge House in London at 2s. 4d. the load, in all 11s. 8d.

To Smith the turner for 4 shovels for the masons, 16d., and for 4 scoops for the boats, 8d., 2s.

To a gardener for 2 days working in the garden, 16d.

To Thomas Monkest, plasterer, for 60 bushels of hair bought by him for the new house in Cheap at 3d. the bushel, 15s.

To James Foster for carriage of 4 loads of stuff to Cheapside and 3 loads home to the Bridge House, 2s. 4d.

To him for carriage of 2 loads to Gracechurch at 2d., 6d.

[Total] of this page 32s. 10d.

Sum total paid £8 2s. 9d.

530. [f. 424v] 8 June

Received of a shipwright for 12 ft. of oak timber by the hands of Robert Gold, 2s. 9d.

Three chaplains 7s. 6d. Five clerks 10s. Roger 12d.

Masons. Bennet 4s. Thomson 4s. Arnold 4s. Fyld 4s. Heron 4s. Jeffrey Orgar 3s. 6d. in apparelling hard stone.

Carpenters. Gold 4s. Cockes the elder 4s. Browne senior 4s. Henry Godfrey 4s. Leonard Holmes 4s. Browne junior 4s. William Wynter 3s. (4s.) Simon Cockes 2s. 6d. Cockes pt 4s. Pasmer 4s. Palmer 4s. Inglydwe 4s. Thomas Browne 4s. John Provest 4s. John Pasmer 3s. in the waterworks and repairs.

Sawyer. Flynt slitting 7 hundred, 7s. 7d.

Porter. Hughet 2s.

Shoutman. Thomas Alen 3s. 4d.

Bricklayers. Swenson 4s. Chorleton 4s. Labourers. Nevell 2s. 6d. Hogett 2s. 6d. Thomas Grene 2s. 6d.

Daubers. Monkest 4s. John Dockett 4s. Labourers. Patrick 2s. 6d. John Tursett 2s. 6d.

Labourers. John S. 2s. 6d. Thomas Alen 2s. 6d. Whythed 2s. 6d. Tanner 2s. 6d. Sherman 2s. 6d. Cloworth 2s. 6d.

[Total] of this page £7 13s. 8d.

[f. 425] To Thomas Dendye of Sussex, boardman, in full payment for 5 thousand 8 hundred of plankboard, 3 thousand 8½ hundred of quarterboard at 20d. the hundred, for 2 loads of quarters at 8s. 6d. the load, and for 3 loads of laths at 10s. 8d. the load, £6 9s. 10d.

To William Bently of Maidstone in Kent for water carriage of 15 tons of pavingstone at 12d., 15s.

To the said Bennett, Thomson, Arnold, Fyld, and Jeffrey Orgar, each for 2 tides out of due time, 3s. 4d.

To John Smyth for 2 new pails for the masons, 6d.

To a cordwainer at the watergate for soling 2 pairs of boots for the masons, 12d.

To Mr Wyndam, parson of (Wolcherc) St Olave for the tithe of Golders for a year ended at Easter, 10s.

To the said Gold for 4 tides, Cockes the elder for 4 tides, Browne senior for 4 tides, Henry Godfrey for 4 tides, Leonard Holmes for (4) 3 tides, Wynter for 4 tides, Simon Cockes for 4 tides, Cocks junior for 3 tides, Inglydwe for 3 tides, Palmer for 3 tides, Pasmer for 3 tides, Thomas Browne for 4 tides, Browne junior for 4 tides, John Provest for 4 tides, and John Pasmer for 3 tides, carpenters working in the waterworks out of due time, between them for 54 tides at 4d. the tide, 18s.

To Tanner for 2 tides, Whythed for 2 tides, and John Cloworth for 2 tides, labourers labouring with the said carpenters, between them for 6 tides at 3d. the tide, 18d.

To 2 labourers for bearing boards, laths, and quarters for 2½ days, 2s. 2d.

Item paid for 4 cart clouts for the cart for the millstone, 9d.

[Total] of this page £9 2s. 1d.

Sum total of the week, £16 15s. 9d.

531. [f.425v] 15 June.

Renter £8   Fishmongers   Butchers   Passage tolls

Three chaplains 7s. 6d. Five clerks 10s. Roger 12d.
(Bennet 2s.)
Carpenters. Gold pt 4s. Cockes the elder 4s. Browne senior 2s. Henry Godfrey 2s. Leonard Holmes 2s. Wynter 18d. Simon Cockes 15d. Cockes pt 4s. Inglydwe 2s. Palmer 2s.
Sawyers. Flynt slitting 3½ hundred, 3s. 9d.
Porter. Hughet 2s.
[Shoutman] Thomas Alen 3s. 4d.
Bricklayers. Swenson (2s.) <13d.> Chorleton 2s. Labourers. Nevell 15d. Hogett 15d. Thomas Grene 15d.
Daubers. Monkest 2s. [Labourers] Patrick Plankeney 15d.
Labourers. John S. 15d. Thomas Alen 15d. Whythed 15d. Tanner 15d. Sherman 15d. Cloworth 15d.
[Total] of this page £3 7s. 6d.
[f. 426] To Robert Nelson, glazier, in part payment of a greater sum for glazing in the new house in Cheap, 40s.
To Brydgs for holing a millstone at Mr Forman's wharf, 3s. 4d.
To Mr Draper for his (quarter) half year's fee ended at the feast of the Annunciation last past, £13 6s. 8d.
To him for his livery due at Christmas last past, 20s.
To Laurence Couper for hooping sundry hogs[heads?], pails and boxes [*Bockks*] by bill, 5s. 4d.
To him for making a new tun for the Crown over against the Bridge House gate, 27s.
To Thomas Bulbroke of Lynn for 2 warps of small and great ropes, weighing 212 lb. at 12s the hundred, 25s.
To Richard Ambrose for his quarter's fee ended at Midsummer next, 50s.
To Richard Olyvers, carter, in part payment of a greater sum for carriage of timber and wood from Petham Court, 65s.
To Thomas Alen for 4 men for heaving [*havyng*] of boats through the bridge at 11 several times, at 1d. the man (3s. 8d. and) to them for 3 men at one time 3d., in all 3s. 11d.
To 8 men for unloading 2 boats, one of stone and one of chalk, 16d., and to 6 men for unloading one boat of chalk, 6d., in all 22d.
To Thomas Wryght for 3 tides placing chalk in the starlings this week, 9d.
To Thomas Monkest for 4 bushels of hair, 12d.
To the wife of James Foster for carriage and recarriage of 9 loads of timber, stone, and other stuff from the Bridge House to Cheap and other places in London at 4d., 3s.
To her for carriage of 1 load to Gracechurch, 3d.
To her for carriage of 5 loads of rubbish from a joiner's house in Southwark at 2d., 10d.
[Total] of this page £25 13s. 10d.
Sum total of the week £29 17d.

532. [f. 426v] 22 June
Renter £30   Fishmongers £5   Butchers £10   Passage-tolls

Received of John Cockes for 27 ft. of oak timber, 5s. 6d.

Three chaplains 7s. 6d. Five clerks 10s. Roger Robyns 12d.

Masons. Bennet 4s. Tomson 4s. Arnold 4s. Fyld 4s. Heron 4s. Jeffrey Orgar 3s. 6d. on a breast for a new arch aforesaid.

Carpenters. Cocks 4s. Robert Gold 4s. Cockes the elder 3s. 4d. Inglydwe 3s. 4d. Pasmer 3s. 4d. Palmer 3s. 4d. Browne senior 3s. 4d. Thomas Browne 3s. 4d. Henry Godfrey 3s. 4d. Leonard Holmes 3s. 4d. John Browne 3s. 4d. John Provest 3s. 4d. William Wynter 2s. 6d. John Pasmer 2s. 6d. Simon Cockes 2s. 1d. on the waterworks and repairs.

Sawyers. Flynt slitting 6 hundred, 6s. 6d. Horton slitting 4 hundred, 4s. 4d.

Porter. Hughwet 2s.

Shoutman. Thomas Alen 3s. 4d.

Bricklayers. Swenson 3s. 4d. Chorleton 3s. 4d. Labourers. Nevell 2s. 1d. Hogett 2s. 1d. Grene 2s. 1d. Sherman 2s. 1d.

Daubers. Monkest 3s. 4d. Labourer. Chorleton 2s. 1d.

Labourers. John S. 2s. 1d. Thomas Alen 2s. 1d. Whythed 2s. 1d. Tanner 2s. 1d. John Clowerth 2s. 1d.

[Total] of this page £5 19s. 11d.

[f. 427] To John Orgar by bill, 114s.

To him for his quarter's fee ended at Michaelmas last, 50s.

To learned counsel for an answer made against a bill of complaint exhibited by the abbot of Tower Hill against the wardens of London Bridge, 10s.

To the aforesaid 3 chaplains and 6 clerks for *Placebo* and *Dirige*, 3s.

To Tanner's wife for washing the said chapel stuff, 12d.

To William Hughwett's wife for weeding the garden for this Midsummer quarter, 2s.

To Henry Mylls, gardener, for 2 days working in the garden, 16d.

To Richard Rudyng, paviour, for paving 21 toises of new paving at the Stocks and 15 toises at the Old Change at 7d. the toise, 21s.

To Peverell, blacksmith, for battering of 34 dozen mason's tools this quarter at 1½d. the dozen, 4s. 3d.

To the aforesaid 6 masons working in the waterworks out of due time, each for 3 tides at 4d. the tide, in all 6s.

To the widow of Richard Pytwyne, glover, for 6 prs. [gloves] for the masons working at the foundation of a new breast, 12d.

To Thomas Alen for 2 tides, Whythed, Tanner, Sherman, and John Southgate, each for 3 tides at 3d. the tide, 3s. 6d.

To Thomas Mason, ordure voider, for cleansing 6 tuns of ordure out of a sluice called *le bragyn* at 18d., 9s.

To Robert Buttler, carter, for carriage of 9 loads of oak timber from Croydon to the Bridge House at 2s. 4d. the load, 21s.

To John Smyth for watching one night with [him] 4d.

To him for 1 pail, 3d.

To Richard Buckerell of Deptford for 4 warps of rope, weighing 3¼ hundred and 11 lb., at 12s. the hundred, 40s.

To Ambrose Wolles for 1 barrel of pitch, 5s. 4d., and for 1 piece of tarpaulin [*bollyng tylt*] for the cement boat, 7s., 12s. 4d.

To the said Thomas Alen for heating 5 pots for the cement boat, 20d.

[Total] of this page £(16) <15> (10) <6>s. 10d.

Sum total £22 6s. 9d.

533. [f. 427v] 29 June

Renter £8   Fishmongers   Butchers   Passage tolls

Three chaplains 7s. 6d. Five clerks 10s. Roger Robyns 12d.

Masons. Bennet (4s.) <3s. 4d.> Tomson (4s.) <3s. 4d.> Arnold 4s. Fyld (4s.) <3s. 4d.> Heron (4s.) <3s. 4d.> Jeffrey Orgar 2s. 6d. on the foundation.

Carpenters. Gold pt 4s. Cockes 4s. Cockes the elder (3s.) <2s. 8d.> Browne senior (3s.) <2s. 8d.> Leonard Holmes (3s.) <2s. 8d.> Henry Godfrey (3s.) <2s. 8d.> Browne junior 2s. 8d. Inglydwe (3s.) <2s. 8d.> Palmer (3s.) <2s. 8d.> Pasmer (3s.) <2s. 8d.> Provest (3s.) <2s. 8d.>. William Wynter 2s. [lost]. John Pasmer 2s. [lost]. Simon Cockes (2s. 1d.) <20d.> Thomas Browne 2s. 8d. in the waterworks.

Sawyers. Flynt slitting 5 hundred, 5s. 5d. Horton in slitting 4 hundred, 4s. 4d. 10s. 10d.

Porter. Hughwet 2s.

[Shoutman] Thomas Alen 3s. 4d.

Bricklayers. Swenson (3s.) <2s. 8d.> Chorleton (3s.) <2s. 8d.> Labourers. Nevell (2s. 1d.) <20d.> Hoget (2s. 1d.) <20d.> Grene (2s. 1d.) <20d.>

Daubers. Thomas Monkest (3s.) <2s. 8d.> Labourer. John Tursett (2s. 1d.) {20d.} <15d.>

Labourers. John S. (2s. 1d.) <20d.> Thomas Alen [blank]. Roger Whythed 20d. Tanner 20d. Sherman 20d. John Cloworth 20d.

[Total] of this page 116s. 9d.

[f. 428] To Jeffrey Haryson for (42) <40> loads of sand delivered to the Bridge House, 14 loads to Cheap, 10 loads to the bridge, 8 loads to Paternoster Row, and 7 loads to Rood Lane, at 6d. the load, 39s. 6d.

To him for 32 loads of loam at 4d. the load, 10s. 8d., for 85 loads of gravel at 4d. the load, 28s. 4d., 39s.

To him for carriage of 6 loads of rag and one of tiles from the Bridge House at 4d. the load, 2s. 4d., for carriage of 19 loads of rubbish from Cheap with his great cart at 2½d. the load, 3s. 11½d., and for 6 loads of rubbish from Old Change and Newgate market at 2d., in all 7s. 3½d.

To the churchwardens of St Olave's for the salary of a priest for this quarter ended at (Michaelmas) <Midsummer>, 26s. 8d.

To Robert Butteler for carriage of 5 loads of timber from Croydon this week at (3s.) 2s. 4d. the load, 11s. 8d.

To the said Thomas Alen for (carriage of) heating 4 pots for the cement boat, 16d.

To Richard Ruddyng, paviour, for paving 3 toises of new pavement at the corner of East Cheap at 7d., 21d.

To the said Richard for 4 days work in mending of *Joks* [?] upon the bridge at 8d. the day, 2s. 8d., and for his labourer for 4 days at 5d. the day, 20d., 4s. 4d.

To Thomas Alen for 5 men helping to get the boats through the bridge for 2 tides at 1d. the man, 10d., to 4 men for helping for 5 tides at 1d. the man, and to 6 men for one time, 6d., in all 3s.

To 6 men for unloading 6 boats of chalk at 1d. the man per boat, 3s., to 5 men for loading and unloading 4 boats of chalk at the bridge, 20d., 4s. 8d.

To Thomas Wright for 9 tides, John a Fen for 4 tides, John Gaston for 2 tides, and Thomas Alen for 2 tides, labourers labouring in placing chalk on the starling, between them for (15) {19} 17 tides at 3d. the tide, 4s. 3d.

To the said John Gaston for placing chalk, 2d.

To John Monke for 1¼ hundred of rope for the boats, 15s.

To the parson of Woolchurch for the tithe of the Stocks for this quarter, 13s. 4d.

In expenses this week to Deptford and Lewisham, to view the tenements and other ground, 3s. 4d.

[Total] of this page £8 15s. 3d.

Sum total of the week, £14 12s.

534. [f. 428v] 6 July

Renter £8   Fishmongers   Butchers   Passage-tolls 20s.

Received of Stacy the bellwright for 69 score of oak timber for All Hallows the Great, 17s. 3d.

Three chaplains 7s. 6d. Five clerks 10s. Roger Robyns 12d.

Masons. Bennet 4s. Tomson 4s. Arnold 4s. Fyld 4s. Heron 4s. Jeffrey Orgar 3s. 6d. in raising a breast aforesaid.

Carpenters. Gold Pt 4s. Cockes pt 4s. Cockes the elder 4s. Browne senior 4s. Henry Godfrey 4s. Leonard Holmes 4s. Palmer 4s. Pasmer 4s. Thomas Browne 4s. Browne junior 4s. John Pasmer (4s.) <3s. 6d.>. William Wynter 3s. Simon Cockes 2s. 6d. John Provest 4s. Inglydwe 4s.

Sawyers. Flynt slitting 7 hundred, 7s. 7d. Horton slitting 6 hundred, 6s. 6d. Plankboard 2 hundred, 2s. 16s. 1d.

Porter. Hughwet 2s.

Shout[man]. Thomas Alen 3s. 4d.

Bricklayers. Swenson 4s. Chorleton 4s. Labourers. Nevell 2s. 6d. Hogett 2s. 6d. Grene 2s. 6d. Sherman 2s. 6d.

Daubers. Thomas Monkest 4s. Labourer. John Tursyt 2s. 6d.

Labourers. John S. 2s. 6d. Thomas Alen [blank]. Whythed 2s. 6d. Tanner 2s. 6d. John Clouworth 2s. 6d. Shepherd 10d.

[Total] of this page £7 15s. 8d.

[f. 429] To Robert for the gibbet gin by 7 [tides] in driving piles at the starling next to St Magnus [church] at 5s. 8d. the tide, 39s. 8d.

To Cockes senior for 5 tides, Simon for 5 tides, Cockes junior for 5 tides, John Pasmer for 5 tides, Inglydwe for 5 tides, Provest for 4 tides, Wynter for 4 tides, Browne senior for 4 tides, Browne junior for 3 tides, Leonard Holmes for 3 tides, Robert Pasmer for 4 tides, Palmer for 3 tides, Thomas Browne for 4 tides, Henry Godfrey for 4 tides, Robert Gold for 5 tides, carpenters working in the works out of due time as the tides have fallen these 3 weeks, between them for 63 tides at 4d. the tide, 21s.

To Sclater of Mile End for 4 new tide-axes at 12d. each, 4s.

To him for 4 new adzes for the tides, 4s.

To him for steeling 6 old adzes, 3s.

To William Drappar of Bromley, deputy steward of Greenwich, Deptford, Lewisham, Lee and Stratford for his retainer to make answer every year in the said court for 12d. at this time, 5d.

To a chantry priest of Paul's for a quit-rent due at Midsummer, 2s. 6d.

To the said 6 masons, each for 2 tides working out of due [time], 4s.

To Whytehed, Playworth [sic], Tanner, and Sherman, each for 2 tides labouring with the masons, 2s.

To John A Fenne for 6 tides, Thomas Alen for 5 tides, Thomas Wright for 3 tides, labourers labouring with the said masons, between them for 14 tides at 3d. the tide in all, 3s. 6d.

To the shoutman for 20 men heaving boats through the bridge at 4 tides, at 1d. the man, 20d.

To 4 labourers for unloading 10 boats of chalk at 1d. the man, 3s. 4d.

To 2 other labourers for labouring placing chalk at the starling, 12d.

(To John Affen for 6 tides, Thomas Alen for 5 tides, Thomas Wright for 3 tides, between them for 14 tides at 3d., 3s. 6d.)

To Robert Buttler, carter, for carriage of 4 loads of timber from Croydon at 2s. 4d., in all 9s. 4d.

To William Carter [? the carter] for carriage of a millstone to Bootes Mill in (Kent) Stratford, 2s.

To the shoutman for heating 6 pots, 2s.

To the gardener for cutting in the garden, 8d.

Sum total of the week £13 4s. 4d.

535. [f. 429v] 13 July

Renter £8   Fishmongers   Butchers   Passage-tolls

Received from St Thomas' chapel on the bridge on St Thomas's [day] in oblations, 5s. 2d.

Received of Nicholas Barker, armourer, for divers sorts of oak shells, 4s.

Three chaplains 7s. 6d. Five clerks 10s. Roger Robyns 12d.

Masons. Bennet 4s. Tomson 4s. Arnold 4s. Fyld 4s. Heron 4s. Jeffrey Orgar 3s. 6d. upon the arch aforesaid.

Carpenters. Gold pt 4s. Cockes pt 4s. Browne senior 4s. Henry Godfrey 4s. Leonard Holmes 4s. Browne junior 4s. Palmer 4s. Pasmer 4s. Inglydwe 4s. Thomas Browne 4s. Provest 4s. Cockes the elder 4s. William Wynter 4s. John Pasmer 3s. Simon Cockes 2s. 6d. in the waterworks.

Sawyers. Flynt in slitting 7 hundred, 7s. 7d. Henry Horton slit 8 hundred, 8s. 8d.

Porter. Hughwet 2s.

Shout[man]. Thomas A. 3s. 4d.

Bricklayers. Swenson [sum erased] Chorleton 4s. Labourers. Nevell 2s. 6d. Hogdett 2s. 6d. Thomas Grene 10d. [over erasure]. Sherman 10d. [over erasure]. Total 6s. 8d.

Daubers. Thomas Monkest (4s.) <3s. 4d.> Labourer. John Turfyld 2s. 1d.

Labourers. John Smyth 2s. 6d. Thomas Alen [blank]. Whythed 2s. 6d. Tanner 2s. 6d. Sherman 2s. 6d. John Cloworth 2s. 6d.

[Total] of this page £7 10s.

[f. 430] To Robert Gold for the gibbet gin for 7 tides driving piles in the starlings aforesaid at 5s. 8d. the tide, except that there lacked 1 man for 1 tide, 29s. 5d.

To Nicholas Barker, armourer, for divers and sundry sorts of nails by bill, £14 14s. 11d.

To Laurence Awen, clerk of the Bridge House, for his quarter's fee ended at Midsummer last past, 50s.

To Sir John Gaynesford, knight, in full payment for 200 loads of oak timber and for carriage of the same, that is to say 100 [sic] loads and for carriage as is aforesaid, £12 14s. 2d.

To the said Thomas Crull and Robert Draper, wardens of the said bridge for their quarter's fee, £13 6s. 8d.

To Stephen Parate for 20 boat[loads] of chalk, every boat containing 12 tons at 6d. the ton, £6.

To the said 6 masons each for 2 tides at 4d. the man per tide, 4s.

To Roger Whythed, John Sherman, John Cloworth, and Tanner, each of them for 2 tides with the masons, 2s.

To Thomas Alen, shoutman, for heating 4 cement pots for the masons, 16d.

To Cockes senior, Cockes junior, Henry Godfrey, Browne junior, Leonard Holmes, Thomas Browne, Palmer, Pasmer, Inglydewe, William Wynter, John Pasmer, and Simon Cockes, each of them for 2 tides, and John Provest for 1 tide, carpenters working in the waterworks out of due time as the tides have fallen this week, between them for 25 tides at 4d. the tide, 8s. 4d.

To 13 labourers for taking (28) <18> loads and 31 ft. of oak timber at 55 ft. the load, at 3d. the man, 3s. 3d.

To Thomas Alen, shoutman, by bill 6s. 1d.

to John Affen, labourer, for labouring with the said masons for 8 tides at 3d. the tide, 2s.

To 2 men for placing of chalk in the starlings at the bridge for 3 tides, 18d.

To Robert Graye, waxchandler, for making of 53 lb. of wax new and old into sundry tapers great and small, and other lights for the chapel on the bridge at 1/2d. the lb., 21 1/2d.

To him for a Paschal of his own wax, weighing 22 lb., 3s. 3 1/2d.

Expenses of the masters this week, 14d.

To Thomas Alen and 3 labourers with him for bringing of a fare of planks from Dartford, sawn at Petham Court by water by drove, 6s. 6d.

To John Alen, mercer, for 1 barrel of pitch for the storehouse, 4s.

To John Heere, waterman, for a great oar [*hoore*] for the cement boat, 14d.

To Thomas Smyth, turner, for 6 mortar trays at 4d. the tray, 2s.

[Total] of this page £52 3s. 7d.

Sum total of the week £59 13s. 7d.

536. [f. 430v] 20 July

Renter £8   Fishmongers   Butchers   Passage-tolls

Received of Mr Symson for the rent of a little granary in Golders [yard] for the year ending at Midsummer, 10s.

Received of Edward Dygbye, plumber, for 409 lb. of lead skimmings [*bettys of skommyng of leade*], 10s. 8d.

Three chaplains 7s. 6d. Five clerks 10s. Roger Robyns 12d.

Masons. Bennet 4s. Tomson 4s. Arnold 4s. Fyld 4s. Heynes 4s. Jeffrey Orgar (4s.) 3s. 6d. upon the arch aforesaid.

Carpenters. Gold pt 4s. Cockes the elder 4s. Browne senior 4s. Henry Godfrey 4s. Browne junior 4s. Inglydwe 4s. Palmer 4s. Pasmer 4s. Leonard Holmes 4s. Simon Cockes 2s. 6d. William Wynter 4s. Cockes 4s. Provest 4s. John Pasmer 4s. Thomas Browne 4s.

Sawyers. Flynt slitting 7 hundred, 7s. 7d. Horton 8 hundred, 8s. 8d.

Porter. Hughwet 2s.

Shoutman. Thomas Alen 3s. 4d.

Bricklayers. (Swenson 4s.) Chorleton 4s. Labourers. Nevell 2s. 6d. James Jacson 2s. 6d. Thomas Grene 15d. at the Crown in Southwark. Labourers. John Smyth 2s. 6d. Thomas Alen 20d. Roger Whythed 2s. 6d. Tanner 2s. 6d. Sherman 2s. 6d. John Cloworth 2s. 6d.

[Total] of this page £7 4s. 6d.

[f. 431] To Robert Gold for the gibbet gin for 6 tides driving piles in the starling aforesaid, except there lacked 1 man for 1 tide, 33s. 9d.

To Belton of Maidstone in Kent for water carriage of 17 tons of hard stone of Kent from [blank] at 12d. the ton, in all 17s.

To Richard Hawlsey of Houndsditch for new casting of 3 old brasses weighing 66 lb. at 1d. the lb., in all 5s. 6d.

To Robert Gold for his costs and charges in going to Croydon with the charges of Cockes with him, 16d.

To William Hughwett for 46 lb. of tallow for the store of the House, at 1d. the lb., 3s. 10d., and for 40 lb. of grease [*greyse*] at 1d. the lb., 3s. 4d., 7s. 2d.

To him for boughs and flowers for strewing the gates at Midsummer, 10d.

To William Sharpeharow, blacksmith, for divers sorts of nails and other by bill, £9 17s.

To John Hughweth, organmaker, for mending a pair of bellows, 5s.

To Thomas Alen for heating 2 cement pots for the masons, 8d.

To the shoutman by bill, 5s. 7d.

To Thomas Alen for 2 tides and Sherman for 2 tides, labourers labouring with the said masons, each of them for 2 tides, 12d.

To Robert Gold for 17 labourers taking timber that came from Colchester, 20 loads 24 ft. at 4d. the man, 5s. 8d.

To 10 labourers for taking up planks that came from Deptford, at 3d. the man, 2s. 6d.

[Total] of this page £14 3s.

Sum total of the week £21 7s. 6d.

537. [f. 431v] 27 July

Renter £8 Fishmongers Butchers Passage-tolls

Received of Mr Temple, the king's fletcher, for certain old timber and shells of oak, 12s.

Received of Mistress Hylles towards the new making of a stall in her house, 9s.

Three chaplains 7s. 6d. Five clerks 10s. Roger Robyns 12d.

Masons. Bennet 3s. 4d. Tomson 3s. 4d. Arnold 4s. (Fyld 3s. 4d.) Heynes 3s. 4d. Jeffrey Orgar 2s. 9d. upon the arch aforesaid.

Carpenters. Gold pt 4s. Cockes pt 4s. Cockes the elder 2s. 8d. Browne senior 2s. 8d. Henry Godfrey 2s. 8d. Browne junior 2s. 8d. Leonard Holmes 2s. 8d. Inglydwe 2s. 8d. Pasmer (2s. 8d.) Palmer 2s. 8d. Thomas Browne 16d. John Provest 2s. 8d. John Pasmer 2s. Simon Cockes 20d. in the waterworks and upon the frame for Simon Lawes' house.

Sawyers. Flynt slitting 5 hundred, 5s. 5d. Horton 2½ hundred, 2s. 8d.

Porter. Hughwet 2s.

Shoutman. Shoutman 3s. 4d. [sic]

Bricklayers. Swenson 2s. 8d. Chorleton [blank]. Labourers. Nevell 20d. Hogett 20d. Thomas Grene 5d.

Daubers. Monkest [blank]. Labourer. John Tursett [blank]

Labourers. John Smyth 20d. Thomas Alen 10d. Whythed 20d. Tanner 20d. Sherman 20d. (Nevell) John Cloworth 20d.

[Total] of this page £4 18s. (4d.) 9d.

[f. 432] To Robert Gold for the gibbet gin for (4) 3 tides driving piles in the starling aforesaid, lacking one man 2 [tides] 16s. 6d.

To John Clerke, pewterer, for 2 fother of lead at £4 6s. 8d. the fother, in all £8 13s. 4d.

To Richard Olyver in part payment for carriage of elm timber from Petham Court at 16d. the load, 20s.

To Robert Nelson, glazier, in full payment of 2 bills, £6 5s. 4½d.

To Thomas Alen for water carriage of a drove of elm timber from Dartford, 12s. 8d.

To John Modell of Reigate for 1 load of Reigate stone for *beketts for loads mouthes* [?] 2s., for 1 load of border with 4s. for scappling 6s., and for carriage of the same 7s., in all 15s.

To 13 labourers for taking up a fare of timber that came by drove from Dartford at 5d. the man, 5s. 5d.

To John Bygges for holing a millstone for the mill at Stratford called Tomson's mill, 3s. 4d.

[Total] of this page £18 11s. 7½d.

Sum total of the week £23 10s. 4½d.

538. [f. 432v] 3 August
Renter £8   Fishmongers   Butchers   Passage-tolls
Three chaplains 7s. 6d. Five clerks 10s. Roger Robyns 12d.
Masons. Bennet 4s. Tomson 4s. Arnold 4s. Fyld [blank]. Heron (4)
Jeffrey Orgar 3s. 6d. upon the arch aforesaid.
Carpenters. Gold pt 4s. Cockes the elder 4s. Browne senior 4s. Henry
Godfrey 4s. Browne junior 4s. Leonard Holmes 4s. John Provest 4s.
John Palmer 4s. William Wynter 4s. Simon Cockes 2s. 6d. in the
waterworks.
Cockes pt 4s. Inglydwe 4s. Pasmer 4s. John Pasmer 4s. Thomas Browne
4s. in repairs at Mr Lewes' house.
Sawyers. Flynt slit 7 hundred, 7s. 7d.
Porter. Hughwet 2s.
Shoutman. Alen 3s. 4d.
Bricklayers. Swenson 4s. Labourers. Nevell (3s.) 2s. 6d. James Jacson
2s. 6d. Thomas Alen 2s. 6d. at the Crown in Southwark.
Daubers. Thomas Monkest 2s. 8d. La[bourers]. John Turfyld 20d.
Labourers. Smyth 2s. 6d. Whythed 2s. 6d. Tanner 2s. 6d. Sherman 2s.
6d. Clowerth 2s. 6d.
[Total] of this page £6 11s. 9d.
[f. 433] To Robert Gold for the gibbet gin for 6 tides, driving piles at
the starling aforesaid, except there lacked 1 man for 3 tides, 34s. 3d.
To John Carter of Colchester, carpenter, in part payment of a greater
sum for oak timber bought of him by Laurence at 7s. the load, 55 [ft.]
to every load, £10.
To Thomas Alen, shoutman, by bill, 20d.
To him for 21 men for 5 tides for heaving out of boats at 1d. the man,
21d.
To him for 10 men for loading and unloading 5 boats of chalk and
placing the same, at 4s. 2d., for 6 men for unloading 3 boats of chalk,
18d., and for 3 men for 4 tides in placing chalk at the bridge, at 3d.
the man per tide, 3s., in all 8s. 8d.
To 10 labourers for taking up 20 loads of oak timber that came from
Colchester at 50 ft. to every load, at 4d. the man, in all 3s. 4d.
To Thomas Mason by the hands of his wife, for carriage of 3 loads of
rubbish from Mr Medley's in Wood Street at 2½d. the load, 7½d.
[Total] of this page £12 9s. 2½d.
Sum total of the week £19 11½d.

539. [f. 433v] 10 August
Renter £8   Fishmongers   Butchers   Passage-tolls
Three chaplains 7s. 6d. Five clerks 10s. Roger Robyns 12d.
Masons. Bennet 4s. Tomson 4s. Arnold 4s. Fyld 4s. Heron 4s. Jeffrey
Orgar 3s. 6d.
Carpenters. Robert Gold 4s. Browne senior 4s. Cockes the elder 4s.
Henry Godfrey 4s. Browne junior 4s. Palmer 4s. Leonard Holmes 4s.
Thomas Browne 4s. John Provest 4s. William Wynter 3s. Simon Cockes
2s. 6d. in the waterworks and in repairs in divers places.
Cockes pt 4s. Inglydwe 4s. Pasmer 4s. John Pasmer 4s.

Sawyers. Flynt slitting 7½ hundred, 8s. 1d.

Porter. Hughwet 2s.

Shoutman. Thomas Alen 3s. 4d.

[Bricklayers]. Swenson 4s. Labourers. Nevell 2s. 6d. James Jacson 2s. 6d. Thomas Grene 2s. 6d.

Daubers. Thomas Monkest 4s. Labourers. John Turfett 2s. 6d. at the Angel, Bishops[gate]

Labourers. Smyth (4s.) 2s. 6d. Roger Whythed 2s. 6d. Tanner 2s. 6d. Sherman 2s. 6d. Cloworth 2s. 6d.

[Total] of this page £7 2s. 5d.

[f. 434] To Robert Gold for the gibbet gin for 6 tides, driving piles in the starling aforesaid, except there lacked 1 man for 1 tide, 33s. 9d.

To [blank] Brygges, wharfinger to Mr Forman, for holing a millstone for Tomson's mill, 3s. 4d.

To Richard Amberous in part payment of a greater sum for a bargain of oak timber bought at Water Okyng, 20s.

To 4 labourers for taking up 7 loads and 17 ft. of oak timber that came from Mr Ambrose, 8d.

[Total] of this page 57s. 9d.

Sum total of the week, £10 2d.

540. [f. 434v] 17 August

Renter £8 Fishmongers Butchers Passage-tolls

Received of Thomas Bayly, grocer, for 8 ft. of elm, 20d.

Received for an old piece of Reigate stone, 6d.

Three chaplains 7s. 6d. Five clerks 10s. Roger Robyns 12d.

Masons. Bennet 4s. Thomson 4s. Arnold 4s. Fyld 4s. Heynes 4s. Jeffrey Orgar 3s. 6d. in apparelling stone for the arch aforesaid.

Carpenters. Robert Gold 4s. Cockes pt the elder 4s. Browne senior (4s.) 3s. 4d. Henry Godfrey 3s. 4d. Browne junior 3s. 4d. Leonard Holmes 3s. 4d. Simon Cockes 2s. 6d. in the waterworks.

Cockes pt 4s. Inglydwe 3s. 4d. Robert Pasmer 3s. 4d. John Pasmer 2s. 6d. in repairs.

Thomas Browne 3s. 4d. Palmer 3s. 4d. at the Angel in Bishopsgate.

John Provest 3s. 4d. William Wynter 2s. 6d. at the Lock bridge on a pale in Clerks' close.

Sawyers. Flynt slitting 3 hundred, 3s. 3d. Horton slitting 4 hundred, 4s. 4d. 7s. 7d.

Porter. Hughwet 2s.

[Shoutman] Thomas Alen 3s. 4d.

Bricklayers. Swenson 3s. 4d. Chorleton [blank] Labourers. Nevell 2s. 1d. Hogett 2s. 1d. Thomas Grene 2s. 1d.

Daubers. Thomas Monkest 3s. 4d. Labourer. John Tursett 2s. 1d.

Labourers. John S. 2s. 1d. Whythed 2s. 1d. Tanner 2s. 1d. Sherman 2s. 1d. Cloworth 2s. 1d.

[Total] of this page £5 8s. 9d.

[f. 435] To Robert Gold for the gibbet gin for 5 tides, driving piles in the starling aforesaid, lacking 1 tide, 28s. 1d.

Paid to Andrew Morrez for wharfage of 2 millstones, 2s., for cranage and portage of the same, 2s. 8d., 4s. 8d.

Paid to Thomas Whyte of Stratford, master wheelwright, for mending the wheels that carried the same stones, 20d.

Paid to Richard Ambrose, carpenter, in full payment for 7 loads and 17 ft. of oak timber that came from Water Okyng at 6s. 8d. the load, 28s. 1d.

Paid to Thomas Devell for cleansing a piece of a sewer on the backside of the Crown in Southwark, 20d.

Paid to the churchwardens of St Nicholas Shambles for a quarter ended at Midsummer, 25s.

[Total] of this page £4 9s. 2d.

Sum total of the week, £10 17s. 11d.

541. [f. 435v] 24 August

Renter £8   Fishmongers   Butchers   Passage-tolls

Received of a stranger for making fast his ship and breaking his way against the wharf, 8d.

Three chaplains 7s. 6d. Five clerks 10s. Roger Robyns 12d.

Masons. Bennet [blank]. Thomson 4s. Arnold 4s. Fyld 4s. Heynes 4s. Jeffrey Orgar 3s. 6d. upon the arch aforesaid.

Carpenters. Gold pt 4s. Cockes the elder 3s. 4d. Browne senior 3s. 4d. Henry Godfrey 3s. 4d. Leonard Holmes 3s. 4d. Browne junior 3s. 4d. Simon Cockes 2s. 1d. in the waterworks.

Cockes pt 4s. Inglydwe 3s. 4d. Pasmer 3s. 4d. John Pasmer 2s. 6d. at Mr Lawes aforesaid.

Thomas Browne 3s. 4d. Robert Palmer 3s. 4d. at the Angel aforesaid. John Provest 3s. 4d. William Wynter 2s. 6d. in repairs on the bridge at [sic]

Sawyers. Flynt slitting 7 hundred, 7s. 7d. Horton slitting 7 hundred, 7s. 7d. 15s. 2d.

Porter. Hughwet 2s.

[Shoutman] Thomas Alen 3s. 4d.

Bricklayers. Swenson 3s. 4d. Labourers. Nevell 2s. 1d. Jacson 2s. 1d. Thomas Grene 2s. 1d.

Daubers. Thomas Monk' 3s. 4d. Labourer. John Turfett 2s. 1d.

Labourers. John Smyth 2s. 1d. Roger Whythed 2s. 1d. Tanner 2s. 1d. Sherman 2s. 1d. Cloworth 20d.

[Total] of this page £6 11s. 11d.

[f. 436] To Robert Gold for the gibbet gin for [blank] tides, driving piles in the starling aforesaid, except [blank]

To Thomas Alen, shoutman, by bill, 4s. 7d.

To the said Thomas Alen for loading 3 boats of chalk in the Bridge House and unloading the same at the bridge, 2s. 6d.

To him for loading 4 boats of chalk stone at the Bridge House, 2s., for 3 men for 4 tides in placing chalk, 2s., in all 4s., 6s. 6d.

To Mistress Foster for carriage of 9 loads of timber and other into divers places in London at 4d. the load, 3s., and for 13 loads of like stuff to the bridge at 2d. the load, 2s. 2d., and for carriage of 14 loads of rubbish from her own house, 2s. 4d., in all 7s. 6d.

To John Browne for 6 men for 4 tides, making scaffolds for the gin to stand in at 3d. the tide, 6s.

To William Hughwett for taking up 2 oars, 2d.

To William Cockes senior for 2 tides, Browne senior for 2 tides, Henry Godfrey for 2 tides, Wynter for 2 tides, Simon Cockes for 2 tides, Leonard Holmes for 1 tide, Browne long [sic] for 1 tide, and Palmer for 1 tide, between them for 13 tides at 4d. the tide, in all 4s. 4d.

To John Cloworth for (1) 2 tides, William Tanner for 1 tide, and Roger Whytehed for 1 tide, between them for 4 tides at 3d. the tide, 12d.

To Robert Bentley of Maidstone in Kent for water carriage of 62 ft. of ogee [*ooge*] stone containing 7 tons, 7s.

[Total] of this page 37s. 1d.

Sum £8 9s.

542. [f. 436v] 31 August

Renter Fishmongers Butchers Passage-tolls

Received of the churchwardens of All Hallows the Great for 49 ft. of oak timber, 10s.

Three chaplains 7s. 6d. Five clerks 10s. Roger Robyns 12d.

Masons. Bennet [blank]. Tomson 4s. Arnold 4s. Fyld 4s. Heynes 4s. Jeffrey Orgar 3s. 6d.

[Carpenters] Gold pt 4s. Cockes the elder 4s. Henry Godfrey 4s. Browne senior 4s. Leonard Holmes 4s. Browne junior 4s. Simon Cockes 2s. 6d. Palmer 4s. Cockes 4s. Inglydwe [4s. blotted]. Pasmer [4s. blotted]. John Pasmer 3s. Thomas Browne 4s. (John Provest 4s.) William Wynter 3s.

[Sawyers] Flynt slitting 3 hundred, 3s. 3d. Horton slitting 8½ hundred, 9s. 2d. 15s. 2d.

[Porter] Hughwet 2s.

[Shoutman] Thomas Alen 3s. 4d.

[Bricklayers] Swenson 4s. Chorleton [blank] [Labourers] Nevell 2s. 6d. Hogett 2s. 6d. Grene 2s. 6d.

Daubers. Monkest [blank]. Labourer. John Turfett [blank].

Labourers. John S. 2s. 6d. Whythed 2s. 6d. Tanner 2s. 6d. Sherman 2s. 6d. John Cloworth 2s. 6d.

[Total] of this page £5 15s.

[f. 437] To Robert Gold for the gibbet gin, driving piles in the starling aforesaid, except there lacked 2 men for 1 tide, in all 5 tides, 27s. 10d.

To William Nevell by the hands of [blank] for carriage of 9 loads of rubbish from the Angel in Bishopsgate Street, 18d.

[Total] of this page 29s. 4d.

Sum total of the week, £8 4s. 4d.

543. [f. 437v] 7 September

Renter £8 Fishmongers Butchers Passage-tolls 20s.

Received of the churchwardens of All Hallows the Great for the *relyns* [sic; ?relief] of a gin to hang their bells, 2s.

Three chaplains 7s. 6d. Five clerks 10s. Roger 12d.

Masons. Bennet [blank]. Tomson 4s. Arnold 4s. Fyld 4s. Heron 4s. Jeffrey Orgar (4) 3s. 6d. in apparelling hardstone.

Carpenters. Gold pt 4s. Cockes the elder 4s. Browne senior 4s. Leonard Holmes 4s. Henry Godfrey 4s. Browne junior 4s. Simon Cockes (4) 2s. 6d. in the waterworks.

Cockes 4s. Inglydwe (4) 3s. 4d. Pasmer (4) 2s. 8d. John Pasmer 3s. Thomas Browne 4s. John Palmer 4s. John Provest 4s. William Wynter 3s. on the house aforesaid.

Sawyers. Flynt slitting 5 hundred, 5s. 5d. Boards 11d. Horton 2½ hundred, 2s. 8d. (13s. 11d.) 9s. 1d.

Porter. Hughwet 2s.

Shoutman. Thomas Alen 3s. 4d.

Bricklayers. Swenson 4s. Chorleton [blank] [Labourers] Nevell 2s. 6d. Jacson 2s. 6d. Thomas Grene 2s. 6d.

Daubers. Thomas Monkest [blank]. Labourer. John Tursytt [blank].

Labourers. John Smyt 2s. 6d. Roger Whytehed 2s. 6d. Sherman 2s. 6d. Tanner 2s. 6d. Cloworth 2s. 6d.

[Total] of this page £6 10s. 11d.

[f. 438] To Mr Ambrose in full payment for 7 loads and 30 ft. of oak timber delivered at the Bridge House at 6s. 8d. the load, 50s. 7d.

To the shoutman by bill, 2s. 11d.

To the shoutman for 4 labourers for loading 3 boats of chalk, 12d., for unloading of the same at the bridge, 9d., in all 21d.

To Robert Gold for the gibbet gin for 6 tides, driving piles in the starling aforesaid, 34s.

To William Cockes, John Browne, Henry Godfrey, Palmer, and Simon Cockes, each of them for 1 tide at 4d., 20d.

To Roger Whythed for 1 tide, William Tanner for 1 tide, John Southgate for 1 tide, at 3d., 9d.

To 8 men for taking up 19 loads and 30 ft. of oak timber at 4d. the man, 2s. 8d., and for taking up 7 loads and 30 ft., 16d., in all 4s.

To 2 labourers at the five-man beetle for 2 tides 12d., to 1 man for 1 tide 3d., 15d.

To 8 labourers for heaving [*halfing*] planks into the storehouse at 2 sundry times, 4s.

[Total] of this page 100s. 11d.

Sum total of the week £11 11s. 10d.

544. [f. 438v] 14 September

Renter £8   Fishmongers   Butchers   Passage-tolls

Received of Mr Maire, clerk of the king's ships, for 18 loads of oak timber taken from Croydon, £4 10s.

Received of Doctor Smyth for 4 loads and 21 ft. of oak timber, 37s. 6d.

Three chaplains 7s. 6d. Five clerks 10s. Roger 12d.

Masons. Bennet [blank]. Tomson 3s. 6d. Arnold 3s. 6d. Fyld 3s. 6d. Heynes 3s. 6d. Jeffrey Orgar 3s. 6d.

[Carpenters]. Gold pt 3s. 6d. Cockes the elder 3s. 6d. Browne senior 3s. 6d. Leonard Holmes 3s. 6d. Henry Godfrey 3s. 6d. Palmer 3s. 6d.

Thomas Browne 3s. 6d. John Browne 3s. 6d. Simon Cockes 2s. 6d. Cockes pt 3s. 6d. Inglydwe 3s. 6d. Pasmer 3s. 6d. John Pasmer 3s. John Provest 3s. 6d. Wynter 3s. 6d.

[Sawyers]. Flynt slitting 7 hundred, 7s. 7d.

[Porter]. Hughwet 2s.

[Shoutman] Thomas Alen 3s. 4d.

[Bricklayers]. Swenson 3s. 6d. Chorleton [blank] [Labourers] Nevell 2s. 6d. Jacson 2s. 6d. Thomas Grene 2s. 6d.

[Daubers]. Monkest [blank]. Labourers. John Tursytt [blank].

[Labourers] John S. 2s. 6d. Roger Whythed 2s. 6d. Tanner 2s. 6d. Sherman 2s. 6d. Cloworth 2s. 6d.

[Total] of this page £6 2s. 11d.

[f. 439] To Richard Ambrose in full payment for 7 loads and 37 ft. of oak timber, 51s. 8d.

Paid for the obit of John Clifford kept at St Olave's, 13s. 4d.

To Robert Gold for the gibbet gin for 4 tides, driving piles in the starlings aforesaid, lacking 1 man, 22s. 5d.

To 16 men for taking up elm timber, planks, and boards, 7s. 6d.

Item for 1 man at the five-man beetle for 1 tide, 3d.

For the steeling of 3 augers 18d., for steeling of an adze 6d., and for 1 new adze 12d., 3s.

To Thomas Alen for 4 men for fetching elm timber from Dartford by drove, 9s., and to 2 men for loading the same timber for 2 days, 2s., 11s.

To children for singing in the chapel on St Thomas's day, 20d.

To 2 labourers for labouring in bringing a boat to Deptford for one whole night, 8d.

To Richard Rooding for paving 10 toises in Friday Street at (10) 8d. the toise, 5s. 10d.

To 7 labourers for taking up 7 loads of oak timber, 14d.

(To William Cockes the elder for 16 men for taking up timber, 7s. 6d., for one for 1 tide at the five-man beetle, 3d., for steeling 3 augers 18d., and for steeling of [an] adze 6d., and for 1 new adze 12d., in all 10s. 9d.)

545. [f. 439v] 21 September

Renter £8. Fishmongers butchers passage-tolls.

Received of the beadle of the bridge for certain stands in the wide rooms at a fair, 14d.

Received of Roland Edwards, clothworker, for his quarter's rent of the tenement that he now dwells in in Cheapside from the Annunciation of Our Lady to Midsummer, because it was not finished, £4.

[Three chaplains] 7s. 6d. [Five clerks] 10s. [Roger] 12d.

[margin, in Latin: <Here begins the new order of the mayor and aldermen>]

[Masons] Bennet [blank]. Tomson (3s. 6d.) 21d. Arnold 3s. 6d. Fyld 3s. 6d. Heynes 3s. 6d. Jeffrey Orgar 3s. 6d.

[Carpenters] Gold pt 3s. 6d. Cockes the elder (3s. 6d.) 2s. 11d. Browne senior (3s.) 2s. 11d. Leonard Holmes 2s. 11d. Browne junior 2s. 11d.

239

Henry Godfrey 2s. 11d. Palmer 2s. 11d. Cockes pt 2s. 11d. Inglydwe 2s. 11d. Pasmer 2s. 11d. John Pasmer 2s. (1d.) 11d. Thomas Browne 2s. 11d. John Provest 2s. 11d. Wynter 2s. 6d.

[Sawyers] Flynt slitting 5½ hundred, 5s. 11d. Board a hundred 12d. Horton 5½ hundred (6s.) 5s. 11d. (13s.) 12s. 10d.

[Porter] Hughwet 2s.

[Shoutman] Thomas Alen 3s. 4d.

[Bricklayers] Swenson (3) 2s. 11d. Chorleton [blank] [Labourers] Thomas Grene 2s. 1d. Nevell 2s. 1d. Jacson 2s. 1d.

[Daubers] Thomas Mon' 2s. 11d. Labourers. John Turfyd 2s. 1d.

[Labourers] John Smyth 2s. 1d. Roger Whythed 2s. 1d. Tanner 2s. 1d. Sherman 2s. 1d. Cloworth 2s. 1d.

[Total] of this page £6 3d.

[f. 440] To Robert Gold for driving piles in the starling aforesaid for 3 tides, 17s.

To Mistress Foster for carriage of 9 loads of (rubbish) <tile stone> [*tygul stone*] from the bridge into divers places of the city, 3s., and for 6 loads carried from the bridge and to the bridge at 2d. the load, 12d., in all 4s.

To Tomson, Bennett, Arnold, and Fyld, masons, for steeling their tools for 3 quarters of a year at 12d. the man, in all 3s.

To Thomas Alen, shoutman, by bill 4s. 9d.

To Philip Miller for 3 loads of sand, 15d.

To him for carriage of timber, boards and other from Deptford to Lewisham, containing 8 loads at 4d., 2s. 8d.

To Tanner, Wynter, and Cloworth for carriage of 1 boat[load] of timber, boards and other from the Bridge House to Deptford for 1 night at 4d. the man, 12d.

To a blacksmith of Lambeth, 1,000 sixpenny nails, 5s., and 1,000 fourpenny nails English, 3s. 4d., 8s. 4d.

To John Goose for 21 ft. of lattice for a tenement at the Minories at 2¾d. [the foot], in all 4s. 9¾d.

[Total] of this page 46s. 9¾d.

Sum total of the week £8 7s. ¾d.

546. [f. 440v] 28 September

Renter £30 Fishmongers £5 Butchers £6 19s. 10d. Passage-tolls 20s.

Received of William Cockes the elder for an elm board 9 ft. long, 4d., of Leonard Holmes for a small piece of elm timber, 3d., 7d.

Received of Richard Bradbury, saddler, for the income of a tenement in Newgate market, late Kellett's, 5s.

Received of William Sutteley, merchant tailor, for the income into a tenement late Johnson's in the prin[cipal] east [part of the bridge], 40s.

Three chaplains 10s. Five clerks 10s. Roger Robyns 12d.

Masons. Bennet [blank]. Heron 3s. 6d. Jeffrey Orgar 3s. 6d. apparelling [blank]

Carpenters. Gold 3s. 6d. William Cockes 3s. 6d. Browne senior 3s.

6d. Henry Godfrey 3s. 6d. Leonard Holmes 3s. 6d. Simon Cockes 2s. 6d. John Browne 3s. 6d. Palmer 3s. 6d. in the waterworks and mill at Stratford.

Cockes pt 3s. 6d. Inglydwe 3s. 6d. Pasmer 3s. 6d. John Pasmer 3s. at Lawes' house.

John Provest 3s. 6d. William Wynter 3s. Thomas Browne 7d. in repairs at Deptford.

Sawyers. Flynt slitting 4 hundred, 4s. 4d. Board 3 hundred 3s. Horton slitting 6½ hundred, 7s.

Porter. Hughwet 2s.

Shout[man] Thomas Alen 3s. 4d.

Brick[layers] Swenson 3s. 6d. Chorleton [blank] Labourers. Nevell 2s. 6d. Jacson 2s. 6d. Thomas Grene 2s. 6d. at Deptford.

[Daubers] Thomas Mon' 3s. 6d. Labourer. John Turfyt 2s. 6d. at Deptford.

Labourers. John Smyth 2s. 6d. Roger Whythed 2s. 6d. Tanner 2s. 6d. Sherman 2s. 6d. Cloworth 2s. 6d.

[Total] of this page 24s. 9d.

[f. 441] To Robert Gold for the gibbet gin, driving piles in the starling aforesaid, for 6 tides at 5s. 8d. the tide, 34s.

In expenses for the obit of Christian Mallyng kept at St Mary Woolchurch, 20s.

To John Orgar, mason, by bill, 117s. 10d.

Expenses of the masters this week to Deptford, 12d.

To Thomas Cooke of Addington in Kent by Richard Maunsell for 600 corner [*cornell*] tiles at 2s. 8d. the hundred, 16s.

To the said John Orgar, chief mason of the bridge, for this quarter's fee, 50s.

To the said 3 priests and 6 clerks for *Placebo* [and *Dirige*] 3s.

To John Ferres for his quarter's fee and singing bread, 5s. 2d.

To Ralph Willott for 60 pints of Gascon wine spent within the chapel, 5s.

To Nicholas Hacker for 9 gallons and 1 pottle of lamp oil, 9s. 6d.

To Thomas Peverell for battering 47 dozen of masons' tools at 1½d. the dozen, 5s. 10½d.

To the wife of William Tanner for washing the chapel stuff this quarter, 12d.

To Hughwett's wife for weeding the garden this quarter, 2s.

To Richard Buckerell of Deptford for [words not clear] 9 lb. of rope for buckets, 4s.

To Richard Amborous, master carpenter of the Bridge House, 50s.

To Laurence for his quarter's fee, 50s.

[Total] of this page £18 4s. 4½d.

Sum total of the week £24 1½d.

[f. 441v blank]

547. [f. 442] Payments made after Michaelmas for the preceding year. 2 October. First paid to the parson of Woolchurch for the tithe of the Stocks, 13s. 4d.

To the masters for a repast made for the mayor, auditors, and certain common councilmen, over and above their old allowances, 110s. 7d.

To William Einerygor, one of the chaplains, by commandment of my lord mayor, for his wages for 13 weeks to end at Christmas next, and in recompense for his discharge 2s. 6d., 32s. 6d.

To Michelson, Vyncent, William Brys' and Stephen Robson, clerks, for their wages by the same commandment, for 13 weeks at 2s. each a week, 104s.

To Roger Robyns for 13 weeks at 12d. a week, 13s.

To John Carter of Colchester in full payment for 80 loads of oak timber delivered by him at the Bridge House, at 55 ft. [the load], £8.

548. 12 October. To a chantry priest of Paul's for a quit-rent due at M[ichaelmas], 2s. 6d.

To the master and convent of St Thomas of Acre, for a quit-rent due at Michaelmas, (3s.) <4s.>

To the prioress of St Helen's for a quit-rent due at Michaelmas last, (3s. 4d.) <13s. 4d.>

To the chamberlain of Westminster Abbey for a quit-rent due at Michaelmas last past, 10s.

To the wardens of St Ethelburga [*Albryht*] within Bishopsgate, for a quit-rent due at Michaelmas, 33s. 4d.

To Jeffrey Haryson for 16 loads of sand, 8s. 6d., for 17 loads of loam, 5s. 8d., and for 10 loads of gravel, 3s. 4d., delivered at sundry places in London, 17s. 6d.

To him for carriage of 12 loads of rubbish from the Stocks at 2½d., 2s. 6d., and for 1 load of bricks from the Stocks, 4d., in all 2s. 10d.

To John Baynton, grocer, for a year's rent ended at [sic], 4s.

549. 21 October. To Johnson, bailiff of Deptford, for a quit-rent yearly from lands in Deptford and Deptford marsh, for a year ended at Michaelmas, 10s. 6d.

To Richard Olyvere of Deptford in full payment for carriage of 74 [loads] of oak timber from Petham Court in Kent to Deptford at 16d. the load, and for carriage of 31 loads of tallwood and billets at 12d. the load, 29s. 8d., for the coming over a man's ground 2s., and mending of our gin 16d., in all 33s.

[Total] of this page £27 13s. 5d.

550. [f. 442v] 26 October 2 November [sic]

To the wharfinger of Deptford for wharfage of 74 loads of timber elm and for 31 loads of tallwood and faggots, 7s. 11d.

To Mr Mustham for a quit-rent by acquittance, 3s. 10d.

To Butler for carriage of 2 loads of timber from Croydon, 4s. 8d.

551. 2 November. To Thomas Alen for 3 men for 5 days and 5 nights away at Dartford, fetching elm timber by drove at 9d. each for the night and day, 11s. 3d.; to him for 3 men helping him to load the same timber at 2 several times, 3s. 11d.; to him for going 3 several times to Petham Court to see the sawyers and to pay them, 2s. 6d. and to him for his charges for twice going there for timber as aforesaid, 2s. 8d.; and for his charges in going to Croydon to see boards, 8d., in all 21s.

552. 5 November. To William Sharpeharowe, blacksmith, for sundry sorts of iron work and other, by bill, £10 14s. 8½d.
To Richard Roberts, plumber, for sundry things by bill [blank]
To (5) <11> labourers for taking up a fare of timber that came from Dartford, at 5d. the man, in all 4s. 7d.
To Henry Knyght of Knights Hill, for 46,000 tiles at 4s. 8d. the thousand, £10 14s. 8d.

553. 9 November. To the King's grace as in the right of the late monastery of St Faith's in Horsham, co. Norfolk, for a quit-rent due at Michaelmas last, 3s.
To Richard Roberts, plumber, in part payment of 3 bills, £4.
To William Stephyns for 4 barrels of pitch at 5s. 4d. the barrel, 21s. 4d., and for 4 hundred 17 lb. of rosin at 4s. the hundred, 16s. 8d., for wharfage of the same ware [*where*] 1d., and for 2 oars 3s., in all 41s. 1d.

554. 9 November. To the churchwardens of St Nicholas Shambles for a quarter ended at [sic], 25s.

555. 12 November. To John Cheseman, esquire, for a quit-rent due to the King's grace at Michaelmas last, for certain lands lying in Lewisham, 15s. 6d.
To Thomas Nelson, glazier, for certain works done by him, as appears by his bill, 7s. 3½d.

556. 13 November. To the King's grace for a quit-rent from certain lands in St George's field, late belonging to Bermondsey Abbey, 14s. 10d.

557. 16 November. To the chamberlain of London for a quit-rent, 12s.
To my lord of Canterbury for a quit-rent, 5s. 2d.
To the masters churchwardens of St Olave's, 26s. 8d.

558. 19 November. To the prioress of the Minoresses for a quit-rent, 20s.
To the king's grace as in the right of the monastery of Stratford, 32s.

559. 27 November. To Stephen Parat of Deptford for 20 boats of chalk, each boat containing 12 tons at 6d. the ton, £6.

560. 30 November. To Richard Roberts, plumber, in full payment of 4 bills, except that 9s. 10d. was deducted from the first bill, £4 16s. 6½d.

561. 4 December. To Mr Caudwell for his year's fee, 13s. 4d.

562. 7 December. To the abbot of Tower Hill and for learned counsel, £42.

563. 10 December. To the duke of Norfolk, the earl of Derby, and lord Bergavenny, 16d.

564. 13 December. To the bailiff of Lewisham for a quit-rent from lands called *the brughous*, 3s.
[Total] of this page £93 12s. ½d.

565. [f. 443] 15 December. Paid to Hugh Brampson, brickburner, for 11½ thousand bricks, received of him by Swenson at sundry places in the city, the bridge and Southwark, between Easter and Michaelmas last, at 4s. 8d. the thousand, 53s. 8d.

566. 18 December. To the said wardens for their quarter's wages, to each £6 13s. 4d., £13 6s. 8d.
To them for their horses for the same year, £4.
To Richard Bryn' by bill, £6 13s. 4d.

567. 4 January [1539]. To the dean and chapter of Pauls' for a quit-rent due at Michaelmas last, 19s.
To the prior of St Mary Overey for a quit-rent due for 3 years ended at Michaelmas last, at 3s. 6d. the year, in all 10s. 6d.

568. 9 January. To William Porter of Weybridge for 8,000 planks and 3,300 quarterboard at 2s. 2d. the hundred, in all £12 6d.
[Total] of this page £28 3s.
Sum total of the payments after Michaelmas (£149 8s. 5½d.) <£161 8s. 11½d.>
[f. 443v blank]

569. [f. 444]
Receipts after Michaelmas [1538] for the preceding year
5 October. Received of Richard Maunsell £8.
13 October. Received of Richard Maunsell £8.
13 October. Received of William Gaston of Lambeth for the rent of a granary in Golders yard for half a year ended at Lammas last, 10s.
17 October. Received of John a Wood for the passage of carts, 20s.
19 October. Received of Richard Maunsell £8.
26 October. Received of Richard Maunsell £8.
16 November. Received of Mr Moore in full payment for certain timber, 2s.
30 November. Received of John a Wood for passage 20s.
7 December. Received of John a Wood for passage 20s.

Glossary

OED: *Oxford English Dictionary*, ed. J.A. Simpson and E.S.C.Weiner (2nd. ed., Oxford, 1989)

LCW: L.C. Wright, *Sources of London English: Thames technical vocabulary* (Oxford University Press, forthcoming 1995)

MED: *Middle English Dictionary*, ed. H.Kuhn *et al.* (Ann Arbor, 1953)

MLWL: *Revised Medieval Latin Word-List from British and Irish sources*, ed. R.E.Latham (Oxford, 1965)

S: L.F.Salzman, *Building in England down to 1540, a documentary history* (Oxford, 1967)

Batch: a brewing vessel: OED

bead-hook: a kind of boathook: OED

beetle: a type of heavy weight with a handle, used for ramming, worked by three or five men: LCW

bollyng, bollyng tylte: probably a tarpaulin

bolster: a metal support: MED

bridge ashlar: a type of stone, hewn like a plank, used in building the bridge: LCW

bunch: a small measure of glass, possibly about 3 sq. ft.: S 184 and n.

cement: the word here clearly means a waterproof mixture including pitch or tar, used to bind masonry, delivered hot to the masons who used it: cf. S 153.

corbel: used in two senses, for baskets (**4–5, 8, 24–6**) and stone projections (**240**)

crests, see hollow tiles

crombes: hooks, crooks: MED

damel: a small dam or wall, possibly a barrier constructed around a starling for protection: LCW

eddering: materials (osiers, hazel-rods) used for interlacing the stakes of a hedge: OED

fare: a load or cargo: OED

forge: probably some kind of stone suitable for forges or furnaces

fyneux: tiles, probably hollow- or ridge-tiles: S 231.

garnet: hinge: OED

gemels: a kind of hinge: S 298–9

gibbet gin, ram: a machine, ?with a projecting beam, for driving piles into the riverbed: LCW

glovers' shreds: leather shreds used to make size: S 158

gyle tun: fermenting vat in brewing: OED

hames: curved part of horse-collar: OED
hassock: soft Kentish sandstone: OED
hollow tiles, crests: ridge tiles: S 231–2
in bowing: cutting to form an arch: S 258
karfe, *kyrffe*, kerf: the act of cutting, a cut; *anthwart kerf*, probably crosswise cuts
lattice nails: used for lattices or windows: S 310
lyre: tape for binding: OED
moty: an earth-based pigment, probably reddish: S 159, 168, OED
mount: a measure of plaster, 30 cwt.: S 155–6
ogees: stone cut for vaulting ribs: S 116
packthread: strong thread for tying: MED
pane: section of a wall: MED
parells: (stone for) chimneypieces: OED
patten nails: used in making pattens: MED
pile-shoe [nail]: [nail for fastening] the metal casing on the end of a pile: LCW
potent': probably a hinge: cf. *potentgarnetta*, cross-garnet: MLWL
puncheons: wooden struts, posts: OED
pynne timber: possibly wood for making pins or pegs
Pysens, pisan: head armour, collar: MED
roda: possibly a roadstead or landing-place (**143**)
rove: a small metal plate through which a nail or rivet is clenched, in boatbuilding: S 313
running ram: a machine for driving piles into the river bed: LCW
scappling: rough shaping: OED
scomour, skimmer: utensil for skimming liquid: MED
seam nails: probably a clenched nail or rivet: S 313
shavehook: a tool for scraping, used on the starling: LCW
shipborde: ship planks, the kind of planking used in boatbuilding
shout: a flat-bottomed river boat, used for transporting goods: LCW, OED scout
shwer, shore: drain: LCW
scoppet, scuppet: a spade or shovel: OED
slitting (wood): lengthwise splitting into planks, probably with wedges rather than sawing: S 243
somer: heavy timber beam across an opening
sortelathe: some kind of lath
spiking: a strong iron nail: OED
springer: the stone from which an arch springs: OED
stampnes, stems: the stem or prow of a boat: OED
starling: a platform of sawn-off piles, upon which a pier was built; subsequently an outwork of piles, projecting from the lower part of the pier: LCW
stop (wood): piece of wood forming rebate, as part of the joinery of a door
swerd', sword: blade of the ram or pile-driver (**57, 80, 87**)
tallwood: (fire)wood
tide-boots: used by workmen in the water

tide-saw: used by tidemen

tideman: a construction worker whose work depends on states of the tide

tilte, tylte: awning, covering of coarse or hair-cloth, especially over a boat: OED tilt

toise, *teys*: a measure of paving, about 7½ sq. ft.: S 147

tontight: a measure of stone, about a ton/2,000 lb. in weight but varying in quantity: see S 122

trasshnaill: wooden pegs: S 202

trenails: wooden pegs or nails

tusserds: some kind of (fire)wood: OED

voussoir: wedge-shaped stone: S 115

wadmal: a coarse woollen cloth, particularly used to cover horse-collars: OED

warelyne: meaning unknown

water-adze, water-auger: tools used for construction work in the water

waterworks: work on the piers, starlings, and arches of the bridge, often at the waterline

Westvale: Westphalian linen

wilkin: pile-driving machine: LCW

wiveling: hair, material for caulking: LCW

wranges for boats (**325**): meaning unknown

INDEX

Variant spellings of one surname have been gathered under a single, modern, head-form, as have surnames based on place-names with a modern form. References are to numbered paragraphs, not pages.

—, Henry, renter of granary in Golders yard, 500
—, Mr, clerk of king's ships, 454
[illegible], Guy, 136
[illegible], John, 152
Abbot (Abbotte), John, 411
Aberford, Richard, 404
Abingdon, Stephen, 303
Abraham, Richard, 133
Absolon, William, carpenters' labourer, 347
accountant, 286
accounts, *passim*; books, 253, 330, 381, 473, 488; keeping and making, 294, 351, 382, 397; writing, 396, 488
actions against tenants, 294
Acton, Mazera, 110
Adam, Geoffrey, 126
Adams, Robert, 413
Adcok, Robert, 141
adzes, 105, 378, 470, 534, 544; water-adzes, 251, 264; steeling, 534, 544
Aes, Ralph, churchwarden of St Mary le Bow, 250, 278
Affen (A Fen), John, labourer working with the masons by the tide, 533–5
Albery, John, clothworker, 514
Alblast'
  Philip, 132
  William, 132
Albon, Richard, 2
albs, 267, 294, 337, 385
alder poles, 257–9
Alderbury, Edward, 122
Aldfold, Peter, Warden, 296, 301
Aldgate, brick-kilns outside, 339
ale, 243–4, 246–8, 254, 256, 259–63, 269–71, 275–7, 278–9, 282, 285–6, 288–9, 291; given at weekly account, 243–94, 331; given for unusual work, 257, 259–64, 277, 282, 284–6, 290; given to carpenters, 244, 246–8, 254, 259–60, 262, 264, 269–71, 274–9, 286–7, 289, 294; given to masons, 248, 254, 256, 274, 276, 286, 292,

386; ale (or drinking allowance) given to tidemen, 265–7, 269–75, 277, 279, 280, 287–93
Alenson, John, 407
Alexander, painter of Wood Street, 474, 506
Aley, John, clerk of chamber of Guildhall, 334
Alford, Thomas, 339
All Hallows Barking, 114, 149, 307, 317, 423
All Hallows Gracechurch, 154, 303
All Hallows Honey Lane, 119, 316
All Hallows on the Wall, 117, 418
All Hallows the Great, 453, 534; church-wardens of, 454, 542–3; work to church, 534
All Hallows the Less, 162, 304, 308
Allarye, John, clothworker, 453
Allen (Alen, Aleyn)
  John, mercer, 535
  Roger, stainer, 262
  Thomas, 453, 467, 473, 495, 496, 518, 525, 527–8, 531–2
  Thomas, labourer, 480, 495–506, 508–28, 530–7; working with the carpenters, 515; working with the bricklayer, 538; working with the masons by the tide, 534, 536; bestowing chalk in the starling by the tide, 533
  Thomas, mercer, 473
  Thomas, shoutman of the Bridge House, 467, 480, 487, 495–546, 551
  Walter, carpenter, 479, 498–504, 506, 508–19, 521–3
Alley, Richard, citizen and skinner, 317
allowance of rent, 371, 463
Allut', Theobald, and wife, 160
Almonte, William, shipwright, 484, 526
alms, 199, 204, 229, 232, 241
Alrede
  Elena, 142
  William, 142
Alwyn, [Nicholas], alderman, 367
Ambrose (Amberous, Amborous), Master Richard, master or chief carpenter of

Ilford, co. Essex, 331
images, 336; at stone gate on Bridge, 261, 264; of St Thomas on the bridge, 290; in Bridge chapel, 283; of St Petronilla, 280
in bowing, 503, 504, 506, 509, 510
incense, 60, 68–9, 82, 91, 105
incomes and fines, 455, 546
increase of rents, 360, 449
indentures of lease, 332
indentures, 334
Ingledew (Inglydw, Inglydw, Inglydwe), —, carpenter, 479, 495–506, 508–27, 529–46
Ingleton, Henry, seneschal of Marshalsea, 333
ink, 330
iron, 293, 312; black, 263; worked, 98, 107, 247, 252, 258, 267–8, 280, 285, 311, 329
ironwork, 254, 264, 329, 378, 470, 506, 516, 521, 552; black, 470; tinned, 378; white, 470. *See also* bolts, garnets, hinges, hooks, hoops, latches, locks and keys
Isaac, John, carpenter's labourer, 331, 347
Islington, Philip, 428
Ivy Lane, 316, 474

Jackson (Jacson)
    James, bricklayer's labourer, 536, 538–9, 541, 543–6
    John, of Oxgate, 376
    William, labourer with the bricklayers/ tilers, 481, 495–500
    William, Queen's bailiff of Southwark, 452, 498
Jacob, Simon, labourer, 332, 347
Jaket, —, stainer, 262
jambs, stone, 240
James, William, 402
janitor of the Bridge House, 349
Jenkin, Richard, 414
Jennyn, William, 415
Jesson, Richard, 425
Joce, John, 402
John, Thomas, 523
Johnson's house on the bridge, 522, 546; work on, 511
Johnson
    —, bailiff of Deptford, 549
    Johan, 380
    John, 136
    John, 430, 464
    John, labourer, 524
    Ralph, 411
    Thomas, 408
    Thomas, butcher, 325
    Thomas, labourer, 480
    William, 403, 422, 456, 503

William, apprentice mason, 386
Joiner (Joynour)
    John, 381
    [? the joiner] Laurence, 259–62
    Robert, 251 [possibly Robert Baker, joiner]
    William, 336
    William, *ducheman*, 122
joiners, 259–63
joints, 378
joists, 247, 390
Jolyf, Thomas, 130
journal of weekly payments, 478, 480, 482
Joy, the, brewhouse, in St Benet Grace- church, 153
Joye, John, 134
Jurdan
    Henry, fishmonger, 303
    Roger, 335
    Thomas, chief mason of the Bridge, 340
justices of *wallas and fossat'*, 331, 333

Katherine Wheel, the, in St Benet Grace- church, 153
keeper of boats and shouts belonging to the Bridge, 330, 346, 395, 487; *see* Donmowe, Thomas
keeper of the chapel on the bridge, 477
Kele, Patrick, 339; dauber, 344
Kellet
    John, 415, 455
    William, of London Bridge, merchant tailor, 404, 453, 514; wife of, 514; work on his house, 511, 513–14
Kellett's tenement in Newgate market, 546
Kelsey, Thomas, ironmonger/smith, 254, 267, 280
Kelynge, William, 404
Kendall, John, wife of, 376
Kent Street, Southwark, 305
Kent
    Richard de, 102
    Richard, 372
keys, 243–4, 248, 256–7, 267, 294, 378, 470
Kidder (Kydder), —, wife of, 405
King (Kyng)
    John, 181
    John, 309, 325
    John, woolpacker, 114
    Richard, 113
    Richard, of Grene, co. Sussex, 375
    Thomas, 130
king, the, 458–60, 553, 555–6, 558; his attorney, 453, 502; his fletcher, 537; his harness, 474, 499
Kingsmill (Kyngesmylle), Thomas, *subs'* [? subseneschal] of Marshalsea, 333
Kingston (Kyngston), Robert, grocer, 119

necessary purchases, 330, 381, 473
Nedeler, Henry, 122
Nedewey, William, 376
needles, 294
Neel
 William, and son, 187
 Henry, plumber, 379
Neffold, Nicholas, 134, 217
Nelson, Robert, 414; glazier, 472
Nelthorpe, John, 411
Neve, Nicholas le, 160
Nevill
 —, labourer with bricklayers, 481
 Edward, knight, 316
 Henry, 330
 Salamon, of Broomfield, 293
Newby, George, labourer, 388
Newgate market, 455, 476
Newman
 Edmund, stock/fishmonger, 301, 332
 John, 137
 John, carpenter: wages, 243–66; other
  references, 254, 264
 John, hardhewer, 386
 John, mason, 340
Newnton, Robert, carpenter, 341
Newys, Thomas, 416, 439
Nicholl, John, 122
Nidygate, —, king's servant, 453
night work, 262, 279–80, 282, 290, 333,
 346, 382, 388, 474, 480, 515–17, 544–5,
 551
Noble, John, 220
Norbury, co. Surrey, 331, 339, 341, 347
Norfolk, duke of, 316, 458
Norman, John, 322
Normavile, John, clerk of the works of the
 Bridge, 395
Northburgh (Northborow), Michael, bishop
 of London 1354–61, 304
Northfleet, co. Kent, 331
Norton
 J., 262
 Thomas, joiner, 260, 263
 William, 170, 176
 William, 304; draper, 306
Norys, Robert, 383
Nynes, Mr [Nicholas], commoner, ?auditor,
 382

Oak timber, 282, 285, 312, 325, 331, 375,
 452–4, 467, 480, 485, 496, 502, 506,
 509–12, 520, 523, 527–8, 530, 532,
 534–5, 538–40, 542–4, 547, 549; sold,
 312, 527–8, 530, 532, 534, 542, 544
 board, 453, 527
 curved, 325
 ends, 528
 planks, 375, 452–3, 496, 502, 509
 quarters, 453, 502–3

shells, 452, 454, 498, 516, 523, 535
oak trees, 347
oakum, 346, 473, 525
oars, 287, 381, 473–4, 535, 541, 553
oats, 338
obits, 331, 337, 382, 474, 501, 544, 546
oblations, 314, 362, 451, 525, 535
Odierne, John, 152, 303
offerings (to employees) at Christmas, 67;
 at Easter, 82
Offold, Walter, 326
oil (lamp-oil), 294, 337, 385, 477, 546
oil and rosin for boat, 79
oil and varnish, 60
oil for chapel, 107
Old Change, 2, 96, 107, 122, 268, 312, 372,
 411, 455, 478, 486, 506, 532–3
Old Fishmarket, the, 121
Oliver
 J., 263
 Robert, mason, 386
 William, 153, 303
Oliver/s
 Richard, carter, 531, 537; of Deptford,
  549
 Richard, of Dartford, 467
ordure, 332; voider, voiding, 382, 474,
 515–17
Orgall, Thomas, 412
organmaker, 477, 525, 536
organs in chapel, 477, 525
Orgar (Orger)
 Jeffrey, mason, 478, 495–506, 509–23,
  525–30, 532–46
 John, 505, 512, 518; chief or master
  mason of the Bridge works, 466, 478,
  519, 527, 532, 546
 John, mason, 386
orphreys, 273
Osbarn, Nicholas, 125
Osemond, Thomas, carpenter, 341
Osgood, Richard, 130
osier-grounds, Stratford, 437
Otley (Oteleye, Otteley), Robert, 130,
 287
Oulegrove, Thomas, alderman, 311; auditor
 of Bridge House accounts, 331, 353
Oune, John, 330
ovens, 312, 329, 383, 392, 466, 513–14,
 521
Owenby, John, carpenter, 387
Oxneye, Salamon, 123
oyster-shells, 330
Oystergate, 303

Packthread, 258, 265, 330
Paddesle, John, 136
Page, John, and wife, 131
pageant on London Bridge, 382, 399
pails, 330, 337, 473, 530, 531–2

271

Painter (Peyntour, Peynter)
  Bartholomew, 116
  Richard [? the painter], 261–2
  Robert, 381
  William, 308
painters, 259–64, 267, 283, 332, 474, 506
paling, 381
Palmer
  John, and wife Joan, 130
  John, carpenter, 479, 495–506, 508–40,
    542–6
  Thomas, of Deptford, 383
Panell (Paynell), Anne, widow, 407, 444,
  522
Panter, John, 116
paper, 262, 293, 381, 473, 503
parchment maker, 473
parchment, 60, 65, 82, 96, 100, 244, 293,
  330, 381
parells for chimneys, 511
Pargeter (Pargit', Pargyter), Lady, 471,
  502
pargetting, 324
Paris (Parys)
  John, carpenter, 243–4, 259–94
  Robert, 171
  William, 332
Parker
  Christine, 122
  John, 171
  Richard, 410
  Stephen, 138
  William, wheelwright, 452, 499
paroffs, 337
Parrot (Parat, Parett)
  Nicholas, 422
  Stephen, of Deptford, 469, 501, 35, 559
Parson, Thomas, 425, 439
parsonage in St Dunstan in the East,
  306
paschal candle, 477, 535
Pasmer
  John, carpenter, 479, 495–506, 508–19,
    521–30, 533–46
  Robert, carpenter, 387
  Robert, carpenter, 479, 495–502, 504–506,
    509–30, 532–46
passage-tolls:
  from carts, 1, 3–54, 188–92, 194, 196,
    198, 200, 202–3, 205–6, 212, 214,
    216–18, 221, 223–241, 569
  from ships, 1, 3–54, 188, 199, 200, 202,
    206, 225–6, 229, 241
  from either or both, 254, 267, 280, 294,
    310, 321, 349, 359, 448, 519–46
Paternoster Row, 123, 184, 328, 371, 412,
  460, 463, 476, 478–9, 481, 497, 499,
  503–4, 506, 513, 519, 533
Pathe, Thomas, 142
Patwey, Richard, 402

Patwyn (Petwyn, Pytwyne), Richard,
  glover, 473–4, 498; widow of, 532
pavement, mending, 332
paving, 256, 261, 265, 268, 280, 324, 386,
  394, 478, 504, 511, 513, 522, 532–3,
  544
paving, lead, 471
paving-stone, *see* stone, paving
paving-tiles, 256
paviours, 256, 265, 268, 280, 345, 394, 486,
  504, 506, 522, 533; labourers, 486
Paxon, Thomas, grocer, 130
payment by bill, 495, 498, 518–19, 521,
  527, 536–8, 541, 543, 545–6, 552–3,
  555, 560, 566; by bill and tale, 506,
  523
payments made after the year of account,
  547–68
Payne
  Christopher, 452, 496
  Henry, 416, 439
  Roger, carpenter, 341
Paynell, Richard, 363, 380; receiver of the
  Bridge, 395
Payse, Mabel, 142
Peacock (Pecok, Peakocke, Peycocke)
  John, 167, 306, 308
  John, 411, 452, 500
Peale, Peter, 414
Peart (Pert, Piert)
  Thomas, carpenter, 330, 369
  Thomas, carpenter, 461
Peckham, co. Kent, 316, 368, 431; fields
  of, 190; Pipers hope in, 430; Wardells
  meadow in, 283, 430
Pegrom (Pygrom)
  John, wife of, 137
  Walter, 137
pegs, wooden [*trasshnaill*], 265
Pelham, Walter, 131
Pellican, Robert, fishmonger, 304
Pellyng, John, 165
Penbrooke, John, chaplain, 316
Pencryche
  Leticia, 136
  Thomas, 136
pendants of the arches of the bridge,
  520–1
pendants, 526–7
Penhertgart, Henry, 329
Penythorn, Richard, carpenter, 387
Percell (Porcell), Philip, 129
Percival (Percyvale), Robert, 131, 135
Percy
  John, 303
  Robert, 155
Perpelett, Robert, 404
Perpoynte, John, attorney in Comon Pleas,
  382
Pery, Richard, chaplain, 173

William, clerk serving in chapel on the bridge, 337

Richardson
Reynolde, 466, 505
Simon, 415

Rickmansworth (Rikmeresworth), William, 274

Rider (Ryder)
John, 145
John, 307
Peter, 267

Rigby, Thomas, under-sheriff, 305

Rillesthorp, William, 123

rings, 248, 260, 378; iron, 60, 470, 516

roadway repairs, 486, 506

Robekyn, William, 62

Robelard, Thomas, 130, 136

Robert
John, 123
William, 330

Roberts, Richard, plumber, 471, 502, 506, 552–3, 560

Robertson, Richard, 426

Robinson
—, 336
William, 422
William, mill-picker, 453, 502

Robson, Stephen, clerk in the chapel on bridge, 477, 547

Robyns (Robynson), Roger, 519–46; clerk in the chapel on the bridge, 477, 547, 477

Robyns, Robert, 422

Roche
John, labourer working with the masons by the tide, 528
Mr, 412

roda [?roadstead, landing-place], 143

Rodbourne, Agnes, 122

Rodley, William, of Deptford, 382

Rogerson, Roger, 412

Rokesley
John, 352
John, chaplain, 297

Roland, Thomas, 343

Rolf, William, 381

Romsen, —, 439

Romsey, John, widow of, 225

Rood Lane, 533

Roofe, John, 409

rope, 250, 265, 277, 294, 330, 381, 473, 531–3, 546; harness [*bakroppes, womberoppes, pyperop'*], 244

Ropkyn, John, 322

Rose, Robert, 145

rosemary, 474, 523

rosin, 79, 265, 330, 381, 473, 497, 553

Rothyng, Isabel, 148, 307

Rotour, William, and wife Christine, 130

Roue, Robert, 122

Roughhead
Peter, 312
Simon, 126
Thomas, carpenters' labourer, 347

Roulys, John, 408

Round House in Deptford, 430

Rous
Robert, 175, 308
Thomas, and wife, 135

Rowe, John, 122

Rower, John, 129

Rowland (Roulande, Roulond)
Henry, 132
John, 123
John, 407
labourer, 388

Rowley
—, blacksmith, 470
John, 378

Roy, Bernard, 124

royal entries
Henry V and Queen Katherine, 1421: 257–66, 278, 280, 287, 294; angels' wings for, 278; donjon for, 260; giants for, 257, 262–3, 265; hoops, *pysens* and garments for, 265; lion for, 262; vanes for, 267; virgins hired for, 267, painted linen garments for, 264
Katherine of Aragon, 1501: 365, 382, 399

rubbish removed or carried, 102, 105, 107, 339, 384, 388, 476, 501, 506, 524–5, 531, 533, 538, 541–2, 545, 548

Ruddyng (Roddyng, Rodyng, Rooding, Rudyng), Richard, paviour, 486, 504, 506, 522, 532–3, 544

Rudmarige, Robert, clerk in chapel on the bridge, 385

Rush Hope, meadow called, in Stratford, 2, 309

rushes, 332, 381

Russell
Thomas, 137
William, 121

Ruston, John, 134

rynde for mill at Lewisham, 383

Rynde, James, bricklayer, 392

Sackcloth, 330

sacks, 311; for lime, 330

saddle (cart), 79

Sadler (Saddeler, Sadeler, Sadiller)
John, 161, 382
William le, 162, 304

Saers Court, 368

sail, 280

St Alban Wood Street, 2, 174

St Andrew Hubbard (Eastcheap), 150, 307

St Audoen *see* St Ewen

St Augustine Papey, 2, 118

LONDON RECORD SOCIETY

President: The Rt. Hon. the Lord Mayor of London

Chairman: H.S.Cobb, MA, FSA, FRHS
Hon. Secretary: H.J.Creaton, BA, MPhil, ALA
Hon. Treasurer: G.G.Harris, MA
Hon. General Editors: V.A.Harding, MA, PhD, FRHS
                S.O'Connor, BA, PhD

The London Record Society was founded in December 1964 to publish transcripts, abstracts and lists of the primary sources for the history of London, and generally to stimulate interest in archives relating to London. Membership is open to any individual or institution; the annual subscription is £12 ($22) for individuals and £18 ($35) for institutions. Prospective members should apply to the Hon. Secretary, Miss H.J.Creaton, c/o Institute of Historical Research, Senate House, London WC1E 7HU.

The following volumes have already been published:
1. *London Possessory Assizes: a calendar*, edited by Helena M. Chew (1965)
2. *London Inhabitants within the Walls, 1695*, with an introduction by D.V.Glass (1966)
3. *London Consistory Court Wills, 1492–1547*, edited by Ida Darlington (1967)
4. *Scriveners' Company Common Paper, 1357–1628, with a continuation to 1678*, edited by Francis W. Steer (1968)
5. *London Radicalism, 1830–1843: a selection from the papers of Francis Place*, edited by D. J. Rowe (1970)
6. *The London Eyre of 1244*, edited by Helena M. Chew and Martin Weinbaum (1970)
7. *The Cartulary of Holy Trinity Aldgate*, edited by Gerald A. J. Hodgett (1971)
8. *The Port and Trade of early Elizabethan London: Documents*, edited by Brian Dietz (1972)
9. *The Spanish Company*, edited by Pauline Croft (1973)
10. *London Assize of Nuisance, 1301–1431: a calendar*, edited by Helena M. Chew and William Kellaway (1973)
11. *Two Calvinistic Methodist Chapels, 1748–1811: the London Tabernacle and Spa Fields Chapel*, edited by Edwin Welch (1975)
12. *The London Eyre of 1276*, edited by Martin Weinbaum (1976)

13. *The Church in London, 1375–1392*, edited by A. K. McHardy (1977)
14. *Committees for the Repeal of the Test and Corporation Acts: Minutes, 1786–90 and 1827–8*, edited by Thomas W. Davis (1978)
15. *Joshua Johnson's Letterbook, 1771–4: letters from a merchant in London to his partners in Maryland*, edited by Jacob M. Price (1979)
16. *London and Middlesex Chantry Certificate, 1548*, edited by C. J. Kitching (1980)
17. *London Politics, 1713–1717: Minutes of a Whig Club, 1714–17*, edited by H.Horwitz; *London Pollbooks, 1713*, edited by W.A. Speck and W.A. Gray (1981)
18. *Parish Fraternity Register: Fraternity of the Holy Trinity and SS.Fabian and Sebastian in the parish of St. Botolph without Aldersgate*, edited by Patricia Basing (1982)
19. *Trinity House of Deptford: Transactions, 1609–35*, edited by G.G.Harris (1983)
20. *Chamber Accounts of the sixteenth century*, edited by Betty R. Masters (1984)
21. *The Letters of John Paige, London Merchant, 1648–58*, edited by George F. Steckley (1984)
22. *A Survey of Documentary Sources for Property Holding in London before the Great Fire*, by Derek Keene and Vanessa Harding (1985)
23. *The Commissions for Building Fifty New Churches*, edited by M.H.Port (1986)
24. *Richard Hutton's Complaints Book*, edited by Timothy V. Hitchcock (1987)
25. *Westminster Abbey Charters, 1066–c.1214*, edited by Emma Mason (1988)
26. *London Viewers and their Certificates, 1508–1558*, edited by Janet S. Loengard (1989)
27. *The Overseas Trade of London: Exchequer Customs Accounts, 1480–1*, edited by H.S.Cobb (1990)
28. *Justice in Eighteenth-century Hackney: the Justicing Notebook of Henry Norris and the Hackney Petty Sessions Book*, edited by Ruth Paley (1991)
29. *Two Tudor Subsidy Assessment Rolls for the City of London: 1541 and 1582*, edited by R.G.Lang (1993 for 1992)
30. *London Debating Societies, 1776–1799*, compiled and introduced by Donna T. Andrew (1994 for 1993)
31. *London Bridge: selected accounts and rentals, 1381–1538*, edited by Vanessa Harding and Laura Wright (1995 for 1994)

Most volumes are still in print; apply to the Hon. Secretary, who will forward requests to the distributor. Price to individual members £12 ($22) each, to non-members £20 ($38) each.